T0366390

The publisher gratefully acknowledges the generous support of the Humanities Endowment Fund of the University of California Press Foundation.

Edgar G. Ulmer

WEIMAR AND NOW: GERMAN CULTURAL CRITICISM

Edward Dimendberg, Martin Jay, and Anton Kaes, General Editors

Edgar G. Ulmer

A Filmmaker at the Margins

Noah Isenberg

UNIVERSITY OF CALIFORNIA PRESS

Berkeley · Los Angeles · London

University of California Press, one of the most distin-
guished university presses in the United States, enriches
lives around the world by advancing scholarship in the
humanities, social sciences, and natural sciences. Its
activities are supported by the UC Press Foundation and
by philanthropic contributions from individuals and
institutions. For more information, visit www.ucpress
.edu.

University of California Press
Berkeley and Los Angeles, California

University of California Press, Ltd.
London, England

Library of Congress Cataloging-in-Publication Data

Isenberg, Noah William.
    Edgar G. Ulmer : a filmmaker at the margins / Noah
Isenberg.
        pages   cm. — (Weimar and now: German cultural
criticism)
    Includes bibliographical references and index.
    ISBN 978-0-520-23577-9 (cloth : alk. paper)
    ISBN 978-0-520-95717-6 (ebook)
    1. Ulmer, Edgar G. (Edgar George), 1904–1972.
2. Motion picture producers and directors—United
States—Biography. I. Title.
    PN1998.3.U46I84 2013
    791.43′0233092—dc23
    [B]   2013025957

Manufactured in the United States of America

22 21 20 19 18 17 16 15 14

10 9 8 7 6 5 4 3 2 1

In keeping with a commitment to support environmen-
tally responsible and sustainable printing practices,
UC Press has printed this book on Natures Natural, a
fiber that contains 30% post-consumer waste and meets
the minimum requirements of ANSI/NISO Z39.48-1992
(R 1997) (Permanence of Paper).

To Melanie, Jules, and Bruno

and in memory of

Jon Irwin Isenberg (1937–2003)

and

Hanuš Georg Rehak (1927–2006)

Contents

Illustrations

Preface

The origins of this project lie in a conversation I had more than a decade ago. I was sitting on the redwood deck at my mother's house in La Jolla, California, and her companion of many years, Bob Lurie, was talking with me about my current teaching and research interests. An adman by profession, Bob had a keen understanding of film, particularly of the glory days of Hollywood in the 1940s and 1950s, when he'd lived in Los Angeles, having moved there from New York to attend UCLA on the GI Bill. I happened to mention to Bob that a director who really intrigued me, whose films I had taught in several of my courses, was one of Hollywood's European transplants, a lesser-known figure among the celebrated lot, a guy named Edgar G. Ulmer. The very mention of his name prompted an outburst. "Don't believe a word he said!" Bob exclaimed. As fate would have it, Bob's first cousin was Shirley Ulmer, Edgar's wife and lifelong collaborator. Bob had sat through many a meal with the director holding court and telling some of the tallest of his tales, and he wasn't buying any of it.

This, naturally, made me only more eager to explore the career of this enigmatic director, a man who clearly had talent but repeatedly exaggerated his accomplishments and affiliations, especially late in life, in such a way as to provoke total disbelief. I needed to find out more, so Bob offered to put me in touch with Shirley Ulmer. My calls went unanswered until one autumn evening in 2001, when I heard from Shirley's daughter, Arianné, a former actor, who told me that Shirley had recently passed away. Arianné, however, had not only acted in several of her father's films but ran the Edgar G. Ulmer Preservation Corp. out of her home office on Stone Canyon Road in Sherman Oaks, California. Not long after that, I boarded a plane from New York to Los Angeles to visit Arianné, whose passion, commitment, and charm came across even over the phone. Together we combed through the many boxes of materials—photos, letters, diaries, other unpublished manuscripts—she and her mother had been holding on to since her father's death nearly thirty years earlier. I gathered as much material as I could, then worked my way through the various papers kept at the Margaret Herrick Library of the Academy of Motion Picture Arts and Sciences. In addition, I watched and rewatched all of Ulmer's movies, some on duped videocassettes, some in brittle 16 mm prints viewed on a flatbed editing table, some on newly released DVDs, and some on the big screen.

From California the journey continued onward to Vienna, where I spent the winter and spring of 2003 as a fellow at the International Research Center for Cultural Studies, trying to uncover details about Ulmer's childhood and initial training in theater and film. While there, I often found myself reaching a series of dead ends: no records at the primary and secondary schools he purportedly attended; no definitive proof of his contributions to various early productions; no confirmation of the formal education he later claimed to have had. I continued to wade through the archives and follow up on numerous leads provided by friends and colleagues at the Austrian Film Museum and by journalist Stefan Grissemann, who had just published his German-language biography of Ulmer, *Mann im Schatten: Der Filmemacher Edgar G. Ulmer* (Man in the shadows: The filmmaker Edgar G. Ulmer) that same year. But the itinerant director seemed, either unwittingly or very craftily, to have covered his tracks. What made Ulmer marginal was not merely that he tended, over his thirty-five-year career as a director, to work in offbeat markets (B studios, Hollywood's underground, European independents), and to traffic in eclectic genres (horror, race pictures, health shorts, film noir, costume dramas, science fiction), but that the details of his own life were tucked away somewhere in the dark corners of history.

I left Austria after four months with a somewhat better picture of Ulmer but many mysteries unsolved. Luckily, in the final days of my stint in Vienna I had made a trip to Berlin, where I discovered a large cache of letters kept in the Paul Kohner Archives between Ulmer and his agent Ilse Lahn at the Kohner Office, mainly documenting his European productions from the 1940s, 1950s, and 1960s. I saw immediately that to tell a fuller story of Ulmer, it would be necessary to include the lively, occasionally tense, discussions that he, Shirley, and Lahn—with periodic input by Kohner himself—carried out during the final decades of his professional life. I knew I would have to return to Berlin, the place where Ulmer had his seemingly auspicious directorial debut three-quarters of a century earlier.

But while Ulmer began his career with such renowned émigré directors as Robert Siodmak, Fred Zinnemann, and Billy Wilder—all of whom collaborated on the celebrated late silent classic *Menschen am Sonntag* (*People on Sunday*, 1930)—he never enjoyed the same sort of commercial success or big-studio backing as did others in his cohort of Austrian and German-born filmmakers in America. To compare Ulmer to those great, triumphant studio careers and to the dominant rags-to-riches Hollywood mythology, though, is in many ways to fail to see Ulmer's career on its own terms. "It isn't as if Wilder remained an unsung outcast in his own time," observes Ed Sikov early on in his biography of Billy Wilder, "a lone artist rubbing against the grain of his culture."[1] Indeed, that's a description far more befitting of Ulmer than of his illustrious counterparts in the film business.

In 2006, when I began writing the BFI Film Classics volume on *Detour*, Ulmer's best-known film, I thought I would write a "little engine that could" tale about how a lowly B picture, made on a shoe-string budget, found its way into the National Registry of Films of the Library of Congress and became one of the most famous films noirs of all time. That was the line champions of his work had taken over the years. "Ulmer chose to make small films on low budgets," writes George Lipsitz in a rather exemplary vein, "because they gave him an opportunity to explore ideas and techniques that would not have been tolerated by the big studios. His entire life history in theater and film testifies to a self-conscious struggle to pursue artistic and social truths at the risk of commercial failure."[2]

But what I learned, especially after spending time with Ulmer's personal writings, was that the truth, as it often is, was a bit more complicated. This pioneering independent filmmaker also harbored genuine, heartfelt aspirations of financial success, recognition, a studio contract, and a steadier paycheck than has often been acknowledged in Ulmer circles. And why not? The two are, to my mind, not mutually exclusive and do not make Ulmer any less of an artist. In 2008 I returned to the Paul Kohner Archives in Berlin and again dove into the papers deposited there by the "Magician of Sunset Boulevard," as Kohner was known. What I found further balanced my understanding of Ulmer. Not exactly a model client, Ulmer often ran into trouble with his agent by making deals of his own, getting into chronic money troubles, and bellyaching intermittently about the lack of proper studio work. His letters show a man who spent most, if not all, of his career moving from one freelance assignment to the next, a man who, in the process, produced a dizzying—in some ways extraordinary, given the limitations placed on him—body of work. As Austrian critic Bert Rebhandl writes, Ulmer was "an Odysseus of cinema, who wasn't destined to return home, but who, on his long voyage through various genres and film cultures, spanned the entire spectrum: cool modernity alongside lascivious speculation, cheap trash beside classic virtuosity."[3]

In *Edgar G. Ulmer: A Filmmaker at the Margins,* I have attempted to track that voyage, to add previously unknown details of the director's life and career wherever I could, and to speculate on the significance of each phase, each picture, and each itinerary. When I first set out to write this book, I was determined to find clear-cut answers to all of the disputed facts and half-truths connected to the filmmaker. But over time I became more comfortable with the impossibility of this task and with the need for a life like Ulmer's to straddle truth and fiction almost the way a literary memoir might. In that sense this is not a straight biography—if there ever were such a thing. In the end I have chosen neither to believe wholesale what I was told on that redwood deck in La Jolla more than a decade ago nor to accept without qualification what Ulmer himself presented as the truth when he was still alive. It hasn't made his life or career any less intriguing to me, which, I suspect, is precisely how he wanted it.

Traces of a Viennese Youth

Vienna is no more. What you seek there, you will not find.
—Josef von Sternberg, Hollywood 1968

Dealing with a subject as elusive as an undocumented childhood is a daunting task, one that requires considerable resourcefulness, tact, and imagination and that ultimately relies on a fair amount of detective work and scholarly conjecture. Yet when it comes to a figure like Edgar G. Ulmer, whose life and career often seem enshrouded in unverifiable claims, some of them quite extravagant—for instance, that he was related to the eminent turn-of-the-century Viennese writer Arthur Schnitzler; that he once served as a case study for Freud's childhood analyses; that he invented the "unchained" camera, the dolly shot, and pioneered German expressionism; or, perhaps most fabulous of all, that he directed the Atlanta fire sequence in *Gone with the Wind* and stepped in for Fellini to execute a long tracking shot in *La dolce vita*—it is perhaps fitting that what we know of his childhood be marked by a similar degree of murkiness, fantasy, and mendacity as his adult life.[1] Indeed, as film scholar Lotte Eisner once claimed in a more provocative spirit, Ulmer might be considered "the greatest liar in the history of cinema."[2]

Ulmer first came to public attention in the mid-1950s, when French critics from *Cahiers du cinéma,* the same unwavering auteurists who took special delight in finding virtues in the depraved, neglected, and misunderstood renegade directors toiling on the fringes of Hollywood (Anthony Mann, Fritz Lang, Nicholas Ray, among others), began to champion the director. In 1956 Luc Moullet dubbed Ulmer "le plus maudit des cinéastes," and though he may not really have been the *most* "accursed" of filmmakers—indeed that same year François Truffaut hailed his work as "a small gift from Hollywood" and soon declared Ulmer one of America's best directors—his largely subterranean career, and even the reception of what is likely his best-known film, *Detour* (1945), has often seemed utterly doomed.[3] Like the *poète maudit* on which the term is based, the *cinéaste maudit* has been commonly understood as a romantic, tragic figure, whose style and sensibility spurn the mainstream, who is self-consciously outré or oppositional. The *Cahiers* critics gravitated toward this idea with uncommon zeal; to label a director or a film *maudit* was to grant a special status (Fritz Lang's M was released in France under the title *M le maudit*), to recognize an aesthetic whose greatness was, perhaps, accepted by a mere few, those who were the true purveyors of the cultural avant-garde. Ulmer would come to embody this very spirit and over the course of his life and career retained his marginal status, a "termite" artist as opposed to a "white elephant" artist, in Manny Farber's famous comparative scheme laid out in the pages of *Film Culture* in 1962. The peculiar force of termite art, wrote Farber, is that "it goes always forward eating its own boundaries, and, likely as not, leaves nothing in its path other than signs of eager, industrious, unkempt activity."[4]

For many decades now, Ulmer has understandably remained something of an enigma in the history of American and European cinema. "Ulmer occupies an unknown, uncharted, and apparently invisible space on the margins of cinema history," remarked John Belton in 1997.[5] Although he was made the subject of several interviews, in *Cahiers du cinéma* in the early 1960s and in extensive conversations with Peter Bogdanovich, recorded only two years before Ulmer's death and first published posthumously, in 1974, in *Film Culture,* and although bits of biographical information have trickled out over the years, the mystery still lingers.[6] Of the many entries contained in Rudolf Ulrich's comprehensive reference guide *Österreicher in Hollywood* (*Austrians in Hollywood,* 1993), there is only a brief and partially inaccurate piece on Ulmer. What Ulrich does get right, however, is his opening assertion: "The first years of his life lie somewhat in the dark, as Ulmer himself gave different years of his birth in different interviews."[7]

Focusing on this aspect of Ulmer's story—both the shadowy details surrounding his life and the fact that he spent his career in the shadows of his cohort of famous Viennese émigré directors, including Fritz Lang, Otto Preminger, and Fred Zinnemann—Austrian film critic Stefan Grissemann published his aptly titled 2003 biography of Ulmer *Mann im Schatten* (Man in the shadows). Regarding the filmmaker's childhood, Grissemann observes the following:

> He grew up in a Viennese rental apartment located on the Hofenedergasse during the early years of the past century. It is a rather quiet, unusually hidden street in the Second District [the Leopoldstadt], only a few minutes on foot from the Praterstern, and yet not quite visible, as if cut off from the city life which begins to assert itself just two blocks away, easily reachable, but only to a person who knows what he's looking for. Edgar Georg Ulmer's childhood matches the kind of cinema that he would later produce: close to all that's timely and popular, very near to that which is big, explicit, and evocative of success, and still hardly visible, kept in secrecy, almost private—something of a mystery.[8]

More enigmatic than all other phases of his life and career, Ulmer's childhood, and what we know of it, has to be traced along a disparate route made up of verifiable facts and assertions that fall somewhere in the murky zone between truth and fiction. As French filmmaker Bertrand Tavernier, who together with Luc Moullet interviewed Ulmer in the early 1960s, has said of him: "He is a character even beyond his films, one of the rare people that when you read what he has said it's practically impossible to be able to write his life because he was everywhere at the same time."[9] Tavernier regards Ulmer as someone given to extraordinary "invention, dream, mythomania," a compulsive liar and inveterate fabulist, "someone who was totally original and sometimes a little mad." Adding a critical rejoinder, however, Tavernier also considers Ulmer someone who, when you least expect it, is capable of telling the most outlandish story that turns out to be "totally accurate," a story almost more spectacular than the patently fabricated ones he was famous for telling. Finally, as he has said of Ulmer more recently, "He seems almost like a fictitious character himself, but I can testify: He lived!"[10]

THE EARLY YEARS

What we do know is that Ulmer was born on September 17, 1904. And even if he often pronounced himself a native of Vienna, sometimes claiming to be four years older than he actually was—presumably as a means of lending greater credence to his assertions of having

worked on various films when he would have barely been a teenager—
the truth of the matter is that he came into the world not in the
Habsburg capital but at his family's summer residence in the provinces, in the Moravian town of Olmütz (Olomouc), in what is today
the Czech Republic. His birth certificate makes it clear that his family
address, which was originally where his paternal grandparents resided,
was Resselgasse 1 (today Resslova 1) in the Olmütz district of Neu-
gasse (today Nová ulice).[11] He was born at home, not at the hospital,
and owing to the story told by his family, that he first appeared completely covered in placenta, he was thought to have emerged from
"underneath a veil," appropriately hidden from direct view.[12] His
younger Viennese-born sister Elvira, known as Elly, used to like to
tease her elder siblings, all of whom were born outside the city, calling
them *Bauernkinder* (peasant children).[13] Soon after his birth, however, Ulmer and his family returned to Vienna, the birthplace of his
mother, where Edgar was raised in the Leopoldstadt, a district known
for its high concentration of Jews, many of them from the outer
reaches of the Austro-Hungarian Empire. There he was provided the
basic petit-bourgeois comforts of his parents, Siegfried (Figure 1), a
Moravian wine merchant, and Henriette (*née* Edels), an unsuccessful
opera singer (Figure 2). In these early years Ulmer's father was frequently on the road, said to return for only brief periods—just long
enough to leave his wife pregnant with the next child—and his mother,
not known for her warmth, earned a lifelong reputation for a nasty
temper and an occasionally brutal punitive streak (when Edgar would
misbehave, his wife, Shirley Ulmer, recounted many years later, "she
would lock him in a dark closet and leave him there for a whole
day").[14] Edgar was the eldest of four children, two boys (Edgar and
Max) and two girls (Karola and Elly) (Figure 3); a fifth child, a daughter, died soon after birth.

Brought up as a thoroughly secular, assimilated Viennese Jew,
Ulmer claimed to have attended a local Jesuit school; in his interview
with Bogdanovich he said he had never known he was a Jew until he
went to high school (B 577). Yet it remains altogether unclear which
school in Vienna he actually attended. It was not, in any case, the
prestigious Akademisches Gymnasium to which he alludes in his
unpublished autobiographical novel, "Beyond the Boundary"; nor
was it the Schottengymnasium, of equally high repute in the world of
Viennese secondary education. There is, as I learned after dogged
efforts to secure information, no record at either school of an Edgar

FIGURE 1. Siegfried Ulmer, circa 1900. Courtesy of Edgar G. Ulmer Preservation Corp.

Georg Ulmer ever having been a pupil there. Yet despite the paucity of hard documentation, it is still possible to speculate—based on correspondence and personal accounts—on the abilities and talents Ulmer possessed as a youngster. "He was an unusual child from all I've heard," writes his wife, Shirley—whom he would marry in 1935 and who would be his lifelong collaborator and ardent defender of his reputation—in a letter of June 1939, to their young daughter, Arianné, then two years old, in an attempt to sketch a personal account of Ulmer's family background, "eager, sensitive, strong willed and periodically morose. His tremendous ego has been fed and nurtured by himself since infancy, and despite all obstacles—all

FIGURE 2. Henriette Ulmer, circa 1900. Courtesy of Edgar G. Ulmer Preservation Corp.

family attachments—all sentimentalities, he could remain unmoved until his purpose be achieved."[15] Indeed, in an early portrait of Ulmer as a teen, taken at a Viennese photo studio located around the corner from his family apartment, near the amusement parlors of the Prater, he has his arms folded and his chin slightly raised, projecting an air of self-confidence and maturity (Figure 4).

The city of Vienna undoubtedly left its mark on the young Edgar, whose early life was thoroughly saturated with the cultural heritage of his time. This was, after all, the same Vienna that fellow filmmaker

FIGURE 3. The Ulmer children, circa 1912. *Foreground from left:* Elly, Karola, Edgar. *Background:* Max. Courtesy of Edgar G. Ulmer Preservation Corp.

Josef von Sternberg, ten years Ulmer's senior, once pronounced a *Kinderparadies* (children's paradise) and that famed turn-of-the-century Viennese novelist Stefan Zweig so lovingly described in his sentimental memoir *Die Welt von Gestern* (*The World of Yesterday*, 1943) as a "golden age of security."[16] As unsustainable as the mythical, near utopian status of the city may have been—Zweig himself admitted that it ultimately proved to be little more than a "castle of dreams"—its cultural landscape helped shape, and was shaped by, a generation of young Austrians, largely of Jewish extraction, who saw the city as their cradle.[17] In the many years since, several critics have drawn attention to

FIGURE 4. Portrait of Edgar as a young man, circa 1916. Courtesy of Edgar G. Ulmer Preservation Corp.

Ulmer's relentless inclusion of high art references (ambitious classical scores, modernist sets, assorted highbrow literary references, and aesthetic flourishes) in even some of his lowliest productions. Ulmer managed to bring "art and culture," as Tavernier observes, "to the most unexpected places."[18] From the outset he was a self-described aesthete, a *Kulturfreak,* as another commentator has remarked, somebody "who engorged himself and his family—and of course his films—with art of all kinds from Schumann's piano concertos to the Venus de Milo."[19]

But Vienna's impact on the blossoming youth was not solely affirmative. In the spring of 1916, before Ulmer had reached his twelfth birthday, his father died of kidney failure while in Austrian uniform fighting on the Italian front in the First World War; like so many patriotic Austro-Hungarian Jews, Siegfried Ulmer had volunteered to serve in Emperor Franz Josef's army. Young Edgar, not quite a full-blown adolescent, is said to have been sent alone, rather mercilessly, to identify the body of his father and to help transfer his remains to Vienna.[20] There can be little doubt that such a devastating loss—a loss he forever associated with the city—was tough to digest for a young boy, and it certainly left an indelible scar, not only personally but also artistically. "In so many of his films," observes Michael Henry Wilson, "the father figure is absent or is dead and is influencing the character from beyond the grave."[21] We merely need to think of some of the most prominent examples from Ulmer's repertoire, such as *Strange Illusion* (1945), *Carnegie Hall* (1947), or *Ruthless* (1948). On April 12, 1916, Siegfried Ulmer was buried in Vienna's Zentralfriedhof.

BEYOND THE BOUNDARY

Some two decades after the death of his father, Ulmer dedicated a draft of his unfinished novel "Beyond the Boundary," which is dated "Hollywood 1935": "To one of the many thousand soldiers, who died in the first World War; In memoriam of Siegfried Ulmer, my father."[22] The ravages of war form not only the backdrop of Ulmer's fragmented, elliptical, and deeply autobiographical text—which follows the psychological and sexual travails of Viennese adolescent George (the Anglicized version of Ulmer's middle name) Weichert on his path through the war-torn capital—but also highlight, to a considerable extent, his own coming of age and his budding creative sensibility. Indeed, he would continue to draw on the war experience throughout his later years. Ulmer's wife, Shirley, who typed much of the manuscript while her husband dictated it to her, has said that the book "was something that he didn't want anybody to know about . . . like it was a diary," or what Ulmer thought of as "[his] little private work."[23] He chose to write a novel, as he explains to Bogdanovich, "because I did not *believe* the literature during and after the war on both sides: in Germany *and* in England, it was very much the heroic thing, where enemies were friends like you never saw. I couldn't believe that" (B 576).

For years, as he continued his labors intermittently between film projects, it became something of a family joke, a book that would be published, if at all, in some later century. Realizing perhaps that this was not his usual métier, and that he needed to write in a style and a language that was not his own, he once confided to his wife, "You know, I'm a bit of a thief, because I'm trying to follow the style of Franz Werfel and [Thomas] Mann."[24] Both Werfel and Mann, who, like Ulmer, had taken up residence in the larger community of German and Austrian-born émigrés and refugees in Los Angeles of the 1930s and 1940s, were names evocative of that golden age of literature and culture with which Ulmer frequently and passionately identified himself. Consider, for instance, the opening paragraphs of the novel:

> It is quiet in the large dark room. The dawn hasn't broken yet. The presence of sleeping humans is obvious. The window is open and past the snow-

covered ledge, streams in the cold winter air. It gets quite cold in Vienna in the winter.

The window looks out upon a back yard. Fore-shortened in perspective, one feels the back wall of the other house alongside. And opposite that bleak back wall, in "L" form runs a wing, housing the servant- and kitchen-quarters. Beyond that . . . the skyline of Vienna.

It's futile to describe it. Listen to Schubert, Johann Strauss, to Mozart and Haydn, and you will feel the strange substance of sentimentality, charm . . . the Spanish court-ceremonial and the Wienerwald . . . the Danube.

The novel follows its protagonist, George, through the streets of the semidestitute city, from the breadlines to the brothels, and chronicles his coming of age—the traumatic death of his father, his sexual awakening in adolescence at the hands of a local prostitute, and his final departure from his maternal home, scenes taken from Ulmer's own life. Although it is far from first-rate in terms of its overall literary quality—the text is littered with errors, frequent ellipses, and handwritten notations suggesting he hoped in vain to return to it later—it does offer something in the way of substance concerning Ulmer's cultural sensibility, which would be adapted, never completely, often as mere traces, into his cinematic output. Indeed the sounds of Vienna, not to mention the "ghostlike" figures and "shadows" ("like thoughts in dreams") that populate Ulmer's oneiric work, would crop up continuously in his aural and visual lexicon.

The novel's heavy emphasis on music not only jibes with the most prominent cultural currents of fin-de-siècle Vienna but also fits the self-fashioned profile of its author, who considered music his first passion and who was known to use a baton—one that originally belonged to Franz Liszt and was passed to Ulmer by the Hungarian-born musician Leo Erdody, a frequent collaborator, whose father had received it as a gift—on the set. A penciled notation ("Why does the discord of an orchestra tuning up never disturb me?") atop the first page of the text is repeated in the closing lines of the chapter, followed by Ulmer's rather heavy-handed, overextension of his chosen metaphor: "And so the boy George became part of the orchestra itself . . . with all its many instrumental sections. . . . He somehow too felt he was being tuned up . . . but did not actually know it." Leading up to this, we are made to witness George's nocturnal strolls with his maid, Poldi—a peasant girl who holds a certain erotic attraction over the adolescent boy—through the city streets and alleys. We are also treated to a critical flashback of George's father in military uniform. His parting words, after explaining to his son that he may not return from the front and that he should be prepared to take care of his mother and siblings, are instructive: "Never forget your and my name . . . our good name." Ulmer himself would bear the burden of upholding his father's name and employs the novel as a means of paying personal homage, from its dedication onward.

Throughout the narrative the trauma of war figures with great prominence. When George visits the comparatively grand, sumptuous home of his friend Heinrich, who "played the piano like a virtuoso" and is two classes ahead of George, they debate the merits of the patriotic fervor—the so-called spirit of 1914—that swept the country in the early years of the Austrian military campaign. Playing on the Latin education of Viennese schoolchildren of Ulmer's generation, George cites Horace's *Odes,* "Dulce est pro patria mori" (It is sweet to die for one's country), and goes on, in one of the more thinly veiled autobiographical moments of the novel, to confront Heinrich: "So my father was killed in your war. What does that make us children? War orphans! . . . My mother was left with four children." George castigates his friend for not being more sympathetic to the predicament in which thousands of women and children found themselves, standing in the breadlines with ration cards and waiting in vain for proper sustenance, an atmosphere perhaps most poignantly captured in Hugo Bettauer's novel *Die freudlose Gasse (The Joyless Street,* 1925), adapted to the screen by G. W. Pabst a year later. The rotten taste of "warbread" serves as a redolent leitmotif in the novel.

Following their heated discussion, George ends up storming off from his friend's home only to find himself with a prostitute called Peppi, whom he recognizes from the breadlines in which he waits with his maid. Peppi offers a kind of familiar, possibly maternal comfort—she affectionately calls George "Bubi" (an Austrian term of affection for a small boy)—that he is willing to pay for. As his first sexual partner, Peppi is accorded special status. George insists, as a means of preserving her status as long as possible, that she accept his extra payment of ten kronen so she can spend the entire night sequestered in their hotel room without entertaining additional patrons. Upon leaving Peppi at the hotel, Ulmer draws again on his musical lexicon and has George observe, "If I were a great composer like Johann Sebastian Bach, I would write another *Passion.* Not with the son of God on the cross, but woman." He then underscores the transformation: "The child George had died; because there had to be room in his soul for the man George."

In a highly compressed chapter, limited to a single typewritten page, Ulmer opens with yet another musical allusion, marking the chosen tempo of his work "allegro con brio," an ostensible reference to the countless Viennese composers, from Haydn through Schoenberg, who were known to begin their symphonies in that same tempo. The setting here, however, is the horrible winter of 1916–17, when rations were cut and the initial war frenzy had begun to wane. "The once gay and noisy people of Vienna had become ominously silent," he writes. "They shuffled like shadows through winter cold streets. . . . A melody like a dirge began slowly to rise." The fateful night with Peppi, now months in the past, remains on the forefront of George's mind: "Somehow he felt that this experience had unnaturally and prematurely brought him to maturity." The young boy retreats inside himself, closing off the outside world and, like Ulmer himself ostensibly did, closing off his relationship to his mother. Ulmer writes of George, "He wanted no part of his home, nor his mother." Over the years, in his personal writings, Ulmer would frequently revisit his animosity toward his own mother and the conflicted feelings that took root in him. "I hated my mother mentally," he writes in a long, introspective letter to his wife, sent from Rome on April 25, 1949, and explicitly indebted to Freud ("The great inventor and prophet of psychoanalysis," as he calls him); yet, he then adds, with the slightly bungled syntax of an émigré, "as a woman I adored her."[25] It is worth recalling that Ulmer wrote this work, in his adopted language, only ten years after arriving on these shores. His general linguistic mastery—minor syntactical errors and, in spoken English, his thick Viennese accent notwithstanding—is impressive.

As for his protagonist, George leaves his mother's house behind and moves in with a Dr. Erika Donat, an avowedly "sexless" woman he meets during a long night of drinking at a coffeehouse and who, according to the narrator, is "one of the very few young human beings who successfully has overcome the inheritance of being Viennese and therefore sentimental and *gemütlich*." George announces, "I haven't any home; never had one," a bold pronouncement with far wider reverberations later in Ulmer's life. Indebted to the precedent of Schnitzler, Freud, and other fin-de-siècle Viennese writers who sought to plumb the depths of the subconscious, Ulmer couches his penultimate chapter in a haze of intoxication and dreams. "This is a dream," asserts George. "This is alcohol speaking through me." Almost clinical in her approach, Dr. Donat engages with George in a kind of dialogic analysis, a talking cure of sorts. "You are in the embryonic development of the intellectual," she tells him, noting that she belongs "to that class of physicians that prefer to tell their patients the truth." She then goes on to explain to George, with more than a subtle nod to Nietzsche: "The intellectualist is perforce an egomaniac and possessing these requirements you shall undoubtedly become a valuable addition to that select circle of critics and oracles."

For Ulmer, as he noted repeatedly in his letters, the pure intellectual or artist, loyal to his or her pursuit—the genius perhaps—forms a separate social class. As he writes to his daughter, Arianné, from Munich, just after Christmas 1955, seemingly glossing *Thus Spoke Zarathustra* once more: "Art is a very high peak which very few people have really ascended. The air is thin, cold, way up there. Practically no people live up there. It's warmer in the valley where all the other people live. There is laughter down there, children and the comfortable house and somebody who belongs to you."[26] To George, who fashions himself "the smartest boy in [his] class," the path is similarly lonely. The penultimate chapter concludes with George lying down to sleep, with a final thought of transformation: "Always something happened to lift him from the greatest despondency to a state of security from which he was able to start the trek of his earthly existence anew."

The novel offers little in the way of resolution. In fact, the fifth and final chapter is just as skeletal as some of the other more compressed parts. There is no formal denouement. Instead, George awakens the next morning, somewhat confused and disoriented, at Dr. Donat's home. A young woman, Miss Ilse, a student at the Academy of Dramatic Arts who was taken in by Dr. Donat two years ago, greets him in her pink robe. She teases George for wearing one of Erika's sleeping gowns, calls him "the run-away" and mistakenly addresses him as "Joseph" instead of George, possibly an allusion to the biblical figure known to be an interpreter of dreams. George is "put properly in his place" by the rhetorical skills of the aspiring actress, and the story essentially comes to a halt there. As elsewhere in the writing process, Ulmer shows a high degree of self-awareness; indeed, the very act of writing a fragmentary, autobiographical work with literary pretensions is itself highlighted throughout the text. For example, George receives Stendhal's *Souvenirs d'égotisme (Memoirs of an Egotist)*, a work that is similarly autobiographical and fragmentary, as a gift for his fifteenth birthday from his friend Heinrich. Dr. Erika Donat, in conversation with George, declares herself to be "good material for a novel or play in the modern vein" and suggests possible affinities to Jakob Wassermann and Henrik Ibsen. "Amusing to be conscious of one's own value as story material," she concludes, with a tacit reference to the nature of the entire project. Long after setting out to write his novel, Ulmer would remain enthralled by notions of self-mythologizing and the vast powers of the human imagination.

BIG CITY OF DREAMS

Like many artists before him, Ulmer felt the need to declare himself a native son of Vienna and, in so doing, claimed a profound attachment—emotional, cultural, and otherwise—to the storied city. "When Truffaut and the critics of the *Cahiers du cinéma* interviewed the man, he gave Vienna as his birthplace," observes Bernd Herzogenrath. "Fashioning himself as a representative of European High Culture, Ulmer almost naturally felt the urge to repress provinciality."[27] By the eve of the Great War, just as Ulmer was approaching his tenth birthday, a catchy tune entitled "Wien, du Stadt meiner Träume" (Vienna, you are the city of my dreams), written by Rudolf Sieczynski, was making the rounds in the Imperial capital and becoming a worldwide hit (Stanley Kubrick would later use it to set the tone for his final film, the fin-de-siècle, Schnitzler-inspired *Eyes Wide Shut,* 1999). The song's refrain goes as follows:

> Wien, Wien, nur Du allein
> Sollst stets die Stadt meiner Träume sein
> Dort wo die alten Häuser stehn,
> Dort wo die lieblichen Mädchen gehn . . .
>
> (Vienna, Vienna, none but you,
> Can be the city of my dreams come true
> Here, where the dear old houses loom,
> Where I for lovely young girls swoon . . .)[28]

As the scene of Ulmer's first metropolitan experience, Vienna certainly attained the status of city of dreams, and he continued to treat it as such long after he left it behind, first for Sweden, then for Berlin to work on Max Reinhardt's stage productions, and still later on for New York, Hollywood, and eventually back to Europe once more. Indeed, the course of Austrian cinema was not unlike the itinerary of Ulmer's life. From the very beginning the industry was necessarily international, with well-trodden paths leading to Berlin, Paris, and, somewhat later, Hollywood.[29] "Austrian film history is a phantasm," the German film critic Frieda Grafe once remarked, "because it is not tied to a fixed place; its cinema is a kind of film without a specific space." In her pithy summation, with a wink to the city's famous literati and psychoanalysts, "Vienna was a reservoir of dreams."[30]

By the time Ulmer reached his teens, the Austro-Hungarian Empire, that vibrant amalgamation of cultures and ethnicities, no longer existed. And even before that, the Jews of Vienna, as Carl Schorske has noted, had become regarded as a "supra-national people."[31] It should perhaps come as no surprise, then, that the Viennese-born, or in Ulmer's case Viennese-trained, film directors were particularly adroit fabulists when it came to dreaming up their pasts in the film world of Hollywood, the factory of dreams. Erich von Stroheim would take on a self-avowed air of Prussian aristocracy; Otto Preminger pedaled the image of a Teutonic tyrant, something he shared with Fritz Lang; Billy Wilder embraced the identity of a former gigolo and star reporter ("In a single morning," he boasted to *Playboy*'s Richard Gehman, "I interviewed Sigmund Freud, his colleague Alfred Adler, the playwright and novelist Arthur Schnitzler, and the composer Richard Strauss. In *one* morning");[32] and Ulmer, no less immodestly, fashioned himself a wunderkind from Reinhardt's renowned drama school and an "aesthete from the Alps."[33] Each of these roles, and there were of course many more, would offer a new identity to the displaced émigré in need of a quick makeover, especially one that might bring more work or, at the very least, some additional grist for the public relations mill. As Ulmer once remarked of Stroheim, with a tone of approval, if not outright adulation: "I loved Stroheim. The man invented his own character—everything" (B 568).[34]

From childhood onward, Ulmer would remain engaged in the process of self-invention; his Viennese youth, the skills he learned, and the cultural mythology that seems to have followed him to the New World featured prominently in this process. "He is a king without a country," insisted Frieda Grafe. "Out of necessity, he made films in Hollywood almost without any means, dark films conjured from his imagination."[35] The Viennese seemed especially well equipped for this task. "The secret affinity that existed between Hollywood on one side and Vienna or Paris on the other," observes Thomas Elsaesser, "was that they were societies of the spectacle, cities of make-believe and of the show. The decadence of the Habsburg monarchy was in some ways the pervasive sense of impersonation, of pretending to be in possession of values and status that relied for credibility not on substance but on convincing performance, on persuading others to take an appearance for the reality."[36]

FIGURE 5. Ulmer with his host family in Sweden, 1919. Courtesy of Edgar G. Ulmer Preservation Corp.

There were, however, real-life events that punctuated the illusion of living merely in a spectacular world of appearances. After his father Siegfried's death—it's hard not to think of the event in mythical, even Wagnerian, terms—with the help of a Jewish aid organization and the U.S. Hoover Commission, Edgar and his sister Karola were sent to a foster family in Sweden, where they remained until the end of the war (his brother, Max, found foster care in England, his sister Elvira in Holland). To qualify for financial support, Ulmer's mother, Henriette, allegedly had to present her children as orphaned nieces and nephews.[37] A surviving photo from that period shows Ulmer, in 1919, with his Swedish host family. Surrounded by mostly smiling young girls, he looks strangely ill at ease, uncharacteristically serious and without any hint of play, staring rather blankly at the camera (Figure 5).

Yet a much later letter, sent in May 1947 and written by Eric Kro-nning (*né* Katz) of Stockholm, one of the children in Ulmer's host fam-ily, tells of the happy times being cared for by various Jewish families in and around Stockholm, and Ulmer himself spoke equally fondly of his time in Sweden.[38] Likewise, Ulmer seems to have left a strong impres-sion on his Swedish foster family, and it is perhaps that positive experi-ence that made it possible for him, upon leaving Sweden, to return *not* to his mother (who, by 1920, had begun a relationship with a new man, something that her teenage son had difficulty countenancing) but instead, much like the character of George in "Beyond the Boundary," to enter into yet another nonbiological family structure.

Returning to Vienna in 1920, Ulmer moved in with the Schildkrauts, a father-son acting duo, Rudolph and Joseph, who were largely responsible for introducing him to the world of theater and cinema. Around this same time, in continued rebellion against his mother, he rejected her plans for him to become a furrier, a trade that Middle European Jews of his genera-tion pursued in relatively large numbers, and instead registered for courses at Vienna's Academy of Fine Arts. This sort of rebellion was not uncom-mon among Ulmer's cohort of aspiring filmmakers. "Indeed, in the Vienna of the Twenties," writes Neil Sinyard in his study of Fred Zinnemann, "there was a great gap between the mostly conservative and tradition-bound professional class and film people, who were definitely not regarded as solid citizens."[39] At the Academy of Fine Arts, Ulmer is said to have taken courses with Alfred Roller, who, like Rudolph Schildkraut, was a close collaborator of Max Reinhardt and helped him to establish the Sal-zburger Festspiele.[40] There is, regrettably, no surviving record at Vienna's Academy of Fine Arts of Ulmer ever having formally enrolled; records of this sort are generally kept only for graduates of the academy, which sug-gests that, assuming he attended at all, he never graduated. In Shirley Ulmer's rendition, written in a personal letter from 1939, "[Ulmer] had wanted to be a symphony conductor, but his widowed mother wouldn't sponsor his education along these lines. Even so, he took the next best route along 'the world of make believe'—the stage."[41]

Regardless of the precise circumstances surrounding his formal studies—as Ulmer tells it, before his time with Reinhardt, "I took my schooling at the Burg Theater in Vienna" (B 562), the city's most his-torically renowned dramatic venue—the true details of which will likely never be known, what is clear is that the Schildkrauts served as an important conduit for Ulmer, an initial apprenticeship of sorts in prepa-ration for his later career. As Ulmer describes it himself, in conversation with Bogdanovich: "In my youth, the first time I ran away from home was with Rudolph Schildkraut and Pepi [i.e., Joseph]. Pepi was at the beginning in the theatre with me. Rudolph was, of course, a fantastic actor, and he understood kids" (B 577). In a slight variation of his own story, Ulmer's daughter, Arianné Ulmer Cipes, a former actress who appeared in several of her father's films, puts it this way: "My father was in Sweden as a war orphan after the First World War, and when he came back to Vienna, Rudolph Schildkraut—'Pepe' [*sic*] Schildkraut's father—took him into his home, and Joseph and Dad (who were pretty much the same age) became close friends. Rudolph Schildkraut was a matinee idol, the Barrymore of that time. He not only took my father in as a teenager, he got him into Max Reinhardt's dramatic school, where Dad started initially as a student to be an actor."[42]

Without relying too heavily on armchair psychoanalysis—or, quite simply, on the symbol-laden absence of a biological father—it would seem to make complete sense that Rudolph Schildkraut, an actor made famous by playing a series of patriarchs and grand Shakespearian figures, from Shylock to King Lear, should be well suited to be Ulmer's surrogate father. "At the core of Schildkraut's art," wrote Weimar-era theater critic Julius Bab, lies the "caring father."[43] For Bab, what was so special, and what remained seared in one's memory after viewing Schildkraut's many performances, was the "Vatergefühl" (paternal feeling) he transmitted. Indeed, Egon Dietrichstein featured the elder Schildkraut in his survey *Die Berühmten* (*The Celebrities,* 1920), calling him one of the last great comic actors, "strong, virtuous, formidable, like the mimes of the old school. But fine, delicate, nuanced. One cries and laughs with Schildkraut."[44] Schildkraut's son, in his autobiography *My Father and I* (1959), cites an unnamed critic, possibly Bab, making a similarly laudatory assertion: "Loving, majestic, kind and cheerful, helplessly crushed and frightening in his anger—always a father. This actor from a little village in Romania put his indelible mark on the German theater because he could rise to the highest levels of his art—whenever called upon to create the character of father."[45]

Alas, in his some 250-page memoir, much of it of the self-serving variety of ghostwritten autobiography, the younger Schildkraut, who enjoyed an enormously successful acting career in the United States and went on to win an Oscar for his portrayal of Captain Dreyfus in William Dieterle's *The Life of Emile Zola* (1937), does not see fit to mention his friendship with Ulmer (admittedly, he also fails to mention other key friendships, including that of Peter Lorre). Yet he does speak at great length about his father and his ties to Max Reinhardt, the so-called high priest of art, and mentions the great import of the Yiddish Theatre on New York's Lower East Side, where Rudolph acted in a number of classic plays and where Ulmer mentions having been introduced to some of the players with whom he would later collaborate on his four Yiddish features made in the late 1930s.[46] Although the Schildkrauts shuttled back and forth to Europe in the 1910s and 1920s, the dates that Ulmer gives in his interview match up, and it is fully conceivable that the Schildkrauts served as another kind of host family and as theatrical mentors to Ulmer for a brief, yet significant time.

MAX REINHARDT; OR, AN AESTHETIC EDUCATION

As was the case with most German and Austrian filmmakers of his generation, Ulmer learned much of his trade in the theater. And like these acclaimed figures (F. W. Murnau, Otto Preminger, William Dieterle, and others), he eventually made his way to Max Reinhardt. "It's very difficult to imagine today what the name Max Reinhardt meant when I grew up in Vienna," notes Preminger in an interview from the early 1970s; and, as he suggests later in the same interview, "nobody who watched him direct and became a director could escape his influence."[47] The Schildkrauts are credited with having arranged Ulmer's formal introduction to Reinhardt, and they both had far-reaching ties to the renowned theater impresario. Ulmer's tenure at Reinhardt's Berlin-based drama school, at the Deutsches Theater, or somewhat later at the Viennese Theater in der Josefstadt, however, has yet to be documented (and, in fact, given the staggering number of students who trained with Reinhardt, it may never be). What can be ascertained with relative assuredness, however, is Ulmer's journey to New York to assist in the staging of Reinhardt's grand production of *Das Mirakel (The Miracle)* at the Century Theatre, which entailed nothing short of the total transformation of a run-of-the-mill theater on the Upper West Side into a Gothic cathedral.[48]

Ulmer himself claims to have been involved in the stage design for the production, and he describes his first trip to New York, at the age of nineteen, as having been organized by the Schildkrauts. Indeed, Rudolph Schildkraut was part of the original cast of *The Miracle* that traveled to New York with the show. It is fully plausible that Ulmer had a hand, perhaps as one of the many designers or simply one of the some seven hundred people enlisted in the play's highly successful ten-month, 298-performance run.[49] The Berlin-born actor Fritz Feld, a principal in the Reinhardt production and a repeat player in Ulmer's pictures of the 1940s, attests to this fact in his eulogy to Ulmer, delivered on October 3, 1972. "Edgar came to the United States in the same year as I did," he begins, "49 years ago. We first met in Salzburg, Austria. Both of us belonged to the staff of Professor Max Reinhardt. Edgar was born in the romantic Vienna and he had all the charm of the true Viennese."[50] Yet the official record at Ellis Island, which indicates his transatlantic passage on the SS *President Roosevelt* and his arrival in New York Harbor on April 12, 1924 (also his place of residence as "Wein" [*sic!*]), puts him in Manhattan long after the opening on January 16, 1924.[51] There are nevertheless a number of plausible scenarios regarding Ulmer's involvement in *The Miracle*: (1) that Ulmer came at the request of his friends Feld and Schildkraut, both of whom were officially engaged in the production; (2) that he came to assist Reinhardt and his chief American collaborator, Norman Bel Geddes, in set design or some other capacity (the ship manifest lists his profession as "actor"), in the ongoing performance; or (3) that he simply seized the chance to travel to the Unites States, like countless other European theater and film people, in search of greater opportunities and financial prosperity.

In an end-of-season review in the *New York Times,* on November 9, 1924, more than ten months after its premiere, and seven months after Ulmer's arrival in New York, critic Stark Young hailed *The Miracle* as "a landmark in the history of American theatre" and went on to note that for the immense and rather lavish production—with outlay costs of more than $600,000 and total earnings of $2 million—"700 people are said to have been employed."[52] Ulmer is not listed in the official entry on *The Miracle* contained in Heinrich Huesmann's *Welttheater Reinhardt*, the most detailed, exhaustive reference guide to Reinhardt's productions. But Huesmann does not account for the hundreds involved and, in fact, lists only those who participated in the play's premiere, when Ulmer had not yet landed on American shores.[53]

Anecdotal evidence from Reinhardt's acclaimed New York production, as conflicting and unreliable as it may be, abounds. For instance, Shirley Ulmer tells how her husband, whose English was quite poor at the time of his arrival, allegedly offended the play's leading lady, Diana Manners, by using expletives unwittingly as stage directions during rehearsal. In that same interview she shares the opinion with Michael Henry Wilson that *The Miracle* was "an inspiration for a long time in his work" and that, as a kind of morality play, it provided an archetype for Ulmer's later projects as a filmmaker.[54] Of course, the success of the

EDGAR ULMER
REGISSEUR UND AUSSTATTUNGSCHEF DER
REINHARDTBÜHNEN

WIEN – BERLIN – NEW-YORK

FIGURE 6. Ulmer's calling card. Courtesy of the Edgar G. Ulmer Preservation Corp.

production, and the breakthrough that it marked for Reinhardt's American career, made it all the more attractive for a young émigré like Ulmer looking to build a strong résumé. The kind of ardent press attention and rave reviews that the production garnered—a bold headline from the *New York Journal* read "Professor Reinhardt Proves He Is Fully as Great an Artist as Heralded" and eminent critic Brooks Atkinson hailed it as "a stupendous enterprise"—are reviews that any aspiring artist can only dream of.[55]

Regardless of the true scope of his engagement with Reinhardt, though, Ulmer clearly identified himself as part of the Reinhardt school. His visiting card from the period (presumably from the early to mid-1920s) boldly asserts his affiliation (Figure 6). Here he lists his self-appointed title as director and *Ausstatungschef* (head of design) for the Reinhardt stage and also gives Vienna, Berlin, and New York as his cities of operation, an early gesture toward the cosmopolitan identity Ulmer embraced until his death (the transatlantic commute he began in the 1920s would resume in the late 1940s, 1950s, and 1960s). As for the aesthetic legacy from Reinhardt, Ulmer's unwavering attention to mise-en-scène, to artifice and aesthetic detail may indeed be attributed to the precedent set by Reinhardt.

Another strand of this legacy is reflected in his continued artistic collaborations (with people like set designer Rochus Gliese, cameraman Eugen Schüfftan, composer Leo Erdody, and émigré actors Fritz Kortner, Felix Bressart, Hedy Lamarr, and Eva Gabor, among others). We can also note his frequent reliance on European sources (stories by Viennese writers Gina Kaus, Fritz Rotter, Salka Viertel, and others) and the shameless inclusion of inside jokes, accented asides, and allusions ostensibly aimed at the sensibility of German-speaking émigrés in Hollywood (for example, his playful characterization of the collapsed Habsburg Empire and the haunted architect Hjalmar Poelzig in *The Black Cat* or his villainous figure referred to as "Karl Kraus" in *Beyond the Time Barrier*).[56] Although much of his work, both before and after migration to America, can be checked against the historical record, there are instances, such as his professed collaborations with Fritz Lang on such acclaimed productions as *Metropolis* and *M*, that have trouble withstanding the glare of critical scrutiny. "Herr Ulmer never worked for me," insisted Lang when asked about the repeated claims of collaboration, "neither as a film architect nor as a set designer, nor in any other capacity."[57]

In the end, then, Ulmer remains something of a phantom figure, a *Phantombild*, as Grissemann has dubbed him. Tracking his early years is akin to tracking a Zelig-like character that seems to have been everywhere and involved in everything all at the same time. As with Woody Allen's *Zelig*, we are often left to ask ourselves whether such a figure could possibly have existed or whether he's merely a figment of our imagination. It is with good reason that the most memorable line from Andrew Sarris's 1968 entry on the director, tucked away in the "Expressive Esoterica" section of his highly influential compendium *The American Cinema*, reads: "But yes, Virginia, there is an Edgar G. Ulmer, and he is no longer one of the private jokes shared by auteur critics, but one of the minor glories of the cinema."[58] Even if Ulmer's work did not always demand a defensive reflex—Sarris calls him "a director without alibis"—his wider reputation as a teller of tall tales never quite left him. When *Film Comment* ran an article, in the spring of 1990, on ten of the all-time greatest apocryphal Hollywood stories, they published the piece under the wicked title "Ready When You Are, Mr. Ulmer."[59]

In his witty musings in "The Decay of Lying," Oscar Wilde comes to an apt conclusion: "The final revelation is that Lying, the telling of beautiful untrue things, is the proper aim of Art."[60] While it may not be the proper aim of life, Ulmer's life and his art often seem to merge, blurring on repeated occasion almost beyond recognition. "Brother, when it comes to lying," boxer Kid Slug Rosenthal (Maxie Rosenbloom) tells his manager Big Time (Roscoe Karns) early on in Ulmer's wartime comedy *My Son, the Hero*, "you're the champ." Another illustrative moment taken from Ulmer's repertoire comes in his acclaimed western *The Naked Dawn*—rated especially highly by Truffaut and his *Cahiers* colleagues—when the rebel protagonist attempts to impress his female admirer. The romantic, wandering outlaw Santiago (played by Arthur Kennedy, still relatively fresh off the set of Fritz Lang's *Rancho Notorious*) tells Maria (Betta St. John) of the legendary beauties of Veracruz: the dancing, the drinking, and the women. Yet, after serving up a series of florid embellishments, he admits to Maria that it is really nothing more than a "fever swamp," a fitting allegory for many of Ulmer's cheapie productions.

Given Ulmer's own proclivity for the romantic, a predilection on which he prided himself—declaring his allegiance to the "art-possessed" directors as opposed to those vulgar enough to consider film a business— it is perhaps worth considering another romantic summation. "Did he have a tendency to exaggerate—as some have accused him?" asks Bogdanovich in the preface to the 1998 reprint of his interview with Ulmer. "Don't most people? Certainly the movies are a fabulist's paradise, because anything *is* possible. Didn't Edgar prove that with nearly every picture? Ulmer was a child of theatre and of the movies in their childhood and he never lost his innocent wonder at the challenge and magic of the medium."[61] Listening to the taped interviews with Bogdanovich, it's hard not to feel the passion that Ulmer had for art, for music, and of course for cinema. He told many elaborate heartfelt stories, not all of them included in the printed text, about his own legendary productions and about such stirring contemporary work as John Schlesinger's *Midnight Cowboy* (1969), a picture he saw multiple times and that left a deep impression on him. "I know that some directors lie," observes Tavernier. "They have to—or they invent things and after a few years, they believe their own lie."[62] While we may not choose to believe wholesale all that has been told by and about Edgar G. Ulmer, the story of his life, in particular his youth, would be impossible without the inclusion of at least a few of the half-truths and fabrications that helped shape him. In the remaining chapters it will be up to us to sort through the persisting myths and balance them with a more judicious, more precise understanding of the filmmaker as he came into his own.

Toward a Cinema at the Margins

Although Ulmer's first stay in New York City, in 1924, didn't last long—he appears to have made his way west as quickly as he could—it nonetheless left several strong impressions on the newcomer. Sometime during the second half of *The Miracle*'s ten-month run, he found his own living quarters, got his work papers in order, and searched for employment outside of Reinhardt's stage production.[1] While still adjusting to life in New York, he came into contact with another *landsman,* the Austrian-born vaudeville promoter Martin Beck, whom he assisted in designing the Martin Beck Theatre, which opened its doors on West 45th Street in November 1924 (B 576).[2] During Ulmer's first months in America the theater remained for him a constant source of intellectual and cultural stimulation. "When I came to New York the first time," remarks Ulmer in conversation with Bogdanovich, "Reinhardt hired [Rudolph] Schildkraut, who had worked for him in Europe, to play in *The Miracle*. And I was taken down to Second Avenue, and met the Jewish Art Theatre troupe, which had some tremendous actors—Muni Weisenfreund [Paul Muni], Jacob Adler, Maurice Schwartz—it was something which didn't exist elsewhere in all of New York. . . . It was a second Broadway down there" (B 577–78).

This early contact with the thriving Yiddish stage on New York's Lower East Side may well have motivated Ulmer, more than a decade later, to sign on to direct the four independent Yiddish feature films he completed in the late 1930s and 1940s. His dear friend Joseph Schildkraut, who had arrived in New York already in August 1920, and who was in large part responsible for introducing Ulmer to life in America—he would go on to introduce Ulmer to his first wife, the Californian dancer Josephine Warner, a couple of years later—writes in his memoir: "My first impression of New York was mixed, more confusing than exhilarating. The skyline, the harbor, the piers, the crowd—all these were exactly as I had seen them in paintings and photographs. Reality was merely copying art."[3] It's rather ironic that Schildkraut should find this relationship between art and reality in the New World, when in many instances theater and film transplants like himself were enlisted in the process of imitating reality in their art, even an imagined reality of the Old World left behind. Émigrés of Schildkraut's generation were often assigned in the New World the productions of Old World plays or films with an explicit investment in projecting a kind of "phantom Europe."[4] Perhaps for Ulmer one of the main attractions of New York was that there were so many fellow émigrés in his midst— the city was, after all, the first destination for immigrants—many of them artists, actors, directors, and crew members, who continued to draw on their pasts as a means of communicating with their new audience. In Ulmer's case it was often his European training and cultural sensibility that linked him to other émigrés working in the United States.

ARRIVAL IN HOLLYWOOD

Studio mogul Carl Laemmle, the influential head of Universal who himself had migrated to America from the Southern German town of Laupheim as a teenager, was known for his deep fondness for recruiting precocious young German-speaking émigrés. In the summer of 1921, while vacationing in Karlsbad, Laemmle hired the Bohemian-born producer and future agent Paul Kohner, then a nineteen-year-old, whose famed office on Sunset Boulevard would later represent, among many other émigrés, Ulmer.[5] He also contracted the future star director, Alsatian-born William Wyler (né Wilhelm Weiller)—whose mother was a distant cousin of the studio head himself and who, like Kohner, was handpicked by Laemmle on one of his annual European trips—in 1923, when Wyler had just turned twenty-one. Laemmle hired Ulmer, then also nearing his twenty-first birthday, a year later. Famous for his robust appreciation of constant company, Laemmle, or "Uncle Carl," as he was more commonly called, often surrounded himself with members of his extended clan—his children, nephews and cousins, sons-in-law and adopted sons—hosting regular Sunday luncheons at his home. As the American writer and poet Ogden Nash once quipped, "Uncle Carl Laemmle has a big faemmle."[6] Owing to his youthful ambition, his proven talent, and his ability to curry favor with Uncle Carl, Ulmer got his start in the lower echelons of Universal's Art Department, thereby earning an honorary spot in Laemmle's extended clan, where he remained more or less in good standing for nearly a decade.

Two photos of Ulmer, both taken on the Universal lot in the mid-1920s, show a proud young man getting his first taste of professional life at one of Hollywood's major studios. The first shot has him standing underneath a sign announcing Art Director C.D. (Danny) Hall's office—Ulmer would go on to employ Hall for the set design of *The Black Cat* (1934) a decade later—and below Hall's name is "Edgar G. Ulmer, Asst." (Figure 7). His hands are tucked into his pockets, his striped tie slightly rumpled, a leather bag draped around his shoulder, all conveying the casual confidence of someone who belongs. The second photo, snapped elsewhere on the lot, shows Ulmer posing in front of a glamorous convertible sedan, a car that symbolizes in unmistakable terms the American dream (Figure 8). He is wearing the same dark suit and striped tie as in the other photo—they appear to have been taken on the same day—and when one views the two snapshots as a pair, there is the implicit logic that with enough hard work at a big studio like Universal, the rewards will no doubt be ample.

"Everyone who met Edgar Ulmer in those years," suggests Grissemann, "must have noticed it, that hunger for meaning that the young man must have exuded, this aggressive form of yearning, the nagging desire to make himself indispensable in the art of creating something enduring, regardless of how, regardless in which position."[7] In relatively large numbers, young European émigrés of Ulmer's ilk seemed to sense, almost to smell, the opportunity in Hollywood, a place where one could make it despite one's non-American origins.[8] As the Viennese-born Fred Zinnemann would write to a friend in Berlin in December 1929, soon after his arrival in Southern California at the age of twenty-two and directly after his collaboration with Ulmer on the production of *Menschen am Sonntag* (*People on Sunday*, 1930): "Hollywood is a marvelously beautiful place, this constantly occurs to me, and then more than anything else I want to hit the ground running!"[9] The excitement and eagerness to succeed, to claw one's way into gainful employment, was quite infectious among the young émigrés, even if the cultural fit between

FIGURE 7. A studio man: Ulmer as assistant art director at Universal, circa 1925. Courtesy of Robert Ulmer.

the American dream factory and the Middle European transplants was not always a perfect one.

Working in Universal's Art Department, from roughly the end of 1924 to the middle of 1928, Ulmer's individual ambitions began to take root. There he not only invested his energy in art direction and design but also came into contact with future collaborators such as the cinematographer Benjamin Kline, cameraman of *Detour* and a regular during Ulmer's PRC years two decades later.[10] While assisting Wyler on a series of small-scale westerns, produced on the Universal lot at breakneck pace and with dizzying frequency, he eventually earned the opportunity to try his hand at direction. In the short obituary that

FIGURE 8. Dreaming of the big leagues: Ulmer posing with convertible sedan on the Universal lot, circa 1925. Courtesy of Robert Ulmer.

appeared in the *New York Times* on October 2, 1972, the unnamed author claims that Ulmer became known at this time for "grinding out 24 Western two-reelers in one year."[11] As Ulmer tells it, "There were two Western streets—on the upper part of one, Willy [Wyler] worked; on the lower part of the street, I worked. When Willy used the horses and the cowboys, I had to do close-ups in my pictures. Then, when I ran out of close-ups, *I'd* get the horses. . . . We had the following schedule: Monday and Tuesday, you wrote your script and prepared the production; Wednesday and Thursday, you shot; Friday, you cut; and Saturday, you went to Tijuana, gambling with the old man [Carl Laemmle]" (B 567). Philip Kemp points out that much of this work with Wyler can be corroborated and that Wyler himself duly acknowledged the partnership with Ulmer (albeit as a junior assistant) during these years.[12] (Small as the family circle seems to have been, it was Wyler's mother who first put Shirley Ulmer—then still Shirley Kassler—in contact with MGM head Irving Thalberg, who encouraged her to pursue a career as a script supervisor, which is exactly how she would meet Edgar Ulmer in 1934.)[13] As Carl Laemmle Jr. recounted in 1969, "He [Ulmer] started as a sketch artist but quickly became involved in production. Thereafter he worked as a second or third assistant director until we gave him a chance to develop in direction by assigning him to direct some of the two-reel series Westerns which we turned out in large numbers. We had quite a few series of one kind or another at the time and we rotated Mr. Ulmer so that he would be widely enough acquainted with all our product in this area to jump into directing wherever needed on the lot."[14]

In his conversations with Bogdanovich, Ulmer managed to recall one of the many B westerns some four and a half decades after the production, an otherwise forgettable, generic picture called *The Border Sheriff* (1926), on which he is credited as assistant director. The film, a five-reeler, features veteran cowboy stars Jack Hoxie as sheriff Cultus Collins and Peewee Holmes as his sidekick, Tater-Bug, with Robert N. Bradbury, who shot a string of westerns for Universal throughout the 1920s, taking the official director credit. As was perhaps demanded at the time, operating under the conditions of such rapid and routinized production, the film has the boilerplate characters, frenetic scenes with plenty of shoot-em-up chases on horseback, and the contrived story line—good guys (Hoxie and Holmes) working to crush the bad-guy border outlaws and shady businessmen—of any cheap 1920s western.[15] It is also, however, a prime example of the kind of pared-down, minimalist filmmaking espoused by such productions and thus an early object lesson for some of Ulmer's future projects.

Wyler tells a mordant tale from his days of churning out westerns on Universal's back lot with Ulmer. Always on the lookout for schemes to supplement studio income, Uncle Carl would charge spectators twenty-five cents to observe the filmmakers, almost like zoo animals, at work. Wyler wasn't especially fond of this practice and would try to come up with ways of scaring off the spectators, simulating violent arguments with his actors, tossing breakaway chairs and bottles, faking a shoot-out, anything to clear the crowd. Without knowing it, Ulmer was made to play a part in one of these stunts involving a staged fight, a series of gunshots, and all lights on the set going off. As Wyler recounts, "When the lights came on again, one of the fellows was lying sprawled in his blood and Edgar stood over him, dumbfounded, with a gun in his hand. He didn't know how he had gotten the gun. As he stood there watching his 'victim' in horror, a studio sheriff, who was in on it, put a hand on his shoulder, telling him he was under arrest for murder."[16] Ulmer allegedly fainted on the spot; when he awakened and was informed that it was nothing but a bad joke, he fainted again.

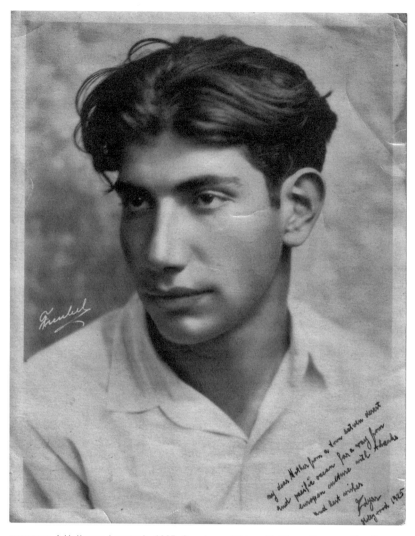

FIGURE 9. A Hollywood portrait, 1925. Courtesy of Edgar G. Ulmer Preservation Corp.

Among the Ulmer family memorabilia from the early years in Hollywood is an elegant photo portrait of the aspiring filmmaker from 1925,
taken at a studio in Los Angeles, that he chose to send home to his mother
in Vienna, perhaps as proof (a "Lebenszeichen," or sign of life) of his
arrival on the West Coast. It shows a handsome young man, with waves
of thick brown hair and inquisitive dark eyes, in a crisp white shirt—open
at the neck, as a true Californian might wear at the time—and a deliber-

ate, focused gaze. In sending the picture home to Vienna, he included a carefully worded dedication, written not in German, but in English, the language of his newly adopted home: "My dear Mother from a town between desert and pacific ocean, far a way from european culture with thanks and best wishes/Edgar/Hollywood 1925" (Figure 9).

Ulmer's early characterization of Hollywood as a place removed from European culture is significant insofar as it suggests the underlying sense of alienation that someone like himself, who so strongly identified with high art and culture, must have felt working on cheap westerns in 1920s Los Angeles. As he would go on to portray it, in such films as *Detour* (1945), Hollywood was for him a place precariously situated between the vast, largely uninhabitable Mojave Desert and the lush, alluring, and affluent California coastline. In the 1950s, in an unpublished piece he wrote called "The Director's Responsibility," Ulmer again located Hollywood "between the desert and the Pacific Ocean," but by then, some three decades after the relatively sanguine, clear-eyed photo portrait had been taken, it is a "sad and confused place."[17]

As for Ulmer's pat salutation on the portrait he sent home—"with thanks and best wishes"—it does not suggest much in the way of affection toward his mother; indeed, relations between the two were quite strained throughout the 1920s, when Ulmer officially left Vienna for America and, in keeping with his initial refusal to resettle in his maternal home after returning from Sweden, continued to assert his independence. On May 10, 1927, Henriette writes to her son, from whom she claims not to have heard anything in more than ten months, "Human beings must be able to forgive, and especially their mothers!"[18] While couched in her plea for forgiveness, what originally prompted Henriette Ulmer's letter was the news she stumbled upon that her son had collaborated with the famous German director F. W. Murnau, whose Hollywood debut for Fox Studios, *Sunrise* (1927), had begun production in September of 1926. What she presumably did not yet know was that her son, only a couple of weeks before the shooting of *Sunrise* commenced, had married a Southern Californian dancer, Josephine (Joen) Warner—a member of *The Fachonettes*, a dance troupe that entertained moviegoers at the Paramount Theatre in Los Angeles—at a wedding chapel in Riverside, California.[19] Ulmer and Warner were married on August 21, 1926, at the St. Cecilia Chapel of Riverside's Mission Inn. Their honeymoon would take place in Lake Arrowhead, the chosen location for shooting *Sunrise,* where, as was often the case for Ulmer, work came before pleasure.

On loan from Universal, Ulmer joined forces with German-born Rochus Gliese in set design at Fox, assisting Murnau, also a former Reinhardt pupil, on his high-profile, and much-touted, production. By his account Ulmer had already worked with Gliese on Murnau's film *Die Finanzen des Grossherzogs* (*The Finances of the Grand Duke*, 1924), made for Ufa in the summer of 1923, before Ulmer had yet reached his nineteenth birthday. Its premiere at the Ufa-Palast am Zoo on January 7, 1924, was just a few months before Ulmer's departure for New York. In her study of Murnau, Lotte Eisner, who is otherwise generally disinclined to believe Ulmer (whom she memorably calls "the greatest liar in the history of cinema") suggests that indeed he "collaborated" on the film.[20] In February 1927 Ernst Chaparral, an editor at the highly influential German trade daily *Film-Kurier,* filed a report from Hollywood—perhaps the same report that eventually reached Henriette Ulmer's hands in Vienna—about the shooting of Murnau's *Sunrise.* He recounts a tour of the film locations, which he took with colleagues from a few other Berlin newspapers. "We are led," he writes, "by the raven-dark, curly-headed, youthfully enthusiastic assistant of Gliese, Herr Ullmer [*sic*], a student of Max Reinhardt, who tries to pull one on us—more is the pity—regarding the joke of the 400,000 dollar production costs. We are poorly guided, as the sudden cries for help soon indicate. The apparently solid and dry, clay-like edge of the road is a gooey swamp, from which the *B.Z.* [*Berliner Zeitung*] and the *Film-Kurier* have to fish out the *Berliner Tageblatt.*"[21] The Germans, who partly resented the fact that Murnau had left Berlin for Hollywood and that he commanded such an extravagant budget, were particularly eager to follow the production. But the American press also paid attention and highlighted some of the same aspects. A report in the *New York Times,* published soon after Chaparral's dispatch, announced that the construction of the studio set alone cost $200,000 (considerably more money than the bottom line on the vast majority of Ulmer's subsequent production budgets).[22]

The collaboration with Gliese proved especially fruitful for Ulmer, who considered him a "partner, a fantastic designer and camera builder" (B 567). Gliese, whose set design for *Sunrise* earned an Oscar nomination, had worked on several early German film productions, including the second Golem film, *Der Golem und die Tänzerin* (*The Golem and the Dancer,* 1917), on which he served as assistant to director Paul Wegener. For Ulmer the significance of *Sunrise,* one of the greatest pictures Murnau ever made and, in Ulmer's words, "the *only* picture

Murnau himself counted" (B 565), cannot be overestimated. The film, based on Hermann Sudermann's short story "Die Reise nach Tilsit" (*The Journey to Tilsit*, 1917), blends European and American styles from the *Straßenfilm* to the early Hollywood melodrama and pits traditional life in the provinces against its radiant counterpart in the big city. The blissful harmony—or dreadful tedium—of family life between the nameless Man (George O'Brien) and Woman (Janet Gaynor) in the country is interrupted, much as in a classic horror film, by the intrusion of an outsider, the Woman from the City (Margaret Livingston—who, as chance would have it, bore a striking resemblance to Ulmer's first wife, Joen Warner).[23] Murnau casts these two worlds in stark opposition, opening the film with a brilliant montage, à la Walter Ruttmann's *Berlin: Die Sinfonie der Großstadt* (*Berlin: Symphony of a Great City*, 1927), and having the city woman lure away the man of the country, indulging him in fantasies of urban decadence.

To achieve this contrast most effectively, Murnau relied on high-quality production design, much of it pioneered in Weimar Germany, as a means of depicting the separate worlds. As Lotte Eisner remarks, "Gliese [and, by extension, Ulmer working with him] had created every kind of landscape, from fields and meadows, through an industrial area and the sparse gardens of the suburbs to the city itself."[24] Monroe Lathrop's rave review of Murnau's "New Masterpiece," published in the *Los Angeles Evening Express* the day after its West Coast premiere, explicitly credits "the art and camera effects to Rochus Gliese and Edgar Ulmer," attributing to them a key role in the overall success of the film, which in Lathrop's words is "to be classed among the cinema masterpieces in sustained beauty, in imagination and in cumulative emotional power as a whole."[25] Murnau's personal aesthetic and his highly cultivated approach to the craft of filmmaking won over countless admirers. In her study of the German filmmaker, Eisner cites Ulmer's assessment of working with him on *Sunrise*, highlighting the unusually collaborative nature of the enterprise. As part of her analysis she includes extracts from an interview she conducted with Ulmer on his tenure with Murnau: "He was a great purist who worked under a sort of hypnosis. . . . 'Good is not good enough.' It was the sort of leitmotiv of his art."[26]

The lessons that Ulmer learned while working with Murnau—the obsessive emphasis, for example, on the aesthetic over mere commercial considerations—would stick. Indeed, four decades later Andrew Sarris would brand Ulmer "the executor of the Murnau estate."[27] One can recognize traces of the German master in several of Ulmer's subsequent films, starting with *The Black Cat,* which contains obvious allusions to the visual mastery of his pioneering work (e.g., *Nosferatu* and *The Last Laugh*), and leading up to his Mexican-themed western *The Naked Dawn* (1955), a film that is, in John Belton's words, "a reworking of Murnau's *Sunrise*—Santiago, with the lure of money for the husband and tales of exotic Veracruz for the wife, taking the part of Murnau's Woman from the City."[28] Not only does that film present a plausible "reworking," but it also picks up on several of Ulmer's own recurrent themes: the false promise of material wealth; the romantic wanderings of a lonely hero; and the struggle to remain loyal to a more noble, if less profitable, calling.

Many of these themes had a place in Ulmer's personal life as well. Not long after Murnau's film premiered in Hollywood, in late November 1927, Ulmer began to feel the pull toward Europe and toward the theater. Sometime early in the next year, he traveled back to Berlin with Gliese—Ulmer's wife Joen also accompanied them but would return to California by 1929, after becoming pregnant—where they worked together on the set design of Max Reinhardt's 1928 acclaimed staging of Ferdinand Bruckner's *Die Verbrecher (The Criminals)* at the Deutsches Theater. Though he often claimed to have had extensive involvement in other Reinhardt productions at Theater in der Josefstadt from the early 1920s onward, Ulmer's contribution to Bruckner's play actually matches the historical record.[29] The play debuted in late October 1928 and ran until early February of the following year. During this time Ulmer also found work on a couple of minor German film productions for Ideal-Film and Merkur-Film, ancillary companies connected to Heinrich Nebenzahl's more prestigious Nero-Film. He is credited, for example, as *Bildassistent,* or production assistant, on Louis Ralph's adventure film, written by Curt (then still "Kurt") Siodmak, *Flucht in die Fremdenlegion (Escape to the Foreign Legion,* 1929). He also earned a credit as set builder on Robert Land's *Spiel um den Mann (Play around a Man,* 1929).[30] In Billy Wilder's contemporary account of the young film scene in Berlin and his creation—together with Ulmer, Siodmak, and others—of the coffeehouse collective Filmstudio 1929, a one-off production company cobbled together by crewmembers and theater impresario Moriz Seeler, he places Ulmer's arrival in Berlin around the time that he would have worked on these other, more marginal productions. In Wilder's thumbnail sketch, "Edgar Ulmer, 23 [*sic*] years old, arrived from Hollywood half a year ago. Worked as a set designer on Murnau's *Sunrise.*"[31]

A LEGENDARY COLLABORATION IN LATE-WEIMAR GERMANY

Shot on the eve of the Great Depression, with essentially no budget to speak of, an equally modest cast of amateur actors, a relatively untested, unknown crew, and no major studio backing, the late silent film *Menschen am Sonntag (People on Sunday)* has a production history like no other of its era. After the more seasoned director Rochus Gliese abruptly abandoned the project, merely a few days into the shoot, the picture was codirected by Robert Siodmak and Ulmer, neither of whom had ever directed a full-length feature film on his own. It was more or less scripted, though not in any formal sense, by Billy (then still "Billie") Wilder, with story input from Kurt Siodmak. The camera was operated by veteran special effects technician Eugen Schüfftan—who would later, after making his way to Hollywood, become a frequent collaborator of Ulmer's during the 1940s—with assistance from Fred Zinnemann, and the project was produced by Filmstudio 1929 with nominal support from Nero-Film boss, and maternal uncle to Curt and Robert Siodmak, Heinrich Nebenzahl.

Almost every person originally associated with the film—in particular, Ulmer, the Siodmak brothers, and Billy Wilder—would later, after migration to Hollywood and after the film's cultural cachet had accrued over time, take more credit for the film than the record allows.[32] In an interview in 1970, for example, Robert Siodmak effectively denied Wilder's involvement, insisting that he worked no more than an hour on the production—his sole idea, in Siodmak's recollection, was that Annie, the model girlfriend in the film, should stay home in bed—and claimed that Ulmer, after eight days on the shoot, returned to America. He asserted, moreover, that Ulmer *really* only worked one day. "On the first day," remembers Siodmak, "he wanted to take the thing away from me."[33] Retrospective accounts of this kind differ quite radically, even those told by the same person. In Siodmak's posthumously published memoir, *Zwischen Berlin und Hollywood (Between Berlin and Hollywood)*, for instance, he refers to Ulmer as his "co-director" and maintains that Ulmer had his true interests at heart.[34]

For his part, Ulmer, who claims to have "organized" the entire production, and to have bankrolled it with money brought from the United States, remembered it as a truly collaborative undertaking: "Our main weapon was that everyone could contribute his bit; even the assistant Zinnemann was allowed to participate in the discussion."[35] Many years later, in Gerald Koll's documentary on the making of the film, *Weekend am Wannsee* (*Weekend at the Wannsee,* 2000), Brigitte Borchert, who plays the girl from the Electrola shop, remarks, with perhaps less of a personal stake: "They didn't have a script or anything. . . . We'd sit at a nearby table while they'd decide what to do that day. . . . It was completely improvised."[36] By her account, Wilder's main function on the set was to hold a sun reflector.

Contemporary journalistic accounts of the shoot add a few critical details and offer further testimony about who was actually involved. During the early weeks of production, in July 1929, a pair of articles published in the Weimar Berlin popular press reported on the unconventional character of the work—its programmatic working title was "So ist es und nicht anders" (This is how it is, and no different)—offering, much like a press kit would do, short profiles of the cast and crew. In the *Filmspiegel* supplement of the *Berliner Tageblatt* on July 25, 1929, Delia Arnd-Steinitz discusses the initial screen tests at Berlin's Thielplatz, not far from the Grunewald forest, and the revolutionary decision on the part of the newly founded Filmstudio 1929 (she names Seeler, Ulmer, and Robert Siodmak as the founders) to use amateurs as a means of expressing real-life authenticity. "The plot," she writes, "should come as close as possible to reality, to the natural course of our days; the events, moods, and conflicts of everyday life should be represented without kitsch, pathos, or sentimentality."[37] Accompanying the article are several photos from the ongoing production, one of which shows Ulmer, together with Siodmak, Gliese (still present in the early days of the shoot), and Seeler, taking the screen test of two of the film's amateur actors, Christl Ehlers and Erwin Splettstößer.

Five days later, in another article published in the afternoon edition of the *Berliner Zeitung,* the cultural reporter Pem (a.k.a. Paul Erich Marcus, a regular at the Romanisches Café, where the project was allegedly first hatched), filed a dispatch, "Film mit Dilettanten" (Film with dilettantes), on the next phase of shooting on location at the Nikolassee train station and at the surrounding beaches and forests of Wannsee and Grunewald. He provides an overview of the film crew, often misspelling or mistaking their names altogether, and giving a cheeky summary of their professional background: "Script: Billie Wider [*sic*], coffeehouse-born journalist and gagman . . . Direction: Rochus Gliese, actually a set designer, but he doesn't need to design the Grunewald. . . . Set professional and jack-of-all-trades: Fred [*sic*] Ulmer, a fiery business hater [*Betriebshasser*] and Hollywood-studio connoisseur."[38] Such descriptions, while meant more as humorous caricatures than professional bona fides, are revealing nonetheless; Pem's portrayal of Ulmer as having both a strong antiestablishment attitude and the insight of someone who had already amassed experience working in Hollywood is itself illuminating. Finally, in the same article the accompanying photo from the shoot on location shows Seeler, Schüfftan, and Ulmer, all of them identified in the caption, huddled around a camera in the middle of the forest. "Here something is evolving," writes Pem, commenting on the transitional and possibly transformative quality of the project, "which can only be thought of as an experiment, a mere signpost; and that's already saying something in our schematized and calibrated age in which technology has grown at a rate over life."[39]

In terms of the formal innovations of the film, *People on Sunday* takes the city symphony film, commonly associated with Ruttmann's *Berlin*—and, in the international arena, with Alberto Cavalcanti's *Rien que les heures* (1926) and Dziga Vertov's *Man with a Movie Camera* (1929), among others—in a new direction. Unconcerned with merely capturing a "Querschnitt," or cross-section, of the German metropolis, the film cannily blends avant-garde documentary and narrative cinema into something that is less abstract and far more improvised, natural, and overtly romantic than its predecessors. While it draws in part on the once dominant trend of *Neue Sachlichkeit* (New Objectivity), with its periodic riffs on popular advertising, design, photography, and technology—and, more generally, on the wider contemporaneous trend in Europe and America of capturing the pulsating life of a city on celluloid—its main conceit is its utter defiance of prevailing modes and industry norms. The film turns its back on studio production, instead allowing the city and its many inviting locations (its boulevards and cafés, lakes, boardwalks, beaches, and other places of leisure and recreation) to substitute for the standard reliance on sets, while at the same time allowing amateurs to play the roles otherwise reserved for film stars. It is, as we are told at the outset, "a film without actors."

The premise of the film couldn't be more basic: in the heart of the city, near the Bahnhof-Zoo subway station, amid the intense bustle of commerce and traffic, a modern boy-meets-girl story seems to be transpiring before our eyes. A chance encounter between two young, slightly aimless urban strollers results in an impromptu scheme for a Sunday outing, which, after each one shows up with a best friend in tow, becomes a frolicsome double date at one of Berlin's nearby lakes (Figure 10); the fifth member of the cast, in a witty twist attributed to Wilder, oversleeps, missing the entire outing. What ultimately unfolds in just a little over an

FIGURE 10. Leisure world: a late-Weimar double date at the lake. *Left to right:* Erwin Splettstößer, Christl Ehlers, Brigitte Borchert and Wolfgang von Waltershausen. Courtesy of the Deutsche Kinemathek—Museum für Film und Fernsehen, Berlin.

hour of total screen time is a remarkably straightforward depiction, by turns affectionate and comical, of courting rituals, leisure activity, and mass entertainment circa 1930. We see the four protagonists listening to music, swimming, enjoying a picnic, riding a pedal boat, alternating their love interests, and trying in general to squeeze the most out of the day. The style of the film is natural, the setting unpretentious, and the atmosphere, perhaps the core of the entire film, shamelessly flirtatious. More than anything, a new kind of directness, an unmediated, unvarnished representation of everyday life as it is experienced by members of a young, urban consumer class is what the filmmakers seem to have been after, in marked contrast to the spectacular big-budget pictures being produced at Ufa at the time. Among the most evocative working titles, in addition to "So ist es und nicht anders," were those of a universal appeal, such as "Sommer 29" (Summer '29) and "Junge Leute wie alle" (Young people like us), a wink at the critics and target audience.

By casting amateurs in roles based on their true day jobs and with their real names still attached to them, all from the minor professions of a burgeoning young, urban workforce, the film crew was able to offer an unusually honest, verité rendering of their world to an audience that was preoccupied with the same values, social mores, dreams, and anxieties as the protagonists on the screen. In the opening credits, following the initial announcement, made via intertitle, that the film's five lead characters appear here before the camera for the first time and are today back at their old jobs, we are immediately introduced to them in their respective pursuits: the jovial taxi driver Erwin Splettstößer, seated behind the wheel of a cab bearing the Berlin license plate "IA 10088"; the charming record salesgirl Brigitte Borchert in front of the Electrola shop on Kurfürstendamm—where Moriz Seeler is said to have discovered her—who last month, so the title reads, sold 150 copies of the hit song "In einer kleinen Konditorei" (In a little pastry shop);[40] the tall, dark and slender Wolfgang von Waltershausen, a former officer, farmer, antique dealer, and gigolo, currently working as a traveling wine merchant, puffing on his cigarette with an air of obvious self-assuredness; the very chic, urbane Christl Ehlers, who enters what appears to be a casting studio and who, we are told, "wears down her heels as a film extra"; and, finally, Annie Schreyer, a model, reclining, filing her nails, and waiting in vain for the next job.

In a similar manner to the early Soviet avant-garde—Ulmer claims to have taken the chief inspiration from Vertov—the film has its characters serve as a series of social types, easily recognizable by the audience. Writing in Weimar Germany's Communist Party newspaper, *Die rote Fahne*, critic Alfred Kemeny extolled the fact that the film evolved "outside the German capitalist film industry" and underscored the influence of Russian cinema: "the plot is plain, as if simply carved out of life, and that here, as in the Russian films, human beings, real, real, real [*sic*] human beings 'play' [their true roles]."[41] The film's five leads participate actively in forming the very mass culture that they represent onscreen, a culture with which Weimar-era cinemagoers readily identified. "The five people in this film," insisted Billy Wilder in a publicity piece he published early on in the production, "that's you and that's me."[42] Admittedly, the film's primary viewpoint, with its occasional flourishes of voyeurism, unabashed prankster sensibility, and boyish bravado, is quite masculine. The audience serves, in part, as witness to Wolfgang and Erwin's youthful exploits: their fraternal bonds, from their chummy card game near the start of the film to their final splitting of a last cigarette, are shown to run deep. Yet the leading women, whose roles shift and evolve throughout the picture, are not without their share of complexity and individual force. Indeed, they challenge their male counterparts, undoing their immature schemes and standing their own ground.

By dint of good fortune, or perhaps good connections, the film enjoyed a well-publicized premiere at the glamorous Ufa-Theater am Kurfürstendamm on February 4, 1930—the elegant letter-press invitations list the official credits: script by Wilder, cinematography by Schüfftan, direction by Siodmak and Ulmer—and was instantly embraced by critics from nearly all the city's leading newspapers. In a cloud of media euphoria they pronounced it "a grand success," "magnificent," and "a delightful film."[43] One review, which declared the victory of the low-budget Filmstudio 1929 (it lists the total cost of production at twenty-eight thousand Reichsmark, the rough equivalent of $7,000 at the time) over the powerful entertainment industry, hailed the film in similarly effusive terms: "A triumph of the artistic element—proof that it works this way as well—a film made from crystal-clear simplicity." The unnamed reviewer then goes on to underscore the film's universal appeal: "Nothing actually happens and yet it still captures that which has to do with all of us."[44] Many critics trumpeted the talent of the young film crew. In the *Berliner Zeitung,* for instance, Kurt Mühsam observed, "Robert Siodmak and Edgar Ulmer wield the authority of a director with remarkable aplomb."[45] In the afternoon edition of the same paper another critic asserted: "Billie Wilder has written a simple, but outstandingly composed screenplay, Schüfftan has performed splendid work on the camera, and Robert Siodmak, together with Edgar Ulmer, has directed very competently."[46]

Although the picture was made at an especially fragile moment in history, between the recent stock market collapse and the rise of National Socialism, it evokes a strange sense of calm, purity, and innocence. "*People on Sunday* can be understood," observes Lutz Koepnick, "as having allowed audiences to take a final breath before being caught in the vortex of violence and mass mobilization."[47] The key concerns of the film, and of the film's characters—fighting over matinee idols, burning one's tongue on a hot dog, having one's portrait taken by a beach photographer, scrounging together enough money to spring for a boat ride—are indeed rather trivial when compared to the grand historical events unfolding offscreen. This does not, however, detach it in any way from its times. Its sustained focus on such comparatively banal matters is entirely in keeping with the Weimar preoccupation with leisure and the still rather new notion of "Weekend." Taken in this vein, *People on*

Sunday stands as a commentary on such hit songs as "Wochenend und Sonnenschein" (Weekend and sunshine)—Otto Stenzeel's original score was replete with pop standards of the day—and on the vivid photo portraiture of August Sander. It is also very much an exploration, in line with Siegfried Kracauer's 1929 study of Weimar Germany's white-collar workers, *Die Angestellten (The Salaried Masses)*, of the new cultural habits of the petite bourgeoisie.[48]

Even if the film's meandering plot, almost more like an episode from a late twentieth-century American television sitcom like *Seinfeld* than from a Weimar-era feature film, eschews a more sophisticated, politically minded critique, *People on Sunday* certainly tested the limits of filmmaking at the time. It broke new ground in the final phase of silent film production, introducing a fresh model of independent cinema— well before the term, as we understand it today, even existed—and a bare-bones realism that had a deep impact both contemporaneously and for many years after. In the *Berliner Tageblatt* the critic Eugen Szatmari took special delight in noting the ways in which the film undid studio production: "Young people got together and with laughably little means—without sets or ballrooms or opera galas, without stars, with a few human beings that they drew from their professions—they shot a film and achieved a total success for which one has to congratulate them and which hopefully will finally open up the eyes of the film industry."[49] Despite the fact that this group of twentysomething cineastes would not effect the change hoped for by Szatmari, either in Weimar Germany or in the Hollywood to which they fled, the model they established with *People on Sunday* is one that has continued to be emulated internationally, from the French New Wave and New German Cinema up to the more systematic efforts in the name of Dogme 95. Filmmaker and critic Luc Moullet tells a story of how when he and Bertrand Tavernier interviewed Ulmer in 1961, Ulmer suggested they all make a film together. "He wanted to remake *Menschen am Sonntag* with young French actors," Moullet remarks. "He wanted me and Bertrand and a few others to write some scenes for that film."[50] It ultimately got tucked away in Ulmer's expansive file of unrealized projects.

For Ulmer, in particular, the production of *People on Sunday*, that fabled cinematic love letter to Berlin, would leave a lasting mark on his life and career. Not merely the improvisational quality of the film, and the need to work on the fly, but also its extreme minimalism (that enduring principle of less is more) and lack of a sizable budget, the tight shooting ratio (in this case, roughly five to one), and the nonexistence of studio enhancement—all of these would become recurrent facets of Ulmer's cinema. Moreover, the highly self-conscious approach to film-making demonstrated here, perhaps most poignantly in the scenes in which Annie and Erwin destroy publicity photos of each other's favorite movie stars and in Schüfftan's use of freeze-frame cinematography when shooting ordinary Berliners on the beach, represents a style and sensibility that he would continue to cultivate in his work, even in some of his cheapest productions.

People on Sunday came at a time in Ulmer's life when he was still positioning himself as a relatively new émigré in Hollywood but also as someone with lingering ties to Europe. His return to Berlin helped him to maintain and strengthen those ties, which, as his later career after the war makes clear, he never had any intention of giving up. Though his marriage to Joen Warner, a girl from Pasadena, signaled a conscious step in the direction of American assimilation, it was a step he took with considerable ambivalence. On December 15, 1929, several weeks before the Berlin premiere of *Menschen am Sonntag,* Ulmer's daughter Helen Joen was born in California; Ulmer rushed back from Europe to join his wife. He then decided, many months later, to allow himself to be baptized along with his new baby at St. John's Episcopal Cathedral, a decision that, while perhaps initially aimed at appeasing his in-laws, gave Ulmer further reason to reconsider his roots.[51]

Even beyond the balancing act necessitated by his evolving American identity, the early 1930s were not easy for Ulmer. At the height of the Depression, work became increasingly scarce. He directed a few musical shorts and otherwise offered his skills to other directors, both in Hollywood and in New York (listed in his "Past Service Record," completed sometime in 1969, are five symphonic shorts from 1930 for a company called Brown-Nagel Productions, operating out of Metropolitan Sound Studios, along with an array of unverifiable work in the Art Department at MGM, when he also purportedly directed the German-language version of *Anna Christie* and assisted on two other films).[52] The tragic death of F. W. Murnau at the age of forty-two, in a car crash in Santa Barbara in March 1931, is said to have shaken Ulmer profoundly; he was one of the few attendees (together with George O'Brien, Greta Garbo, Salka and Berthold Viertel, and Herman Bing) at Murnau's American funeral.[53]

Around this same time, his family life reached a crisis point. His commitment to Joen became increasingly tenuous and ultimately damaged beyond repair. Like his own father, Ulmer was frequently on the road,

FIGURE 11. This man for hire: ad placed in the 1932 *Film Daily* Yearbook. Courtesy of the Edgar G. Ulmer Preservation Corp.

lending a hand to assorted film productions on the East and West Coast—even in Bora Bora, in the South Pacific, to help with Murnau's final picture, *Tabu* (1931)—and generally absent from home. By 1932 he left behind his first wife and young Helen Joen for good; his brother, Max, having migrated from Vienna to New York at the time, stepped in to provide for them until they were able to relocate to California. Helen Joen would later visit her father just once, at the age of eighteen, when he was shooting *The Strange Woman*. They would have champagne and dinner at a Hollywood restaurant, something that impressed the young girl, but owing to the pressure of her mother, that would be their one and only encounter.[54] Ulmer maintained a single-minded focus on securing new work and building a reputation for himself. A notice published in *Film Daily* in February 1932 proclaimed, "Edgar George [*sic*] Ulmer, who was associated with the late F. W. Murnau as chief art director on *Sunrise* . . . will handle the next Peerless picture, to be made in the East."[55] That same year, and in the same publication, Ulmer took out an ad announcing his many skills (director, general manager, supervisor), his past glory *(Menschen am Sonntag)*, his current affiliation with Peerless Productions, and his alleged past association with Ufa (Figure 11).

The new picture for Peerless referred to in the *Film Daily* notice, initially known as *The Warning Shadow,* "a cinema fantasy with a

New York background," was shot by turns in New York's Metropolitan studios; in Fort Lee, New Jersey; and on location at the Waldorf Astoria in New York City. The picture was never released. Instead, parts of it were later incorporated into *Mr. Broadway* (1933), an Ed Sullivan vehicle directed by American silent film actor and producer Johnnie Walker. That film, in its final form, was little more than a tour with showman Sullivan of New York's entertainment hubs and celebrity destinations, the kind of tour that would serve as fodder for Sullivan's column. "About two reels of Ulmer's film were interpolated," asserts Richard Koszarski in *Hollywood on the Hudson,* "into this travelogue as a flashback narrated by Sullivan himself."[56] Although such experiences were likely a source of frustration at the time, Ulmer was inching closer toward the goal of directing his own American feature film.

THE ART OF OUTCASTS

While Ulmer was still shuttling between New York and Hollywood, trying to land what little work there was to be had, he found himself directing a film that wasn't exactly the kind of project an ambitious émigré might have first imagined for himself in Hollywood. *Damaged Lives* is not a thriller, not a love story, neither a horror film nor a melodrama. Rather, it's a cautionary film about syphilis, billed for education purposes but with the inherent appeal of a protosexploitation picture—an ambiguous genre whose borders Ulmer would cross again, at least in a nominal capacity, in his sub-B *Girls in Chains* (1943) and his McCarthy-era "nudie" *The Naked Venus* (1959). A Canadian-American coproduction, it was made in a little more than a week in April 1933, at the behest of the Canadian Social Hygiene Council and Columbia Pictures of Canada, for an independent production company called Weldon Pictures. Like Filmstudio 1929, Weldon was a one-off enterprise—a front, really, whose name was a play on "well-done" pictures—set up by Columbia to produce and distribute the film and to deflect any possible associations between a respectable studio and a project that, for a considerable segment of the American population, would be judged as morally dubious.[57]

Damaged Lives has a particularly odd reception history. It was produced by J. J. Allen and Max Cohn ("the born schlemiel of the family," as Ulmer later called him, though misremembering his name as "Nat" Cohn), whose brothers Jack and Harry ran Columbia Pictures. The film was budgeted, like many Ulmer films in that vaguely poverty-stricken zone, at under $100,000 and shot at General Educational Studios (Harry Cohn refused to have the film shot on the Columbia lot).[58] It enjoyed a relatively wide U.S. release in 1933—a couple of months in Boston, from mid-September to mid-November, with further screenings in such key cities as Chicago, Hartford, Milwaukee, Spokane, Baltimore, and Los Angeles, eventually being shown in twenty-two states and reaching some 650,000 viewers—but in New York it faced opposition by the New York State Board of Censors that effectively blocked its distribution and exhibition there until 1937. The Canadian debut in Toronto had already taken place in late May 1933, and the film was then shown in London in August—in both cities, screenings were augmented by a half-hour filmed lecture by Dr. Gordon Bates, head of the Canadian Social Hygiene Council, who had also served as the clinical supervisor on the film, amplifying the message of the film in a more scientific vein (in Canada, audiences were restricted by sex, with two separate lectures for each audience).[59]

In its American premiere at Boston's Majestic Theater, on September 15, 1933, the film supplement by Dr. Bates was replaced by an entirely new condensed lecture, "Science and Modern Medicine," which, as stipulated by the American Social Hygiene Association, was given *not* by an actual medical doctor but by the British-born actor Murray Kinnell, who plays the infectious-disease specialist Dr. Leonard in the film. Yet, despite an unabashedly positive response in the popular press—a critic in the *Boston Globe* gushed, calling it "the most amazing product of all the sound screen"[60]—the film's American distribution was offset by the initial efforts at censorship. By the time it reopened in New York City, some four years after its debut in Boston, it traded on its former reputation as a banned film, now with an "Adults Only" designation and a string of attention-grabbing taglines (e.g., "Daring! Timely! Tells All!") aimed at driving people to the box office.[61] Around that same time, during a highly successful two-week run at Philadelphia's palatial Erlanger Theatre, *Damaged Lives* reportedly took in $26,500 and was beaten at the box office only by the Marx Brothers' new release, *A Day at the Races* (1937).[62] Overall, in its new guise, severely truncated from the 1933 version, the film is said to have grossed a staggering $1.4 million worldwide.[63]

Before its initial release *Damaged Lives* bore the slightly ominous working title "Dark Waters," a marked contrast to the sugarcoated title "Happy Ending," which was attached to it while the project was still in preparation (many years later, on its rerelease in 1958, there was discussion of giving it the more sober, more didactic title "The Shocking Truth"). The film's story, as conceived by screenwriter Donald Davis and Ulmer, and loosely inspired by French playwright Eugène Brieux's turn-of-the-century *Les avariés* (Damaged goods), takes shape around a harrowing case of syphilis in high society; the Brieux play, with an Austrian cast that included Salka Viertel, had enjoyed a successful run in Vienna during Ulmer's youth.[64] Though the disease was commonly—and often mistakenly—thought to be restricted to the lower classes and "foreign" populations, Ulmer's film, which is cast in a basic exploitation mold, makes it frighteningly clear to the target audience that even America's most glamorous set is not immune. The sensationalized slogan used to draw in viewers, "His life of debauchery brought disease to his wife," encapsulates in bold the more sedate plotlines of the film.

Amid the upper echelons of New York City, which Ulmer ably depicts in visual shorthand, coupling aerial shots of the animated skyline with a low-angle shot of the towering buildings along Manhattan's grand avenues, we are introduced to the protagonist, Donald Bradley Jr. (Lyman Williams), son of a shipping magnate, who wears his ambitions on his sleeve. From the moment that Donald Bradley Sr. (George Irving) gives complete charge of all ships at Bradley Steamship Co. to his son, toward the start of the film, Donald Jr. calls the shots with the zeal of a renegade. He is soon shown presiding over a board meeting, earning the praise of his father and the satisfaction of other board members. In what turns out to be the beginning of the end for Donald Jr., a board member named Nat Franklin (Harry Myers) invites him out for dinner under the pretense of discussing business, yet, as Nat leaves Donald's office, another board member ribs Nat, asking whether "that blonde baby of yours" will be there, too, a "baby" who unsurprisingly plays a critical role in the action that transpires during the remainder of the film.

The invitation to dinner with Nat, accepted in the spirit of business before pleasure and with his father's encouragement, is predicated on Donald's canceling his theater plans with his fiancée, Joan (Diane Sinclair). As the logic of the story would have it, a married man who knows to cherish the vows of fidelity is less likely to surrender to the temptations the unmarried Donald soon faces and, by extension, to expose himself and his loved ones to such risks. Part of the tragedy, then, is that Joan does not recognize soon enough the urgency to marry—her friend Laura Hall (Marceline Day) asks her this early on, and Laura's husband, Bill (Jason Robards), raises the question again at a more fraught moment in the film—thereby protecting her husband from the traps into which he inevitably falls. In terms of its emotional and visual character, the film, under Ulmer's competent direction, establishes two distinct worlds, one in which upstanding citizens like Laura and Bill live and the other in which people quickly lose sight of their principles and allow their base urges to gain the upper hand. Ulmer has his cameraman, Allen Siegler, lead us through the well-appointed, unmistakably bourgeois interiors of the Halls' apartment, evocative of security and stability, before cutting away to the swank speakeasy nightclub in which Donald and Nat are seated at a table with Elise Cooper (Charlotte Merriam), the "blonde baby" whose arrival we have been anticipating. The atmosphere of the nightclub, by contrast, conveys a space in which strict social codes are temporarily suspended, where business becomes pleasure and vice versa. It is a seductive world repeatedly featured in the *Straßenfilme,* or street films, of the Weimar years, films like Fritz Lang's *Dr. Mabuse, der Spieler* (*Dr. Mabuse, the Gambler,* 1922) and Karl Grune's *Die Straße* (*The Street,* 1924), films Ulmer would have known quite well from his youth, and its seductiveness often serves as a potent lure for unmoored citizens, generally men, who cannot maintain sufficient control over their primal urges.[65]

As the narrative threads of the film's prologue continue to unravel, so do its characters. Donald's host, Nat, who in a drunken stupor plunges headlong into further debauchery, becomes drawn to a woman at another table, while Donald and Elise lose their bearings altogether. They are soon seated together—in a handsomely framed two-shot, a shadowy, ominous staircase looming in the background—at a private after-hours gathering, where they observe the anonymous crowd of party people in their midst while swigging their cocktails. The repeated battle cry "Let's go places!" propels them from an after-hours bar, a Prohibition-era gin joint called Joe's, where the syncopation of the cocktail shaker matches the jazz playing in the background, to Elise's thoroughly urbane art deco apartment, where the steady consumption continues until things reach their inevitable conclusion. By the time they retreat to the bedroom—with Siegler's camera focusing first on Donald's coat draped over the sofa, then on the closed doors of the room itself, then back to the abandoned garment one more time—the offscreen radio broadcaster announces it's 3 a.m., and we begin to grasp the formula for Donald's downfall: drink too much, indulge one's pleasures with reckless abandon, and you *will* be punished. The modest, though highly effective, use of the searching camera in *Damaged Lives* almost anticipates, as Grissemann astutely notes, the famous scene in *Detour,* following the death of Vera, in which cinematographer Benjamin Kline focuses in and out on objects around the bedroom as a means of evoking Al's traumatized state.[66]

The remainder of the film shifts focus to Donald's rude awakening, a "morning after" with more than a mere hangover to account for.[67] Guilt, panic, and remorse set in for Donald, as he owns up to his transgression, realizing in turn that he and Joan should have been married long ago. ("If we had," he tells her, "this never would have happened.") But rather than rebuke Donald for his misdeeds, Joan takes on her own share of responsibility for not having married him earlier. She is soon seen behind the wheel, rushing Donald through the dark night to a county justice of the peace for a $2 insta-wedding. Almost as fast as the wedding itself, the urgent news of Elise's illness spreads. On the heels of a failed suicide attempt, Elise confesses to Donald her discovery of having contracted "it"—she refuses to name the disease, preferring instead to say, "I've got *it* . . . and for all I know, I passed *it* on to you . . . and your little wife"—and of not having known she had *it* during their ill-fated evening together. Donald represses the truth—in the full-length rendition of the film he enlists the service of a quack doctor, only briefly alluded to in the truncated version, who assures him of his health—but he cannot unburden himself of the legacy of Elise, who shoots herself soon after making her confession, or of the headline that follows him: "Shipowner's Son Involved in Suicide." Donald only begins to face the truth, the *shocking* truth, when his friend Bill, a medical doctor by profession, intervenes on his behalf, escorting him to the clinic of Dr. Leonard, where Joan, who has by then caught *it* from Donald, is being treated. There the film shifts focus once again, becoming something of a health short, a documentary almost like the anti-TB films Ulmer would direct in the late 1930s and early 1940s, as we enter the clinic and are introduced to the horrors of the disease.

Dr. Leonard's instructional tour of the clinic, presenting a series of patients in examination rooms, each one evidently worse off than the last (severe motor ataxia, a festering skin infection on a man's leg, an even more acute infection contracted by a man who visited a "streetwalker," a woman who harbors chronic symptoms of rheumatism, another woman who has given birth to seven children, one of them

FIGURE 12. Clinical precision: Edgar G. Ulmer *(left)* and Dr. Gordon Bates, with Diane Sinclair (Joan) at the center, on the set of *Damaged Lives* (1933) during the filming of the clinic sequence. Courtesy of D. J. Turner.

dead and all the others spectacularly, tragically syphilitic), gives the most graphic component of the film's educational mission (Figure 12). It is, however, hard to ignore a voyeuristic dimension as well—the diseased patients exhibited, perhaps unwittingly, as "freaks," a form of "shock treatment" or "sideshow attraction," as Dr. Leonard's cabinet of horrors.[68] Each case is presented with clinical precision, not terribly different from the sequence in *People on Sunday* in which we suddenly are presented with freeze-frame photo portraits in the style of August Sander, temporarily halting the pace of the film and sparking deeper reflection on the part of the spectator. In the end Donald can hardly endure the successive confrontations, nervously looking away whenever possible, and has to be propped up by his friend Bill.

Looping back, then, to the underlying story of Donald and Joan, the sequence takes us to a final examination door opening on to Joan, noticeably uneasy and in a trancelike state as she takes a few steps before fainting. Donald's rude awakening—and, of course, the audience's awakening with him—is tempered by Dr. Leonard's comforting assurance that proper treatment will remedy the illness and, with an immediate and concerted effort by Joan, will have no impact on the birth of the child they are now expecting (only obliquely glossed in the truncated version); this is, presumably, the "Happy Ending" once considered an apt title during the film's planning stages. Yet it takes time for *Damaged Lives* to hit a final upbeat note, as Dr. Leonard gloomily announces his fears of what might happen to Donald and Joan during their continued reckoning with the disease: "They're so likely to lose faith with the world they thought was beautiful." By the end of the film, after narrowly escaping Joan's desperate attempt at taking their lives, the final burst of levity comes as comic relief in a phone call from Joan's pregnant friend Marie. She shares with her friend the fear that eating pickles will harm her unborn baby, a scene that is repeated virtually untouched, in a striking case of self-citation or cinematic recycling, by the equally neurotic figure of Rosie in Ulmer's Yiddish comedy *Amerikaner shadkhn* (*American Matchmaker*, 1940). Donald and Joan cannot control their laughter, mitigating their earlier feelings of helplessness and depression, and they assure one another that they will be fine after all.

With specific regard to its formal qualities, *Damaged Lives* belongs—together with Ulmer's later TB shorts, made for the National Tuberculosis Association, and his nudie *The Naked Venus*—to Andrew Sarris's category of "expressive esoterica."[69] These seemingly random, unconventional productions, all of them work for hire, somehow manage, despite their paltry budgets, ham-handed scripts, and other limitations, to offer a few unexpected stylish moments that can arguably be credited to a director's vision.[70] Indeed, these may not be the kind of films that invite the heroic championing of an auteur—the total achievement is, admittedly, rather modest—but they are part of a career that often defied industry-imposed standards and norms. Ulmer's *Damaged Lives* is no cinematic triumph, and to speak of any production values per se is to overstate the case. As a reviewer in *Motion Picture Daily* wrote, "The fiction story, however ineptly told from the standpoint of production value, is nonetheless not tawdry, cheap or vulgar."[71] In fact, *Damaged Lives* contains a few noteworthy moments, scenes that reflect, on a more basic scale, the director's refined approach to his craft.

Consider, for instance, the surprisingly artful sequence, when Joan, still in her trancelike state, leaves Dr. Leonard's clinic and, seeing a young child in the waiting room, recognizes the gravity of her condition. Ulmer executes the scene by way of an evocative montage, intercutting the image of Joan's face with those of the doctor and his suffering patients, an aesthetic touch of a surreal nature, something that almost could have been borrowed from Luis Buñuel.[72] There is also the particularly stirring scene at the end of the film, a near-six-minute sequence, theatrically choreographed without dialogue and, apart from the background music and the subtle hissing of a gas stove when turned on by Joan, is basically silent—or "mit out sound," as the German-speaking émigré directors in Hollywood were known to say at the time—up until its climax. In this sequence Joan rises from her dressing table and lumbers through the apartment, clearly anguished and despondent, with a series of gestures that together suggest her ultimate plan for a double suicide (closing the drapes, windows, and doors; sealing the apartment off from oxygen), and finally lies down next to Donald, who is asleep on the couch, unaware of Joan's plan. The scene has an altogether different pacing from the rest of the film and an essential theatricality that distinguishes it from other sequences.

Owing perhaps to such flourishes of creativity on the part of its director, *Damaged Lives* tended to win over contemporary reviewers. "I cannot but admire the deep sincerity with which producers, author, director and cast carry through: not once is there a false note, a jarring tone," remarked one critic in 1933; "to see it is to realize afresh the tremendous power of the cinema for direct propaganda of any kind; a discovery which for many years seems to have been exploited only by the great Russian producers," asserted another.[73] When the film was finally released in New York City, opening in June 1937 at the Central Theatre—where it played for several consecutive weeks—the *New York Times* applauded it: "Perhaps the most outspoken motion picture ever made for general release, it is the decisive stroke in the struggle to free discussion of venereal disease from the sotto voce, where Ibsen found it." The same review went on to note, "In their use of the dramatic form, the makers of 'Damaged Lives,' cannot be considered Ibsens, but their motion picture is certainly a lot more graphic than 'Ghosts,' and probably as important in its time. . . . Considered as a discussion of a social problem, it is forthright, frank, and unforgettable."[74] The comparison of *Damaged Lives* to Ibsen's *Ghosts*—Ibsen was a personal favorite of Ulmer's and an author he repeatedly turned to for artistic inspiration—is indeed a flattering one, which could not in any way have been anticipated for the formerly banned educational film. Not exactly known for his modesty in his final years, Ulmer, in conversation with Bogdanovich, pronounced his picture "an excellent film, really very good."[75]

In retrospect, the title alone, *Damaged Lives,* evokes both the social ostracism experienced by those infected with the disease and a kind of motto, so Marcel Arbeit argues, "that would fit many other Ulmer films as well."[76] "Reflections from damaged life," as Theodor W. Adorno would call his aphorisms written in American exile in the mid-1940s, lie squarely at the heart of many of Ulmer's film productions. "Every intellectual in migration," insists Adorno, "is, without exception, damaged"; his or her character is permanently stained, bruised, scarred.[77] The experience of social estrangement—whether inflicted by disease, by the experience of war, or by banishment from one's home—recurs over time in Ulmer's work and is one of his dominant motifs. As John Belton has argued, "Ulmer frequently builds his films around the entry of innocent, uncomprehending characters into a decadent or corrupt world that is moving slowly but inevitably towards its own destruction. Finding themselves in this world, Ulmer's innocents are unable to resist its evil, become entangled in the deadly web spun by its inhabitants, and almost share their fate."[78] Throughout his career he gravitated toward the depiction of subjects at the margins of society—outsiders, pariahs, exiles of varying kinds. "Edgar always had sympathy for any outcast or anybody who had a disability or was a fugitive," recalls Shirley, "whether it be for justice reasons or others, it didn't matter. Any outcast was one of his children."[79] Indeed, as Michael Henry Wilson puts it in his summation of the director's career:

> Other damaged lives, other staring eyes quickly come to mind of course. Haunted survivors, all of them: Hedy Lamarr, the small-town jezebel lighting all the candles in her manor as she senses hell opening under her feet *(The Strange Woman)*; John Carradine, the perverted painter driven to strangle his model because she will never meet his ideal of perfection *(Bluebeard)*; Paul Langton, the hardboiled cop who feels his existence unraveling when he begins questioning his work and falling for his suspect *(Murder Is My Beat)*; Robert Clarke, the jet pilot whose features have shriveled after experiencing the post-atomic horror of the year 2024 and who can only whisper: "Prevent the cosmic plague!" *(Beyond the Time Barrier)*. . . . Theirs are nightmares one never wakes up from.[80]

Damaged Lives depicts a nightmare of a terrifying, specific sort. Donald Bradley serves as the stand-in for millions of otherwise respectable citizens who, like him, are equally capable of being infected and who, fearing ostracism and stigmatization, fail to pursue proper treatment. That is, of course, the moral crux of the film and what the institutional underwriters from the Canadian Social Hygiene Council and their American counterparts no doubt hoped to achieve with the production.

These early projects with which Ulmer associated himself apply pressure to the predominant limits of genre, of conventional style, and of all national designations (a string of disposable two-reel westerns shot on the back lot at Universal, a highly improvised late silent from Weimar Berlin, and a largely forgotten Canadian-American hygiene film). In other words, they are not merely transnational but are also transitional, made en route to the next project—or, in some cases, with the hope of reaching that next project, aiming for the next level or quite often merely to earn a much-needed paycheck—and completed, by and large, on the fly. Despite the inconsistent nature of the projects, all of them are films whose production histories and formal qualities have, to varying degrees, a bearing on the director's life and career. Over the next three decades, toiling in Hollywood, New York, and again in Europe, Ulmer's cinema remains eclectic, unpredictable, filled with surprises, and forever on the move. The chance to establish himself as a mainstream studio director, as we will observe, would quickly pass him by.

3

Hollywood Horror

Don't hurry. Oblivion will be there eventually.
—Ed Wood Jr.

The year 1934 brought a number of surprises for Edgar Ulmer. On January 17, just a little over a month before the shooting of *The Black Cat* would commence, and just days after the formal studio announcement of the production was made public, Universal City was abuzz with festivities surrounding the celebration of Uncle Carl Laemmle's sixty-seventh birthday. All members of Laemmle's extended clan, including many of the studio's leading casts and crews (Universal's new starlet Margaret Sullavan, the character actors Andy Devine and Ken Maynard, among others), cheered on the studio patriarch as he blew out candles on an enormous chocolate cake—one pound of pastry for each year of his life—adorned with the Universal insignia.[1] In the VIP front row, just to the right of Laemmle himself, sat Boris Karloff (*né* William Henry Pratt), one of the studio's most decorated stars, by then already selected for the lead in *The Black Cat.* Karloff had been recently loaned out to headline a couple of external productions—John Ford's *The Lost Patrol* (1934) for RKO and Alfred Werker's *House of Rothschild* (1934) for 20th Century—and Universal was hoping to provide him with a vehicle that would forever link him to the House of Laemmle. Seated in the back row, among the less prominent guests, was the twenty-nine-year-old Ulmer, waiting to get his chance at directing his own feature with a capable film crew, talented actors, studio backing, and, perhaps an unintended consequence, a good bit more independence than was normally accorded to first-time Hollywood directors. That opportunity would finally come—at the time of Uncle Carl's birthday Ulmer was already slated to direct *The Black Cat*—but not before several obstacles were surmounted, making this otherwise thoroughly unlikely venture somehow plausible.

Although Ulmer was not particularly close to Laemmle père, he and Junior, then poised to assert himself and climb out from underneath his father's shadow, had developed a loyal friendship and a sound working relationship. Known for his "toothy smile," his notorious bouts of hypochondria, and his skirt chasing, not to mention a deep distaste for reading scripts and a weakness for the track, Junior was a tender twenty-five-year-old at the time of production. He had already been named general manager of the studio on his twenty-first birthday, an infamous case of Hollywood nepotism that didn't do much to help his reputation as "Crown Prince."[2] Junior had managed to make a mark a couple of years earlier by producing Lewis Milestone's award-winning *All Quiet on the Western Front* (1930), which he undertook, as Ulmer explained it to Bogdanovich, "against all advice from his father" (B 575). Owing to the success of that production, Ulmer fed him a follow-up idea to adapt another powerful novel from Weimar Germany, Hans Fallada's *Kleiner Mann—was nun?* (*Little Man, What Now?* 1932). While Ulmer had his heart set on directing the Fallada adaptation, which was completed around the same time as *The Black Cat*, it went to veteran director Frank Borzage (Ulmer was left to build the sets for the film, drawing on skills he had first acquired as a young man working in Weimar Germany, in a largely uncredited capacity). This wasn't the first time Junior had let down his Austrian-born friend. In December of the previous year he enticed Ulmer with a chance to earn a writing credit on a project called "Love Life of a Crooner," for which he'd begun drafting a scenario but which ultimately fizzled.[3]

It isn't clear whether either of these two disappointments prompted the young producer to make good and hire his friend to direct *The Black Cat*, or whether this was merely another case of Junior rebelling against his conservative father, a man who was constitutionally suspicious of all horror productions—let alone a subversive little picture like this one—despite their obvious earning potential. Regardless of such speculation, Junior was, by all accounts, not your average Hollywood studio executive. "He was a very strange producer," according to Ulmer, who ostensibly steered his friend toward "intellectual picture making" with projects like *Little Man, What Now?* "He didn't have much education, but he had great respect for intelligence, and for creative spirit" (B 575). Shirley Ulmer later recalled things somewhat differently: "Junior was a very psycho, mixed-up young man, and Edgar was playing psychiatrist for him."[4] During the film's preparation, shoot, and postproduction—with Uncle Carl conveniently on vacation in Germany and Junior himself, for a good part of the time, tied up in court (facing charges of salary gouging) in New York—Ulmer made the most of the anomalous situation and capitalized on the free pass unexpectedly handed down to him.[5]

THE BRIEF LIFE OF A STUDIO DIRECTOR

It has been a *good* game.
—Vitus (Bela Lugosi) in *The Black Cat*

With *The Black Cat*'s fifteen-day shooting schedule set to begin on February 28, and both Laemmles otherwise occupied, supervision of the production went to E. M. Asher, a moneyman from the studio's front office who served as associate producer on both *Dracula* (1931) and *Frankenstein* (1931) and on Universal's other recent Poe-inspired horror film, *Murders in the Rue Morgue* (1932). Asher had plenty of experience, but he also had a rather hands-off approach; he wasn't one to meddle or to prevent a director from pursuing his vision. And like Junior, Asher was known for his share of eccentric traits, among them meeting his directors while seated on the toilet. (Shirley Ulmer once recalled of the oddball producer: "There'd be Asher, having a 'b.m.,' holding up a copy of the script and saying to Edgar, 'I've read it—and I think it's *great!*'")[6] Though the original production budget of $91,125 was unquestionably modest in comparison to other successful Universal films of its kind—under a third of the budget of *Frankenstein,* for example, and around a quarter of the budget of *Dracula*—and the shooting schedule comparatively tight (less than half the total number of days given to either *Dracula* or *Frankenstein*), Ulmer had at his disposal a gifted crew of seasoned professionals.[7] Behind the camera was John Mescall, who had shot Ernst Lubitsch's *The Student Prince in Old Heidelberg* (1927)—on which Ulmer is said to have had a hand, albeit uncredited, in art direction—and would later earn an Oscar nomination for his cinematography in Mitchell Leisen's *Take a Letter, Darling* (1942). British-born Charles D. (Danny) Hall, who would later also pick up a couple of Oscar nominations of his own and who had formerly been Ulmer's superior during his first years in Universal's Art Department, offered up his talents as chief art director.[8] By the time the production began, Hall had already served as art director on *All Quiet on the Western Front, Dracula, Frankenstein,* and *Murders in the Rue Morgue,* among others. Together with Ulmer, who designed some of the film's most elaborate sets (e.g., Poelzig's mesmerizing compound, constructed in miniature), Hall created what Donald Albrecht, in his *Designing Dreams,* aptly hailed as an "architectural tour de force." As Albrecht notes further, "Ulmer's unexpected use of modern design for a horror film is just the sort of idiosyncratic, almost surreal touch that distinguishes the work of this remarkable director."[9]

For the music, which would play a far more important—and, in the sneering opinion of Uncle Carl, more contentious—role in *The Black Cat* than in any other horror film of its era, Ulmer was fortunate to have the former director of Universal's music department, Berlin-trained composer Heinz Roemheld, at his side. Roemheld had scored *All Quiet on the Western Front* and composed the music for the Universal release of G. W. Pabst's *Die weiße Hölle vom Piz Palü (The White Hell of Pitz Palu,* 1930)—he would later win an Academy Award for the music he composed for Michael Curtiz's *Yankee Doodle Dandy* (1942). Given his formal education in Berlin, he was intimately acquainted with the canon of Central European classical music.[10] Perhaps more important still, Roemheld shared with Ulmer an appreciation of the darker, romantic strains, in particular those of Franz Liszt, whose music—notably, his Hungarian Rhapsody no. 3, his symphonic poem *Tasso,* and the allegro from his Piano Sonata in B Minor, colloquially known as "The Devil Sonata"—sets the tenor of the film (the *Hollywood Reporter* published an account of the production in which it rhapsodized about the fifty-piece orchestra that Roemheld had assembled for his score).[11]

Finally, in the writing department Ulmer teamed up with Peter Ruric (*né* George Sims), a New York transplant who was relatively new to the art of the screenplay, having started out penning mysteries and detective stories under the pseudonym Paul Cain for *Black Mask* and other pulp outlets. (His one and only novel, *Fast One,* championed by Raymond Chandler as the high point of ultra hard-boiled crime fiction, has largely been forgotten.) As Ulmer recalls of Ruric, he was "a very intelligent boy who should have been a great playwright but got lost" (B 575). (In Paul Mandell's far less charitable quip, he "was more of a third-rate Mickey Spillane than a budding Arthur Miller.")[12] Though not a veteran at Universal, Ruric was a frequent guest at Uncle Carl's Sunday luncheons, affording him access to other experienced writers and crewmembers.[13] When the assignment arrived in Ruric's hands, numerous treatments had already come and gone. There was, for instance, the initial idea by Universal's story editor Richard Schayer, hatched in early 1932, to remain loyal to Poe's story and cast Karloff as the alcoholic sadist "Edgar Doe," who keeps his wife and cat locked up in the cellar. At the end of the same year, Junior's brother-in-law Stanley Bergerman and his writing partner Jack Cunningham submitted an eleven-page treatment called "The Brain Never Dies," which boasted a mad scientist with a penchant for brain transplants and a cat with a half-feline, half-human brain.[14] This was followed, in February 1933, by a sixty-eight-page adaptation of Poe's story by Tom Kilpatrick and Dale Van Every (the same writing team that in 1940 would create *Dr. Cyclops* at Paramount), in this case more of a fusion with *Dracula* than *Frankenstein,* set in the Carpathian mountains in the castle of Count Brandos—the film was to feature Karloff as its headliner and German director E. A. Dupont at the helm. All of these ideas were scrapped in favor of Ruric's. What he ultimately put forward, with substantial input from Ulmer (they shared the writing credit), was a version that, despite certain affinities with Universal's past glories and some of its more recent schemes—notably, the treatment by Kilpatrick and Van Every, with a rather heavy dose of the occult à la Aleister Crowley and a dash of Viennese discourse on psychosexuality imported via Richard von Krafft-Ebing—was something entirely unto itself.

The essential story, thoroughly enhanced by Ulmer's insistence on abundant visual and musical flourishes by Mescall, Roemheld, and the technical crew, can be summed up in a couple of sentences. A young American couple honeymooning in the Carpathian Mountains becomes trapped by two feuding madmen, both of them native born with a shared dark past. The innocents are subjected to a series of deranged, unsavory schemes by their lunatic captors but in the end narrowly escape. Even before the formal writing began, it was clear that Karloff, whose name had attained such profound recognition by then that it would appear on its own (like "Garbo" before him) in the opening credits, was to star in the film. Yet he still had to be convinced to play a part as sadistic and truly monstrous as engineer Hjalmar Poelzig, one of the two madmen, especially when he was increasingly eager to break out of being typecast. In an interview conducted in late 1966 by *Modern Monsters* magazine, Ulmer spoke of wooing Karloff through the elegant outfits he'd designed especially for his portrayal of Poelzig: "He knew he would be playing 'Karloff,' but also felt in these duds, he could

FIGURE 13. Teatime: on the set of *The Black Cat* (1934) with Karloff, Ulmer, Manners, and one of the extras from the film's Black Mass scene. Courtesy of the Edgar G. Ulmer Preservation Corp.

employ a sort of 'out of this world' appearance. That, as you know, was exactly how he appeared."[15]

At the time that the production was first conceived, Karloff was for many "the apostle of fright," the true successor to Lon Chaney. His screen persona was not only tied to his iconic performance in James Whale's *Frankenstein* but reinforced in such films as T. Hayes Hunter's *The Ghoul* (1933), which was still playing to packed houses during the shooting of *The Black Cat*. A brief profile, "Boris Karloff's Career as a Monster in Films," published in the *New York Times* shortly before the shooting began, noted the marked contrast between the macabre roles he played and his demure, genteel behavior offscreen: "For diversion he does not eat babies; he plays golf and cricket and fancies a pot of tea in the afternoon."[16] True to form, while embodying the sinister spirit of Hjalmar Poelzig in front of the camera—tempered, of course, by his dry sense of humor and the refined subtlety of an English gentleman—Karloff observed his afternoon tea ritual throughout the shoot (Figure 13).

From the outset Ulmer had given Junior his word that Karloff would get top billing and that the other perceived major box-office draw, the title of Poe's original story, would be duly retained—even if the credit sequence of the release print would announce "suggested by" rather than the usual "based on" in reference to Poe's text. Ulmer's idea to cast Hungarian Bela Lugosi (né Béla Ferenc Dezso Blaskó) opposite Karloff, the first of eight such appearances, was all the more attractive, given the added potential of such a pairing to lure audiences. The blustery publicity included in Universal's press kit sought to exploit this advantage: "The monster of *Frankenstein* plus the monster of *Dracula*, plus the 'monstrousness' of Edgar Allan Poe—all combined by the master makers of screen mysteries to give you the absolute apex in super-shivery."[17] Yet, like Karloff, Lugosi was acutely concerned about having his screen image tarnished by playing cruel and frightening characters. Ulmer had to charm him—owing to their shared Austro-Hungarian background, the two communicated throughout the production in the lingua franca of the former empire—and to assure him that his part, as Hungarian psychiatrist Vitus Werdegast, would include benign traits. Rather different from Karloff, however, was the acting style of the Hungarian, who had a well-known proclivity for exaggeration. "You had to cut away from Lugosi continuously," recalled Ulmer; "[he] nearly ate my set up!"[18] The differences did not stop there. Karloff and Lugosi had separate pay scales (Karloff earning $1,875 per week to Lugosi's $1,000), prompting certain feelings of inequality; they also enjoyed unequal levels of collegiality with other actors on the set (Karloff the consummate professional and source of inspiration, Lugosi more of a ham). Some of the overblown tensions in which the film wallows were already made palpable during the shoot, where bickering and petty rivalry were the order of the day.

In the role of the youthful, romantic American mystery writer Peter Alison, Ulmer cast Canadian-born David Manners, a regular at Universal who had spent his share of time on horror sets, having costarred as Jonathan Harker in *Dracula* and played the equally wide-eyed protagonist Frank Whemple in Karl Freund's *The Mummy* (1932). Although Manners, much like Karloff and Lugosi, was eager to secure a breakout role and to leave behind horror films for good, he later conveyed his fondness for the production, in particular for the film director, who "spent considerable time with the cast, discussing his overall intentions and the effects he desired."[19] As Peter Alison's patently innocent wife, Joan (the tag "hyper-virginal" is attached to her name in the original shooting script), one of the thirteen so-called Baby Stars selected in 1934, in what would be the last of the annual competition of the Western Association of Motion Picture Advertisers, Jacqueline Wells, later known professionally as Julie Bishop, was selected. Another Baby Star of the same year, Lucille Lund, was cast in the role of Werdegast's beautiful daughter Karen (she was also the body double for the other Karen, Werdegast's dead wife, whom Poelzig has hauntingly preserved in his basement). While both Manners and Wells would comment, many years later, on the genuine pleasure of working with their director ("I thought Edgar Ulmer was excellent," recalled Wells), Lund, who was made to endure various forms of harassment (hanging by her hair in a glass coffin, being forced to wear impossibly sheer costumes, and, with the combined effect of her kinky hair and makeup, projecting the unseemly air of "Rapunzel after a shopping spree at Frederick's of Hollywood"), remembered her eight and a half days on the set in late February and early March 1934 as "the most horrible experience in my life."[20]

At different stages in the writing, both Ulmer and Ruric would incorporate various personal asides, inside jokes of sorts, into the script. In Ruric's case, for instance, there is the American male lead as mystery author, a man who with considerable irony pronounces himself "one of the greatest writers of unimportant books" and who, like Ruric, bears the name Peter (the film's final scene, with the couple sitting in a train compartment poring over a barbed review of Peter's latest novel, *Triple Murder,* is just one of the film's many self-reflexive moments). In Ulmer's case there was the naming of the innocent American female lead, Joan, as he had done the year before in *Damaged Lives,* after his former wife, Joen Warner (Ulmer also managed to sneak in other allusions to his own past, mordant in-jokes, and additional forms of self-referential trivia). Yet, despite discernible signs of levity in the act of writing, there was an overriding seriousness to the enterprise. Indeed, Ruric stuck to the tight schedule and submitted his 333-scene script on February 19, 1934.

Exactly one week later to the day, Joseph I. Breen of the still embryonic Production Code Administration wrote his response to the script, following up on a conference he'd held earlier in the day with Asher, Ruric, and Ulmer. He began his memorandum on a mildly optimistic, if cautionary, note: "The blue script which we have read of this production suggests no difficulty, from the standpoint of our Production Code, but there are a number of details which ought to be carefully handled, to avoid mutilation of your picture by the censor boards."[21] The two key issues highlighted in Breen's report—and the point at which the censorship czar sharpens his tone—concern the anticipated "gruesomeness" of the scene, late in the film, in which Poelzig is skinned alive ("It is our understanding that you propose to suggest this merely by shadow or silhouette, but as we suggested this morning, this particular phase of your production will have to be handled with great care, lest it become too gruesome or revolting") and the sequences in the script that call for the killing of a cat ("Mr. Ulmer understands, I think, that any definite suggestion of cruelty to animals will invite considerable trouble, both for your studio and this Association").

In his full report Breen went on to list nineteen additional scenes from the script that, in his view, required special attention and should either be revised or omitted altogether. He expressed particular concern about any possible "suggestion of homosexuality" between Lugosi and Karloff or, as he puts it elsewhere, "perversion of any of the characters." The portrayal of heterosexuality, however, also prompted red flags ("The scene of a man in bed with a nude woman and all it implies should be omitted"). Breen further underlines his concern regarding potential defamation of church and religion (e.g., in the film's Black Mass scene). From today's standpoint, some of his suggestions seem almost to verge on parody or even to be drawn from a spoof of a horror script ("It might be wise to change this derogatory reference to Czech Slovakians [sic] as people who devour the young"). In the end, though, after final shooting—and after the imposition of three and a half days of retakes—Breen expressed his satisfaction with the production. In a letter composed on April 2, 1934, he declared, "The picture conforms to the provisions of the Production Code and contains little, if anything, that is reasonably censorable. We are particularly pleased with the manner in which your studio and director have handled this subject, and we congratulate you."[22] It's difficult to imagine that Breen was referring to the same film that, upon final approval, made its way into theaters the following month. Although Breen praised the film's director, Uncle Carl had failed to muster any words that could be understood as affirmative when he first saw the rough cut and even struggled after the retakes were complete. It didn't much matter that *The Black Cat* would end the year as Universal's top-grossing film, for this was a production that would wreak considerable havoc for the studio and its director.

The release print of the film, which premiered in theaters in May 1934, opens with an evocative prologue of images of transit. Within the walls of an elaborately constructed European railway station, presented as Budapest, we see a porter riding atop a trolley filled with luggage. This shot dissolves to throngs of passengers funneling into the respective tracks of the station, while trains emit billows of steam. The camera then zeros in on a couple of workers, one man with an armful of oversized pretzels and another with his hands around a large sack of potatoes, as the two load supplies into the dining car. Finally, after catching the few last glimpses of officials and travelers preparing for departure, the shot dissolves once more to the wheels of the steam engine set in rapid motion—all of this drenched in the resonant chords of Liszt's Hungarian Rhapsody no. 3.[23]

When the frame gives way to a point-of-view shot of a passport, with a woman's picture on the left-hand page, we are suddenly aboard car 96, compartment F of the Orient Express, as the conductor's voice tells us, en route from Budapest to Vizhegrad. Here the newlywed, consummately naive, American couple, mystery-thriller writer Peter Alison and his young bride, Joan, sit as if posing for a studio portrait; they're bound for a holiday resort in the Carpathian Mountains, a destination not otherwise known for its romantic retreats. As soon as the door closes, the honeymooners cozy up to one another, spouting lovey-dovey banter while trying to respond appropriately to each other's bashful behavior, each move more contrived than the previous. They soon face an intruder, Dr. Vitus Werdegast, who does in fact become a guest, as his name—in German, literally "I shall be a guest"—tells us, whether he's welcome or not, and whose jarring screen presence disrupts the illusion of harmony projected by the Alisons. The grim words of the conductor (André Cheron), that there has been "a terrible mistake" made in the inadvertent sale of a seat in the Alisons' private compartment, may seem initially overstated. But Werdegast's odd behavior soon makes the pronouncement more apt. He finds himself enraptured at the sight of Joan, which Ulmer captures in a striking point-of-view shot, a first taste of the film's recurrent voyeuristic leering directed at the young bride. This is followed by a shot of the unhinged doctor caressing the curls of Peter's wife while she unknowingly sleeps, Peter drowsily witnessing the transgression. We soon learn in conversation that Werdegast left a wife of similar beauty when he went off to fight in the Great War, for "Kaiser and country," as he tells us, eighteen years ago. He was then interned for three years, as a prisoner of war, and yet now, he states triumphantly, "After fifteen years, *I* have returned." Not unlike his role in *Dracula*, Lugosi's Werdegast invokes the return of the undead.

As the twisted plot of the film continues to gain momentum, it doesn't take terribly long—following, in rapid succession, a severe rain storm, a quick journey by bus, an accident, the death of the bus driver, and the injury of Joan—for the three passengers, who continue their extended journey together, to end up in another prison of sorts, the home of engineer Hjalmar Poelzig, built directly atop the mass graves of Fort Marmaros, a wartime battleground. With its clean modernist lines and stylish mystique ("very much out of my Bauhaus period," Ulmer would later boast [B 576]), Poelzig's compound, which shares notable affinities with Frank Lloyd Wright's 1924 Ennis-Brown House in the Hollywood Hills, stands perched on the hillside, in marked contrast to the more primal, forested landscape below. There is, we are told, "still death in the air." The house becomes a new battleground, the space in which the two European "monsters" vie for power and control over their American prey (Joan, in particular, left temporarily unconscious from her roadside injury, becomes the principal object of desire). Werdegast has a score to settle with Poelzig, a former army commander who abandoned his troops, Werdegast among them, resulting in countless deaths and prolonged prison terms. "You sold Marmaros to the Russians," he declares in one of his early confrontations with Poelzig. "You scurried away in the night and left us to die." Not only did Poelzig betray Werdegast in the trenches, but he also stole his wife, eventually killing her, preserving her corpse behind glass, and marrying his rival's daughter Karen, who has not seen Werdegast since before the war and whom Poelzig mendaciously claims to be dead.

With a heavy emphasis on the recurrent motif of the black cat, and Werdegast's crippling phobia ("an intense and all-consuming horror of cats," as Poelzig calls it), the film moves along a narrative axis of rivalry and revenge. Time and again Poelzig and Werdegast square off, as the helpless American couple remains captive. At night, while the Alisons are asleep, the two men descend to a basement vault, into the old military bunker, where Poelzig has Werdegast's wife, among others, embalmed in a glass shrine and where Werdegast challenges Poelzig once more, only to be rendered powerless by the presence of a black cat. The next day they wager Joan's life, in which they both take obsessive interest, over a game of chess. Finally, during an aborted midnight pagan Black Mass ceremony led by Poelzig, in what is undoubtedly the film's most gruesome scene, Werdegast hangs his rival on his own embalming rack while attempting to skin him "slowly—bit by bit."

Because the film was made in America in the early 1930s, and was produced by a leading Hollywood studio, the more frightening scenes had to be tempered by lighthearted, if also somewhat corny, moments. "Absurdity—campy absurdity—was probably the only way Hollywood could deal with horror," observes Otto Friedrich, "because that was the only way it had ever known. Hollywood horror films, no matter how gory or pseudo-gory they were to become, never approached real horror."[24] In the case of Ulmer's picture, the occasionally stilted dialogue adds to this effect in such scenes as the chess game, when the Alisons, wishing to flee Poelzig's compound, attempt to place a call only to discover that the line has been cut. "Did you hear that Vitus?" asks Poelzig impishly. "The phone is dead. *Even* the phone is dead." Finally, in keeping with the American tradition of happy endings, the Alisons escape the reign of terror, while the entire fortress explodes with the two European "monsters" inside it.

Leading up to the film's premiere was a shrewdly orchestrated media campaign. The pressbook, sent out to all exhibitors, gave firm instructions on how to generate interest: "Announce a black cat show to be staged in your theatre with prizes going to the biggest, the most beautiful, the weirdest-looking specimens." Or, as it affirms elsewhere, "Don't play down the sensational angles—capitalize on them! Flash the town with ballyhoo! Send your message through the city, cry to the skies that you have the biggest, triple-barreled, non-stop, emotion-wrangler that ever stalked the screen!" As if that weren't enough, the pressbook also offered tips on how to enhance the screening experience: "It will be a good idea at least for the first few showings of *The Black Cat* to plant a few women in the audience with instructions to scream at certain high spots of the picture. Screams put the audience in the right mood for enjoyment of the picture and also serve to start word-of-mouth advertising which spreads like wildfire."[25] This kind of sensationalism was incorporated into the poster art for the film, trading on the iconic status of the two protagonists (Figure 14).[26]

In the end the film was released to mixed reviews. In a positive vein *Variety* cited its earning potential as a result of the star power of the two leads: "Because of the presence in one film of Boris Karloff, that jovial madman, and Bela Lugosi, that suave fiend, this picture probably has box office attraction."[27] This was, however, the only real upside in the eyes of the leading trade daily, for as the same reviewer put it, "On the counts of story, novelty, thrill and distinction, it is sub-normal." A piece published in the British *Film Pictorial,* nearly a year after its

FIGURE 14. Art of the super-shivery: original poster for *The Black Cat* (1934). Courtesy of the Edgar G. Ulmer Preservation Corp.

American debut, suggested that the audience for such a picture was limited to a self-selecting group of those who were already fans of Hollywood horror: "Does the shadow of a black cat make you cry out in fear? Does the heavily decorated face of Boris Karloff make you cringe away, terrified? In fact, are you horror-film conscious, and never mind the probabilities? If you are, this somewhat unlikely film will be worth your money."[28] Similarly, the *Los Angeles Examiner* noted the innate curiosity the film held for horror fans: "If you have ever wondered what would happen should Frankenstein and Dracula meet on a dark night, the Pantages Hollywood Theatre now offers an opportunity to find out."[29] Ulmer himself had hoped to profit from the famous pairing. As he remarked, in his interview in 1965 in *Midi-Minuit fantastique,* "My idea, at first, was: Lugosi and Karloff had such success in their respective films, why not bring them together in one film. I sold the film to Laemmle, Sr. on this idea."[30] Yet the single unqualified rave review, published soon after the film's release in the *San Francisco Examiner,* ignored the stars altogether, focusing instead on the aesthetic significance of the work undertaken by Ulmer and his crew: "*The Black Cat*

... is the most cultured horror film this department has yet witnessed. ... Technically [it] is one of the most handsome pieces of cinema construction of the season."[31]

Overall praise for the film among contemporary critics was anything but lavish. Following the New York premiere at the Roxy Theatre, on May 18, 1934, some two weeks after the West Coast debut, in an unambiguously titled review, "Not Related to Poe," the *New York Times* dismissed the picture with a single sentence: "A clammy and excessively ghoulish tale of hi-jinks in a Hungarian horror salon."[32] The same reviewer went on to note, "As for the cats, they hardly stay in front of the camera long enough to give the title a good workout." Calling the film "more foolish than horrible," the reviewer offered just one positive observation, more of an afterthought on style than a central point of the review: "The staging is good and the camera devotes a proper amount of attention to shadows and hypnotic eyes." Years later, however, eminent film historian William K. Everson argued that *The Black Cat* came closer to Poe, in terms of its evocation of evil and devil worship inherent to the original story, than earlier critics had suspected.[33] Despite the lukewarm press attention, the film attracted a large audience and was a sleeper for Universal, where it finished the year as its top-grossing picture. According to a recent calculation, *The Black Cat* brought in close to $500,000 at the box office, no small feat for a picture that had cost less than $100,000 to make.[34]

CALIGARI IN AMERICA

Junior gave me free rein to write a horror picture in the style we had started in Europe with *Caligari*.
—Edgar G. Ulmer

One of the chief attributes of *The Black Cat* that sets it apart from its cohort of 1930s horror films is its copious, almost boundless, references to German art cinema of the Weimar period and to the film professionals responsible for its venerated reputation. As Paul Mandell puts it, quoting parenthetically from the shooting script: "*The Black Cat* is a grand summation of the decade of cinema that preceded it. Woven into it are the echoes of Murnau, of Robert Wiene, of Wegener and the pioneers of the Bauhaus. In his overall appearance, for example, Karloff was meant to resemble Cesare the Somnambulist in *Caligari* . . . and his rising motion mimicked the awakening of the vampire in Murnau's *Nosferatu* ('the upper part of his body rises slowly, as if being pulled by wires').”[35] Mandell argues, more fundamentally, that throughout the film, “images are keyed . . . to European films whose styles Ulmer revered and claimed to have worked on.”[36] Barely beneath the surface are a host of motifs—the fashioning of various figures, the choice of formal style and lighting, the general mood of the picture, not to mention the music chosen for its score—that point to Ulmer’s cinematic and cultural heritage. J. Hoberman’s memorable quip, riffing on the famous title of Siegfried Kracauer’s study of Weimar cinema, still rings true: “From Caligari to Hitler in one lurid package.”[37]

For Ulmer *The Black Cat* afforded the chance to revisit both the glories and the horrors of his youth, to draw on a vast compendium of source material he had brought with him from interwar Europe, and to digest some of the still undigested trauma wrought by the Great War. In this respect it was an intensely personal project. It served to bridge—and, in the end, to disrupt—the European and American phases of his life. As he would later comment, in his conversations with Bogdanovich, the proper cinematic lineage was for him self-evident. “For those artists driven into exile after the advent of Nazism, and obliged to remake their careers in alien countries,” writes David Robinson in his companion to *The Cabinet of Dr. Caligari,* “it was often especially important to be able to stake a claim in creating *Caligari,* an infallible calling-card.”[38] The ostensible affinities with Wiene’s groundbreaking film—the frame narrative, the stark undercurrents of war trauma, the stylized sets, and the dramatic low-key lighting—and with other well-known films of the Weimar period, even if mere citations, were deliberate. In Ulmer’s universe the associations he frequently professed to have with the greats of Weimar cinema (*Caligari,* among others) were not merely a matter of padding his cinematic curriculum vitae; they were the measuring stick of greatness.[39] Even if his ties to the actual films may not have been as deep as he often claimed, he aligned himself with them and with the celebrated film professionals who made them.

Consequently, we have among the many Weimar-inspired figures that populate *The Black Cat* Hjalmar Poelzig, named after famous German architect Hans Poelzig, whose film credits include the masterful set design of Paul Wegener’s *Der Golem, wie er in die Welt kam* (*The Golem: How He Came into the World,* 1920). In distinctive makeup by Jack Pierce, evocative of the menacing intensity of a Max Beckmann self-portrait, Poelzig also embodies a sadistic personality that Ulmer purportedly modeled on Fritz Lang.[40] Additionally, Werdegast’s man-servant Thamal (Harry Cording) was, in Ulmer’s words, to resemble "an enormous Tibetan, slant-eyed, with the cold, impassive face of an evil Buddha," a description that would apply equally well to Paul Wegener's portrayal of the Golem, played by Wegener himself, in his 1920 rendition.[41] Even if Ulmer did not occupy the same spotlight as the luminaries from Weimar cinema, he could at least aspire to recreate some of their sparkle both on and off the set. Lucille Lund recalled the director promising her, in one of his more inventive advances, "If you will be my 'girlfriend,' we will be a combination like Dietrich and von Sternberg!"[42]

Arguably, Ulmer's greatest debt is paid to Murnau, his former mentor, who left a profound impact on the young director. In John Belton's words, "Ulmer, like Murnau, shows characters thinking and transforms physical action into mental experience. His camera, again like Murnau's, becomes an intelligence through whose mind the action is viewed and whose movements echo a character's thoughts more than physical movements. They both photograph thought."[43] In one of the film's most evocative sequences, filmed during retakes, the disembodied voice of Poelzig reverberates as Mescall's omniscient camera tracks slowly, deliberately, and creepily through the vault:

> "Come, Vitus. Are we men or are we children? Of what use are all these melodramatic gestures? You say your soul was killed, that you have been dead all these years. And what of me? Did we not both die here in Marmaros fifteen years ago? Are we any the less victims of the war than those whose bodies were torn asunder? Are we not both the living dead? And now you come to me playing at being an avenging angel, childishly thirsting for my blood. We understand each other too well. We know too much of life. We shall play a little game, Vitus. A game of death, if you like. But under any circumstances, we shall have to wait until these people are gone, until we are alone."

Murnau's enduring influence, in visual style and technique, is indeed palpable throughout the film, making it in numerous respects an homage to Ulmer's beloved teacher.

Another allusion of a more explicit nature occurs quite early in the film, when the three passengers aboard the Orient Express descend from their train compartment in Vizhegrad, entering into the stormy night escorted by a porter who couldn't look any more like Emil Jannings in Murnau's *Der letzte Mann* (*The Last Laugh*, 1924). With his Kaiser Wilhelm mutton chops and imposing uniform, the Dutch-born actor George Davis wields his big umbrella—the Hotel Atlantic of Murnau's film has been replaced here by the Hotel Hungaria Gömbös—conveying the same palette of gestures as Jannings's memorable character.

He subsequently doubles as a driver, navigating the slick roads in the rickety hotel shuttle bus and describing, in thick German-accented English, the history-laden signposts along their journey. ("This, too, was built by the Austrian army. All of this country was one of the greatest battlefields of the war. Tens of thousands of men died here.") After going on to describe the gory details ("The ravine down there was piled twelve deep with dead and wounded men. The little river below was swollen, red raging") and pronouncing Fort Marmaros the "greatest graveyard in the world," he crashes the bus, adding himself unwittingly to the long list of casualties at the site.

Ulmer's choice of locale for the film similarly gives a nod to his own past. Indeed, in an early version of Ruric's shooting script, the opening sequence was not to be set in the Budapest railway station, as the release print has it, but in the heart of Vienna at a cathedral where the marriage of Peter and Joan Alison was taking place. The opening shots were to help establish the innocence of Joan (as the language of the script made plain, "camera tilts up to face of Madonna, dissolve to face of Joan").[44] Yet, despite the eventual move from Vienna to Budapest—the next point on the Alisons' European itinerary—the general locus is still very much identifiable as Ulmer's former home. "The Orient Express makes tracks," asserts Stefan Grissemann, "on a round-the-world journey that cuts directly through, as is readily apparent, an imaginary Eastern Europe reconstructed in Hollywood, that is, directly through Ulmer's old, gloomily conveyed Austro-Hungary."[45]

Beyond the choice of location there was the acting talent that the director opted to work with on the project. As Mandell suggests, "It was Ulmer's intention . . . to form a stock company of European émigrés à la Ingmar Bergman as backup talent for projects that went unrealized. As a result, several class names popped up in *The Black Cat* in the most peculiar roles."[46] In the role of Poelzig's creepy majordomo, for example, the acclaimed theater actor Egon Brecher, a native son of Ulmer's Olmütz and also, like the director, a Viennese transplant, was cast; he would go on to play a minor part in Ulmer's *The Wife of Monte Cristo* (1946) a decade later. In the original script there was also the ancillary part of the maître d'hôtel aboard the Orient Express, played by Frankfurt-born character actor Herman Bing, whose lines were to convey a degree of Old World charm and a steady stream of comic asides. Bing's twenty odd scenes got clipped in the end, however, and he is nowhere to be found in the release print. Finally, for the film's single overtly comical scene, the arrival of the chatty local gendarmes to Poelzig's compound—preceded by a few animated notes from what composer Roemheld calls "Hungarian Burlesque"—Ulmer selected the Sicilian-born Henry Armetta, whose name was flagged on the original script as the ideal choice for the part, and Albert Conti, another native of Austro-Hungary, to play a kind of trumped-up vaudeville skit. The two bumbling officers quickly forget about the case at hand (i.e., the investigation of the roadside accident) and instead sing the praises of their respective provincial hometowns as must-see destinations for the American honeymooners. The scene, which goes on and on until Armetta finally remarks, with a sudden burst of self-awareness, "I think you're carrying it a bit too far," not only delivers a comic interlude but allows Ulmer and his two actors to trot out an old Borscht Belt routine on petty small-town rivalry (Pinsk versus Minsk or, in the case of the film, Gömbös versus Pisthyan).

Throughout all of this Ulmer never loses sight of his aesthetic ambitions for the film. As Herbert Schwaab has remarked, "*The Black Cat* is obsessed with art and Ulmer wants to put as much as possible into the film—a mixture of expressionism (something in the style of *Caligari*), some Bauhaus, and the music of the composers he admired so much."[47] The set design, Ulmer suggested in his interview with Bogdanovich, was inspired by conversations with Gustav Meyrink, the Prague novelist who wrote his own rendition of *The Golem*, on which Wegener's film of 1920 was nominally based, and who had allegedly considered setting a play in a French military fortress from the Great War much like Marmaros. The fortress name might also be understood as a play on the great *Marmorhaus* (Marble House) of Berlin, the famed modernist picture palace on Kurfürstendamm at which such films as *Caligari* enjoyed their lavish premieres.[48] Indeed, despite the fact that the film's supposed location is far removed from an urban world, the highly stylized interiors—the digital clock, as well as the many other objets d'art strewn about—evoke something more out of the European metropolis than out of the provincial hinterland. It is, moreover, a style that had already attained renown in Ulmer's cultural orbit. The same is true of Ulmer's rich catalogue of music, selected in consultation with Roemheld, which bestowed on the film, much to the chagrin of Carl Laemmle Sr. (who thought film music was merely "a passing fad" and classical music a guarantee for failure), an unmistakably European flavor.[49]

Of the film's sixty-five minutes, all but ten are enhanced by music—Brahms, Liszt, Schubert, Tchaikovsky, among others—making it by far the most ambitious score of the Universal horror cycle. In his "Music for the Monsters," music editor William Rosar's incisive analysis of horror film scores of the 1930s, Rosar explains the division of labor between Roemheld and Ulmer. "Before the score was recorded," he notes, "Roemheld played his selections on the piano for Ulmer while Ulmer viewed the film on a Moviola. This enabled Ulmer to judge whether the music matched his own conceptions."[50] Already in the shooting script Ulmer highlighted various compositions he hoped to include, several of which (e.g., parts of the "Transfiguration" from Wagner's *Parsifal,* the opening bars from Beethoven's Fifth Symphony, and a portion of Dukas's *Sorcerer's Apprentice*) never made it into the final score that Roemheld composed. In the end, taking Roemheld's lead, Ulmer assigned a set theme to each of the key players of the film: for Karloff's Poelzig there are the lush chords of Liszt's "Devil Sonata"; attached to Lugosi's Werdegast is the opening theme from *Tasso;* and for Peter and Joan Alison, Roemheld playfully invented what he called the "Cat Love Theme," derived from Tchaikovsky's *Romeo and Juliet* (some of the music, such as that of Tchaikovsky, Roemheld tended to paraphrase rather than cite directly, since he wasn't sure at the time if it was public domain and was eager to avoid fees);[51] finally, Karen moves about to the sounds of Brahms's *Sapphische Ode.*

Beyond the individual themes, music saturates the film at nearly every turn. When we enter Fort Marmaros, we hear Chopin's Second Piano Prelude, and when Werdegast hurls a knife at the first black cat, in a state of panic, the dramatic chords of Schubert's *Unfinished Symphony* emanate from the radio. When Poelzig bangs away on the keys of the organ, during the Black Mass ceremony, he plays the opening bars of Bach's Toccata and Fugue in D Minor—whose anthem-like quality would continue to be used in American horror film for decades to come—just as Ulmer noted on the shooting script. "Classical music in films has rarely been used with such grand effect and understanding [as in *The Black Cat*]," suggests film historian Calvin Thomas Beck, "anticipating Kubrick's successful use of it in *2001* and *A Clockwork Orange*—two generations later."[52]

Just as the film score seems to have been drawn in no small measure from the soundtrack of Ulmer's past, so, too, the film's sustained preoccupation with the aftershocks of the First World War appears to have been dredged up from the director's experience of war as a youth in Vienna. To be sure, Werdegast's entry into battle, eighteen years previously (i.e., 1916), as he reveals early in the film, coincides with the year that Ulmer's father died in Austrian uniform. We should be careful not to exaggerate the significance of such an otherwise minor point, but it shouldn't be skipped over either. "The shadow of the Great War," notes David Skal in *The Monster Show,* "haunted horror movies of the twenties and thirties, and was depicted in unusually sharp focus in Edgar G. Ulmer's *The Black* Cat."[53] As Skal argues, not only was Ulmer himself working through his own rendition of war trauma, but Lugosi, who often claimed to have been employed as a hangman in the Austro-Hungarian army, had his own past to deal with; as an infantry captain wounded at battle several times, he had to feign insanity in order to be discharged. Lugosi once told his girlfriend, Hungarian actress Anna Bakacs, that he "escaped death on the battlefield by hiding in a mass grave under a pile of corpses," a line that almost could have been lifted from bits of dialogue in the script.[54]

Among the film's many scenes set in the gloomy atmosphere of inter-war Middle Europe, the Black Mass ceremony—especially as it was originally conceived—was to evoke a tableau of images that recalled the bloody past. According to Ulmer's notes in the shooting script, even before the assembly formally begins, while Karloff is still dressing, Lugosi was to greet the motley crew of cultists. "They are to be as aberrant as possible," asserted Ulmer, "a stable of misfits, members of a decadent aristocracy of the countryside. . . . They are all dressed in keeping with their twisted natures, and give the impression they have been made of old pieces of celluloid, wire, *papier maché,* flesh and red plush."[55] These figures were, according to the script, to bear such names as "Count Windischgraetz" and "Fräulein Krug," "Graf Trivers" and "Hauptmann Eichel" (all poking fun at the Habsburg overinvestment in otherwise meaningless aristocratic titles). There is even a "Herr Sternberg," which, as Gerd Gemünden has recently observed, is "most likely a jab at the phony nobility of Josef von Sternberg,"[56] and, with an eye toward the gathering threat of National Socialism, a "Frau Goering," who, as Ulmer would have it, "was to be played by a woman, the dark fuzz on her lip suggesting Hitler's moustache."[57]

All of these named figures would ultimately be cut from the film. (The few remaining nameless cultists who made their way into the release print, most of them bit players from the Universal lot, include as organist the young John Carradine, who would go on to star in Ulmer's *Bluebeard* a decade later.) What sets the mood of the scene, beyond the dark chords of the Adagio in A Minor from Bach's Toccata, is Poelzig's faux Latin discourse ("Cum grano salis, fortis cadre, cadre non protest" or "With a grain of salt, the brave may fall but cannot yield")—harking back to Ulmer's classical Jesuit education in wartime Vienna—which only heightens the element of ironic self-reflexivity and underscores the Habsburg roots of the film. The orgiastic ritual that nearly ensues, as Grissemann suggests, cuts against the grain of American morality and, to a considerable extent, anticipates the ritual orgy scene in Stanley Kubrick's bold adaptation of Viennese writer Arthur Schnitzler's interwar "Traumnovelle" (Dream story, 1926) in *Eyes Wide Shut*, some sixty-five years later.

Given the repeated references to Austrian culture and society, not all of them especially flattering, it should come as little surprise that *The Black Cat* received an immediate ban, by a unanimous vote of the Austrian State Board of Censorship, in Ulmer's former home. According to a press notice in the *New York Herald Tribune*, "The reason for the ban was that the Universal Film Company, American Producers, introduced a scene in which some of the actors appeared in the uniforms of Austrian army officers."[58] Two month later, Joseph Breen reported that the film had been rejected on the following grounds: "Because religious feelings are hurt by the broad showing of the devil services and by the fact that the one main figure, an Austrian, is shown as a military traitor and the main criminal, thus offending the national feeling of the people."[59] Of course, there wasn't much to laugh about, but Ulmer—who at this point in his life, with fascism on the rise across the continent, was increasingly alienated from his former home—must have found the Austrian ban darkly amusing.

Ulmer's last laugh, kept from the release print, was a scene that would have surely been the film's most self-referential moment of all. In the script, as the two fleeing Americans try to hail a car on the road leading from Poelzig's compound, the driver that stops for them—as if anticipating a signature touch of Hitchcock—was to be none other than the director himself. "Will you take us to Vizhegrad?" inquires Peter. The driver then offers the tart response: "I'm not going to Vizhegrad, I'm going to a sanatorium to rest up after making *The Black Cat* in fourteen days!"[60] Needless to say, Ulmer was unable to end the film with this scene. What he does instead, however, may be more indebted to his Weimar forerunners than to his original idea. Having us revisit the Alisons' train compartment on the return leg of their horrific journey gives the film a bookend to the frame narrative adapted à la *Caligari*. Furthermore, it leaves us to question—just as the critic of Peter's latest novel, *Triple Murder,* does in the newspaper he quotes from—the believability of their journey. Was this, so the imagined critic asks, all merely the product of the author's overly melodramatic imagination?

FROM *BLACK CAT* TO BLACKBALL

Trouble, nothing but trouble.
—Talking parrot, *From Nine to Nine* (1936)

The liberties that Ulmer took with *The Black Cat,* though a great source of praise among his champions, did not earn him much respect at the studio. Because of its emphasis on visual style and modernist aesthetics, a film like *The Black Cat,* as William K. Everson has suggested, can come off as "too tricky for its own good," adding that "the striking, pictorial quality of the film creates a decidedly non-Hollywood and non-stereo-typed horror film."[61] In fact, as Shirley Ulmer explains it, "When Old Man Laemmle came back from Germany, he nearly had a heart attack! He raised holy hell with Junior, because he had allowed Edgar to make this picture and use that music. He didn't want to *hear* of scored classical music; he felt it wasn't commercial. But Junior stood up for Edgar and said 'It's going to be just as it is.' This was just prior to its release."[62] Junior may have come to Ulmer's defense, but Uncle Carl was not one to forget, especially since it wasn't merely the classical music that earned his ire; in his view Ulmer was the cause of considerable unrest in the House of Laemmle. Indeed, if there was any shine at all left on Ulmer's star as a promising young studio director, it faded very quickly. Within ten days, in April 1934, Ulmer would go from being announced in the *Hollywood Reporter* as Universal's chosen director for *Bluebeard*—a project he would, in fact, go on to direct during his stint at PRC in the 1940s, *not* at Universal—to someone who had, allegedly of his own voli-tion, chosen to "freelance."[63] Indeed, the early characterization of Ulmer as a lousy company man [*Betriebshasser*], as reported during the filming of *People on Sunday,* turned out to have some long-term validity.[64] He was conspicuously absent at *The Black Cat*'s premiere at the Pantages Theater in Hollywood, on May 3, 1934, presumably no longer welcome in the company of Laemmle and his entourage, and would remain absent from the Hollywood limelight for many years to come. He was forced to serve out a sentence in what John Landis, speaking in Michael Palm's 2004 documentary *Edgar G. Ulmer: The Man Off-Screen,* dubs "movie jail," when a director is no longer called.

Among the other surprises that the production brought for Uncle Carl, apart from the unconventional score and the litany of broken industry taboos, was that while working together with his extended cast and crew, Ulmer had fallen in love with a woman. She was a young writer and aspiring script supervisor who was assisting the veteran script clerk, Moree Herring, and who happened to be married to Laemmle's beloved nephew Max Alexander. Her name was Shirley Alexander (*née* Kassler), a New Yorker, not yet twenty years old, who until recently had been living with her parents on Kings Boulevard in Brooklyn (the Kasslers had returned to New York, after having spent the first years in the wake of the stock market crash living in Los Angeles, when Shirley was just a teenager). In the summer of 1933, less than a year before she would appear on the set of *The Black Cat,* Shirley returned to Hollywood to marry Uncle Carl's favorite nephew. Like his uncle, Alexander was born in Germany and came to Hollywood as a youngster. He was bosom buddies with his cousin Junior, just months apart in age, and yet had more of an independent streak, running his own company, Beacon Productions, and overseeing a small studio on Santa Monica Boulevard. Max and Shirley had met already the previous summer, when Shirley, then still living with her parents in Los Angeles, put on a small play she wrote at the Pasadena Playhouse. Backstage at the theater, Max and cousin Junior came to introduce themselves after the show. Later that night, Max, Junior, and Shirley went out on a double date with a friend of Shirley's in tow; it's almost as if the story line of *People on Sunday* had been transposed to 1930s Los Angeles. It wasn't long after that evening that Max—when Shirley had begrudgingly landed back with her family in Brooklyn (without knowing the near-nomadic life that Shirley and Edgar would later lead, her mother voiced her negative opinion of showpeople as "Gypsies" and sternly warned Shirley of the "no good circus" it was)[65]—was proposing to her over the telephone, long distance, anticipating another story line from an Ulmer production: the frenzied proposal of Al Roberts to his Hollywood-based sweetheart, Sue Harvey, in *Detour* a good decade later. "I married him to get away from home," admits Shirley in her 1998 interview with Tom Weaver. "I *was* very fond of him, he was a nice guy, but a very simple man."[66]

Ironically enough, it was Max who introduced Shirley to Edgar, inviting him to dinner when the two were in discussion about a picture called *I Can't Escape,* starring Lila Lee, which was released by Alexander's Beacon Productions in summer 1934 (Ulmer served, uncredited, as second unit director). As Shirley recalled their fateful encounter:

> I was in the kitchen making a pot roast when I heard this man's voice that was so exciting to me—not just the timbre of his voice. I thought, "Oh, what

a crazy, exciting man, what a beautiful voice!" I went into the living room and Max introduced me. . . . Then after dinner, Max made the mistake of saying he was very tired and he had a headache, and that I would entertain Edgar, go out to the movies or something with him. Well, I entertained Edgar . . . and that was the beginning of the end for Max.[67]

Instead of going to the movies, Edgar and Shirley went for a drive to the beach, where Shirley talked about the pulp novel she was finishing, *Sinners in Sight*—a title with a strikingly close connection to the budding adulterous affair—and Ulmer told of his wartime experience, living in Sweden, and about all the luminaries he'd come into contact with over the years.[68] "It was a very exciting evening. He started me out on a tremendous journey," Shirley later recounted.[69]

Unfortunately for Ulmer, the ties between Uncle Carl and his dear nephew ran deep. Max and Shirley initially lived together in Beverly Hills at the Benedict Canyon home of Laemmle, before finding their own apartment in Hollywood. They were also considered regulars at Uncle Carl's table during his Sunday luncheons, often seated directly next to the family patriarch.[70] And although Max ran his own production company, he worked for his uncle, helping to collect the rent on his commercial properties at the corner of Hollywood and Vine. Uncle Carl in turn helped the young couple get started, supplying them with furniture and assorted gifts, giving their marriage his unwavering support and his blessing. Anyone who came between them would have to reckon with Uncle Carl's fury. According to Shirley, "he *never* forgave Edgar for taking me away from his nephew Max. . . . We were told that we'd never work in Hollywood again. He [Ulmer] couldn't get a job—that's why we went back to New York."[71] Or, as she confided elsewhere: "Nobody would even keep an appointment with him or answer a phone call. It was really like being blackballed."[72] Some three and half decades after Ulmer's false start as a contract director at Universal, Junior Laemmle, in a letter assessing Ulmer's cumulative work there, failed to recall—you might say chose to omit—the 1934 feature film, and instead merely spoke of Ulmer's minor assignments on the lot in the mid to late 1920s.[73] Had it been left to the Laemmles, Ulmer likely would have been forever excised from the studio's history.

The effect of all this on Max Alexander, who was perhaps kept from witnessing the initial flare-up with Uncle Carl, seems to have been comparatively small and rather delayed. In what in retrospect can only be understood as a strange twist of fate, in the immediate months after *The Black Cat*, using the pseudonym Joen Warner (the name of his former wife), Ulmer directed for Alexander's Beacon Productions, *Thunder over Texas* (1934).[74] This deeply impoverished, long-forgotten B western—costarring Texan hero Guinn "Big Boy" Williams and Marion Schilling, both of them regulars of the B-western circuit—was scripted by none other than Sherle Castle (i.e., then still Shirley Alexander, soon to be Shirley Ulmer) and billed as "A Max Alexander Production." Although Max's brother Arthur Alexander, co-owner of Beacon Productions and production manager of *Thunder,* later attested to Ulmer's service at Beacon lasting "four or five months," the film, which was shot in under a week and released in October 1934, was presumably finished before divorce proceedings and the total fallout from them were in full swing.[75]

For Ulmer the film was essentially grunt work, a step backward in the direction of the two-reel westerns he had made at Universal in the mid to late 1920s. The production attempts in vain to blend a saccharine love story between an upstanding, do-gooder cowboy fittingly named Ted Wright (Williams) and the equally virtuous teacher Helen Mason (Schilling)—and their adoption of a young orphaned girl called Tiny (Helen Westcott)—on the one hand, and a tale of small-town corruption, bank robbery, and kidnapping on America's western frontier on the other. Gone is the big studio; gone, too, are the talented cast and crew with which Ulmer worked on *The Black Cat.* While he managed to squeeze as much out of veteran cameraman Harry Forbes as he could—and even so, the use of severely unmatched stock footage and assorted gaps in continuity mar his achievements—the acting is frequently so wooden as to suggest a throwback to the earliest days of cinema. Without the aid of a musical score, Ulmer's chase sequences in particular seem imported from the silent era; one has the feeling that at any moment the cowboys on horseback might ride right off the set, and the visual incongruity is frequently halting. As Bill Krohn has observed of the film, "stray expressionist conceits dart out like moonbeams from sequences of incredible platitude and technical impoverishment."[76] Unlike his later entry into the western genre, *The Naked Dawn* (1955), the film contains none of the lyricism or sensuality that made it possible for him to transcend the utter lack of financial means. "In its composition," one critic has aptly noted, "the film comes off as half baked, not fully thought through until the end; it threatens, from the very beginning, to fall apart."[77]

Despite such obvious shortcomings, however, the film contains a few halfway redeeming scenes, due perhaps to Shirley's original work on the script and to the constant dialogue that she and Ulmer were known to have on the set. Early on in the film, for example, when Ted returns home to his ranch for the first time with Tiny, having saved her from a car wreck that takes place in the opening sequence, his sidekicks Tom, Dick, and Harry—yes, those are their names, and their main role, unsurprisingly, is that of a Yiddish-style vaudeville trio—are practicing a comedy routine based on the German legend of Baron von Münchhausen fancifully adapted to the life of the cowboy. Dick (Victor Potel) hams it up playing the baron with a hilariously heavy German accent: "Unt zer I vas schtanding in ze middle of sewenty-fife million cattle schtampeding!" Not unlike the scene in which the Emil Jannings doppelgänger jabbers away in his accented English in *The Black Cat,* here the traces of German can be understood, as Grissemann has suggested, as a kind of "Ulmer self-parody, an ironic tribute to the director, whose thick Viennese accent startled many of his actors."[78] Tiny later steals the show with her Garbo imitation ("I *vant* to be alone!") from *Grand Hotel* (1932), Edmund Goulding's acclaimed film adaptation of Viennese novelist Vicki Baum's best seller, another veiled allusion to Ulmer's larger cultural heritage and to his claimed record of professional experience.[79] Finally, when Tiny eventually offers her words, while kneeling and saying grace ("And please, God, make Tom a better actor"), the audience has no choice but to share her hope. If *The Black Cat* signaled for Ulmer enormous possibility, *Thunder over Texas* represented an omen of a very different sort. Ulmer's career as an independent and itinerant filmmaker, toiling on the outer fringes of Hollywood, had officially begun.

Soon after *Thunder over Texas,* and after Shirley had temporarily returned on her own to New York, Edgar and Shirley were living together—living in sin, as it were, as Shirley's divorce would not be finalized for a full year—at the Christie Hotel on Hollywood Boulevard. Ulmer was out of work, and his chances of making films in Los Angeles looked increasingly bleak. After the divorce was final, sometime late in 1935, Shirley and Edgar loaded their belongings into the back of an old Plymouth station wagon and drove from Hollywood to New York; they would make their way to City Hall, to New York's municipal marriage chapel, on December 15 of that year and would remain married for nearly four decades. As for employment opportunities, their sole lead was a British-born producer named Kenneth Bishop, who had his own company and worked in collaboration with other studios. Together with associate producer William Steiner, Bishop would offer Ulmer his debut assignment in the East, *From Nine to Nine* (1936). Shot over the course of nine days in Montreal in late February 1936, under the auspices of Coronet Pictures, it was conceived as a "quota quickie," a film that would help to meet the total number of pictures that the British government, as stipulated by the 1927 Cinematograph Films Act, considered to be fair trade. That it was made in Canada didn't matter, as Canada was part of the British Empire and films made anywhere in the empire qualified under the act; the film was thus released in the United Kingdom as part of Universal's quota compliance.[80]

Originally given the working title "Death Strikes Again," but also referred to as "The Man with the Umbrella" on the shooting script, the film eventually took a title that stems from a popular German novel by Prague-born writer Leo Perutz (*Zwishen neun und neun*, 1918), the adaptation of which F. W. Murnau was ostensibly planning before he moved from Germany to Hollywood in 1927.[81] Ulmer was not only responsible for the selection of the title *From Nine to Nine*—which he likely borrowed from Murnau—but he and Shirley also wrote the original story for this boilerplate whodunit that takes place in a Montreal hotel. According to film archivist D. J. Turner, who was responsible for the film's restoration in the late 1990s, "*From Nine to Nine* was a considerable change of pace for Ulmer after *Damaged Lives* and *The Black Cat*, not to mention *Thunder over Texas*, and he seems to have been having fun with this modest tale of jewel thieves, murder, and blackmail."[82]

Filmed in the Associated Screen News studios and on location at the Mount Royal Hotel, *From Nine to Nine* was supported by technical crew that was largely Canadian and a cast of Broadway stage actors that Ulmer had brought with him from New York, as well as a few locals. The popular if aging serial actress Ruth Roland was chosen for the film's critical role, the intrepid sleuth Cornelia Du Play (Figure 15).[83]

Du Play is the type of woman able to crack the case while offering a few wisecracks of her own along the way (her remark, late in the film, "Will you two act like a couple of movie villains!" bears the same kind of metacommentary as Tiny's observation on Tom's poor acting in *Thunder over Texas*). The rather flimsy structure of the film can barely sustain the convoluted plot, which revolves around the murder of a wealthy jeweler named Balsac (Julian Gray), the theft of his precious stones, and the attempted extortion on the part of a rough-and-tumble international crime syndicate whose members ultimately turn on each other. As the American-employed private investigator, Du Play has the

FIGURE 15. Sleuthing in Canada: Cornelia Du Play (Ruth Roland) in *From Nine to Nine* (1936). Courtesy of the British Film Institute Stills Collection.

task of shedding light on the various agents of deception at work in the jewel heist. The limitations of the genre, not to mention the budget, did not, however, keep the director in a straitjacket. In the words of Bill Krohn, Ulmer "was able to use the conventions of the fake-English detective story to paint a subtly corrosive portrait of Canadian society."[84] But it's unlikely that the film was ever screened in Canada (there is no evidence of a theatrical release there, and it seems more probable that it merely served the utilitarian purpose of filling Britain's demands for Universal); likewise, there are no extant reviews of it from the American trade papers.[85] What's most enduring about the film has little to do with its formal achievement—apart from a few interior shots aided by decent production design, there isn't much to speak of—but rather stems from a witty line uttered by a talking parrot, words that could almost serve as a motto for Ulmer's flagging career at this juncture: "Trouble, nothing but trouble."

While *Thunder over Texas* and *From Nine to Nine* both represented a clear step down from Ulmer's auspicious beginnings at Universal, they nevertheless foreground a new station of his life and career. They mark a transition from a short-lived contract director at a renowned Hollywood studio to the status of a free agent—for better and, indeed, for worse—a kind of itinerant director whose work for hire in the mid-to-late 1930s included everything from industrial shorts, newsreels, and instructional films to a string of generally obscure features aimed at minority audiences. When he finished work on *From Nine to Nine,* he was no better off than he was at the start of the production. During the shoot, Shirley wound up in the hospital with acute appendicitis and, as she recalls of the unexpected costs of the operation, "all our money that we had earned was suddenly wiped out."[86] The return to New York would bear the obvious pressures of needing to find additional film work of any kind upon their arrival. Needless to say, the arc of Ulmer's career trajectory did not match that of his more successful émigré peers working on the West Coast, several of whom either landed long-term contract work at the studios soon after arriving in Hollywood or were brought over with a contract in hand. While they were able to plant their feet firmly on the ground, he would remain, throughout the next phase of his increasingly independent career, very much at sea.

4

Songs of Exile

Just weeks after the shooting of *From Nine to Nine* wrapped in Montreal, in early spring 1936, American producer and distributor Joseph Steiner invited Edgar and Shirley, who was then still convalescing from her unplanned appendix operation, to return to New York City.[1] The project he had in mind for the itinerant director was something so outré, so completely obscure that, were it not for the surviving print of the film, it would stand to reason that Ulmer cooked it up in one of his more embroidered memories: a Ukrainian-language operetta called *Natalka Poltavka* (*The Girl from Poltava*, 1937). The story, whose origins lie in a popular play of the same name written in 1819 by the grandfather of modern Ukrainian literature, Ivan Kotlyarevsky, was thought to possess a special national appeal among Ukrainian immigrants living in North America, who numbered close to a million at the time.[2]

As it turns out, the project didn't belong solely to Steiner, whose name appears nowhere in the credits. The real force behind it, the creative and financial mastermind, was a charismatic Ukrainian folk-dance teacher and impresario named Vasile Avramenko. Through his boundless energy and his savant-like talents in grassroots fund-raising—hocking, among other things, ticket presales and separate shares of the independent production while maximizing the support of a Ukrainian window-washers' union—he rounded up $18,000 in donations in Canada and the United States. The Ukrainian-born Avramenko, who migrated to Canada in 1925, soon after Ulmer's own migration from Europe, made New York

City his home in the 1930s.[3] Although he had no experience working in the film industry, what he lacked in experience he made up for in guts, chutzpah, and a proven ability to talk his way into high places.

By the time the rehearsals for *Natalka* began in summer 1936, not only had Avramenko introduced thousands of students to the art of Ukrainian folk dance, establishing dozens of dance schools across North America, but he also performed at New York's Metropolitan Opera in a widely cele- brated Ukrainian program in the early 1930s. More impressive still, he danced on the White House lawn for Eleanor Roosevelt at the 1935 White House Easter egg hunt.[4] It wasn't terribly long after his performance for the First Lady that he established a Canadian-American film company bearing his name, Avramenko Film Productions (sometimes credited as Ukrainian Films). He immediately hired Russian filmmaker Leo Bulgakov, a trans- plant from the Moscow Art Theatre who had made a handful of B pictures for Columbia the year before, to direct *Natalka*. In mid-September 1936 the *Hollywood Reporter* ran a short notice with a promising headline given in industry shorthand: "6 Ukrainian Musicals for Prod'n at Biograph." *Natalka* was thus initially conceived as but one in a series of half a dozen features to be made at the Bronx-based studio by "Azra Menko [*sic*] Film Productions."[5] Not exactly a man of restraint, Avramenko had high hopes—delusions of grandeur, one might say in retrospect—that *Natalka* would form a cornerstone of a "Ukrainian Hollywood."[6]

How Ulmer came to the project still remains, like other vagaries that dot the director's service record, rather cryptic. Maybe Steiner set up a meeting with Avramenko in the days after *From Nine to Nine*, or maybe the true conduit was Bulgakov, whom Ulmer knew from the latter's suc- cess with his staging of *One Sunday Afternoon* during his days on Broad- way. As Shirley Ulmer remembers it, the acquaintance with Avramenko was made through the owner of a film lab that Ulmer frequented at the time (the owner's wife was Ukrainian and ostensibly had ties to the tightly knit émigré community).[7] Equally plausible, if equally nebulous, is the story that Bill Krohn relates in his early profile of Ulmer in which he describes a fortuitous encounter between the émigré director and Avra- menko while shooting a newsreel—on one of the odd jobs, as a freelance cameraman for Pathé Newsreel, that Ulmer held after moving to New York—in Coney Island. The chance meeting, as Krohn has it, led to a fifty-dollar advance and a commitment on Ulmer's part to direct *Natalka*.[8] By Ulmer's own hazy account, Avramenko first hired him as associate producer, but after Bulgakov—who purportedly was "playing the big director" *à la* "Mr. DeMille"—proved impossible to work with, just two days into the shoot, Ulmer took the helm (B 580–82). Avramenko ultimately took the main director credit with Ulmer and Michael J. Gann, a Ukrainian Jew who was later responsible for the New York arm of Avramenko's production company, credited as motion picture directors.[9]

Regardless of the finer details of its production history, what matters most about *Natalka* is that it marks the beginning of an unusually prolific, if financially inauspicious, period in Ulmer's career, spanning half a decade, when he found himself directing a string of pictures aimed at minority audiences: at Ukrainian immigrants; at Yiddish-speaking Jews; at African Americans, Mexican Americans, and Native Americans. During this time Ulmer earned the moniker "the director of minorities," as acclaimed documentarian Pare Lorentz once dubbed him.[10] What links these films, beyond their shared mission of promoting a culture at the margins of the American mainstream, are the many songs of exile— of political banishment, of social and cultural alienation, of ostracism and discrimination—that resonate both onscreen and off.

VIVA POLTAVA!

Avramenko and Ulmer proved a good match, the one filling in for the other's conspicuous gaps, both marshaling their proven talents and both sharing the gift of gab, albeit in different languages. The dance impresario took full advantage of his far-reaching influence to assemble masses of volunteers for the production. "He called rally upon rally and would speak endlessly," remembers one of Avramenko's early dance students. "Such was his appeal that people would sit for hours, hypnotized, enthralled, and fascinated. He would then ask for donations and always received ample funds."[11] In addition to the help he received from the window-washers' union, and from the Ukrainian immigrant communities scattered across North America, he delegated a small army of craftsmen, many of them members of a Finnish carpenters' union, to recreate the town of Poltava—thatched roofs, church spires, and all— on a farm in Flemington, New Jersey.[12]

When it became clear that the script with which Bulgakov had been working was inadequate, Ulmer showed some of his own entrepreneurial skills, which seemed to offset his complete lack of linguistic ability, seizing the opportunity to collaborate with Avramenko's Ukrainian crewmembers on a thorough rewrite. "I sat down and wrote the shooting script with about eight men," he recounts in his interview with Bogdanovich, "the dancer, a designer, a window washer—everybody wanted to put everything they could think of into the script! I was being paid the magnificent sum of thirty-five dollars a week, and now found myself writing the script. This is a big, huge musical comedy: you had to have a ballet; you had to have an orchestra of at least forty-eight human beings; you had to have singers! But nothing was impossible for Avramenkov [*sic*]" (B 580). Perhaps more than anything else, that abiding faith in limitless possibility is what linked the two collaborators. As Ulmer remembered it, looking back on the production many decades later, "The picture had one thing which I could never recapture again— the enthusiasm of that mad bunch, it showed on screen" (B 583).

Even if ultimately falling short of his dream of creating a Ukrainian Hollywood, Avramenko and his collaborators had, within a short span of weeks in the summer of 1936, completely transformed an otherwise unremarkable Flemington farm into a brilliant replica of Poltava (when a summer storm demolished the sets in the middle of the shoot, they promptly rebuilt them). Feeding off of Avramenko's infectious zeal—a potent mixture of nostalgia, nationalist fervor, and a profound belief in the urgency of the production—carloads of Ukrainians from across the United States and Canada made their way to New Jersey to volunteer, to serve as choir members, dancers, costume designers, and cooks. In conversation with filmmaker Michael Henry Wilson, more than half a century after *Natalka,* Shirley Ulmer recalls the extraordinary atmosphere in Flemington, almost like a Ukrainian Woodstock, with the masses of immigrants descending on the grounds: "From all over, they unloaded onto this field where we set up tents, actually, and long tables and big things full of soup. They were making all kinds of wonderful sausages. It was like living in a foreign country."[13]

The division of labor between Avramenko and Ulmer was relatively clear from the start. Avramenko handled the finances, the oversight of various constituencies of Ukrainian sponsors, and the recruitment of cast and crewmembers. In return Ulmer brought to bear his experience as an independent filmmaker, helping to rework the script, to edit the final picture, and to ensure that the musical integrity of the original operetta— "very much in the style of the early Tchaikovsky," as he recalled (B 580)—was retained onscreen. "Ulmer threw himself into the project with enthusiasm," observes American cultural critic George Lipsitz, "even though he knew nothing about Ukrainian culture. He believed that cinema as a medium had a responsibility to educate and communicate, that it belonged as much to people striving to define their ethnic identity as it did to investors seeking profits from whatever product Hollywood could convince the public to buy."[14] Nearly all of the actors—not to mention the hundreds of extras—were amateurs (the most notable exception, Thalia Sabanieeva, who plays the title character, was a soloist with the Metropolitan Opera), a situation Ulmer knew quite well from his work on *People on Sunday* several years before. Like that storied late-Weimar production, the actors in *Natalka* worked for next to nothing, and if there ever happened to be a sudden change in plans or personnel, Ulmer and his crew had little choice but to improvise.

One such moment involved Shirley Ulmer, the script supervisor on the film, who without any advance notice had to jump in for a missing actress. "One of the girls," she recounts, "was ill, so my husband threw the costume at me and said, 'get in there!'" An extant production photo of her in floral Ukrainian folk costume, a wig of long, blonde braids, almost like a Slavic Rapunzel figure, and barefooted, as any girl living in the nineteenth-century Ukrainian provinces would ostensibly be, provides a window onto the film's makeshift setting and onto the generally relaxed, unpretentious mood shared by members of the cast and crew and ultimately conveyed on the screen (Figure 16). "We all lived on the location," explains Shirley. "It was summertime and my daughter Arianné was conceived during the shooting period."[15] Conceived on *Natalka,* during what appears to have been something of a summer of love, and born before Ulmer's second Ukrainian picture, *Cossacks in Exile,* had hit the screens, Arianné Ulmer grew up on the sets of her father's films. Like her mother in *Natalka,* she, too, would appear before the camera (her first cameo, as a mere baby, would take place on the Yiddish feature *The Singing Blacksmith* in 1938, with many more appearances to follow).

In the course of the shoot, which largely took place on location in Flemington in late summer, and included limited studio photography at Biograph in the Bronx in mid-September, Ulmer's professional training proved to be even more indispensable than he had initially imagined. Avramenko, it quickly became clear, had no idea about the craft of filmmaking. Ulmer tells a story about how during the first days of the production the dance impresario looked into the viewfinder of the camera and worked himself into a lather over the shocking size of the image: "he didn't want this *small* picture in the finder, he wanted a picture you could see on the screen!" (B 582). Although in the credit roll of the existing print Avramenko appears as director, Ulmer's proper role in the production is clarified in the precise wording of the credit ("motion picture direction") that is attached to his name. It is a term that evokes, as Richard Koszarski has pointed out, the old German conception of

FIGURE 16. Going native: Shirley Ulmer as a Ukrainian extra in *Natalka Poltavka* (*The Girl from Poltava*, 1937). Courtesy of the Academy of Motion Picture Arts and Sciences, Edgar G. Ulmer Collection.

Bildregisseur that Ulmer once understood as his rightful title. That is, in Ulmer's own words, "the director for the *picture* itself who established the camera angles, camera movements, et cetera."[16] Given that there is no credited director of photography on the film, it is quite likely that Ulmer had even more of a hand in such matters than he did on the films he made with a seasoned cinematographer behind the camera. Beyond the strength of the amateur cast, and their impassioned musical numbers, it's the visuals—the exquisite long takes and slow panning shots of the pastoral setting, alternating with affectionate close-ups of the film's protagonists—that distinguish the film and that can be attributed to the *Bildregisseur* himself. "Ulmer's camera lingers over these landscapes," writes Koszarski, "supporting or illustrating musical texts and occasionally providing visual echoes of the work of Ukrainian artist Alexander Dovzhenko (several of whose pictures had been screened in and around New York)."[17] What Vertov had ostensibly done for *People on Sunday,* with respect to aesthetic precedent, Dovzhenko did for *Natalka.*

Yet despite the national sentiment that Avramenko aimed to arouse in his audience, the story of *Natalka* is rather modest in comparison to the grand, sweeping epics of Dovzhenko, Eisenstein, Pudovkin, and other Soviet directors and is ultimately a lighthearted romance, a tale of love's triumph over adversity. (As poor timing would have it, at the very moment that the Avramenko-Ulmer-Gann film was being shot, a Soviet adaptation of *Natalka,* directed by Ivan Kavaleridze and distributed by Amkino, was just months from being released in the United States, opening at New York's Roosevelt Theatre on Christmas Day 1936.)[18] In their adaptation, the Gann-Avramenko screenplay sticks close to Kotlyarevsky's original operetta: young sweethearts Natalka (Sabanieeva) and Petro (Dimitri Creona) set their sights on marriage only to have Natalka's father intervene, keeping his daughter from marrying a man without proper means by banishing him from the town of Poltava. Using a shot of flowing water as a vehicle for rendering an elegant dissolve, Ulmer has Natalka indulge her rueful memories, staring into the well as she does chores, singing arias to her beloved Petro and conjuring up scenes of their past. Similarly, the orphan Petro, who is condemned to wander, cannot keep the beautiful Natalka from swirling around in his mind, as he sings ballad after ballad to his unconsummated love. Natalka's commitment to Petro is put into further jeopardy when Vozny (Mathew Vodiany), an unscrupulous town official with deep pockets and lecherous eyes—his most poignant line of dialogue ("Who does not lie and cheat in our times?") would seem to have wider application in

Ulmer's orbit—asks her for her hand. Though she initially rebuffs his offer, when her doubts of Petro's return begin to grow, she acquiesces. Mercifully, if also predictably, Petro's status as a banished figure lost in the wilderness proves temporary, as a good-hearted friend and fellow orphan Mykola (Theodore Swystun) guides him back home to Poltava.

Much of the film's dramatic action, and its charm, rests on the affecting song-and-dance numbers steeped in pathos and sentiment and evocative of an idealized past. "*Natalka Poltavka* came into existence in an atmosphere of cultural euphoria," remarks Stefan Grissemann. "One celebrates, in front of and behind the camera, in the magnificent costumes and backdrops, the resurgence (and the filmic conservation, the 'immortalization') of a culture that is thought to be lost, of a distant sound."[19] Toward the end of the film, in a ritual wedding dance, there is an exchange of scarves between bride and groom, but the disembodied, offscreen voice of Petro—almost anticipating the famous scene of Mike Nichols's *The Graduate* some three decades later—disrupts the ill-fated union between Vozny and Natalka, and Petro returns to his legitimate place as groom. The audience has no choice but to cheer as Natalka and Petro reunite, giving the picture its redemptive ending, the couple rendered triumphant, captured in a low-angle close-up that serves as the iconic final image left in viewers' minds.

The finished film that Avramenko, Ulmer, and company released in New York City in mid-February 1937 exceeded all expectations. The audience, consisting largely of Ukrainian émigrés, couldn't contain itself during the screenings at New York's Belmont Theatre, in midtown Manhattan, where the film enjoyed a successful run before moving uptown to the Ascot, in the Bronx, in July of that same year. (In a curious twist, when *Natalka* ran at the Ascot, the *New York Times* placed its listing opposite an advertisement for Ulmer's *Damaged Lives*, which was then playing at the Central Theatre on 47th and Broadway, in its "5th Big Week" and with a "Children Under 16 Not Admitted" tag attached to it.)[20] Perhaps more surprisingly, the attention the film received in the industry trades and in the popular press was also exuberant. Nearly all of the critics compared the Avramenko-Gann-Ulmer collaboration to its Soviet competitor in the most favorable of terms, perhaps in some measure a reflexive defense of the American picture at a time when U.S.-Soviet relations were cooling off, but also a stamp of approval on formal grounds. Calling it "amusing and entertaining" (words reprinted in boldface type in subsequent ads printed in their pages), the unnamed critic for the *New York Times* declared, "The made-in-America product is more enjoyable than the imported article. This is due to the fact that it contains more funny incidents and is photographed much better than the 'Natalka Poltava' shown at the Roosevelt Theatre during Christmas week."[21] Two days later, *Variety* followed suit, declaring the home-grown version to be "head and shoulders above the other feature." The reviewer went on to note in a similar vein: "The American-produced picture has even tempo, a nice mixture of humor with the more serious moments, and above all—action.... Avramenko, Gann, and E. G. Ulmer were responsible for the swift directorial pace maintained."[22] Finally, the review in *Film Daily*, which in an earlier notice had misidentified it as a "Hungarian operetta," suggested that the American release of *Natalka* "is generally more pleasing than its immediate predecessor because of better technical handling, particularly the photography."[23]

Even the somewhat cranky advance review it received in the *Daily Worker*, the house organ of the American Communist Party, offers a few kind words. "Usually filmed operettas leave us cold as a tombstone," remarks David Platt, the newspaper's film critic, employing the collective pronoun throughout his review. "Not so this splendid piece of Ivan Kotlyarevsky which even Avramenko's obviously vulgarized conception of the basic idea of the Ukrainian classic could not totally destroy. Despite the numerous distortions of this émigré version, we could not help enjoying the lovely melodies of Kotlyarevsky."[24] Platt makes a point of calling Avramenko's version "corrupt," which is to say unfaithful to the Soviet model of filmmaking, but also calls the American production "a music-lover's film" (which certainly makes sense given its status as an operetta but may also be a backhanded compliment of sorts, a symptom of false consciousness or of a dubious susceptibility to bourgeois taste).

Buoyed by the success of *Natalka*, Avramenko, Gann, and Ulmer would test their luck once more in the production of *Zaporozhets za Dunayem (Cossacks in Exile)*, another nineteenth-century operetta launched a little more than a year later. A press notice in *Motion Picture Daily*, in July 1938, announced that the production was set to begin in mid-July and was to be filmed on location at the Little Flower Monastery in Newton, New Jersey.[25] As before, the film was financed on a shoestring budget (costs were initially given at just over $30,000 but came in at somewhere near double that figure), with funds raised by Avramenko in the same piecemeal fashion, with smalltime individual shareholders. Included in the extended list of investors were "Mykola Pasiechko—farmer, Stefan Mudlo—carpenter, Stepan Syvak—carpenter, Vasyl Lozovsky—shoemaker, and Pavlo Tesliuk—worker."[26] Similarly, the schedule of production and the basic constraints under which the cast and crew were expected to operate were tight. "I was pressured to make it in one summer," recalls Ulmer, "and have it ready in the winter" (B 584). Rather than limiting his energies to the single film, Ulmer pooled resources, including his technical crew and several cast members, by shooting both *Cossacks* and the second of his four Yiddish films—about which more follows in the subsequent section—on the same location, one that seems in retrospect to have been peculiarly well suited to the eclecticism of Ulmer's life and career. The Little Flower Monastery happened to be sandwiched between a nudist colony and Camp Nordland, an outpost of the pro-Nazi German-American Bund. In the middle of production the *New York Mirror* ran a piece titled "Hollywood in Miniature" in its Sunday supplement. The pull quote from the article said it all: "There's Freedom in the Newton Hills—for Jewish and Ukrainian Actors, Monks, Nudists and Nazis."[27]

Originally given the working title "Cossacks across the Danube," the film builds on the 1863 operetta by Semen Hulak-Artemovsky, another classic of Ukrainian literature guaranteed to hold a similar attraction for the Ukrainian immigrant community as Kotlyarevsky's *Natalka.* As if the timing of the production had to be outdone yet again, the Soviet director Ivan Kavaleridze, with the same backing he had from Amkino for his rendition of *Natalka,* released a competing version of *Cossacks* nearly a full year before the Canadian-American production premiered in New York. In both cases the plot revolves around the Artemovsky-inspired portrayal of the historical destruction of the Zaporogian Sich, a Cossack military stronghold, by Catherine the Great and the ensuing expulsion of the Cossacks to Turkey. Set in 1775, the year before U.S. independence, the Avramenko-Ulmer picture is very much about the desire for Ukrainian political and cultural liberation. As a prominent intertitle used in one of the film's early songs tells us, "For 200 years the Cossacks languished in bondage." After being forced into exile, "a luckless people" living "in a strange land" among the Turks, pressed to assimilate and left to the mercy of the sultan, they are finally able to journey home, almost like Petro's dramatic return to Poltava at the close of *Natalka.* The cast, whose primary task is singing a medley of nostalgic songs highlighting, as was the case in *Natalka,* an imperiled romance and the Cossacks' rueful state of banishment, features several members, including Michael Shvetz and Dimitri Creona, who play in both of the Avramenko-Ulmer-Gann productions.

As in the earlier film, Avramenko makes full use of his skills as a choreographer, showcasing one vibrant folk-dance number after the next, often captured in a long shot of the ensemble and then intercut with close-ups of the principals and of the faces of the peasant spectators. In lieu of the Metropolitan Opera's Thalia Sabanieeva, who got top billing in *Natalka*, Avramenko casts the full-figured and headstrong Maria Sokil, a renowned Ukrainian singer who happened to be on tour in North America during the production, as the chief matriarch and personification of Old Ukraine (allegedly, because of her traveling schedule, her scenes had to be shot in advance and edited in).[28] Visually speaking, like *Natalka,* the camera tends to privilege the rich landscape, as well as the ominous clouds above it, while zeroing in on the gallant Cossack cavalry and their graceful horses, of which there is no shortage of shots—a critic from *Variety* appropriately bemoans "too much of the galloping horse feet" (the shots themselves are reminiscent of Ulmer's cheapie western *Thunder over Texas*).[29] Ulmer has William Miller photograph his protagonists, especially the lovely Odarka (Sokil) and the boisterous, soulful Ivan (Shvetz), with the camera at a slight low tilt amplifying their significance for the viewer and capitalizing on the emotional and folkloric core of his source material.

Yet despite the film's obvious limitations—a notable lack of major dramatic action, apart from a strikingly incongruous color fire sequence lasting a little over a minute, with hand-painted red flames cast against a blue-black sky, and the repeated reliance on song and dance to make up for this—it was released in New York in late January 1939, at the Belmont Theatre (where *Natalka* had enjoyed its debut a couple of years before). It was considered yet another minor success, at least in the eyes of critics and the viewing public, although it did not match *Natalka*'s figures at the box office. Ulmer, who this time takes the sole director credit on the film, was singled out for moderate praise by an unnamed critic for *Variety,* who formulated his words as if registering surprise: "Production has fairly good direction."[30] The critic in the *New York Times* was less restrained: "Once again, the Ukrainian-Americans . . . have turned out a made-in-New Jersey film operetta that is highly agreeable to both the eye and the ear."[31] And although the *New York Herald Tribune* offered an unflattering comparison between *Cossacks* and the films made by the studio professionals employed in America's major studios, the pastoral beauty reflected on the screen, not unlike that of *Natalka,* receives due attention: "The motion picture has not the directional skill and smooth continuity of a Hollywood production, but New Jersey's meadows and lakes offer grand backgrounds for earnest producers."[32]

Of course, such comparisons to Hollywood are, despite Avramenko's own grand aspirations for Ukrainian cinema, rather misplaced. The political aims, not to mention the material conditions of the film (with the Depression bearing down on the industry, the making of feature-length motion pictures on the East Coast that summer was nearly impossible), are of a different ilk.[33] "Instead of treating film production as a business venture, delivering entertainment to the paying public," notes Ukrainian historian Bohdan Nebesio, "its sponsors perceived *Zaporozhets za Dunaiem* [*sic*] as an undertaking of great national importance." He then adds: "From the Hollywood perspective, *Zaporozhets za Dunaiem* was a mismanaged financial failure that suffered from artistic flaws. But from the perspective of the Ukrainian community, it was a success of unprecedented magnitude, showing the immigrants what they could accomplish in adapting their traditional cultural forms to the cultural forms of the new world."[34]

Far from being a glossy big-studio feature, Ulmer's Ukrainian films resemble much more the verité simplicity and the heightened sense of lyricism, of sentiment and organic beauty conveyed in a film like *People on Sunday*. Both *Natalka* and *Cossacks* invite wistful reflection on the part of émigré Ukrainian viewers, indulging their weighty memories of their homeland. Both make full use of song—these are operettas, after all—as a means of conjuring up the past and, in terms of their narrative function, as a means of propelling an otherwise sluggish story line. In each case it is impossible to forget that Ulmer, together with Avramenko, was addressing an audience of Ukrainian immigrants in North America—in the United States and in Canada, which provided the bulk of the funding—far from home (a poignant line from *Cossacks*, delivered by Ivan, underscores this: "Remember, we live in a strange country among strange people"). We also cannot overlook the fact that these films, while perhaps on one level completely foreign to Ulmer, were films that spoke to his condition as well: as someone who was displaced from his home, a nation that at this precise moment in time was invested in the destruction of the ethnic group to which he himself belonged, and also displaced from the professional "home" that his fellow directors, American and European-born alike, inhabited. Thus, Ulmer's foray into ethnic pictures in the late 1930s and early 1940s "permitted him to explore his own condition of exile," as Krohn has astutely pointed out, "and his mixed feelings about being the inheritor of an alien tradition"[35] This exploration was not limited to the pair of Ukrainian operettas he directed but also encompassed his four Yiddish features and other ethnic pictures he directed during the same period. In each of these small ventures Ulmer would continue to position himself in such a way as to render his subjects in a sympathetic light, revealing his own personal solidarity and, perhaps, his identification with a shared plight.

A DREAM COMES TRUE

In a short director's note, "A Dream Comes True," which was included in the original press kit for *Grine felder (Green Fields, 1937)*, the first of Ulmer's four Yiddish productions, the self-identified Viennese director remarks:

> Unfamiliar with the Yiddish language and its literature, the name Peretz Hirschbein meant for me only a successful writer in a strange idiom. But I happened, many years ago, to see a production of "Greene Felder" [*sic*], starring Jacob Ben-Ami. I did not understand what was being spoken, yet there was something so unusual, so fascinating, which came across the footlights, that through all these years "Greene Felder" remained indelibly imprinted on my mind. Here was something not specifically Jewish, but universal in its ethical and romantic aspects. . . . Its simplicity and deeply rooted honesty bars every violent or even dynamic conflict.[36]

Ulmer could have been talking about *People on Sunday*, about its candor and directness, while the financial constraints of the production, not to mention the relaxed liberal sensibility, are not far removed from the Berlin precedent. With a purported budget of $8,000 ($300 of which went to the director's fee), a shooting schedule of under a week, and not much more than a one-to-one shooting ratio, he once again made use of the countryside around Flemington, New Jersey, for his Yiddish debut (B 586). Based on Peretz Hirschbein's celebrated play of the same name, written in 1916 and performed in New York throughout the 1920s, *Green Fields* initially landed in the hands of stage actor Ben-Ami, who had starred in the theater production at Maurice Schwartz's Yiddish Art Theatre a decade and a half earlier.[37] A left-leaning independent producer name Roman Rebush—formerly head of Amkino, which ironically had been responsible for the distribution of the Soviet competitors of *Natalka* and *Cossacks*—and his partner, Ludwig Landy, founded a company called Collective Film Producers. They hired both Ben-Ami and Ulmer and left it to them to work out the details of direction (a small notice published in the *Hollywood Reporter* on July 12, 1937, called Collective a "co-operative outfit" and announced that Ben-Ami was signed to codirect with Ulmer).[38]

Like the situation with Avramenko on *Natalka,* the relationship between Ben-Ami and Ulmer on *Green Fields* was that of the cultural insider to the professional outsider. Though the Yiddish actor, who was pushing fifty at the time, had initially hoped to give a repeat performance as the lead Levi Yitskhok (Hirschbein allegedly made this a condition of the agreement to relinquish film rights), his age prevented him from doing so (B 579). Instead, he served mainly as "a dialogue coach," working with the actors and serving as an intermediary between them and Ulmer.[39] The role that Ben-Ami ultimately played in the production may be best understood as dialogue director or perhaps even "dramaturge," as J. Hoberman has suggested, recognizing the significance of the theatrical precedent and Ben-Ami's talent in that area. "Ulmer directed the actors for the camera," explains Hoberman, "and handled the technical aspects—setting up shots, designing sets, choosing locations."[40]

Since all the acting talent selected for the production came from the stage, from Schwartz's Yiddish Art Theatre and from Artef (the so-called *Arbeter Teater Farband* or Workers' Theater Union), Ulmer's primary task was instructing them on how to make the transition from stage to screen. Helen Beverley, who plays the female lead of Tsine, a feisty country girl who falls for the wandering yeshiva boy Levi Yitskhok, tells of her first encounter with Ulmer while working on the film. "He was watching us," she recalls, "because after I enter we line up and do our scene à la stage direction. . . . He had a bit of an accent and a lot of temperament and he said, 'My God, you can't do that in front of the camera, standing in a line like that.' Of course he proceeded to restage it and redirect it."[41] Similarly, Hershel Bernardi, who plays Tsine's little brother Avrom-Yankov, fondly remembers the experiences he had under the tutelage of Ulmer: "Over the course of a few weeks with Ulmer, I learned more than college kids do in four years."[42]

Yet the arrangement between Ulmer and his chief collaborator, Ben-Ami, was not quite so rosy. "He had to make a deal with Ben-Ami," recounts Beverley. "And the deal they made was that they would co-direct it. But of course that never happened. Edgar directed the film and Ben-Ami was a very gentle man so he didn't make a fuss or fight about it. But he didn't speak to Ulmer throughout the shooting."[43] As Ulmer told his side of the story, with a slightly puffy chest, "I declared war the first moment I went into this picture: I'm not going to do what [Maurice] Schwartz does; I'm not going to do the cheap things [Molly] Picon does; I'm going to have my own style and I'm going to do it as I see it—dignified, not dirty—not with beards where they look like madmen. The same decision which [writer] Sholem Asch made, which [painter Marc] Chagall made. That was quite an affair, and in the darkest of the Depression" (B 578–79).

Shooting officially began, according to a report in *Film Daily,* in early August at Producers Service Studios in Ridgefield, New Jersey.[44] The small studio had been established a couple of years earlier by cinematographer J. Burgi Contner, who, along with Miller, photographed *Green Fields* (he would go on to work behind the camera on Ulmer's *The Light Ahead* and *Moon over Harlem,* as well as on a couple of Ulmer's health shorts of the same period). The bulk of the film, however, was shot on location in Flemington, where *Natalka* had been filmed, and extended over several days. In an attempt to drum up money for the production, Ulmer claims that he and his fellow crewmembers sold their possessions and that for the duration of the shoot he and an assistant shared a bed in a Newark flophouse (B 586–87). Whether or not we choose to believe this tale, it's clear from all accounts that the finances for the film were tight and that a considerable amount of personal investment was required. "In a depression-era equivalent of paying for the film on credit cards," asserts Richard Koszarski, "Ulmer and his associates raised money from the Household Finance Company by mortgaging their own furniture, kited as many laboratory charges as possible, and finally turned to the International Ladies' Garment Workers Union for completion money."[45]

Even during postproduction, as Koszarski suggests, Ulmer had to come up with a quick solution to cover lab costs. He made an appointment to see Abraham Cahan, the powerful editor of the *Forverts* newspaper, one of New York's largest Yiddish dailies, who then, so the story goes, put him in touch with a Mr. Dubinsky, head of the International Ladies' Garment Workers Union. Dubinsky agreed to purchase a set number of advance tickets (upwards of seventy-five thousand) for a cut-rate price (forty cents per ticket) in return for the freedom to sell them to members of his union at the price of his choosing and to reserve set days of the week for members-only screenings.[46] Ulmer received a large enough portion of the money in advance to pay the outstanding lab bill and to allow for the final editing by Jack Kemp and the scoring of the film by Vladimir Heifetz— whose younger brother, star violinist Jascha Heifetz, would appear a decade later in Ulmer's tribute to musical virtuosity, *Carnegie Hall*—to be finished in time for the film's long-anticipated premiere, on October 11, 1937, at the Squire Theatre in midtown Manhattan.

Opening with a poignant shot of Jewish peasants, men and women, harvesting hay in the fields of a New Jersey stand-in for the Russian Pale, lush choral music reverberating in the background, the dramatic prelude makes the film's primary focus on "community and nature" plain within the first few seconds.[47] The string of credits that immediately follows, the choral music continuing uninterrupted, not only gives proper attribution of the story to Peretz Hirschbein but pronounces the film "An Edgar G. Ulmer Production" (following the primary credit given to Collective Film Producers). We are soon introduced to the protagonist, Levi Yitskhok (Michael Goldstein), clean shaven, square jawed, and vaguely handsome (more Liev Schreiber than Lubavitcher), shot inside a dark synagogue—using the minimalist sets that Ulmer and his crew were able to piece together at Contner's studio—as he dozes off during prayer. His two fellow yeshiva boys, similarly beardless and dignified, as Ulmer demanded, are shown praying fervently through the night. They are unable to grasp Levi Yitskhok's restlessness and his professed need to search for the "light of truth" outside the synagogue. As he packs up his personal effects and silently nods farewell, Levi Yitskhok finally ambles across the room, making his way for the door; the moment he opens it, a stream of radiant sunlight pours in and envelops him, symbolically ushering him forth on his path toward enlightenment.

Along his journey, which Ulmer renders in shorthand via a montage of pastoral images superimposed over a one-shot conveying Levi Yitskhok's body in transit, the Talmud scholar will encounter precisely what he's looking for. A young farm boy named Avrom-Yankov (Bernardi) soon arrives, gripping a horse's bridle, and promises to show Levi-Yitskhok the way to his home—or, more generally, to show him the collective way home—to the shtetl community of Jews like himself. With the help of Contner and Miller's skilled cinematography, Ulmer indulges the audience in an additional montage of pastoral shots, evoking the path toward Avrom-Yankov's family dwelling with images of fruit trees, flower blossoms, a horse-drawn plow, and women planting potatoes and other crops. This is a new world for Levi Yitskhok, one that will forever transform him.

The narrative hinges on this transformation, which comes about not only through the full immersion of Levi Yitskhok in the authentic, primitive, self-sustaining lifestyle of the peasant Jews in his midst but also by his falling in love with the prime embodiment of that lifestyle, Avrom-Yankov's older sister Tsine (Beverley). Like her brother, Tsine seems almost symbiotically attached to the soil. She is first seen harvesting vegetables in the open field standing next to a young calf. She then, rather mischievously, proceeds to spy on her older brother Hersh-Ber (Saul

Levine) and his girlfriend Stera (Dena Drute) as Stera steals a kiss from
her sweetheart, and finally she tears barefoot across the open field, nearly
falling, in a state of total glee over what she's just observed (Beverley
recalled in a later interview how her feet bled from repeated runs through
the fields).[48] By the time that Avrom-Yankov leads Levi Yitskhok to his
home, Tsine, who initially expresses fear at the sight of a stranger, is
thoroughly smitten; his restrained, deliberate movements stand in
marked contrast to her wild, playful, and spontaneous behavior. And
just as the wandering Talmud scholar serves as an emissary from the
rarified world of the urban yeshiva, so Tsine embodies the earthbound
beauty of the countryside. In an early scene, as she carries a sack of potatoes over her shoulder, her mere presence within the frame triggers yet
another montage of wild flowers, a brook, the forest, and the sky.

As the village Jews bicker over the privilege of hosting the coveted
stranger, who agrees to stay in the countryside as a teacher and a guest,
Levi Yitskhok undergoes his own conversion of sorts. He comes to recognize, as did countless European romantics before him, the near-divine
quality of the earth and to prize the free existence of Jews toiling in the
fields. In a role reversal, the Talmud scholar asks Avrom-Yankov to teach
him to till the soil (once more, Ulmer augments this plotline with an affecting montage). But the final conversion comes when Tsine, in a symbol-
laden scene, offers freshly picked apples to Levi Yitskhok, pressing them
to her breast as she hands them to him. At first an occasion for the yeshiva
boy to teach the lessons of resisting temptation, he soon finds himself less
impervious to such forces than he imagined (when Tsine shows him that
she, a girl, has defiantly learned to write, she has Levi Yitskhok close his
eyes only to plant a kiss on his cheek as Stera had done to her brother).
Earthly pleasures find their match in bodily pleasures, and Levi Yitskhok
is immune to neither. The film's well-composed final shot has Tsine and
Levi Yitskhok walking hand in hand, a plow lingering in the foreground
of the frame, almost as if, as Helen Beverley has commented retrospec-
tively, it were the final scene of a western with the heroes riding off into
the sunset.[49] "In this film," suggests Beverley, "the Jews were beautiful
people and they were people of the land. They worshipped the sun, the
sky, the fields, so it was a very pastoral and a beautifully lyrical film."[50]

Especially noteworthy in *Green Fields* is its recurrent emphasis on
natural landscape and the profound connection between the common
people *(proste yidn)* and their idyllic surroundings, an affinity that the
film shares with the two Ukrainian pictures. Its core political message—
with the repeated invocation of the Talmudic dictum "A man without

land is not a man"—amplifies this connection, while the ultimate union between Levi Yitskhok and Tsine, between Talmud and labor, reveals the triumph of a kind of utopian socialism (or labor Zionism), and of the *folksmentsh* (man of the people), over the alienated, all-consuming devotion to sacred texts within the walls of an urban yeshiva. In his pioneering study of Yiddish cinema, Hoberman contends that the politics of the film belong to the concomitant culture of the Popular Front and American antifascism. For him, it is no mere coincidence that the film's premiere was held at the same New York theater—run by Edward Kern of the Workers Film and Photo League—that first screened *The Spanish Earth*, a 1937 partisan documentary on the Spanish Civil War narrated by Ernest Hemingway and John Dos Passos, and was made part of a double bill featuring another Popular Front documentary, *China Strikes Back*.[51] The political leanings of the central figures behind the production were indeed sympathetic to such causes.

At the film's October 1937 premiere at the Squire Theatre, Peretz Hirschbein, who had remained active in leftist circles and who had published his provocatively titled novel *Roite Felder* (Red fields) just two years earlier, took to the stage and announced, "twenty years ago, the play *Grine Felder* marked the beginning of a better Yiddish theater in America." Likewise, he continued, the adaptation by Ulmer and Ben-Ami should "mark the beginnings of a better Yiddish film."[52] The critics, especially those writing in the Yiddish-language press, which was by and large socialist in orientation, couldn't have agreed more. "The appearance of Peretz Hirschbein's 'Green Fields' was a red-letter day in the history of Yiddish film in America," proclaimed *Morgn frayhayt*'s culture editor Nathaniel Buchvald in a summative evaluation of American Yiddish film published in the New York–based monthly *Yidishe kultur*, the house organ of the activist Yidisher Kultur Farband (Jewish Cultural Collective). In his estimation *Green Fields* "was the first film that carried over the best tradition of Yiddish theater onto the big screen. The film was greeted with real joy in the Yiddish cultural circles and instantly captured the hearts of the Yiddish mass observer. Without the advertised stars and without the element of operetta and spectacle, the film became the most popular and most profitable of all Yiddish talkies, including 'Yidl mitn fidl.'" (Buchvald goes on to remark of Ulmer, "although he is not especially soaked with Yiddish, he is the true creator of 'Green Fields.'")[53]

In his New York dispatch for the Warsaw-based *Literarishe bleter*, critic Nakhman Meisel wrote, "For the past ten weeks, many New York movie theaters have been showing the film 'Green Fields' to great success . . . unparalleled in the history of Yiddish film in America."[54] He dutifully reported to his Yiddish-speaking Polish audience that the film was playing in seventy different movie houses in New York and would eventually be shown at more than one hundred theaters in total. Meisel, who had seen Hirschbein's play performed in Poland and in Tel Aviv, insists that "the homey small-town feeling [*heymisher dorfishkeyt*]" that he witnessed on the screen far exceeds that which was first conveyed onstage. Finally, he comments on the trend of which Ulmer suddenly found himself a part, namely, the rise of minority cinema: "In an age when the native 'minorities' in different countries obtain good, artistic films, which can somehow compete with 'King' Hollywood (like, for example, the Russian, German, Italian, French, Polish films), the Jews have not had something about which they could brag."[55]

Ulmer's own boastful account seems in this instance almost well placed amid such ardent praise. "The first weekend we sold out," he crowed. "Nobody could get into the theater. The Jews came . . . in the morning and wouldn't get out! We had to plead with them to please leave the theater so other people could see the picture!" (B 589).[56] The bragging doesn't end there. According to Ulmer's triumphant account of his Yiddish debut, "it broke every record in New York. Over eighty thousand dollars on a sixteen-thousand-dollar negative. It broke the Garbo record up in Bronxville. It was like a fire"—ultimately earning, as he tells it, a Best Foreign Film Award in Paris in 1938 (B 587). Yet the film's closest brush with fame and fortune was perhaps having Paul Muni, who won the 1937 Oscar for Best Actor in William Dieterle's *The Story of Louis Pasteur,* and who reportedly provided some financial backing for Ulmer's film, give his stamp of approval in the form of a rhapsodic blurb in the press kit. "There's nothing to add to the comments I have heard all around me," he intoned, "GREAT! GREAT! DITTO!"[57]

Even the non-Yiddish press was enthusiastic in its evaluation of *Green Fields*. "If the production standard set by this film is maintained," asserted an unnamed critic in *Motion Picture Daily,* "a fresh brand of entertainment for a specialized audience may appear on the market. It is first rate in every respect."[58] Hailing the picture as "one of the finest pastoral films ever produced," *Film Daily*'s critic observed that Ulmer's direction "has caught the beauty and poetry of the classic work and transferred it to the screen in a masterful manner."[59] The one dissenting voice was *New York Times* critic Frank Nugent, whose sarcastic and slightly snarky tone colors his sheepish admission of having been utterly perplexed by the whole affair. "With 'The Spanish Earth' successfully ploughed under," begins his review, "the Squire Theatre (Eighth and Forty-fourth) turned last night to 'Green Fields,' the first of a series of Yiddish pictures to be produced here by Collective Film Producers." He then proceeds to bemoan the "bovine complacence" of the film's pacing and what he calls the "incessant grouping of its characters for conversational thrusts and parries." "These thrusts and parries," he continues, employing some of the film's own vernacular, "although gayly received by those in the know, unfortunately sailed well above this goyishe kopf." Nugent aims his final jab at Michael Goldstein, who in his view "carries Levy-Yitzchok's [sic] unworldliness to the point of imbecility—a better word for him, possibly, would be schlemiel."[60]

 Ulmer suggested to Bogdanovich that Nugent's review was a bald case of anti-Semitism and that *Times* publisher Arthur Hays Sulzberger fired him for his infraction (B 589). In truth, however, Nugent continued to write film reviews—some of them positive, others, like his barbed evaluation of *Green Fields,* less charitable—for the *New York Times* throughout the 1930s and subsequently wrote many successful Hollywood screenplays, including John Ford's *The Searchers* (1956). The final word on the film, however, was not left to Nugent, whose lone dissent was drowned out by the far louder chorus of praise. In the last lines of his review of *Green Fields,* Nakhman Meisel voiced the hope that Ulmer's picture would signal the "beginning for truly artistic Yiddish films."[61] Indeed, in the many years since, Ulmer's Yiddish debut has been favorably compared to the work of such cinematic visionaries as Jean Renoir, Paul Fejos, and Jean Vigo and has been hailed as a singular achievement in the history of Yiddish cinema.[62]

OF CANTORS AND CHOLERA

Perhaps it should come as little surprise, in light of Ulmer's unwavering, lifelong attachment to music and of the seeming natural affinities between his ethnic pictures and the songs that convey their longing, that music should play such a central role in nearly all of the films that he directed for a minority audience.[63] The dramatic choral arrangements by Russian-born Vladimir Heifetz in *Green Fields* are matched by casting the great Russian-born cantor Moishe Oysher in the musical *Yankel der schmid (The Singing Blacksmith,* 1938), the second venture undertaken by Collective Film Producers and the second star vehicle for Oysher, after his screen debut in *Dem khazns zundl (The Cantor's Son,* 1937). Like the Ukrainian operettas, *The Singing Blacksmith,* which reworks

David Pinski's eponymous play of 1906, provides another opportunity for an immigrant audience to indulge its memories of the Old Country via song—and like those films, a replica of the Old World, a Russian shtetl, is utilized to powerful effect—and to allow Oysher's baritone voice to transport them back in time. As for Ulmer's specific role, he appears to have viewed himself as something akin to a conductor, hiring another Russian-born artist, composer Jacob Weinberg, to handle a score that made maximum use of Oysher's signature voice. Aptly enough, on the set of his Yiddish films (and his other pictures as well), Ulmer was known to wield a baton, allegedly one formerly used by famed Austro-Hungarian composer Franz Liszt. "He never put this down," attests Helen Beverley, who starred in two of Ulmer's Yiddish productions, "and he would direct the actors the way you direct music."[64]

As was the case with *Green Fields,* the actors for *Blacksmith* came largely from the Yiddish stage. Quite a few of them (Michael Goldstein, Anna Appel, Max Vodnoy, Hershel Bernardi) had appeared in the earlier film, and several (Ben-Zvi Baratoff, Goldstein, and Appel) were busy performing Sholem Asch's *Three Cities* for Maurice Schwartz's Yiddish Art Theatre by the time the film wrapped.[65] Shooting began in the first week of July 1938, on the same locations used for *Cossacks*—that multipurpose patch of land that Ulmer and his crew stumbled upon while driving around in an old woody on the back roads of Newton, New Jersey, in June of that year—whose production had formally commenced just a couple of weeks prior (B 585). The overlap of exteriors, of stock shots, and of extras used in both films is indeed detectable to the discerning eye.[66] A contemporary account of the shoot and its location appeared in the Yiddish daily *Morgn frayhayt* about a week into the production. Reporter Ber Green told his readers that the "homey Russian shtetl transplanted bag and baggage to the green fields of New Jersey" (a direct allusion, so it would seem, to Ulmer's celebrated Yiddish debut but also a tacit recognition of the shared backdrop for *Cossacks*) and noted, offering a glimpse of the inner workings, Ulmer's repeated struggles to maintain order on the set: "The film director shouted for the hundredth time that day: 'Everybody quiet!' . . . 'Action!'"[67]

The story, adapted from Pinski's play and reworked by Pinski himself together with stage actor Ben-Zvi Baratoff and screenwriter Ossip Dymow, is, like many of Ulmer's ethnic features, a tale of redemption. The title character, Yankel, we learn in the prologue, is left as a young teen (Bernardi) to apprentice with the town blacksmith, Bendet (Baratoff), who instructs him in his trade and helps him on the path of life. Yet, as an adult, after inheriting the smithy from his mentor and acquiring some of his bad habits, Yankel has to overcome his reputation as a notorious philanderer and drinker—a reputation that the cultural hero Oysher ostensibly shared with the character he played onscreen—in order to enjoy a settled existence with the beautiful and patently bourgeois Tamara (Miriam Riselle).[68] Before he reaches this point, Yankel lives the life of a self-satisfied bachelor. When approached by the matchmaker Chaye-Peshe (Appel), he responds tartly, "Why do I need stale bread when I can get fresh rolls?" In turn, we observe Yankel donning a costume that resembles silken pajamas, serenading his various love interests with schmaltzy ballads ("A dream, a dream, I dreamt a dream"), seducing the married Rivke (Florence Weiss, who also happened to be Oysher's real wife off the set), and leading a group of attractive young seamstresses in song with the devious air of a fox in a henhouse. Until Yankel encounters Tamara—which Ulmer conveys in a forceful reaction shot of Oysher, mouth agape, his singing coming to a complete halt, and a pair of affectionate close-ups of each figure balancing the sequence—he is someone who would never be thought of as the marrying type. This is what makes his uncharacteristically rash decision to ask Tamara for her hand the perfect test of his abilities: to repress his base urges, to deny Rivke the chance to steal him away, to prove the suspicions of his family and of the town members to be misplaced, and ultimately to become a faithful husband and father. The film's final shot captures the newlywed couple in a tender embrace, all past infractions forgiven, glancing happily at the bassinet containing their slumbering newborn son (played by Ulmer's infant daughter, Arianné).

With his unmistakable swagger and bare-chested machismo, Oysher's Yankel is, as Hoberman puts it, "almost as much Cossack as Jew."[69] How fitting, then, that two of the film's most provocative scenes—those in which the crossover between *Cossacks* and *Blacksmith* is quite transparent and which are nowhere to be found in Pinski's original play—have Yankel engaging with a group of Ukrainian peasants at the town's local tavern. In both scenes the shtetl is not the insular world depicted in *Green Fields* but instead a place of cultural mixing (perhaps owing as much to the practical realities of the shoot as to a principled stance on the part of the director); the Ukrainians are thus portrayed not as the instigators of pogroms but as friends and coinhabitants. The first of these two scenes introduces Yankel as a Jewish troubadour of sorts, sitting at a piano next to a fair Ukrainian maiden and singing a ballad (in Yiddish) about a blonde shepherd named Vanka who has lost his beloved white sheep. Cinematographer Miller, who also photographed *Cossacks*, assists Ulmer in creating a poignant montage of close-ups of the peasant onlookers (played either by extras from Avramenko's bunch or by monks from the monastery, as Ulmer claims), one of whom, bald and muttonchopped, vaguely recalls Michael Shvetz's jovial Ivan. "When watching the Ukrainian dancers in *The Singing Blacksmith*," asserts Claudia Pummer, "the Jewish viewing public caught a glimpse of *Cossacks in Exile*. The Yiddish film's tavern scene, in turn, projects this image of an *other* audience in its reversal by depicting a Ukrainian audience watching the performance of a Yiddish entertainer."[70] Minutes later, after a short interlude concerning the matchmaking that is now afoot, we return once more to the tavern. In yet another seeming mash-up of the two productions, Avramenko's choreography still operating at full tilt, Yankel and a group of Ukrainian dancers entertain a crowd of onlookers. In between swigs of schnapps, Yankel attempts, halfheartedly and clumsily, to emulate a Ukrainian folk dance. While he may not be able to go completely native, and become a Cossack, Yankel clearly embodies a number of shared traits.

Given the proletarian trappings of Yankel's character, and the relatively pronounced class-consciousness of the film as a whole (even the bourgeois Tamara cites the folk expression "work, work, work makes life sweet"), the film's appeal to New York's labor circles was quite natural. The *Sunday Worker* proudly announced the premiere, on November 1, 1938, at the Continental Theatre on Broadway, highlighting the personal appearances by Moishe Oysher and David Pinski for a special midnight screening and reception ("Not since *Marie Antoinette* opened has a night film premiere attracted such an enthusiastic crowd," attested another local paper).[71] Film critic David Platt of the *Daily Worker*, who had given a favorable review of *Natalka* two years earlier, immediately welcomed the arrival of *Blacksmith*, which in his eyes "advance[d] the art of Yiddish film." As he puts it more programmatically: "Collective Film Producers are to be warmly congratulated for their efforts in trying to build up an honest Jewish film tradition in America. It is a far cry from the usual embarrassing Yiddish film of the type of 'I Want to Be a Mother' to this tragic-comic story of life in old Russia, with its splendid people, its back-breaking poverty, its class divisions, its fascinating folk songs, dances and humor."[72]

The desire for a more sophisticated art cinema, and a conscious move away from the sentimental kitsch, or *shund,* often thought to be standard fare in Yiddish theater and film, was something that not only contemporary critics such as David Platt and Nakhman Meisel articulated but also that Ulmer seemed unusually well suited to undertake. Even in

Blacksmith, which is not the most visually striking of his Yiddish films, Ulmer makes dramatic use of chiaroscuro lighting, effectively rendering an array of stylish shots of Yankel's face, accentuated by a latticework of shadows, as a means of highlighting the moral ambiguity of his character and his questionable judgment (the traces of a style that Ulmer would continue to hone in his later films noirs). Ulmer's third and final Yiddish feature for Collective Film Producers, an imaginative rendition of *Fishke der krumer* (*Fishke the Lame,* or in the seemingly inconsonant English title under which it was released, *The Light Ahead,* 1939), is also the most visually ambitious of his Yiddish films, allowing him greater freedom to incorporate an aesthetic that is more self-consciously indebted to his European background and training ("The Shtetl of Dr. Caligari," as *Village Voice* critic Carrie Rickey memorably dubbed it).[73]

Based on the writings of S. Y. Abramovitsh, the so-called grandfather of modern Yiddish literature, who was known mostly by his pen name and fictional persona Mendele Moykher Sforim or Mendele the Book Peddler, Ulmer's film recasts the shtetl as a fever swamp of dogma, corruption, and narrow-mindedness. "He subjected the shtetl to a scathing exposé and presented its traditional culture as deeply flawed," notes Yiddish scholar Dan Miron of Abramovitsh's writings, "and yet he also managed, as an artist, not to remain at a distance from the object of his aesthetic exploration and to allow the shtetl to speak for itself, to use its own authentic voice, to project its own inherent priorities, values and fantasies."[74] In keeping with Abramovitsh's approach, Ulmer's adaptation contains none of the predominant nostalgia for a romanticized version of Jewish life in Eastern Europe so often imagined in the New World (reaching its apex in postwar Hollywood in such films as *Fiddler on the Roof*); instead, he presents what is perhaps the only overtly negative representation of the shtetl in an American-made film.[75]

With the help of prizewinning scriptwriter and children's book author Chaver Paver (*né* Gershon Einbinder), who had initially conceived of the idea for the stage, Ulmer and his wife, Shirley, drew liberally from Abramovitsh's literary repertoire. They gathered bits and pieces from several texts—one of the early Yiddish titles under which the film was released was *Di klyatshe (The Nag),* was borrowed from one of Abramovitsh's novels—and transformed them into a tale of intense social alienation at the hands of religious superstition, communal corruption, and archaic shtetl practices. Shot over several days in late spring 1939, on the same New Jersey location as *Cossacks* and *The Singing Blacksmith,* with the interiors photographed at Contner's Ridgefield studio, postproduction was completed in New York just as the Nazis were invading Poland.[76] Featuring highly stylized, painted, angular sets, along with heavy shadow play and a nightmarish atmosphere (Hoberman calls it "Chasidic gothic"), the film comments not only on the artistic antecedents from interwar Europe (Robert Wiene, F. W. Murnau, Marc Chagall, and El Lissitzky [né Lazar Markovich], among others) but also on the increasingly oppressive, volatile, and lethal situation in Europe at the time of production. The spread of cholera, depicted in *The Light Ahead,* and the desperate need of the film's protagonists to flee, may be construed as an allegory of European emigration during the Nazi regime. Similarly, when the film's young protagonists are told to "go forth and prosper," at the close of the film, we can hear a faint echo of Horace Greeley's legendary exhortation, "Go West, young man."

The main story line of the film takes shape around the lives, and the love, of two community outcasts, the titular Fishke (David Opatoshu), a downtrodden bathhouse attendant, and his soon-to-be fiancée, the blind orphan Hodel (Helen Beverley). Their dreams of leaving behind Glubsk ("fools' town") for the big-city life in Odessa are met with derision by the town inhabitants, except for Mendele (Isidore Cashier), a true *folksmentsh* and raconteur who serves as the film's narrator—his opening and closing monologues frame the film—and who ultimately helps the couple elude their fate as the "cholera bride and groom." A significant strand of the narrative concerns the outbreak of disease, due to the lack of modern sanitation, and the age-old superstitious rite of holding a midnight wedding between the two community outcasts at the town cemetery. These kinds of antiquated rituals were not limited to the realm of fiction. During the nineteenth-century cholera outbreaks in Eastern Europe, reports a Jewish encyclopedia entry, such "marriages often took place within the cemetery, as that in Kovno of a lame young man to a deaf-mute or hunchback woman. At Pinsk, and in other communities, two orphans were married."[77] In the case of *The Light Ahead,* the urban-rural contrast between Odessa as the modern metropolis and Glubsk as a backwater town of beggars, cripples, and thieves, helplessly stuck in the dark ages, fuels the quest of Fishke and Hodel. It also drives the primary confrontation between the religious dogma promoted by the town's rabbinical court and the secular countermovement that gathers around Mendele and whose chief slogan, uttered by a fiery clean-shaven upstart, is "Better a Jew with no beard than a beard with no Jew."

Through a sympathetic lens, shot frequently in soft, muted light, Ulmer renders the town pariahs, in particular Beverley's Hodel, almost

FIGURE 17. Noodle soup: Ulmer (standing) and David Opatoshu (Fishke) look on as an unknown crewmember feeds Helen Beverley (Hodel) in *Fishke der krumer* (*The Light Ahead*, 1939). Courtesy of the National Center for Jewish Film.

angelic. ("I think Edgar had a great sympathy for them," observes Beverley in an interview from the 1990s. "He did not show them grotesquely.") In this regard the director seems to have shared Abramovitsh's profound allegiance with *dos kleyne mentshele* (the little man), as an early novella of his was called; this sensibility is deeply embodied in the fictional figure of Mendele, who in turn may be seen as a kind of "on-screen surrogate" for Ulmer.[78] "Edgar always had sympathy for any outcast," recalls Shirley Ulmer, "or anybody who had a disability or was a fugitive—whether it be for justice reasons or others, it didn't matter. Any outcast was one of his children."[79] An extant production still shows Ulmer on the set with his actors, helping 'to establish the proper tone for an affecting scene in which Fishke and Hodel share a communal pot of chickenless noodle soup—all that the poor can afford—on Sabbath eve (Figure 17).

Perhaps unwittingly, the poverty of the production comes across in such scenes as this, both on a narrative and visual level. In this particular sequence the otherwise static camera tracks in and out on the abject bowl of soup, while the paupers dip their oversized wooden spoons into the broth and talk about how much nicer it would taste with a real chicken. Similarly, the dream that Fishke and Hodel pursue, in leaving Glubsk for Odessa, the golden medina of their minds, is little more than a dream of eating herring and potato under a roof of their own and being free of the shackles of their dejected existence in Glubsk.

As for the lack of embellishments on the set, Ulmer made do with what he could. Known for his demonstrated ability to recycle, he confected a musical score—which includes bits of Joseph Cherniavsky, Anton Bruckner, various klezmer numbers, even strains of Wagner—that was, as Hoberman points out, prepared entirely from existing recordings.[80] These kinds of creative low-budget solutions extended to the acting department as well. As in the case of *Natalka*, when Shirley Ulmer was made to step in for a no-show, *The Light Ahead* contains another family cameo, this time by Ulmer's two-year-old daughter, Arianné, in the role of Yentele (Figure 18). She wanders, with her unsteady gait, across the frame of the first shot in which we are introduced to Hodel, and her diminutive presence on the set—indeed, in the first production still, she is barely visible at her father's side, seated at the table beneath him—was felt. As the adult Arianné Ulmer Cipes remembers it:

> *The Light Ahead* always had a very special meaning for me. It is my earliest memory of childhood. If you look carefully, you can see a little goat herder toddling over the path in front of Helen Beverley as she sits plucking her chicken. I remember my mother behind the camera coaxing me to cross from one side of the set to the other. I hated the sensation of the dirt on the floor on my bare feet, and even more I hated the smell of goats and spoiled several shots by complaining loudly 'No Goats, No Goats.' They finally managed an acceptable take, but I still recall the smell of that set. This was my debut as a two-year-old actress.[81]

Although not as much of a winner at the box office as *Green Fields*, despite auspicious forecasts in the *Exhibitor* that the "superb Yiddish photoplay . . . should set new records where Jewish films can be played," *The Light Ahead*, which debuted in New York in late September 1939, was by all counts a critical success for Ulmer and his extended cast and crew.[82] In the Yiddish-language press William Edlin of the New York–based daily *Der Tog* declared the film "one of the best to appear in the past several years" and hailed Ulmer's direction as "entirely successful."[83] In other reviews the historical significance of the film, appearing as it did against the backdrop of the Nazi incursions in Europe, caught the critics' attention. The *New York Times*' Frank Nugent called the

FIGURE 18. Early cameo: Arianné Ulmer as Yentele in *Fishke der krumer* (*The Light Ahead*, 1939), with Anna Guskin (Gitel) in the background. Courtesy of the National Center for Jewish Film.

film "remarkably honest and forthright in its portrayal of the trials and tribulations of the Jew" and drew attention to what he saw as "a strong parallel between the sufferings of the past and those of the present," ultimately underscoring the element of hope in the film and "the reassuring message it contains for World Jewry."[84]

Finally, the week before Christmas the *Hollywood Reporter* ran a short dispatch from Kansas City under the title "Yiddish Picture a Sensation in K.C.," which told of the sleeper that Ulmer's film had unexpectedly become in that offbeat market. "The surprise sensation of the picture business here," began the report, "is the trade being done at the Vogue by 'The Light Ahead,' a Yiddish dialogue picture. The show was given rave notices by the local press, which urged Gentiles to enjoy it with their Jewish neighbors, resulting in picture fans of all creeds and nationalities buying tickets."[85] In his ongoing efforts to reach a minority audience, and in the process encouraging a more universal embrace of humanity, Ulmer couldn't have hoped for better press. As for the precise subject that he took up in his third Yiddish feature, the spread of illness and the damage that it has on those who are most vulnerable, he was at that same time working on several educational shorts aimed at preventing the spread of tuberculosis among minority populations in America and finishing up work on his two final features made for ethnic audiences.

REDISCOVERING AMERICA

Under the auspices of the New York–based National Tuberculosis Association and, from August 1940 to July 1941, on a one-year contract from a small production company called Springer Pictures, Ulmer directed a series of health shorts. These films include, among others, *Let My People Live* (1938), aimed at African Americans; *Cloud in the Sky* (1940), aimed at Mexican Americans; and *Another to Conquer* (1941), aimed at Native Americans.[86] Ulmer made each of them on location, in Tuskegee, Alabama; San Antonio, Texas; and Window Rock on the Navajo reservation in Arizona, respectively. Unlike the bulk of his Ukrainian and Yiddish features, these semidocumentary films present the viewer with an authentic American locale, not a fictional reproduction of Old Europe. In this respect they demand of both the viewer and the director a deeper, more explicit, engagement with America, a further step toward acculturation but also a reckoning with America's imperfections. At the time, tuberculosis was a disease that afflicted tens of thousands of Americans each year, a disproportionate number of them members of minority groups. As Dr. Gordon (Rex Ingram) tells his student audience in *Let My People Live:* "We, as Negroes, seem to be particularly susceptible to this disease. The reason is that the great majority of our homes are poor; our work is hard; and we don't have money to get treated when we should." During the thirteen-minute film, shot in a week in April 1938 on the campus of the Tuskegee Institute and its local environs, Ulmer shows the same kind of deep sympathy for his subjects, the siblings Mary (Peggy Howard) and George (Merritt Smith), who fear they may have inherited the disease from their mother, as he does for Fishke and Hodel in *The Light Ahead*. Together with

Dr. Gordon, they earn the focus of the film's few close-ups, and they are the righteous characters with which the audience is made to identify.

As is the case in each of the three shorts, the narrative is presented in a very simple, didactic framework. Consistent throughout is the need—rather similar to the dominant motif of *The Light Ahead,* but with more of an educational mission à la *Damaged Lives* or perhaps of "a Jesuit morality tale," as Ulmer would have it (B 590)—to set aside folk ritual in favor of modern science, including regular medical examination and X-ray technology. In *Let My People Live* the underlying message of Dr. Gordon is that science must be allowed to triumph, that treatment, if effectively sought and administered, can cure the people. Ulmer underscores this in the visuals, but he also amplifies it in his choice of music. We move from an opening sequence that features a Negro spiritual ("I Know the Lord Has Laid His Hands on Me") sung in the university chapel by the college choir to a gospel rendition of "Let My People Go," while George travels home by bus to visit his sick mother. From there we move onward to another spiritual at the funeral of Mary and George's mother and in the last shot back to the same college choir singing the Hallelujah chorus of Handel's *Messiah,* which, as Ulmer tells Bogdanovich, "I had to have as a finale" (B 590). As he does elsewhere in his shorts, he cannily blends "native" and European traditions (in *Cloud in the Sky* Ulmer includes the Spanish folk song "Cielito Lindo" alongside symphonic numbers played by the fifty-piece Tipica Orchestra). The film, which was made in cooperation with Roosevelt's Works Progress Administration and the U.S. Veterans Administration, was submitted by the U.S. Health Department to the 1939 World's Fair in New York, where it reportedly picked up an award for best documentary.[87]

Each of the three TB shorts aimed at an ethnic audience shows, in contradistinction to *The Light Ahead,* a compatibility between organized religion and science or, more broadly, between religion and modernity. A black pastor (Erostine Coles) in *Let My People Live* encourages Mary to see a doctor. Similarly, in *Cloud in the Sky,* it is the church padre (Rev. Frederick J. Mann) who tells Consuelo (Rosario de la Vega) to seek help from a medical professional, while in *Another to Conquer,* the Navajo tribal elder Slow Talker (Howard Gorman) ultimately, painfully recognizes the importance of modern medicine over tribal ritual.[88] "While characters are tempted to rely on folk medicines or the consolations of prayer," writes Bill Krohn, "it is always a priest or minister who recommends that they have a skin-test."[89] Taken together, these shorts are, like *Green Fields, Cossacks in Exile,* or other of Ulmer's ethnic pictures, testimonies to the strength of the common folk. They draw our attention, specifically in such instances as the panning shots of the rich open landscape of *Another to Conquer,* ably photographed by Robert Cline, to the inherent beauty of America's neglected corners. As the final line, spoken by that same film's offscreen narrator, emphatically announces, "The people will conquer again."

Returning closer to home, to the New York City in which Edgar and Shirley Ulmer had resided since the mid-1930s, a similar focus on the triumph of the people in the battle of good over evil, and on the pressing needs for greater modernization and acculturation, appears in the two final feature-length films Ulmer made for a minority audience, the all-black musical drama *Moon over Harlem* (1939) and his final Yiddish film, a comedy, *Amerikaner shadkhn* (*American Matchmaker,* 1940). Both pictures were deeply personal undertakings for Ulmer, collaborations that involved an extended crew of family members. Shirley (credited on both films as Sherle Castle) wrote each of the scripts, the second of which was based on a story by Ulmer's dear cousin from Vienna, Gustav Heimo (*né* Horowitz), who also served as production manager on both pictures. Shirley's brother Fred Kassler was, together with Heimo, assistant director, and Peter Kassler, Shirley's father, was associate producer on *Moon over Harlem.* Both of these films offer critical insight into Ulmer's ethnic period of filmmaking, conveying a new kind of timeliness, a bolder and more direct engagement with current affairs, and with the wider popular debates concerning American assimilation, than do his other features of the same period.

It's not completely clear how Ulmer came to direct *Moon over Harlem,* which was among the first all-black features with a white director at the helm. George Lipsitz claims that a black producer who saw Ulmer's short *Let My People Live* asked the émigré director to take on the project. Yet an article published in November 1937 in the *Chicago Defender,* a leading black newspaper, attaches Ulmer to an early script ("Blues in My Heart") by black playwright Mathew Mathews, who is credited with the original story and dialogue of the finished film.[90] By his own account, Ulmer was asked by composer Donald Heywood, who provides the music for the film, to take on a script (presumably Mathews's) and to shoot the picture in four days with a budget of under $8,000, approximately the same amount he had to make his short *Another to Conquer* (B 591). Using his standby cinematographer Contner once again, together with Edward Hyland, Ulmer shot the film in a cigar warehouse in New Jersey, as well as on location in Harlem at a nightclub, the Lido Ballroom on 146th Street, after its doors closed for the evening. In the absence of costly 35 mm film stock, Ulmer and his crew were left to use the 16 mm short ends of previous productions— leftovers, in other words—which meant, as he tells it, reloading the camera nearly every two minutes and shooting no long takes (B 591). Ulmer seems also to have returned in this picture to a mode of filmmaking he first explored in *People on Sunday,* what he calls in his interview with Bogdanovich the "Rossellini style: we didn't use actors, we used real people, and they were very natural" (B 591). The only marquee name is renowned jazz clarinetist Sidney Bechet, credited as "Sidney Bechet and his Clarinet," whose brief cameo appearance bestows on the film an added layer of authenticity.

Catering to its target audience of African American cinemagoers, the film offers a bird's eye view of the famed neighborhood "black Manhattan," as its upstanding protagonist Bob (Carl Gough) pronounces it. Already in the first seconds of the opening sequence, with its city symphony of neon images—an amalgamation of stock shots capturing the flickering lights of Blumenstein department store, the Apollo nightclub, the Savoy Theater, all shorthand visual testimony to the mix of Jewish and black cultures onscreen and off—combined with the rhythmic sounds of Heywood's jazz score, the unmistakably urban milieu of the film emerges. As we soon learn, this is a world of gangsters and mob control, characters from rival gangs with names like Dollar Bill and Wall Street, but also one of an aspiring middle class represented by Bob and his like-minded fiancée, Sue (Ozinetta Wilcox). From the credit sequence onward, the music and cityscape work together in a kind of syncopated unison. Later in the film, when Sue sings Heywood's "Teach Me How to Sing Again" at the Plantation nightclub, the song serves as a centerpiece and an anthem for Bob and Sue, who, like Fishke and Hodel in *The Light Ahead,* dream of a better life than the one that has been handed down to them (Figure 19). "Music takes on the function of social glue," remarks Frank Mehring, "and spiritual self-empowerment."[91]

In the film's pivotal sequence Ulmer brings his audience into the apartment of Minnie (Cora Green), a widow working as a maid at Broadway Slick's nightclub, who lives together with her daughter, Sue, and whose wedding to a sweet-talking racketeer named Dollar Bill (Bud Harris) is taking place amid the melodious sounds of Sidney Bechet's clarinet. Dollar Bill's crew roughs up the place, destroying a photo of Minnie's late husband and drawing the contrast between the

FIGURE 19. Dreaming of a better life: Bob (Carl Gough) and Sue (Ozinetta Wilcox) in *Moon over Harlem* (1939). Photofest.

righteous folks of Harlem, allied with Bob and Sue, and the thugs who bring corruption and vice to the neighborhood. No sooner is the wedding ceremony over than Dollar Bill makes a pass at Sue, but he is rewarded with a slap across his face (he boasts to one of his onlooking pals, "When I moves in on a deal, I moves in"). By contrast, Bob's repeated invocations of hope for Harlem ("There's so much to be done here. This place is screaming for leadership") serve as a rallying cry for the audience, just as his unwavering fidelity to Sue forms a bulwark against the evils of those like Dollar Bill, who is shown to be cheating on Minnie with a much younger (and lighter-skinned) woman (a floozy named Connie [Audrey Talbird]) and gambling away all his wife's hard-earned wages. Minnie refuses to heed the abundant warnings about Dollar Bill, declaring to a friend of hers that "it's me and him against the world" and throwing her own daughter out after blaming her for the continued sexual advances made by her new husband. Unsurprisingly, Minnie ultimately falls victim, taking a bullet from mobsters who come to collect a debt from Bill. A final shoot-out and bloodbath among the gangsters leaves the racketeer dead and allows the film to strike an upbeat note, giving the forward-looking Bob the last word (the same prerecorded dialogue, "This place is screaming for leadership," with the dramatic chorus from "Teach Me How to Sing Again" playing over the same montage of neon images from the opening sequence).

Shot over several days in February, *Moon over Harlem* held its first previews in New York in late May and premiered in mid-June; this was followed by wide release at movie houses of the black circuit, including RKO's Alhambra Theatre, whose flickering marquee is captured in the montage that starts and ends the film, throughout the summer and into fall of 1939.[92] Yet before it officially hit the screens, the film was submitted to the Production Code Administration, which issued Mercury Film Laboratories—where the print was processed—a stern warning about its content. As the letter of June 1, 1939, states, "We cannot approve this picture in the form in which it was presented to us."[93] Among the given reasons were lack of clear punishment for the perpetrators (they recommend shooting a new scene with police officers arresting the gangsters); the critical question of Connie's skin color (though advised that she was in fact a "negress," the PCA screeners find that she looks rather white in her scene with Dollar Bill and demand confirmation); excessive drinking during the "wake scene," when Sue tries to drown her sorrows; sexual suggestiveness at the wedding party with, in their words, "the little negro placing his head on the bosom of his female dancing partner" (one of the few overtly comical scenes); and partial nudity in the sequence in which Sue bathes in front of two friends. "This afternoon we had the pleasure of conferring with Mr. Ulmer," the letter concludes, "and we have gone over with him in detail the objectionable material contained in the picture, and he has agreed to make an attempt to re-edit it."

Whether out of lack of proper funding or pure defiance, there were no retakes, and it appears that the very same print submitted to the PCA made it into New York theaters some four months later. Although the film received considerable attention in the black press, it didn't elicit much of a response in the industry trades or the popular press. The one notice it garnered in the *Exhibitor* was largely dismissive. "Another entrant in the ever-growing number of pictures made with all-Negro casts," the review began, "'Moon over Harlem' turns out to be just another yarn about a petty racketeer who wants to become the local big shot, but finally gets a belly full of lead for his pains."[94] Just a few months later, in January 1940, *Variety* ran a seemingly belated headline forecasting a "Negro and Yiddish Film Boom."[95] By this time Ulmer was finishing up work on *American Matchmaker,* his "ethnic swan song" and final contribution to the so-called "boom," and this branch of niche market filmmaking was nearing collapse.[96]

Almost a New World sequel to *The Light Ahead,* Ulmer's foray into Yiddish comedy, *American Matchmaker,* brings us directly to the world of the metropolis—not Odessa but New York—and introduces us to the different roles that Yiddish-speaking Jews occupy there. "It's about time to stop looking back at the past, the Old Country, on the other side of the ocean," wrote *Der Tog*'s film critic, William Edlin, "and turn our eyes toward life here, where you can find more than four million Jews."[97] Quite fittingly, *Matchmaker* was billed as a "story of American-Jewish life" and may be seen, as one critic trenchantly noted, as a "comedy in which we see what became of Fishke and Hodel's descendents in the city."[98] The film's protagonist, Leo Fuchs, the so-called Yiddish Fred Astaire, plays the suave, upwardly mobile, highly assimilated business-man Nat Silver, who in the process of continuing to climb the social ladder of New York City effects a late-career makeover ("human relations" or what is sardonically called "human relishes"), becoming a matchmaker and changing his name from Silver to Gold. Despite his prowess in the world of business, when it comes to romance, he is more of a "schlemiel," as his sister Elvie (Anna Guskin, who plays Gitel in *The Light Ahead*) calls him. At the outset we are informed that Nat has been engaged seven times—it's the occasion of the eighth engagement, to a cheekily named bride, Shirley (named after Ulmer's own wife), that brings his friends together to celebrate one more time Nat's soon-to-be-failed graduation from bachelorhood. The Viennese-born psychoanalyst Theodor Reik conceived of the "schlemiel" in his book *Jewish Wit* as "the hidden architect of his own misfortune."[99] This is an appropriate description of Nat, who cannot seem to overcome his inability to commit to a woman (it is only in the final scenes of the film—when a woman who is equally sophisticated and modern as he, played to stunning perfection by Judith Abarbanel, enters his life and essentially guides him to the *khupe*—that he is able to beat his protracted and seemingly undying stroke of misfortune).

After a quick montage of New York's skyline, not unlike that of *Moon over Harlem,* the film opens inside a sumptuously designed apartment on Central Park West—a street on which Edgar and Shirley Ulmer had in fact lived during the mid-1930s—where Nat's bachelor party is under way. The elegant setting, lavish decoration, and self-consciously urbane mannerism together conjure a milieu that is anything but specifically Jewish; for a bargain-basement film like this, shot inside a Bronx studio, these images also help to distract attention from the absence of camera movement or other formal embellishments. The only thing that marks the film as Jewish at all is the fact that Yiddish is spoken; and even that is highly Americanized, and urbanized, with continuous references to contemporary idiom ("come on," "toots," "old boy," etc.) evocative of street-savvy sophistication.[100] There are, however, running gags within the story line that explicitly address the vexed issue of assimilation. There's the faux-English butler Maurice (Yudel Dubinsky, who played the stuttering *shadkhn* in *Blacksmith*), Nat's "man Friday," who insists on speaking a stilted British English. And then there's the well-groomed, ascot-wearing Nat, who harbors the fantasy of becoming his Uncle Shya (also played by Fuchs)—a bearded *shadkhn* from the Old Country, anticipating Woody Allen's Hasidic drag in *Annie Hall*—which serves as an inspiration for his career change.

Fuchs tells in a 1982 interview how Ulmer had approached him in his dressing room, while he was still acting in Sholem Asch's Yiddish play *Salvation,* and how this "young, sensitive moviemaker" offered him the chance to return to comedy.[101] As Nat Silver, he hams it up, singing a drunken bachelor number, one of the few bits of music in the film, dancing arm in arm with his chums. Similarly, his relationship to Maurice, sharing an apartment and enjoying a quasi-married existence, has a playful subtext of homosexuality that Ulmer's cousin Gustav, who wrote an unpublished memoir in America on being gay, may have worked in with Shirley (when Maurice talks with the canary, singing to the *feygele,* a Yiddish term for small bird and for homosexual, or when he declares himself heartbroken at Nat's announcement of his marriage to Judith at the close of the film, additional veiled allusions to his sexual orientation may be detected). In more ways than one the film represents a personal response to the dilemmas of assimilation in an urban setting, a coming to terms with the "craziness" of America, as Nat's mother (Celia Boodkin) remarks. For Ulmer this was a dilemma with which he could no doubt identify. "The immigrant from the Old World," writes Grissemann of the director, "adjusted to America, and adopted America. The conversion [represented by *American Matchmaker*] is as good as fulfilled."[102]

When the film opened on May 7, 1940, at the National Theatre, the cultural "boom" of which Ulmer partook was enjoying its final hurrah.

"Eight acts of Yiddish vaudeville were on the bill," remarks Stefan Kanfer of the opening, "including acrobats, singers, and comedians. They represented the last of a dying breed."[103] Not even the additional acts, however, could make up for the inauspicious timing of the film—on the eve of Hitler's invasion of France—or the lukewarm response it received in the press. The *New York Times*' reviewer insisted that the "best thing" about *Matchmaker* was the performance by Judith Abarbanel, lamenting the fact that Ulmer "makes the spectator sit through almost an hour of tiresome comedy before Judith comes on the screen."[104] The film fared no better in the Yiddish press. William Edlin's review in *Der Tog* similarly singled out Abarbanel, who "lights up the action" and is "a real American girl." Although he found Contner's cinematography to be fine, Edlin concluded: "The film is directed by Edgar Ulmer, who already excelled with a number of Yiddish talkies, but as it proves, comedy is not his specialty."[105] Perhaps aware of this shortcoming, Ulmer mostly avoided comedy in the years to come.

This general period, however, was not without deeper significance for Ulmer's life and career. It enabled him to pursue subjects that, in a roundabout way, helped him to become more deeply assimilated into the fabric of America. "Ulmer's movies," asserts Tag Gallagher, "are a series of ethnic studies: Hungarians, Yiddish, blacks in Harlem, blacks in Alabama, Wall Street tycoons, Navajos, Mexicans, Berliners, Neapolitans, New York Dutch, Boston WASPS, Spaniards, Caucasians, Armenians, and Brabantians. But they are also studies in ethnic faith and conviction."[106] This is perhaps what makes the ethnic pictures transcend their particularity and communicate something larger for Ulmer. A film like *Matchmaker* represents, in Krohn's words, "Ulmer's readiness to become finally what he had set out to be seven years earlier [i.e., when making *The Black Cat*]: an American filmmaker, one who had found his own version of the American Sublime, but only after an exuberant and often downright wacky pilgrimage through all the cultures and conditions which had somehow gotten left out of the American Dream."[107] Indeed, only a circuitous path such as the one Krohn describes, with its full share of detours, is befitting of a director like Ulmer, a director whose entire life and career can be properly understood in a constant state of transit and reinvention.

Later in life, Ulmer continued to maintain some of the friendships he made during his stint directing ethnic films. In 1947 he and Shirley received an inscribed copy of Maurice Schwartz's play *Shylock and His Daughter* encouraging them to return once more to the cultural terrain they had explored in the cycle of Yiddish pictures. Schwartz, who was best known for his role as Tevye in the 1939 film adaptation he directed of Sholem Aleichem's beloved work of the same name, writes in his inscription: "Read this book and think of the great world success this play can be as a picture, and you should make this your great mission to show to the world the real character of the Jew Shylock."[108] Ulmer's mission in 1947, and throughout much of the 1940s, was to find decent work—in some cases, any work—as a director, but none of it ever brought him back to the Yiddish films. Helen Beverley recalls meeting periodically with Edgar and Shirley Ulmer during the later years, remembering in particular Edgar's penchant for eating at Gypsy restaurants. "Ulmer was," as she puts it, "a kind of Gypsy anyway."[109] Throughout the 1940s, and into the 1950s and 1960s, there was a seeming nomadic quality—almost "like a circus family," as Arianné Ulmer once remarked—about Ulmer's life and career as a director.[110] After more than half a decade of scrounging up work in the East, it was time for Shirley and Edgar Ulmer to return to Los Angeles, where they set up shop for the next sustained phase of professional reinvention.

Capra of PRC

I was offered the picture [*Hitler's Madman*, 1943] which was
to be shot at some speed: I was given one week's shooting
time. . . . I realized that it was both a chance and a danger. It
could be useful, and it might launch me. Or it could stick me
as a B-feature director. And when this happens to you, no
matter how good you are, you can just get stuck. Ulmer, for
example, I think he's a very good director, but he got stuck
with B-features all his time in Hollywood.

—Douglas Sirk

Around the same point at which Ulmer's cycle of ethnic pictures and
educational shorts began to slow down, in the middle of summer 1941,
he paid a visit to Hollywood to test the waters and follow up on any leads
he could find. Writing on stationery from the Hollywood Plaza Hotel,
located at the storied intersection of Hollywood and Vine—home to the
Pantages Theater (where *The Black Cat* had its portentous premiere in
May 1934), the Laemmle Building, and the offices of the Academy of
Motion Picture Arts and Sciences—Ulmer conveyed to his wife, Shirley,
his great enthusiasm for their planned return to the West Coast. He confided in her his true hope, fleeting though it may have been, that this
could be the beginning of a new era for him, a chance to regain his foot-
ing in the big-studio fortresses from which he'd previously been banished.
"Sherle darling I feel like a child," he intones in the first of two letters. "I
am myself again, that old Edgar with all his love for art, not that loafer
who tried to sell himself and went goofy like any other common money-
grubbing Jew. Sweetest—things are happening . . . appointments with
L.B. Mayer, R.K.O. and Paramount. . . . Your old Edgar has not been
forgotten." As the language of the letter suggests, Ulmer saw himself in a
semifictional, semidocumentary universe not unlike the one depicted in

Budd Schulberg's contemporary novel *What Makes Sammy Run,* a blistering portrayal of Hollywood ambition, published earlier that same year. But even as he senses that this could be his big chance, and that he might rehabilitate his former self, so, too, he remains aware of the odds, something he relates in a final utterance of desperation: "Dearest pray—pray here is our chance. . . . I *must* make it. I am happy and I know you are. We are coming home."[1]

No more than a couple of days later, in a letter dated July 1, 1941, and written again on Hollywood Plaza stationery, he announces to Shirley: "The prayer has worked. Sweetest I am so excited I hardly can hold the pen in my hand. I just returned from Paramount. Sherle, they have not forgotten. Sherle, I am as good as signed with Paramount. Producer—director—good God! Sweets we are home again and on the way." He then proceeds to assert, reiterating what the studio executives presumably told him: "Well, Ulmer, I am sold on you 1,000%. . . . You are going to be one of the big men on the lot. Dearest, I hardly could keep from crying out. So seven years [1934–1941] I had to suffer and starve. I nearly sold you out, you, [the] picture business, my family, myself. Oh, I am so excited I hardly can think."[2] In the last lines of the letter Ulmer announces the two pictures he hopes to make for Paramount: first, an idea called *Beggar on Horseback,* based on the eponymous play by George S. Kaufman and Marc Connelly, an update of Paramount's silent release in 1925; and second, a throwback to late Weimar, a remake of Sternberg's *The Blue Angel,* starring the young Veronica Lake, a contract player at Paramount who had just landed her first major role in Mitchell Leisen's *I Wanted Wings* (1941). Neither of the two projects ever panned out, and Ulmer's fantasy of becoming a redeemed and celebrated studio director at Paramount remained just that: a fantasy.

Rather than securing a lavish contract with one of the majors, Ulmer found work at Producers Releasing Corporation (PRC), one of the lowliest outfits on Hollywood's Poverty Row, its diminutive lot located on Santa Monica Boulevard near Fairfax.[3] Together with Monogram and Republic, PRC formed what was known as the B-Hive, a loose conglomerate of bargain-basement studios that existed in the shadows, sometimes on borrowed scraps, of the majors. The American B movie, which emerged during the Great Depression and thrived throughout the 1940s, was conceived as the bottom half of a double bill, in many cases as mere filler for a three-hour film program that included newsreels, shorts, and trailers for the price of a single admission. Generally limited to six reels, or a runtime of roughly between fifty-five and seventy minutes, B pictures were made quickly and efficiently—often shot at night, repurposing sets from other productions, with plenty of stock footage, fog, mirrors, and rear projection—and utterly devoid of frills.[4] In other words, these were modest boilerplate features made on a slim budget, the kind of movies "in which the sets shake when an actor slams the door."[5]

PRC was famous, if not infamous, for churning out cheap wartime entertainment, its three-letter company abbreviation sometimes mockingly referred to as "Pretty Rotten Crap," and even imagined to be "a front for organized crime."[6] With its banner logo of cement-like block letters, implying the kind of strength and permanence it yearned for, it existed in various guises for less than a decade: from 1939, when it was briefly known as Producers Distributing Company headed by Ben Judell, with backing from Sigmund Neufeld; into the mid-1940s, with support from Pathé Laboratories, when Leon Fromkess emerged as the studio's industrious head of production; and finally up until late 1946, when it was folded into the British Eagle-Lion Films and eventually absorbed into United Artists in the early 1950s.[7]

WARTIME LIES; OR, THE ART OF THE SECOND BILLER

Not long after Ulmer wrote to Shirley confessing his desperate wish to become a contract director at Paramount, he brought his family out to the West Coast, where he channeled what was left of that same feverish energy into directing a string of eleven pictures in four years, 1942–46, at PRC. He also wrote scripts, generated titles and story ideas, had a hand in producing, and ultimately became something of a big man on a small lot. He and his family initially took up residence in a couple of rentals, first on Orange Grove and then on Courtney Avenue just above Hollywood Boulevard. But once he was working at a more regular interval, with a steady stream of income from the studio, Ulmer purchased a relatively spacious Spanish-style house on Kings Road, nestled in the hills that rise up north of Sunset Boulevard—later referred to as "Mortgage Hill," after Ulmer had to refinance the property, on repeated occasions, to help fund his films—where he and his family lived for almost a decade.[8] "One can imagine," remarks Stefan Grissemann of the evocative street name, "how its sound alone would have appealed to Edgar Ulmer."[9] In his interview with Bogdanovich, Ulmer tells of his fortuitous encounter with Leon Fromkess, an accountant by training and the former treasurer at Monogram Pictures who began producing in the early 1940s, one day at Pathé Laboratories while still working in New York. They had a good friend in common, producer Seymour Nebenzal, whose father Heinrich Nebenzahl (the German spelling still intact) had helped produce *People on Sunday* and whose own Weimar-era production company, Nero-Film, boasted such illustrious screen credits as G. W. Pabst's *Die Büchse der Pandora* (*Pandora's Box*, 1929) and Fritz Lang's *M* (1931).[10] Ulmer considered Nebenzal "a man of exquisite taste" and a brilliant producer, dubbing him the "Selznick of Europe" (B 592).

As Shirley explains it, in conversation with filmmaker Michael Henry Wilson more than half a century after Ulmer's PRC years, her husband met Fromkess during "that slack period when we were in New York."[11] The only extant letters from the period—from late summer 1940, when Ulmer's main sources of income were the TB shorts and the meager fees from his ethnic pictures—betray his deep-felt worries about remaining adrift. In mid-August 1940, on letterhead from the Brooklyn Tuberculosis and Health Association, Ulmer writes to Shirley from work on location in Philadelphia: "I am very lonesome, and miss you and my daughter [Arianné] very much."[12] Days later he relays in a couple of missives, once more underscoring profound feelings of desolation, how he is merely trying to finish up odd projects, more instructional films for Springer Pictures, a company from which he would soon resign, biding his time without giving up all hope. From this particular vantage point the alliance that Ulmer formed with Fromkess marked a considerable improvement over his languishing state. ("This was *big time!*" he insisted to Bogdanovich.)[13] "It was a nice studio," recounted designer and puppeteer Bob Baker, who worked with Ulmer on *Isle of Forgotten Sins* and *Bluebeard*. "It was clean and it was well kept. Yet, you felt—you felt a kind of [strangeness] there because as you looked around, most of the people in the way of actors and actresses were on the rebound . . . or just beginning. It wasn't like going into Paramount, MGM, or Fox or even Universal."[14] Despite the lack of studio polish and fat contract, the PRC years represent a relatively happy time for Ulmer. "He was," in Shirley's words, "pretty much his own boss. . . . It was a great, great little studio."

Shirley and Edgar Ulmer's individual recollections more or less match those of the higher-ups at the studio. "Edgar G. Ulmer came to us early in 1942," recounts former PRC boss Fromkess in a letter of 1969, "with the Atlantis-Nero-Nebenzal group. He directed *Tomorrow We Live, My Son the Hero,* and did substantial second unit direction on Arthur Ripley's *Prisoner of Japan.* He also prepared to direct and did commence principal photography on *Minstrel Man,* but the film was turned over to Joseph H. Lewis four or five days into production. Thereafter Mr. Ulmer directed the stage sequences operating in effect as a second unit director."[15] Fromkess continues, outlining the rest of Ulmer's time at PRC:

> Isle of Forgotten Sins, Girls in Chains, and Jive Junction followed in 1943. Ulmer left us for a short time in late 1943 to make films for the Army via Raphael Wolff Productions returning early in 1944. . . . He prepared, directed and edited Bluebeard and Strange Illusion in 1944 and prepared Club Havana as well as working on other product for later production. In 1945 he directed Club Havana and was then placed on a one-year contract extending to approximately mid-1946. During this time, he did Detour, Her Sister's Secret, Wife of Monte Cristo and we loaned him to Hunt Stromberg to direct Strange Woman with Hedy Lamarr.

Of the eleven features Ulmer directed for Fromkess and PRC, quite a few of them, especially the early pictures (*Tomorrow We Live, Girls in Chains,* and *My Son, the Hero*) were shot in less than a week with a budget of under $30,000 and a director's fee of $1,000 per picture.[16] Both the shooting schedules and budgets increased, to approximately two weeks per shoot and anywhere between $50,000 and $150,000 in production costs, toward the middle of his stint at PRC (with *Isle of Forgotten Sins* and *Jive Junction* in 1943, and *Bluebeard* of 1944). Although some of the later films at PRC—in particular *Detour,* but also *Club Havana,* both of 1945—are thought of as Ulmer's quickest and cheapest, they spanned two full weeks of shooting and well surpassed $100,000 in total production costs. By 1946, his final year at PRC, the Dumas-inspired costume drama *The Wife of Monte Cristo* extended nearly three weeks and cost more than $300,000, an unfathomably high figure for a B-list production. With some minor discrepancies (e.g., *Detour*), Ulmer's director's fee, which ostensibly also covered pre- and postproduction, remained relatively constant.[17] "You didn't fit the shoe to the foot," observed Jimmy Lydon, the lead in *Strange Illusion,* in a 2001 interview. "You fit the foot to the shoe. You made the budget first, and then you made the picture fit into the budget."[18]

In Hollywood, after an ill-fated venture with the majors, producing the Dalton Trumbo–scripted *We Who Were Young* (1940) for MGM, Nebenzal founded an independent company, Angelus Pictures (later known as Atlantis Pictures), and coproduced with Fromkess a number of low-budget films for PRC. These included, among others, Ulmer's directorial debut at the studio, *Tomorrow We Live* (1942), and Douglas Sirk's *Hitler's Madman* (1943), for which Ulmer served, without formal credit, as second unit director; the latter film was based on a story by German émigré novelist Emil Ludwig and was reworked into a script by Peretz Hirschbein of Ulmer's *Green Fields* days.[19] What at first glance may seem like a relatively arbitrary sequence of events would shape Ulmer's career for many years to come. "I drifted into PRC and couldn't get out," he told Bogdanovich. "This was my home and I could operate and bring any idea immediately to the top echelon. I suffered, of course, from one thing. I was so tied up that I couldn't take any contracts on the outside" (B 593). Earlier in the same interview, he phrases things somewhat differently: "I was known all over town—I could have gone anywhere—but was under exclusive contract" (B 573). Regardless of the wording, this new situation was, as Sirk attests, a mixed blessing—it meant consistent work at a studio that offered Ulmer plenty of freedom, where he would have the kind of creative control normally limited to a head of production, yet at the same time it would forever stigmatize him as a B director.[20]

Ulmer's first assignment at PRC, commencing in the first months of 1942, was not to direct but rather to rewrite an existing screenplay that, like much of his early work at the studio, had an obvious and essential link to the war effort. Arthur Ripley's *Prisoner of Japan,* made in the immediate wake of Pearl Harbor for slightly more than $20,000 and for which Ulmer carried out second unit direction (purportedly filling in for Ripley in the final stretch of production), is a tawdry war melodrama set in the Pacific (B 593). The film stars Alan Baxter in the title role, an astrophysicist held captive by a Japanese secret agent played by the Prague-born Ernst Deutsch (credited as Ernest Dorian), a transplant from the Weimar film scene who at the time was best known for his role as the shifty rabbi's assistant, Famulus, in Paul Wegener's *Der Golem: Wie er in die Welt kam* (*The Golem: How He Came into the World,* 1920) and who would later play Kurtz in Carol Reed's *The Third Man* (1949). Ripley's picture, produced by Nebenzal, delivers in less than an hour a period-specific story of good against evil. In the belligerent rhetoric of the industry trade press, it was called a "slap-the-Jap yarn [that] presents the rice lice as a cruel and cunning enemy," while the tagline that graced its posters similarly thundered, "TOKYO TREACHERY FOILED . . . AND A SPY PAYS THE PRICE!"[21] The war is made palpable, as it is in most of Ulmer's subsequent films at PRC, leading to the conspicuous exhortation, tacked on at the end of the final reel, for millions of American moviegoers to buy war bonds and support the Allied effort.

Indeed, that is precisely how Ulmer's directorial debut at PRC, *Tomorrow We Live,* shot on the lot in six days in early summer 1942 and released just two months after *Prisoner of Japan*, reaches its dénouement. The unusually saccharine score by Leo Erdody, Ulmer's versatile standby composer at PRC, gives way briefly to an exultant military march intercut with stock shots of army brigades cruising mightily across the screen. We return for the last bit of blustery dialogue ("I'll be there!"), with a tight low-angle shot of heroine Jean Parker framed against the washed-out prairie sky, before the end credits roll and the critical announcement comes: "CALLING 80,000,000 AMERICAN MOVIEGOERS! BUY WAR SAVING STAMPS AND BONDS! On Sale in this Theatre!"[22] All that precedes this final moment, in the hour or so of rudimentary entertainment, is similarly aimed at galvanizing popular support for the larger cause. "The war impacts almost everything done at PRC between 1942 and 1945," asserts Grissemann. "The pathos of the moment, the battle for freedom and against the tyranny of fascism, flow almost unfiltered into the productions of the studio."[23]

One of many potboiler melodramas made for the Poverty Row studio, *Tomorrow We Live*—written by Bart Lytton (*né* Bernard Shulman), who would also help craft the story for *Hitler's Madman* a few months later—pits an unsavory "girl-crazy" gangster and desert casino owner known as the Ghost (Ricardo Cortez, *né* Jacob Krantz) against the young, innocent, aspiring teacher Julie Bronson (Parker) and her uncompromisingly decent fiancé, Lt. Bob Lord (William Marshall). The tension of the odd love triangle gives the film its essential structure and light suspense. "Strange, very strange," remarks Ulmer of the film. "I was very much influenced at the time by Grand Guignol, which took me twenty years to get out of my system. The melodrama and the absolute theatrics was very tempting: a horror picture in the desert, with Ricardo Cortez" (B 584).

As was even more dramatically the case with *The Black Cat*, made eight years earlier, the most extreme impulses of his characters in *Tomorrow We Live* are fueled by the presence—or, in the first instance, the traumatic past—of the war. The Ghost, who in his debonair white dinner jacket runs the Dunes nightclub like a low-rent Rick Blaine of *Casablanca*, emerges as the consummate villain, a figure whose very name links him to horror. "He's got a bullet in his brain and a slug in his chest," warns the streetwise waitress Melba (Roseanne Stevens) when talking with Julie. The Ghost holds Julie's vulnerable father, Pop Bronson (Emmett Lynn), in his merciless grip and uses all the powers at his disposal, including extortion and deadly force, to keep him there. More significant still, he threatens to come between Julie and her upstanding fiancé (Figure 20).

FIGURE 20. Tainted love: The Ghost (Ricardo Cortez) and Julie Bronson (Jean Parker) in a publicity still from *Tomorrow We Live* (1942). Photofest.

In stark contrast, Bob Lord, forever photographed in uniform, serves as the self-appointed advocate for the "little men, honest men, big with the dignity of toil and strong with the courage of decency." Almost as if Ulmer were offering an unsolicited entry to the U.S. Army's *Why We Fight* series, headed by Capra, *Tomorrow We Live* is a parable of heroism in distilled form. Lieutenant Lord stands strong, eager to defend the nation against oppression in a war that he insists is worth our effort. ("Thousands of us, millions maybe, will have to go out and fight," he explains to Julie with a sense of urgency and conviction, "so that life can go on. It must go on.") When Bob faces off with the Ghost at the Dunes nightclub, the implications of his actions are made haltingly plain. "It must be your kind that makes a Hitler," he asserts, adding in the same incriminating breath, "Berchtesgaden must be something like this!" Vaguely reminiscent of *Moon over Harlem,* and of Bob and Sue's noble battle against the mob, the struggles of Julie and Bob are unmistakably, if rather simplistically, those of good against evil.

Given the political exigencies of wartime propaganda, the symbolism of the film is unsurprisingly short on nuance. In one especially memorable scene, with Julie in a state of mental anguish over the diabolical machinations of the Ghost, Ulmer has Jack Greenhalgh's camera track in on what appears to be a miniature doll in a glass case—a handwritten card from her beloved Bob noticeably attached to it—an unintended reminder of the ghoulish embalmed corpses of *The Black Cat* with the threat of the Second World War now replacing the trauma of the Great War. When it comes to Hitler, Ulmer, together with scriptwriter Lytton, exploits the opportunity for asserting the putative gangster associations to Nazism (President Roosevelt, in a public address from early October 1941, famously spoke of Hitler and his henchmen as "a band of gangsters").[24] To do so in a 1940s American B movie, however, he had to employ an identifiable gangster argot or stylized speech harkening back to such pre-Code marvels as *Scarface* (1932) and *Little Caesar* (1931). When compared to the *Führer*, the Ghost, whose given middle name, as the script would have it, is "Caesar," and whose mannerisms recall the slick gunrunning gangster Cortez played in Michael Curtiz's *Mandalay* (1934), retorts: "That cheap punk, he's an amateur!"

Off the set Ulmer was deeply shaken by the war, which appears to have been both professionally and psychologically unsettling for him. In an untitled poem, signed and dated "on the 21st day of the Second World War" (i.e., in late September 1939), he writes:

When man,
created in the image of the maker
sallow and barberously primevil [*sic*]
sulks in the darkness
of his hatred . . .
And
that slow running blood
coagulates on the shiny metal
covering that misled land
forming a pattern
a design
a Swastika—
let him
that sallow barberously primevil
in that darkness
be conscious of that
eternal truth
He who sits and slinks in
the morass of the darkness of
destruction
may reach into the light
drag many down into his swampy ground

attempting to use them
as stepping stones into that
light.

As in the case of his unpublished novel "Beyond the Boundary," composed in Hollywood some four years earlier, the poem is not important so much as a literary document—with its many stylistic and syntactical peculiarities—as it is a testimony to the sensibility of its author. The core idea, not to mention its cinematic images, might be viewed as the germ of Ulmer's anti-Nazi efforts at PRC, in particular in such films as *Tomorrow We Live* (and, even if not attributable to Ulmer alone, in *Hitler's Madman*). He ends the poem with the following lines, returning to the chosen leitmotif:

And thus that
sallow and barberously
primevil man in hatred
sinks back
and must remain
in that Dante-esque inferno
of world historical despicability
which hatred
thus deserves.[25]

This sentiment is echoed in the morally righteous words of Lt. Bob Lord, who admonishes the Ghost: "Mad dogs die of their own venom."

In a similar vein the synopsis of *Tomorrow We Live* that Ulmer, Fromkess, and Nebenzal submitted for review by the Production Code Administration in June 1942, a historical document that is impossible to read today without recognizing the allusions to Nazi Germany and to such diplomatic blunders as the Hitler-Stalin pact, begins with the following statement: "You cannot do business with a killer, you cannot appease a madman." Upon submission, the script bore the title "The Time Has Come," evoking more transparently its proper place within the context of Hollywood's contribution to the Allied propaganda machinery and America's late entry into the war.[26] "During the Second World War, Dad refused to have any German spoken around him," recalls Arianné Ulmer. "He only counted in German when we played piano together or when he lost his temper and was cursing at me."[27] By 1942, Hollywood had been enlisted in the fight against the Nazis. German and Austrian émigré film directors were among the first to lend a hand: Lubitsch released his acerbic *To Be or Not to Be* in 1942; Billy Wilder his *Five Graves to Cairo* in summer 1943; and Fritz Lang, in unharmonious collaboration with Bertolt Brecht, his *Hangmen Also Die!* in spring of that same year. The industry celebrities like Viennese-born Hedy Lamarr, who just a few years later would star in *The Strange Woman,* collected substantial donations, purportedly $25,000 per kiss, for war bonds, while studio bosses continued to think up ways to create industry product that would both help the cause and turn a profit.[28] Ulmer's *Tomorrow We Live* was made the same summer in which such big-budget war pictures as Michael Curtiz's *Casablanca* (1942) and Herman Shumlin's *Watch on the Rhine* (1943) were also in production.

Yet far different from the movies being made at Warner Bros. and other top studios, Ulmer's directorial debut at PRC would neither earn him the accolades nor the wide review attention. If the industry trade press was any indication of the film's potential appeal, it was essentially dead on arrival. As the unnamed critic for *Daily Variety* wrote in late September 1942, the week before the film's release: "Because of the times and conditions alone this unbelievable tale of gangsterism and Freudism [*sic*] on the plains will suffer from audience apathy. Morbid theme is not what is wanted these days, particularly when it is carried to the extreme. And in this entry it goes beyond that, being an altogether dreary and depressing tale of folks who are sick at heart and mind, who never let you forget it, and who will finally get audiences down with it, too. That's not entertainment for any but psychos. Strictly double-bill fodder if not just a flopper."[29] Regardless of its nonexistent production values, from today's standpoint, the idea that a film of this kind should be a downer for audiences may seem absurd. Its sole purpose, as it were, was to awaken viewers from their complacency and to inspire them to support the great battle against tyranny. Sure, the story line is schmaltzy, the acting wooden, and the camera work negligible. But it seems darkly ironic that the *Variety* reviewer would forecast audience apathy, when that's exactly what Ulmer, Nebenzal, and Fromkess were attempting to combat. "How slow we are to learn," they poignantly wrote in their synopsis.

The most fundamental difference between films made for Hollywood's major studios and those made for the Bs was, as the name Poverty Row suggests, the capital—money that would pay for, among other things, A-class actors, expensive technical support, and ultimately the publicity machine that would ensure proper press coverage. The mantra on Poverty Row was "fast and cheap," and the PRC films stuck to that. Once a title was selected, often without a proper script or story idea, and a budget made, the shooting soon followed. According to Ulmer, he had "a perfect technique worked out: no set of mine existed in these pictures where there was not one wall without any paintings, without anything, just a plain wall in gray. I shot my master scene, but left close-ups for the last day: they would play against that one flat, blank wall" (B 573). The pressures were such that given the scarcity of film stock ("fifteen thousand feet for a feature," in his recollection), the shooting ratio was as small as two to one. This prompted Ulmer to incorporate as much stock footage as possible. Near the start of *Tomorrow We Live,* for example, there is a thirty-second sequence of discontinuous exterior shots—galloping horses, a couple of cowboys herding sheep, a horse-drawn carriage—that comes across as a medley of outtakes from Ulmer's B western *Thunder over Texas;* from one of his late TB shorts, *Another to Conquer,* filmed on the Navajo reservation; and perhaps a shot or two borrowed from *Green Fields* or *The Light Ahead.* Whatever their true derivation, they spare him the need, let alone the cost, of shooting these scenes and help convey a little extra local flair, a quick flash of naturalism that's otherwise completely absent (they are among the very few exterior shots).

If we think of the film, as we might think of other Ulmer cheapies made at PRC, as a tacit meditation on the material conditions of the production—the total production costs came in at under $25,000, a paltry sum even by B-picture standards—and on Ulmer's marginal status working at a Poverty Row studio, then such declarations by the Ghost as "I'm a desert exile!" have greater relevance to the director sweating it out in the lower trenches of Gower Gulch. (Several decades later, in his 1984 film, *Paris, Texas,* Wim Wenders opted to cast aging German filmmaker Bernard Wicki, famous for his West German anti-war film *Die Brücke* [*The Bridge,* 1959], as a desert exile named, with wicked irony, Dr. Ulmer.) For many of the German-speaking refugees who relocated to Southern California during the war, Hollywood represented something of a wasteland—a corrosive, desiccated, money-obsessed culture industry. "Scratch it a bit," remarked Brecht, who arrived in San Pedro, California, in July 1941 and whose relationship to the dream factory was notoriously fraught, "and the desert comes through."[30] In a letter to Siegfried Kracauer, then living in New York, the recent Hollywood transplant cinematographer Eugen Schüfftan wrote in January 1942: "It's 300% worse than we imagined it."[31] While Ulmer may not have been quite as overtly critical as some of his compatriots, he remained suspicious of the business throughout the 1940s, even up to his final years—as he once memorably quipped, "I did not want to be ground up in the Hollywood hash machine" (B 592). That same suspicion comes across in many of his films from the period.

FAST AND CHEAP

In 1943 alone, working with Fromkess and Dutch-born producer Peter R. Van Duinen, Ulmer directed a Damon Runyon–inspired comedy, *My Son, the Hero,* a farce whose main conceit is being able to project wealth where there is none; a barebones reworking of Liontine Sagan's Weimar-era *Mädchen in Uniform* in an American B-exploitation mold, *Girls in Chains;* the South Seas drama *Isle of Forgotten Sins* ("a hold-over" from Murnau's *Tabu,* as Ulmer called it), whose tangled plot hinges on gaining possession of $3 million in stolen gold; and, sans Van Duinen, the frothy musical drama *Jive Junction,* which pits commercial, trend-driven jive against classical music of the Old World. Each of these films retains a notable degree of self-consciousness, an awareness of the B movie's limits and possibilities, that occasionally gives Ulmer the upper hand when wrestling with flimsy scripts (most of which he helped cowrite or rewrite) and facing the perennial need to work at breakneck speed with only minimal support.

Equally important, like *Tomorrow We Live,* the four features from 1943 emerged at a time when the war was becoming more deeply ingrained in the American psyche, when patriotism was on the rise, and when Hollywood's output bore greater responsibility with respect to the Allied effort. Rather fittingly, during this same phase, Ulmer cowrote with Doris Malloy the South Pacific propaganda film *Corregidor* (1943), assisted Sirk on his anti-Nazi picture *Hitler's Madman,* and directed a couple of instructional shorts, "Hymns from Home," as they were then known, for the U.S. Air Force's Turbosupercharger series: *Master of the Skies* and *Flight Operation.* By the time the *New York Times* ran a joint review of *Hitler's Madman* and *Watch on the Rhine,* in late August 1943, alongside the review appeared a small announcement that renowned émigrés Kurt Weill and Otto Preminger had taken the oath of citizenship in New York City the day before. There is no notice of Ulmer, but he too had become a naturalized U.S. citizen, in an unpublicized ceremony in Los Angeles two weeks earlier, and his deepening loyalties to his new home continued to reach articulation in his assorted projects of the period.[32]

The war backdrop of *My Son, the Hero*—a film that was thrown together on the lot at PRC in six days in early December 1942—though more comical than propagandistic, informs the film's overall mood and propels its story line. Fast-talking Hollywood con man Big-Time Morgan (Roscoe Karns, a character actor who had earned a name for himself a decade before in Capra's *It Happened One Night*) receives a telegram that his beloved son Michael (Joseph Allen Jr.), a decorated army correspondent serving in the Pacific, is returning home for a visit. We learn that Big-Time, a habitual gambler and crooked fight manager who shares a flophouse room with dimwitted boxer Kid Slug Rosenthal (Maxie Rosenbloom) and Italian wise guy Tony (Luis Alberni), has long deceived his son into thinking that he's "rolling in dough." The sudden announcement of Michael's return sends him scurrying to cook up a scheme. He joins forces with Kid Slug's equally fast-talking and unscrupulous ex-wife, Gerty (Patsy Kelly), who secures a Beverly Hills mansion on loan and enlists the others as bit players in their elaborate ruse. Much of the comedy stems from the characters' inability to carry off their new roles, enacted in the play-within-a-play *Lady for a Day* farce, as members of the wealthy elite. Gerty stumbles as Big-Time's nouveau riche wife—his ex-wife Cynthia (Joan Blair), a Philadelphia socialite, together with the true mansion owner's Vassar-educated daughter Linda (Carol Hughes), drop in unexpectedly and threaten to blow their cover—while calling in a nightclub cigarette girl named Nancy (Lois Collier) to pose as her daughter. When Tony, who hams it up as the operatic majordomo, greets Nancy with "Welcome to our family of phonies," he not only divulges the prime element of disguise that undergirds the entire film but also hints at the fact that, on a more implicit level, what we really have is a B-picture cast pretending to be the stars of a top biller.

Viewers of *American Matchmaker,* Ulmer's previous foray into comedy, will recognize a similar proclivity for social farce and for playing up the great drama of cultural assimilation. On a very rudimentary level, *My Son, the Hero* is all about passing and the bonds of class and ethnic difference. Gerty's unalloyed Brooklynese and habitual reliance on street slang ("Who bounced for that?" she asks Cynthia, when admiring her diamond ring), despite her aristocratic garb, serves as a constant reminder of her scrappy origins, while Kid Slug pockets the silverware, sleeps in the bathtub, and never misses an opportunity to exude oafishness ("I may be a dope," he admits, "but I ain't stupid!"). In collaboration with scriptwriter Doris Malloy, Ulmer laces the dialogue with a number of sardonic jibes rooted in the wartime climate. "Look, Big-Time," remarks Kid Slug, when complaining about sharing a bed with Tony, "why must we sleep with these enemy aliens?" (Ulmer's own status during the production, months before his naturalization, was indeed the same.) Tony tartly replies: "I come here in this country 1929 with [Italian heavyweight champion] Primo Carnera. I *stay* in this country! I *love* America! I *hate* Benny Deluxe [Benito Mussolini]!"

As with *Tomorrow We Live,* there are several key moments in the film, similarly lacking in aesthetic prowess, when the poverty of the production bleeds into the narrative. When Big-Time's scheme starts to unravel, about two-thirds of the way in, Kid Slug stares straight at the camera, operated by PRC regulars Robert Cline and Jack Greenhalgh, and says, "What a screwy picture!" A question that critic David Thomson raises in reference to the protagonists of *Detour* seems equally apt here: "Were these actors, hoping for careers, or derelicts resolved to treat the idea of a movie with contempt?"[33] All that is performed in *My Son* is as artificial and deceptive as Kid Slug's own poorly played knockout in the film's opening sequence. "The whole thing has been put together by mirrors," announces Big-Time, perhaps more damningly than he knows, in the film's closing moments, "and anyone could kick it down." Somewhat surprisingly, the limited press attention the film received wasn't quite as discouraging as that for *Tomorrow We Live.* "Picture is filled with laughs," wrote a charitable critic for *Daily Variety.* "Direction which is well-sustained is in the hands of Edgar G. Ulmer, with screenplay his and Doris Malloy's."[34]

Of Ulmer's other films directed for PRC that same year, *Girls in Chains* is the rawest of the lot. A fly-by-night prison drama made during the first days of February 1943, it had a budget under $28,000, or roughly the same amount allotted to *My Son, the Hero.* Yet in comparison with *My Son* and other films made that same year, it has a grittier, more primitive feel to it, more like Ulmer's Canadian quota quickie *From Nine to Nine* or even some of the Weimar-era productions with which he identified. Ulmer furnished the story, which he purportedly lifted from the tabloids ("there was some political graft in one of the women's jails") and whose mock headlines are cited in a montage sequence during the final minute of the film. As he did with other PRC productions, he invented the sensationalized title, or what he thought of as the piece that "*made* the damned thing" (B 594), well in advance of composing the script (PRC would soon follow up with *Delinquent Daughters*). Thematically, it's as if Ulmer attempts a fusion between *Mädchen in Uniform,* Sagan's 1931 film set in an authoritarian girls' reform school, which similarly follows the struggles of a single benevolent teacher in pursuit of fairness and decency, and another generic 1940s morality tale of mobsters and racketeering.

The film opens on the big-city streets—its painted skyline, like that of *Moon over Harlem*, provides the setting for the credit sequence and later returns, at the close of the film, as the backdrop for an incommensurately stylized noir shoot-out scene—with a stock shot of traffic intercut with another shot of a car careening down a curvy night-lit highway. It's a matter of seconds before we're inside the car of mafia boss Johnny Moon (Allan Byron), shrouded in thick fog in place of rear projection, as he's about to make a hit. The ensuing dialogue between Johnny and his driver, Pinkhead (Sidney Melton), never moves beyond cliché. ("You sure can pick dames, Johnny!" meets its match in "Why not? I got a whole town to pick from.") Ulmer quickly cuts to a montage of shots of spinning axles at a printing press, a lone worker occupying the foreground, and the bold headlines "Johnny Moon's Fate in Jury's Hands" gracing the front page. He then dissolves from a photo of Moon tucked underneath the newspaper headline to the mobster seated in a courtroom, fidgeting nervously with a pen as he awaits the verdict on his latest murder rap. Despite the overwhelming evidence pointing at Moon's guilt, he is found not guilty.

Much like *Tomorrow We Live,* and *Moon over Harlem* before it, there must be someone who stands up to corruption, someone who follows the straight and narrow. That person is Helen Martin (Arline Judge), a devoted schoolteacher with a bird's nest–style pompadour and a Nancy Drew gift for sleuthing, whose sister is married to Moon and who loses her job at a public school as a result of her presumed ties to the mobster. Helen urges her sister, Jean (Patricia Knox), to "get out before it's too late," but like Minnie in *Moon over Harlem,* Jean remains a loyal moll. With the support of do-gooder cop Frank Donovan (Roger Clark), Helen eventually agrees to take a position at the county correction school in the hope of preventing girls from following the same path as her sister. Yet, like all other branches of municipal life, the oversight of the school is in cahoots with the gangsters. The deputy director, Mrs. Peters (Dorothy Burgess), carries herself like the proto-Nazi headmistress in *Mädchen,* contriving a faint Germanic accent and insisting that the girls of the reformatory are irredeemable. Helen infiltrates the correctional system and, like the goodhearted Fräulein Bernburg of *Mädchen,* inspires rebellion among the girls. She rebuffs Johnny Moon's overtures, uncovering his crew of chiselers and turning his own mistress against him. "What we need is a Paul Revere," announces the drunken whistle-blower (played by Emmett Lynn, with the same overblown pathos he showed in his performance as Pop Bronson in *Tomorrow We Live*), "to ride through the world like a hurricane." Detective Donovan and Helen together serve that role, dismantling Moon's vast network, exposing him as a brutal murderer, and restoring faith in justice.

What makes *Girls in Chains* so raw, so threadbare, is its rough-hewn composition and the odd mix of bland studio photography with a wild array of visible backdrops and stock shots. This aspect is apparent from the opening sequence through the various transitions (in which Ulmer intercuts, among others, an exterior stock shot of the Pantages Theater opposite the Hollywood Plaza Hotel) up to the rather spectacular final murder scene. "Indeed, perhaps the most audacious use ever of stock footage," note Todd McCarthy and Charles Flynn in their *Kings of the Bs,* "occurs in Ulmer's *Girls in Chains* (1943, PRC), a classic women's prison picture, incidentally. A murder scene supposedly takes place at night atop a dam. The actors involved play the scene in medium shot, with appropriately dim lighting, on a minimal set representing a cat-walk atop the dam. This scene is *intercut* with stock footage of Hoover Dam, shot at high noon (take that Alain Resnais)!"[35] Though these imperfections were presumably not lost on audiences ("Picture lacks spectacular attributes and dialog is stilted," remarked the critic for *Daily Variety*), the film did rather well at the box office, where it traded on its sensationalized title.[36] "The little *Girls in Chains* was such a gigantic money success," recalled Ulmer, "that we could have bought the PRC studio" (B 593).

As with the other cheapies made for the studio, there is arguably a deeper element of self-consciousness that demands our attention. Somewhat akin to J. Hoberman's discussion of Oscar Micheaux in his influential essay "Bad Movies," we might think of Ulmer's many obvi-ous imperfections—his frequent recycling of inconsonant footage and casting a blind eye to various continuity blunders, blown lines and botched editing—as part of a severely constrained, minimalist art-istry.[37] Other critics, examining the PRC films, have suggested a similar line of inquiry. "*Girls in Chains,*" notes Bret Wood in his reappraisal of the director, "a seemingly ordinary exploitation picture patterned after Warner Bros. social problem/prison films (specifically Archie Mayo's *The Mayor of Hell* and Howard Bretherton and William Keighley's *Ladies They Talk About*), shines in a brighter light if one eyes the plot as a self-referential spin on the B-movie."[38] In other words, as with *My Son, the Hero,* there is an implicit invitation to take Wood's lead, or even Hoberman's, and think of the film as another sly commentary on the act of producing such dross. "Thus the plight of Helen," Wood continues, "is not that she's caught between the bureaucracy of the prison and the criminality of the street, but that she's trapped within a B-movie. Lost in a universe of stock footage and stock characters, the beleaguered protagonist navigates this artificial movie universe to which she doesn't belong."[39]

Commanding a budget of nearly three times that of *Girls in Chains,* and more than double the number of days in production, *Isle of Forgotten Sins* represents a small step forward for Ulmer, who in addition to directing also supplied the original story. The idea is said to have come from nothing more than a chance to borrow palm trees used in John Ford's adventure film *The Hurricane,* made for Samuel Goldwyn in 1937. Bob Baker, at the time a nineteen-year-old puppeteer, worked with Ulmer on the miniature diver used in the film and went on to help design the marionettes used on *Bluebeard* a year later. He had a cousin who was the special effects man on *Hurricane,* and through him they were able to borrow the palm trees from MGM. "I hate to tell you something," Baker later recounted; "a lot of the films at PRC . . . this way was how a lot of them came about."[40] Baker was largely responsible for the shots of the puppet scuba diver that Ulmer, with cameraman Ira Morgan, shot inside a fish tank toward the beginning of April 1943. "We had to be careful, because we had to move slowly; otherwise it didn't look real." Realism, admittedly, is not the film's strong suit. It's hard today not to scoff at the underwater shots ("we were blowing bubbles down the line," explains Baker, "so that it looked like the guy was having oxygen in the old deep sea diver"), with the puppet—more GI Joe than Jacques Cousteau—bobbing around in what is to be taken for seaweed and making the kind of jerky movements that only a stiff puppet's body would make.

The plot of the film was no less waterlogged. Onetime Warner Bros. contract player Gale Sondergaard, who starred opposite Paul Muni and Joseph Schildkraut in William Dieterle's *Life of Emile Zola* (1937), is cast as the madam of a South Seas brothel—or what, for the sake of the Production Code, had to be presented as a female-run "saloon and gambling house"—called the "Isle of Forgotten Sins," where sailors drop by for entertainment and distraction. As the business-minded Marge Williams, Sondergaard instructs her mermaid-like harem of women, dolled up in Polynesian dresses and flowers in their ears, to bring in money from the newly arrived ships; they're told to lure their men to the roulette table, but also warned against any "rough stuff."

Unsurprisingly, the casino attracts plenty of criminally dubious characters. First, there are a couple of deep-sea-diving toughs, Jack Burke (Frank Fenton) and Mike Clancy (John Carradine), pirates in the guise of sailors (in the story synopsis, their ship is known as *The Vulture*). Jack and Mike share the same romantic interest in Marge and express their love for her with their fists in several drawn-out, tedious brawl scenes. Then there's a wide-grinning, lecherous plantation owner with a "banshee laugh" called Carruthers, a.k.a., Captain Krogan (Sidney Toler, of Charlie Chan fame), who deceitfully lures the divers with the promise of sunken treasure buried at the bottom of the sea intercepting it as soon as they complete their dive. Krogan's sidekick, the hilariously named Johnny Pacific, played by Russian-born Rick Vallin (*né* Eric George Efron), serves as a displaced piano prodigy who performs a couple of concertos from Old Europe for the nightclub audience— anticipating the handiwork of Al Roberts in *Detour*—but who also has designs on the buried treasure and on Krogan's native paramour, Luana (Veda Ann Borg). Finally, there's a gun-toting vamp named Olga (Betty Amann, who played the lead femme fatale, in 1929 Berlin, in Joe May's *Asphalt*), whose plucky personality and quick trigger finger set her apart from the other girls, putting her at the center of a murder at the shady nightclub near the start of the film and later allowing her the chance for a repeat performance when the pot of gold is up for grabs.

Beyond the mildly seductive musical numbers, the synchronized nocturnal swimming and light murder suspense, *Isle of Forgotten Sins* is just another jaundiced Ulmerian universe of liars, double-crossers, and cheats. Perhaps its most redeeming feature, one that had more lasting value for the director, was that it allowed Ulmer to establish a close working relationship with John Carradine ("a person I could hang on to," as he later told Bogdanovich). Carradine was a classically trained actor who shared with Ulmer a passion for art and theater—known to recite Shakespeare late night at the Hollywood Bowl, later touring with his own company—and who showed potential for greater performances than the one to which he was limited in *Isle* (he had played a bit part in *The Black Cat*, as an organist sitting with his back to the camera, and in early summer 1944 would play the title role in *Bluebeard*). In the Ulmer family lore Carradine figured with considerable prominence. He was sometimes teasingly referred to as "The Man Who Came to Dinner," as he and his first son, Jack (later known as actor David

Carradine), moved in with the Ulmers on Kings Road for almost two months while he was dodging alimony payments to his first wife. He later fell in love with Sonia Sorel, who would become his second wife, on the set of *Bluebeard* and married her in a Shakespeare-themed wedding in an Episcopal church on Wilshire, with the entire Ulmer family in the wedding party. He even saved young Arianné from drowning in the swimming pool at the fabled Garden of Allah on Sunset Boulevard, where Carradine kept an apartment.[41] In *Isle,* the mustachioed, pipe-smoking Carradine, photographed in striped fisherman shirt and white sailor slacks, offers a few hints of dashing charisma but otherwise has his arms tied as he's aptly portrayed in the first shot introducing him in the film.

Showing themselves to be true cinematic bottom-feeders, PRC films attempted to capitalize on trends and drive audiences to the theaters by adopting titles or ideas that had already demonstrated robust currency. Ulmer explains, for instance, how when Billy Wilder's *Double Indemnity* became a colossal hit at Paramount, he proposed doing *Single Indemnity* at PRC—an idea that was eventually reworked by Raymond L. Schrock, who cowrote *Isle of Forgotten Sins* with Ulmer, and released as the independent Martin Mooney production *Blonde Ice* in 1948 (B 595). In the case of *Isle* we likewise see how, based on the spectacular success of a film like *Casablanca,* Ulmer arrived at the core idea he supplied to Van Duinen and Fromkess in late March 1943, just months after Curtiz's film had made a huge splash. Although Ulmer makes no mention of the Warner Bros. hit in any of his interviews, the nightclub setting can readily be taken for a South Seas variation of Rick's Cafe, with Marge as a kind of hard-boiled female Rick Blaine.[42] The cabaret numbers, the exotic battleground setting (a local magistrate and other naval officers frequent the "Isle of Forgotten Sins"), and the heavy dose of romantic intrigue were presumably thought of as surefire commercial elements that Ulmer could replicate in his low-budget production.

Despite the avowed connection between *Tabu* and *Isle of Forgotten Sins* there is none of the lyricism, fluid camera movement, visual dynamism, or sensuality that one finds in Murnau's film. Visually speaking, one of the few notable scenes comes right at the start, with Ira Morgan's mobile camera snaking through the brothel corridor and directing our gaze at the rooms occupied by Marge's sleeping maidens—not quite the dazzling opener of *The Last Laugh* but nonetheless showing faint signs of indebtedness to Ulmer's mentor. This sequence alone, however, does not make up for the film's sluggish pace and general lack of coherence.

An acid-tongued critic for the *Hollywood Reporter,* in an unambigu-ously titled review "'Forgotten Sins' Better Forgotten," lambasted the film as "an unconscious burlesque of South Sea Island dramas."[43] Ulmer himself may have hoped to forget it, like a failed romance, though his final film to round out the year at the Poverty Row studio was not much of an improvement.

"I had to compromise to keep PRC in business," he later explained. "Now I admit to myself that I was somehow schizophrenic in making pictures. On one hand, I was absolutely concerned with box office and on the other I was trying to create art and decency, with a style. I could not completely get out of the commercial, though I knew it limited me. There was no real reason for me to make *Jive Junction,* except that the picture had to be made, and had to be done quickly, and we couldn't jeopardize a penny."[44] The war-themed musical *Jive Junction* was made for less than $50,000 in the final days of September 1943 and to some extent picks up where *Isle of Forgotten Sins* leaves off. The film stars former matinee idol Dickie Moore as child prodigy Peter Crane, a classically trained pianist who becomes the leader of the Clinton High School swing band—almost like an extended flashback to Johnny Pacific's former life—with the hope of entertaining the troops and boosting army morale.

In the film's first seconds, following an artfully designed credit sequence with painted dancers and big-band tunes resonating in the background, the iris of Ira Morgan's camera opens up on a cluttered music store, as much a shrine as a place of commerce, and follows Gerra Young while she dusts off memorabilia and sings "In a Little Music Shop" (the panning camera jerks a bit at one point, and what appears to be Morgan's shadow is detectable in the foreground). This is but one of the film's many popular jazz numbers, composed by Erdody with Lew Porter, introducing us to the central conflict of the film: the face-off between classical music and jive, or, as Young sings it for us, "Mendels-sohn, Bach, and Beethoven must be turning in their grave." On Peter's first day of school at Pasadena's Clinton High, having just moved from New York, where he studied at a music conservatory under the aegis of Viennese maestro Dr. Feher (Frederick Feher, *né* Friedrich Weiss-Féher, who at Moore's age had costarred in *The Cabinet of Dr. Caligari*), he's an outsider in speech, dress, and manners, stilted and out of touch with the Southern California hepcats in his midst.

When Peter steps in to help teach a music lesson, in an early scene in the film, one of the onlooking schoolgirls responds to his bossy directives: "Who does he think he is? Toscanini?!" Soon after, he narrowly eludes a schoolyard brawl. "I'm a musician," he responds to a taunting bully, reiterating the same alleged anxieties of Robert Schumann; "my hands are my future."[45] In truth, the real Dickie Moore—who would soon after play the deaf-mute in Jacques Tourneur's *Out of the Past* (1947)—could not play piano and had to fake it. "I remember it was total horror," he recalled in a recent interview. "Maybe the most uncomfortable experience of my entire career. I felt terribly self-conscious." As for the director, Moore suggested, despite his "bombastic" accent, "Ulmer was very pleasant. He tried to make me feel as comfortable as anyone could."[46] Moore appears in several dramatic sequences at the piano, usually shot from the chest up, moving his upper body ever so gently, occasionally lifting his right hand or not touching the keys at all, and looking vaguely confident as he plays on. (Two years later, in *Detour*, Tom Neal faced the same task, while the close-ups of his supposed virtuoso hands banging the keys in a Brahms-to-boogie-woogie medley belong to none other than Erdody.)[47] Both Ulmer and the Berlin-educated Erdody, closest of friends during the PRC years, held the European classical composers in high esteem; they often conducted the studio musicians together, and they made their selections in tandem, with Ulmer having the final say.[48] "I think Brahms and Mozart were his favorites," recalls Shirley Ulmer of her husband. "Schubert and Schumann—he loved all of them. He loved Bruckner and Mahler, too. And Tchaikovsky."[49] Ulmer is said to have kept among his prized possessions, next to the Franz Liszt baton he received from Erdody, a copy of the score to Wagner's *Parsifal,* with a 1928 personal inscription by eminent German conductor Wilhelm Furtwängler.[50]

Regardless of its musical emphasis, *Jive Junction* cannot be separated from the war context. As its story unfolds, Peter faces a profound loss: he returns from his first day at school to find his mother weeping, hunched over a Western Union telegram announcing that her husband, Major Robert Crane, "was killed in action in defense of his country in the South Pacific February 12, 1943." Although the film's script was crafted by a team of writers, including Malvin Wald, certain links to Ulmer's own life, such as the loss of a father on the battlefront, can be discerned. There is, for starters, the intense love of music, Ulmer's first passion, embodied in Peter. As the young boy mourns the death of his father, he awakens to the faint chords of a Bach cantata, only to have a neighbor play his father's most cherished selection—the second movement of Schumann's Piano Quintet in E-flat Major, op. 44, a composition Ulmer also used in *The Black Cat,* when Lugosi descends furtively into Karloff's dungeon—on a phonograph. Ulmer dissolves from this scene to a shot of Peter seated alone in an empty rehearsal room playing the same composition on the piano, Morgan's camera tracking backward to the doorway where Peter's classmate Claire Emerson (Tina Thayer) arrives. Claire urges Peter, who's been playing "that tune" every day since his father's passing, to stop brooding and take action, to show his patriotic duty by entertaining the troops. Despite his initial reservations ("I'm afraid that anything that I'd conduct would sound like a Schumann symphony"), Peter agrees to conduct an all-girl jive band.

To a large degree the film aims to mobilize the youth on the home front. In one illustrative scene, as Gerra Young sings "Mother Earth," we observe the high school kids picking oranges in unison. The sun-dappled exterior shots that Ulmer appropriates to punctuate this sequence—vast fields, rolling hills, a working plow, and a few billowy clouds, alternating long shots with close-ups—look more like scenes taken from *Green Fields* or Pare Lorentz's *The Plow That Broke the Plains* (1936) than the citrus farms they're meant to evoke. Yet the collectivist spirit, echoed in the song "Just Do Your Share," is captured once more as the high school students clean up a barn that they transform into the Jive Junction dance club. The banner hanging outside the barn-turned-juke-joint makes their mission plain: "Servicemen Welcome . . . and How!" The corny story line has Peter and band members, now all male, enter a contest in which they play their own original patriotic compositions, with the winner getting a tour of the army camps. When they suddenly lose access to the barn, the teen musicians head to the Hollywood Bowl to meet with Peter's former mentor, Dr. Feher, who happens to be conducting Bach, Vivaldi, and Verdi. The maestro saves the day, loaning his orchestra's instruments and learning to appreciate the latest craze ("I'm getting jivey in my old age," he announces in accented English); as in other Ulmer productions for PRC, the path that music travels in *Jive Junction,* from rarified European to popular American, might be seen to reflect "allegories of a typical emigrant situation."[51] The winning composition, a choral number that blends elements of jazz and classical, is fittingly titled "We're Just In Between." Conducted by Peter with a solo given by Gerra Young—a musical bookend to her opening song—its refrain, "I'm just in between/will someone tell me where I fit in," gives the film an easy resolution, met with approval by the maestro and the contest judges.

Even if Ulmer himself may have preferred to regard *Jive Junction* as a compromise, a film he really didn't need to do or perhaps shouldn't have done, the industry trade papers saw things differently. The *Hollywood Reporter* ran its review under the effusive headline "PRC's 'Jive Junction' Has Pep, Youth, Topical Value." The review's opening sentence, modulating the idiom used in the film, declares: "Your audiences do not have to be cats to dig entertainment from 'Jive Junction.'" The same critic goes on to praise Ulmer's "imaginatively staged" sequence in which Gerra Young sings her "Mother Earth" number, asserting finally, "Ulmer directs with pleasing authority throughout, and there is an excellent job of musical direction by Erdody."[52]

A mere week after the *Reporter* ran its laudatory review, when Ulmer was busy on loan-out to Raphael G. Wolff Studios, directing a couple of training shorts for the U.S. Air Force, he received less fortunate news. His mother, Henriette, then living in San Francisco with her American husband, Karl Edwards, a man she met on the ship to the United States in the late 1920s, had died of heart failure; she was sixty-one years old. Always fraught, Ulmer's relationship with his mother never quite overcame the deep rift that set in during the First World War, when she sent him and his siblings to live in foster care in Sweden. Known for her narcissism, for her mood swings, and for harboring dark secrets—young Edgar had been stunned to discover her with a new man when he returned to Vienna in 1919, and much later, as Henriette Edwards, she had kept her Jewish identity from her husband, who only learned of it posthumously when finding Siegfried Ulmer's prayer shawl and yarmulke among her possessions—Henriette abandoned her two teenage daughters, after their transatlantic passage, and ran off with Edwards to California. Ulmer's sisters, Karola and Elly, remained in New York, both marrying members of the Hakoah Wien Jewish soccer club they had met on the ship to America; the two sisters, who were still in their late teens when their mother took off for the West Coast, both worked for a time as waitresses at Schrafft's lunchroom in Manhattan to keep themselves afloat.[53] "Edgar adored and hated his mother," remarks his daughter Arianné, "who left him a terrible letter on her passing and the only item of inheritance was a down pillow she sent for him. He always slept on this pillow for the remainder of his life."[54] Henriette was buried in Ferncliff Cemetery in New York's Westchester County near the home of Edgar's sisters. All four siblings were said to have been in attendance. Edgar, however, was immediately back at work, burying the past, or repressing it, while working on his next round of films.

SHADOWS OF WEIMAR, SHADOWS OF NOIR

When trying to rationalize some of the choices he made over the years, in particular with a film like *Jive Junction,* Ulmer remarked: "I have nothing against commercialism, but it cannot outweigh the creative urge" (B 570). In his attempt to balance these two seemingly irreconcilable aims, he often struggled. Explaining in retrospect which of his films made for PRC mattered to him as a director, he suggested that one could often recognize this by the cinematographer he chose to work with. In other words, with the single exception of *Detour,* those films featuring the German-born cameraman Eugen Schüfftan, who made *People on Sunday* with Ulmer and company in Berlin a decade and a half earlier, were the ones that allowed him to explore that "creative urge" more fully; they were, he insisted, his "serious pictures" (B 594). Having fled to France after Hitler's ascent, working on such films as Max Ophüls's Goethe adaptation *Le roman de Werther* (produced by Seymour Nebenzal's Nero-Film in 1938), Schüfftan narrowly escaped Nazi-occupied Europe. He arrived in America on one of the last ships to leave the Port of Lisbon for New York in late spring 1941. By that point he was known not only for the special effects he pioneered during the Weimar years—for the so-called Schüfftan Process, manipulating mirrors and miniatures to convey an illusion of enormous scale, used in *Metropolis*—but also for a deeply refined, painterly approach to shadow and light.

"I represent a special kind of camerawork," Schüfftan wrote (in German) to émigré agent Paul Kohner in late June 1941, shortly before leaving New York for Hollywood. "I try to create the character of a scene with the image, to support the technical work of others in a visual manner, and visually to develop individual scenes with strength."[55] Although he quickly made his way to California, he was unable to join the professional union, the American Society of Cinematographers, and thus had to work mostly in an uncredited capacity—sometimes listed as technical director, production designer, or production supervisor. At PRC he started with *Hitler's Madman,* in 1943, and continued in collaboration with Ulmer over the next couple of years on *Bluebeard, Strange Illusion, Club Havana,* and *The Wife of Monte Cristo.* (Schüfftan would gain admission to the union in the state of New York a decade later, and for his magnificent location photography on Robert Rossen's *The Hustler* he would earn the 1961 Academy Award for Cinematography [Black-and-White].)[56] The first three films that Schüfftan made with Ulmer, all of them shot at PRC in 1944 and 1945, have a mysterious shadow-laden quality, stylized as they are with notable flourishes of chiaroscuro lighting à la German expressionism, and with various aspects of German silent cinema more generally, evidencing a style and sensibility that would later become known as film noir.

Beginning with *Bluebeard,* Ulmer's cinematic mash-up of *Faust,* Jack the Ripper, and the nineteenth-century French folktale by Charles Perrault from which it takes its title, Schüfftan worked his magic helping to project an atmospheric Paris of the Second Empire in turmoil over a serial killer on the loose. Reminiscent both in theme and setting of Fritz Lang's *M,* the film opens with the sound of a church bell (in lieu of the gong employed by Lang), Schüfftan's camera tracking slightly outward on the painted backdrop of Notre Dame and other buildings lining the Seine, lit for night, then cutting and dollying in on the shimmering water below, a female body floating into the frame and ultimately being hoisted onto a rowboat by two gendarmes. This visual prologue immediately dissolves to the gendarmes posting a wall placard, again like *M,* warning the citizens of Paris: "A murderer is in your midst! A criminal who strangles young women."

Referred to as "Bluebeard," the unknown murderer turns out to be puppeteer and frustrated painter Gaston Morel (John Carradine), photographed by Schüfftan in a string of poignant close-ups using low-key lighting to accentuate Carradine's chiseled features and to draw increasing attention to his mercurial eyes (the distorted focal point during the murders we witness). Morel is a hyperobsessive artist with a beaux arts education and a haunted past, presented late in the film in a hallucinatory flashback sequence—replete with Weimar-style canted angles, menacing shadows, silent nonnaturalistic acting, and forced perspective—in which we learn of his first love and the emotional scar that causes his compulsion to murder. He works with puppets as a means of breaking the cycle of strangling the women he paints. At an outdoor theater he stages several scenes from an English-language rendition of Charles Gounod's *Faust* opera, using marionettes for the characters of Faust, Mephistopheles, and Marguerite. This play-within-a-play allows Ulmer to frame the story of Bluebeard, and of serial killer Morel, as a Faustian allegory: with Morel as a stand-in for the overambitious Faust; Morel's duplicitous art dealer Lamarté (Ludwig Stössel, the Austrian refugee actor best known for his small comedic routine as Herr Leuchtag in *Casablanca*), a scheming Mephistopheles figure; and the dressmaker Lucille (Jean Parker, playing in a far more complex, challenging role than in *Tomorrow We Live*), a Marguerite-like muse and Morel's true love interest, the woman he hopes will help him to overcome his murderous impulses.[57]

The three-minute Faust sequence, placed near the start of the film, sets the parameters for the remaining story—the fiery finale onstage is replayed, following the flashback that Morel narrates to Lucille, with the Wellesian camera placed behind the fireplace—and also helps amplify the visual complexity to which Ulmer and Schüfftan aspire, not to mention the musical significance of Erdody's symphonic score. The scene pivots on Morel stepping away from the strings of his marionette for a moment and staring through a peephole at the audience; panning slightly to the left, we see Lucille standing next to her two sisters, then a quick reaction shot of Morel looking into the peephole, only his face illuminated in an otherwise completely black frame, then an amorous close-up of Lucille followed by another such reaction shot. "This approach, which illustrates Schüfftan's predilection for graphic visual effects," remarks Robert Müller, commenting on the film's self-reflexivity, "comes across as a circular aperture."[58] It is, moreover, just one of many aesthetic touches in the film that harken back to the era when Ulmer and Schüfftan first met in Berlin, and indeed further back to the years that first brought German expressionism to the screen. Near the end of the film, after strangling Lucille's sister Francine (Teala Loring) in a set-up, and exacting revenge on Lamarté, Morel escapes from the gendarmes through the Paris sewers. The elegant chiaroscuro lighting, oblique angles of the evocative set design, and Carradine's menacing silhouette recall Robert Wiene's touchstone of German expressionist cinema *The Cabinet of Dr. Caligari* (Figure 21).

On a personal level Ulmer seems to have harbored much sympathy for the obsessive artist Gaston Morel, and he poured all of his own obsessive energy into what he later called "a tremendously challenging picture" (B 595). He already had a long-standing interest in the Faust legend, going back to Goethe's tragic play, to Gounod's opera, and to Murnau's great cinematic adaptation in the mid-1920s. Moreover, the Faustian bargain, the selling of one's soul—or, in the case of Gaston Morel, one's art—to the devil, was something with which Ulmer could no doubt identify (as his 1941 letters from the Hollywood Plaza attest). Morel finds himself trapped, unable to break free of his pact with Lamarté, equally unable to fulfill his love for Lucille, and ultimately chased to his tragic demise in the Seine, a predicament that bespeaks the horrors of an artist searching in vain for salvation in Hollywood.

FIGURE 21. From Hitler to Caligari: John Carradine in a publicity still from *Bluebeard* (1944) bearing a striking resemblance to Robert Wiene's acclaimed Weimar production, *The Cabinet of Dr. Caligari* (1920). Photofest.

This moral bind can perhaps be paraphrased in a few caustic lines from fellow refugee Brecht's poem "Hollywood":

> Every day, to earn my daily bread
> I go to the market where lies are bought
> Hopefully
> I take my place among the sellers.[59]

The market-driven hope at PRC, irrespective of the Faust material, was that a film like *Bluebeard* would cash in on the Jack the Ripper trend set by 20th Century–Fox's *The Lodger* released earlier that year.[60]

By the time that principal photography for *Bluebeard* began, on the last day of May 1944, Ulmer had signed a one-year contract at PRC. Yet the genesis of this particular project lay a full decade earlier, when he was still at Universal and Schüfftan was still living in Paris. In April 1934 the *Hollywood Reporter* announced, prematurely as it turned out, that Ulmer was slated to direct the picture, "an elaborate production," for Universal.[61] As we now know, by that time Ulmer's romantic and professional indiscretions on and off the set of *The Black Cat* surfaced, and studio patriarch Carl Laemmle severed all ties to the director and exerted his powers to keep Ulmer at bay. Although a great champion of Ulmer, and in all other respects the true good cop to Laemmle's bad, Leon Fromkess was not keen on acquiring the project for PRC, especially when it came to the play-within-a-play *Faust* opera that Ulmer insisted was essential to the story. ("Now I know what you can do with deep sea divers and regular puppets," Ulmer told Bob Baker, in whom he confided his secret hope of filming the entire opera, "this [project] is *very* special.")[62] For Fromkess the *Faust* sequence was little more than "stuffy high-brow music and marionettes."[63] Yet on the question of classical music Fromkess proved just as mistaken as Laemmle had been before him.

Regarded as a prestige film for Fromkess and PRC, *Bluebeard* ultimately brought greater attention to the little studio, its head producer, and its star director. As the review in *Hollywood Reporter,* published under the banner headline "PRC 'Bluebeard' Excellent, Distinctive Class Film: Ulmer Mega Scores, Carradine Fine," summed it up:

> It has been the avowed and advertised purpose of PRC for some time to lift itself above the status of an organization devoted to the making of lower-budget films and strike out for a better trade by pouring into the market films with a "flexible budget," which means, of course, that cost is not the consideration as compared with quality. PRC has done this with "Bluebeard." It is the kind of picture any company, or any producer, would like to release. It is a class product from start to finish, with every opportunity to entertain, regardless of expense, utilized to the fullest. In comparison with other movies with the same premise, it is head and shoulders a superior. . . . Producer Leon Fromkess and his associate, Martin Mooney, have taken pains to see that no detail—in whatever department—was overlooked in making this film a sombre, gripping melodrama which moves toward its conclusion relentlessly. . . . Edgar Ulmer's direction is studied and exact. There is a gentleness and an understanding permeating the entire film that can be attributed to him.[64]

Unlike Ulmer's previous features made for PRC, *Bluebeard* had required a full nineteen days of shooting and bore production costs amounting to nearly $170,000.[65] Ulmer's stubborn persistence and deep attachment to the material—he purportedly beat out Chaplin, who later gave his own spin on the Bluebeard legend in *Monsieur Verdoux* (1947), for the title ("I think my picture was nicer," Ulmer offered unabashedly)—paid off in the end (B 596).

Buoyed by the success of *Bluebeard,* Ulmer's next feature for PRC, *Strange Illusion* (a cinematic paraphrase of *Hamlet*), was no less personal, no less ambitious. While still in New York, sometime in late December 1941, he had seen a production of Viennese playwright and composer Fritz Rotter's *Letters to Lucerne,* featuring the Berlin-born actress Grete Mosheim, during its short run at the Cort Theatre. Owing to his initial interest in the material, he convinced Fromkess to buy the rights. Yet the final script that veteran screenwriter Adele Comandini produced in the fall of 1944 had no resemblance to Rotter's three-act play (Ulmer insists that he and Fromkess later sold the rights back to Rotter). Far more transparent is the indebtedness to Shakespeare's renowned drama of murder, madness, and revenge—or at least to a Freudian interpretation of it, Oedipal tension and all. "I was fascinated at the time with psychoanalysis," Ulmer remarked, "and this story was about a father-son relationship" (B 596).

Ulmer wastes no time introducing his chief theme. The film's opening sequence is one long take of Paul Cartwright (Jimmy Lydon) walking toward the camera—on a thirty-foot treadmill that the director built for the scene—in a seeming trance, clouds of smoke swirling around him while he delivers a meditative voice-over narration amid the ominous sounds of Erdody's score: "I am Paul Cartwright. My father was Judge Albert Cartwright, once lieutenant governor of the state. He was killed two years ago in a mysterious accident. We were not only father and son, but friends. The *shock* of his violent death still haunts my mind, my nights are troubled by strange dreams." Against this oneiric backdrop, Ulmer cuts to additional ghostlike figures populating the same smoky frame, their disembodied voices now in conversation with Paul while his primal nightmare is reenacted amid faint violin chords: we witness Paul's mother, Virginia (Sally Eilers), announcing her happiness that Albert has finally returned to her newly incarnate, followed by Paul's adamant rejection of this shadowy apparition; we hear his impassioned plea for his sister, Dorothy (Jayne Hazard), to come to his aid, while she instead happily accepts their new ersatz father and the fancy bracelet that comes with him; we finally observe Paul replaying in his tormented mind the lurid images of his father's car being hit by an unstoppable train, the voice of his nameless, faceless successor rejoicing while a few bars of the father's favorite Schumann concerto—a holdover, perhaps, from *Jive Junction*—are played on the piano. The fever dream reaches its climax with Paul blurting out the symbol-laden catchwords: "My father! The train! You! Mother! Mother! Mother!" (Ulmer would later boast, in his 1961 *Cahiers du cinéma* interview with Luc Moullet and Bertrand Tavernier, that his film was fifteen years ahead of Hitch-cock's *Psycho*.)[66]

At the close of the film's prologue Paul awakens to the comforting hand of old family friend Dr. "Doc" Vincent (Regis Toomey, who would soon after play Bernie Ohls in Howard Hawks's *The Big Sleep*), a psychologist who has taken him on a fishing trip. Doc consoles Paul and then, dressed like a logger and armed with a tackle box, allows him to retell the dream on their way to the lake (*Strange Illusion* has by far the most location shooting of Ulmer's PRC films up to that date). Although Doc encourages Paul to forget about it, the connections between his dream and reality pile up to the point that he can no longer stop. When he receives a letter, one that his father has arranged to be sent from the office of his estate, Paul realizes he must return home. "It will be your responsibility," the letter states, "as the man of the family to protect your mother and Dorothy by being constantly vigilant of their associates. I have always guarded your mother, who is so much younger than I, for in my experience I have had ample opportunity to observe the cunning of unscrupulous imposters." As soon as he arrives home, he senses something is awry. The all-knowing black butler, Ben (George H. Reed), who later assists Paul in his investigation, informs him that his mother is spending time with a man named Brett Curtis (Warren William), the kind of man of whom Judge Cartwright would not approve. It turns out that Curtis is really Claude Barrington, or in *Hamlet* terms Claudius, who was responsible for the murder of Cartwright *père* and who, like Dollar Bill of *Moon over Harlem*, has an insatiable appetite for young daughters. Coupling elements of the psychological thriller with a noir gumshoe caper, *Strange Illusion* spends the rest of its time allowing Paul to use his wits and persistence to unmask the "imposter" ("the Romeo," as Paul first refers to him), saving his mother from disgrace and his sister from sexual molestation.[67]

In his dogged, quasi-pathological pursuit of the truth, Paul increasingly takes on the role of his father, wooing his mother (whom he calls "the princess"), professing his plan to finish writing his father's greatest work of criminology, and doing everything within his power to upend Curtis. After meeting Curtis in the Cartwright living room, standing beneath an oversized portrait of his father (shot from a slight tilt to emphasize its totemic weight), Paul becomes convinced—especially after seeing Dorothy show off her new bracelet and falling unconscious when he hears the Schumann concerto being played on the family piano—that his dream is actually occurring, almost like "a hyper-extended déjà vu."[68] A few scenes later, Paul retreats to his father's study, where the same portrait now looms large on the wall, and unlocks his filing cabinet; several bars from Schumann return as Paul opens the Claude Barrington file, a case his father had been pursuing before his death, reading aloud sordid details from the legal records while Schüfftan's omniscient camera surveys the room and slowly, inexorably directs our gaze back to the portrait.

As a means of cracking the case, Paul, who fittingly keeps a textbook in psychoanalysis on his desk, checks himself into a sanatorium run by Curtis's crony, the evil Professor Muhlbach (Charles Arnt), Barrington's co-conspirator in the murder of Paul's father. Working with Muhlbach at the darkly lit, labyrinthine clinic—the perfect spot for a little extra retro-expressionist lighting and set design—is the conniving nurse Miss Farber (Sonia Sorel, by then married to Carradine), the first to be captured by the police, in a scene visually overexposed by the beams of a flashlight, after Paul's premonition proves to be fact. Finally, Paul and his *Jive Junction*–like gang of wholesome friends succeed in thwarting Curtis's plan to sneak off with Dorothy to the family cottage for a romantic interlude.

The otherwise plot-heavy and comparatively long film, running close to an hour and a half, is interspersed with a number of visually taut scenes. Near the midway point, for example, when guests are gathered at the Cartwright home to celebrate the engagement of Mrs. Cartwright and Brett Curtis, Paul and his girlfriend, Lydia (Mary McLeod), sneak off to the pool to chat. As they stroll into the inky night—an alternative title for the film was the more thoroughly noir "Out of the Night"—their mirror reflections follow them while they circle the perimeter of the pool. When they finally take a seat at the edge, as Lydia reveals to Paul that the previous day in the pool Curtis got her in a "stranglehold" and started kissing her underwater, Ulmer cuts to a shot of greater emotional intensity, their inverted reflections glistening in the water, as if Schüfftan suddenly hoisted the camera up over the pool (Schüfftan would further hone his skills in noir distortion and split images in Robert Siodmak's *The Dark Mirror* a year later). Shooting this scene, filmed at an estate in Beverly Hills, proved tricky for the actors as well. "It was wintertime," recounted Lydon in a 2001 interview, "and when we rehearsed, the cameraman went to Edgar and said, 'Edgar, I can see their breath.' This was supposed to be a summertime scene." Ulmer purportedly gave it some thought and with help from the prop man came up with an inventive solution: "the leading girl and I put an ice cube in our mouth, and when they said 'speak' or 'go' or 'action!' you'd spit it out and play the scene," explained Lydon. "And if you could play the scene quickly enough, in a minute or a minute and a half, you can get away with it before your mouth warms up and you can see your breath again."[69]

Like *Bluebeard*, the film's formal design intimates the legacy of German cinema of the 1920s. "It lies slightly closer to the 'Haunted Screen,'" remarks Alexander Horwath, invoking the title of Lotte Eisner's famous history of Weimar cinema, "than to film noir, with its non-naturalistic ambience and peering into the soul, its sleepwalkers and the 'man without a face,' its low-key lighting and centrifugal movement that implies an oppressive, controlling external force."[70] In terms of its proper place in the visual lexicon of film (the 1980 German release title *Stimme aus dem Jenseits* [Voice from the netherworld] would imply horror), there is considerable slippage between German expressionism and noir. The film's arresting final image, recalling the opening prologue, bears a surplus of noir style—a backlit two-shot of Paul and Lydia walking toward us on the same treadmill, smoke pots off-camera spewing vast amounts of swirling smoke into the frame, that anticipates the oft-reproduced, iconic image of Joseph H. Lewis's *The Big Combo* a decade later. Even if Ulmer's subsequent noirs earned him more of an enduring reputation, *Strange Illusion* already showed considerable strength in that department.

Also like *Bluebeard*, it represented a bounce for the little studio, at least in the eyes of the industry trade papers. "This Leon Fromkess production is PRC's undisputed entrant in major league competition," asserted the *Hollywood Reporter*, "a big and handsome production reflecting its unlimited budget [*sic!*] and—even better than that—reflecting infinite pains and care to make a good picture." After recommending that the film be considered for top billing (or running at the "preferred time," as the trade magazine puts it), the review reserves much praise for Ulmer himself. "So perfectly has mood been created that Edgar Ulmer's direction creates its own illusion of having been done all in one day, with actors playing at one intense pitch; not one single lapse of audience interest comes to mind in looking at Ulmer's job in retrospect."[71] In this instance Ulmer's own recollections of the film's success match the record, while also hinting at some of the lingering professional ambivalence he felt. "The picture was very well received critically," he observed decades after its release. "Whether it made

money, I do not know. At the time, I was already chafing at the bit and
wanted *out* of PRC" (B 596).

It would be another few pictures before Ulmer was able to leave PRC
behind for good. His next film, the ultraminimalist *Club Havana*, shot
in a single locale constructed on a rented soundstage during the second
half of May 1945, afforded him the chance to continue working with
Schüfftan and to cast Tom Neal, known about Hollywood's B-movie
circuit as "a poor man's Clarke Gable," as one of the film's protagonists.[72] (He would immediately cast Neal again, in near back-to-back
productions, for the lead in *Detour*.) Despite any desire Ulmer harbored
to break free of his obligations to Fromkess, he managed to enjoy retest-
ing his skills at improvisation in what was to be regarded as "PRC's
Grand Hotel"—without the stars, without the sets, without the script,
and without the deep pockets of Irving Thalberg and MGM (B 596).
The project was said to have been slated to go to the same writing team
that would later script Rudolph Maté's *D.O.A.* (1950), Russell Rouse
and Clarence Greene (they are, in fact, listed on the production budget
as having received $1,500 for their idea), but instead arrived in Ulmer's
hands as a one-page outline (perhaps the same short synopsis submitted
to the Production Code Administration, still bearing the working title,
"Out of the Night"). On the release print Raymond Schrock, who
helped write *Isle of Forgotten Sins*, is credited as screenwriter, though
Ulmer claims, as he does elsewhere, that he made this one entirely on
the fly. "I had no script," he told Bogdanovich. "I did a Rossellini
again. . . . Schüfftan did that picture for me, too. I really had fun on that
one—we shot the whole picture on one set. We had quite a musical success with the cockeyed thing: 'Tico-Tico' [by Brazilian composer
Zequinha de Abreu and more famously sung by Carmen Miranda in
Copacabana, 1947] was used in that for the first time" (B 596–97).

Much like the acclaimed Weimar-era novel by Viennese author Vicki
Baum, *Menschen im Hotel* (*Grand Hotel*, 1929), from which Edmund
Goulding's award-winning adaptation took its material, *Club Havana*
depicts a social microcosm—a ritzy Miami nightclub in lieu of a Berlin
luxury hotel—in which the stories of its individual inhabitants are told
alongside one another, sometimes converging with one another. The
nightclub that Ulmer depicts, as J. Hoberman wryly suggests (playing
on the name of a 1940s Manhattan hotspot), "might be generically
termed The Ulmerocco."[73] It is, once more, a universe of liars, double-
crossers and cheats but also of crestfallen lovers and of budding, aging,
and rekindling romances. The film begins in the darkness outside the

nightclub, the muffled sounds of Latin music seeping through its glass doors as waves crash gently against a beach in the foreground. Ulmer cuts to a close-up of the club's neon sign before dissolving to a lone violinist playing a solo, the vague outlines of a cabaret audience and a tropical facade discernible in the background. This brings us inside the club, where we remain until the film's final moments, the full orchestra and performers—shot from stage level and from overhead, in shadow and in light—now doing the first of five extended musical numbers that help embellish the hour-long drama. Musical director Howard Jackson fills in for Erdody, using his highly choreographed song-and-dance routines ("Tico-Tico," "Bésame mucho," and others) less as a way to propel the narrative—they are sung mostly in Spanish and Portuguese—than to project an exotic air of authenticity, recalling the approach Ulmer took in his ethnic pictures. The suave, accommodating maître d'hôtel Mr. Charles (Pedro de Cordoba), with his fastidious dress and foreign accent, embodies the spirit of the club, whisking his regulars to their given tables, allowing a pleading guest a few extra days to settle his tab, and urging his performers to put on their best show for the overflowing crowd.

In due course the ensemble of players trickles into the club, where they each have their respective moment in the spotlight. There's the goodwilled pianist—or "ivory tickler," as a sassy cigarette girl calls him—Jimmy Medford (Eric Sinclair) and his girlfriend, the songstress Isabelita (Lita Baron); Hetty (Gertrude Michael), the powder-room attendant who doubles as psychotherapist and confidante to the women she serves; the nervous, naive model Lucy (Dorothy Morris), on her first date with medical intern Dr. Bill Porter (Tom Neal); the recently divorced Rosalind (Margaret Lindsay) and her unrequited love interest, businessman Johnny Norton (Don Douglas); the high-rolling Clifton Rogers (Paul Cavanagh), currently short on cash, and his well-heeled if homely date, Mrs. Cavendish (Renie Riano), who shows up with her three bespectacled, docile children in tow; the mobster Joe Reed (Marc Lawrence), another Johnny Moon of *Girls in Chains*, recently freed from jail on a murder charge; and the shifty nightclub receptionist Myrtle (Sonia Sorel, who pretty much stays in character as Miss Farber from *Strange Illusion*). Their stories intersect and overlap, providing a loose, meandering structure for the film. The heartbroken Rosalind swallows a fistful of sleeping pills left in the powder room by a giddy Mrs. Cavendish. Dr. Porter gets a chance to test his medical degree—or, really, to administer black coffee and continuous walking inside Mr. Charles's private office—helping to lead Rosalind from a near-comatose state back to full consciousness. Jimmy confides in Isabelita about witnessing Joe Reed fleeing the murder scene, eventually phones the Miami police headquarters (informing an eavesdropping Myrtle in the process), and then just barely survives the hit that Joe puts on him.

A film like *Club Havana,* however, is not so much about plot—at least not in the hands of Ulmer and Schüfftan—as it is about movement, milieu, and atmosphere. "To a much greater extent than in his previous films," remarks film historian Müller of Schüfftan's cinematography, "he avails himself of the mobile camera that follows the arriving guests to their tables or follows the ladies into the checkroom where they powder their noses. In the process these figures traverse alternating light and shadow zones so that—as is often the case with Schüfftan—only half of one's face is lit."[74] This is as true of the powder room, where women flow in and out of the dim hallway and sit in front of the table lamps illuminating the vanity, as it is in the main hall of the club, where the guests and performers fluctuate between being partially exposed and shrouded in complete darkness. "My own recollection of the PRCs," observes film historian William K. Everson, "is how dank and dark most of them were. Interior sets were often so threadbare that the lighting was deliberately kept low to hide the fact that there really was nothing to look at. An Edgar Ulmer could answer the challenge and turn darkness into a film noir asset, but many directors couldn't."[75] With the aid of "Schuffie," as Ulmer liked to call his German cameraman, he continuously accentuates this aspect. When Isabelita makes her way to the stage to sing "Tico-Tico," for example, the camera follows the movements of her dark silhouette twirling gracefully, her body undulating behind a backlit gauzy screen. This sort of sexually laced shadow play, whose progenitors include such Weimar-era classics as Arthur Robison's *Schatten: Eine nächtliche Halluzination* (*Warning Shadows,* 1923), enhances the atmosphere and shifts emphasis from the poverty of the production to the richness of imagination, just as we're made to plumb the depths of Paul's unconscious in *Strange Illusion.*

When the film finally returns to the pitch-black world outside the club, after the guests and showgirls have left, we witness another sharp, if less subtle, confection of shadow and light. The devious Myrtle, now dressed entirely in white, gets into her convertible in the unlit parking lot; upon hearing the lurking hit man whistle "When Johnny Comes Marching Home" (a tune that Erdody had made efficient use of in *Girls in Chains*), she has an inexplicable burst of moral rectitude. She runs back into the illuminated entryway of the club searching for Jimmy, only to return to her car—the sole source of light is the faint reflection on the chrome and paint—one last time; she prevents the hit by shrieking ("Look out, Jimmy, look out!") and plowing her car into the gunman as she takes a bullet between the eyes. This totally unvarnished scene, more relentlessly bleak and explicit compared to what one normally finds in films of the period—far harsher, say, than the murder scene in *Double Indemnity* (1944)—anticipates the brutality of Ulmer's later noirs.[76] This didn't, however, guarantee any greater popular or critical appeal. "PRC's top production team dolls 'Club Havana' up in sophisticated fashion, and then, apparently, has no place to go," insisted one mixed review.[77] For his final two pictures for PRC, made in rapid succession after *Detour*, Ulmer would shift gears dramatically, leaving behind the world of street crime for a swashbuckler and a weepie and returning once more to well-trodden source material from Old Europe.

BETWEEN PARIS AND VIENNA

The first of these two films, *The Wife of Monte Cristo*, was made in the final weeks of summer 1945 and marked the farewell contribution of Schüfftan—officially credited as production supervisor—to Ulmer's PRC cycle. It also represented an unusually large-scale creative effort on the part of Middle European refugees in Hollywood. In addition to Ulmer and Schüfftan there was the acclaimed German composer Paul Dessau, who supplied the classical score (and served as Arianné Ulmer's piano teacher off the set), while the vast majority of the large ensemble cast—including Martin Kosleck, Fritz Kortner, Lenore Aubert (*née* Leisner), Eva Gabor, Egon Brecher, and Fritz Feld—were born either in Germany or countries from the former Habsburg Empire. The entertainment journalist Hans Kafka, whose column *Hollywood Calling* appeared regularly in the German-Jewish émigré newspaper *Aufbau*, called the production "an almost exclusive job of our colony."[78] Ulmer cowrote a loose adaptation of Alexandre Dumas's eponymous novel—the credit aptly reads "*suggested* by" Dumas, just as *The Black Cat* was "suggested by" Poe—with Austrian compatriot Franz Rosenwald (credited as Francis Rosenwald, who later wrote television episodes for *Lassie*) and did much of the set design, constructing another nineteenth-century Paris, with his beloved cameraman. "We utilized the genius more than at any other time," recalled Shirley Ulmer of Schüfftan's contribution to the film. "He made sets that were all on wheels and they were able to be moved around very rapidly. Edgar did them, but it was Schüfftan with him."[79] The idea for the picture came from a scheme by Fromkess, in what would be his final PRC film, to capitalize on another profitable trend, the Monte Cristo pictures—notably, *The Son of Monte Cristo* (1940), costarring future Ulmer actors Louis Hayward and George Sanders, which had ostensibly made a financial killing for producer Edward Small (B 598).

What Ulmer and company produced, despite the talented cast and technical crew, and the unusually large budget (more than $300,000 in production costs, PRC's highest budget to date), was a generally uninspired genre picture with a few modest gestures of import. Without the same grace or formal intricacy as *Bluebeard*, the film opens in Paris—an intertitle reads "Paris 1832," in case we fail to recognize the setting—inside the grand halls of the Sûreté Générale, in the office of police prefect de Villefort (John Loder). There a meeting is in progress between Villefort and his nervous business partner, Baron Danglars (Charles Dingle), who worries about how to keep the next shipment of their phony plague-vaccination pills from being intercepted by a mysterious bandit known as "The Avenger." This masked man, who appears in public wearing a cape and wielding a saber, is the self-appointed champion of the people. Prefect Villefort runs the corrupt pill-peddling business with Danglars and the equally unscrupulous Monsieur Maillard (Fritz Kortner). From the beginning, he rightly suspects that the Avenger is the Count of Monte Cristo but cannot prove it. Meanwhile, the Count (Martin Kosleck) leads an underground movement, something of a *Beggar's Opera*-style group of revolutionaries, and together with his equally talented, courageous wife, Haydée (Lenore Aubert), attempts to protect the plague-suffering Parisians from injustice.

When his left hand is wounded in a sword fight with the loyalist gendarmes, near the start of the film, the Count goes into hiding to preserve his identity. The Countess does his bidding, replacing him at an official dinner at the palace of Villefort, along with Maillard and Danglars—who, as an otherwise unremarkable flashback informs us, was one of the men responsible for the wrongful torture and imprisonment of her husband—and borrowing her husband's mask and cape while he is away. In due time the lecherous Villefort ("There are so many beautiful women in Paris," he quips, as if importing a line from *Johnny Moon*, "and so little time"), who has been having an affair with Maillard's fetching wife, Lucille (Eva Gabor), makes a move on Haydée (perhaps an in-joke, as John Loder was at the time still married to Hedy

Lamarr, whose first name is pronounced with exactly the same intonation).[80] He eventually ferrets out her true identity, unmasking the Avenger. But we don't reach this point before first being subjected to a series of generic sword duels—the climactic one between Villefort and the Count—and outdoor battles on horseback, photographed in near darkness with the basic look of a B western.

At its best moments the film allows Schüfftan to work his magic, helping Ulmer to conjure up a few poignant street scenes—shot among the moody low-key gas lamps—and to recall once more some of the glories of German cinema between the wars. One scene in particular, a sequence of barely a minute and a half, takes all its cues directly from Lang's *M*. After Maillard comes to visit Haydée to ask for a loan, she arranges to have him pinched and taken to a dark, cavernous meeting-house of the underground, where he faces a people's court that merely shuffles the deck played in *M*'s kangaroo court. Maillard stands trial for the brutal crimes of distributing poisonous medicine, which has resulted in the deaths of "scores of poor people." When he mounts his feeble defense ("I'm merely a salesman," the rhetorical equivalent, in 1946, of "just following orders"), the shadow of the Avenger, Haydée in her husband's hat and cape, suddenly looms in the background. At this point, Kortner's gestures begin uncannily to resemble those of Peter Lorre as child murderer, on the stand in Lang's film, as a small girl, blinded by tainted medicine, is brought before the accused; in a fit of misplaced defiance, he turns around to find the Avenger standing behind him, his reckoning with justice ineluctable.

At another point in the film, during the dinner held by Villefort, Haydée refers to her husband, the Count, as "something of an internationalist," a clue perhaps to Ulmer's own sensibility when retrofitting his swashbuckler, as he would do again when filming *The Pirates of Capri* in Italy just a few years later. "Recurrently contracted by the studios to mimic their past and provide some kind of European flair," writes Lutz Koepnick in *The Dark Mirror*, "émigré directors exploited their peculiar state of in-betweenness, not only to complicate the relation of individual films to their genre but also to reflect, refract, reconstruct the image of German cultural identity—of German music, literature, and cinema history—within the American imaginary of the time."[81]

With the two final pictures he made for PRC, Ulmer began to garner attention in the popular press. "Although the road to Paris in 'The Wife of Monte Cristo' is strangely reminiscent of the trail to Eagle Pass," notes a generally favorable review in the *New York Times,* "the youngsters and, probably, some of their elders, will find this adventure familiar but exciting."[82] Writing in the *New York Herald-Tribune,* critic Otis Guernsey gives the film a fair if unflattering evaluation, calling it "a plainly stylized and ingenuous cloak-and-sword melodrama."[83] The film fared considerably better among the critics from the industry trade papers. "This elegantly mounted, carefully constructed production," observes the critic for the *Hollywood Reporter,* where Ulmer frequently seems to have found a sympathetic eye, "is probably the foremost 'class' effort to come from that lot to date." The same effusive reviewer goes on to suggest that Ulmer "has fully demonstrated here that he deserves better opportunities than the stock assignments heretofore open to him at PRC."[84] This must have been music to the director's ears, even if he still had one more picture to complete before moving on.

The spirit of internationalism prevails in Ulmer's final production for PRC, *Her Sister's Secret,* an emotionally wrought melodrama based on a novel by Viennese writer Gina Kaus and filmed at the studio over four weeks in fall 1945. In conversation with Bogdanovich, Ulmer mistakenly suggests that the film was "a remake of a German picture," but in truth it was a French adaptation of Kaus's novel *Die Schwestern Kleh* (1933; in English, *Dark Angel,* 1934), released in 1938 as *Conflit,* that inspired its producer, Arnold Pressburger, to introduce the idea to an American audience (B 598). As early as November 1944, the Bratislava-born Pressburger, who had migrated to the United States in 1941 and still owned the rights to the novel, submitted a draft of the script (with the working title "Once and for All") to the Breen Office for approval. He produced Lang's *Hangmen Also Die!* the year before and would later produce Sirk's *A Scandal in Paris* (1946), with Schüfftan behind the camera, along with Peter Lorre's enigmatic German feature *Der Verlorene (The Lost One,* 1951). Given the perceived lack of an identifiable "voice for morality," Breen rejected the script outright. "The general overall objection to the present story," he wrote to Pressburger, "is that it is, basically, a story of illicit sex and illegitimacy, without sufficient compensating moral values."[85] After resubmitting a revised script a couple of weeks later without success, Pressburger gave up on the project, passing it on to his brother-in-law, transplanted Berlin businessman Heinz Brasch (credited as Henry Brash), who produced the film for PRC a year later.[86]

Rather than setting the picture in interwar Vienna, as Kaus's novel does, the screenplay developed for PRC by Anne Green takes the world of contemporary New Orleans as its primary locale and concludes the story on New York's Upper East Side. It is the peak of Mardi Gras when the film opens, and the vibrant combination of euphoria, pageantry, and pandemonium that accompanies that annual rite radiates in the first shots. In place of Schüfftan, Austro-Hungarian émigré cameraman Franz Planer works to convey the proper mood of celebration and romance, capturing the costumed revelers as they stream into the confetti-drenched ballroom of the café Chez Pepé. After trying to shoo his ardent customers so he can close up for the night, the endearing Pepé, played by German-born character actor Felix Bressart, of *Ninotchka* fame, shrugs his shoulders and sighs, "Once a year!" The real focus, however, is on the masked Antoinette "Toni" DuBois (Nancy Coleman), granted several flattering close-ups early on, who persistently casts longing glances and pieces of confetti in the direction of the uniformed serviceman Dick Connolly (Phillip Reed).

Within seconds Toni and Dick abandon their dates and dance cheek to cheek to a big-band version of "Bayou Serenade." Toni playfully introduces herself as Marie Antoinette, while Dick, an army soldier based nearby, gives a hurried sketch of his life, desperately urging Toni to accompany him into the night. As they are whisked away in a horse-drawn carriage, enveloped in their enchanted milieu, Planer compresses time and space in a suggestive montage, allowing the ambient sounds of Mardi Gras to fill in for dialogue. With the help of Planer's camera work, Ulmer succeeds in highlighting the thrill of fresh romance (something Planer shrewdly repeats, with Ophüls, in *Letter from an Unknown Woman* a couple of years later). When Dick kisses Toni in a passionate embrace, after removing her mask, Planer cuts away to a star-filled sky, while the sentimental notes of Hans Sommer's string-heavy, chorally enhanced score sound and the sun gradually rises, brightening the frame.

The most controversial subject of the film, which provoked Joseph Breen's ire when vetting the script, is that after their fateful night together—a night in which Antoinette "lost her head, but not her heart," as Dick explains it—Toni finds herself pregnant out of wedlock. Worse still, she is never condemned for her actions, as the Breen Office dictated, and instead goes ahead with the birth of her son, agreeing to have her childless older sister, Renée (Margaret Lindsay), raise the baby with her husband, Bill (Regis Toomey), in New York. The film's pathos intensifies after the pregnant Toni shows up at Pepé's toting a kewpie doll—despite the Breen Office's waggish admonition that "this business with the doll in the box is unacceptable"—hoping to reunite with Dick as planned six weeks after their Mardi Gras encounter. Their botched rendezvous (Dick's letter announcing the hasty deployment of his company never reaches her) prompts a despondent Toni to seek comfort with Renée. The DuBois sisters reconnect at Renée and Bill's glamorous deco apartment on Fifth Avenue, and with Bill commissioned to a Virginia naval base, they decide "once and for all" (a pivotal line of dialogue, formerly the working title of the film) to have Renée stand in as mother.

Though the agreement suits the immediate needs of both women, tensions remain: Toni's independence looks enviable to her older sister, yet it's clear from their first encounter that Toni feels bereft ("I wouldn't mind having somebody to weep on," she admits). A stray line from the source novel encapsulates the very spirit of the weepie: "Woman's love is a strange thing," writes Kaus. "It brings suffering in its train, suffering, and yet again suffering."[87] When, a couple of years later, Toni can no longer bear the absence of her young son, she breaks the agreement, returning surreptitiously to New York and watching young Billy Jr. play with his nanny in the park; she nearly kidnaps him in a moment of deep psychological turmoil. Before final resolution is reached, with Toni and Dick locked in a redemptive embrace, the two sisters dig in their heels in a go-for-broke feud over the child (Figure 22).

"For a B-picture," remarks Jan-Christopher Horak in his survey of German exile cinema, "the film demonstrated an unusual sensitivity for the complexity of human emotions, for the giddiness of great love affairs, for the difficulty of motherhood, and for the barely repressed jealousy between siblings."[88] Although it may not have been able to compete with A-list films made in the same vein, Ulmer's melodrama has some of the same emotional and visual panache found in Sirk's more refined, renowned weepies of the mid-1950s such as *All That Heaven Allows* and *Written on the Wind*.

Part of what gives *Her Sister's Secret* its charm and simplicity is the international undercurrent. Like *The Wife of Monte Cristo*, the cast of émigré actors, here used in supporting roles rather than as leads, lends a hint of cosmopolitanism with a subtle foreign accent. The scenes in which this comes to the fore are easily overlooked and nonessential to the plot. For instance, the hammed-up haggling routine, in accented French, between Pepé and the boisterous wine merchant played by another German character actor, Fritz Feld (*né* Feilchenfeld)—a lifelong friend of the director and the person who, in 1972, would deliver the eulogy at his funeral—who first demonstrated an aptitude for American

FIGURE 22. Sibling rivalry: Renée (Margaret Lindsay) *(left)* and Toni DuBois (Nancy Coleman) in *Her Sister's Secret* (1946). Photofest.

screwball comedy as the high-strung psychiatrist, Dr. Lehman, in *Bringing Up Baby* (1938). Yet, perhaps the most revealing scene in this vein is the very brief encounter that Toni has with a man seated on a bench at the playground in Central Park feeding his beloved pigeons as part of a daily routine. In a form of self-parody, the birdman (Rudolph Anders) speaks to her in noticeably accented English extolling the virtues of punctuality, a stereotype often attributed to Germans and Austrians. His fleeting appearance almost works as a director cameo or another such authorial touch, an implicit reminder of the time and place in which the film was made. "At their edges," asserts Grissemann, "nearly all of Ulmer's films are a form of émigré cinema."[89]

Ulmer's one and only foray into the weepie proved quite successful in the eyes of the critics. In the *Hollywood Reporter* he received hearty praise for his "knowing and sensitive direction," while *Variety* and *Film Daily* followed suit, hailing his work as director and the achievements of the film as a whole.[90] Like *The Wife of Monte Cristo*, the film also received further attention in the popular press, with the *Los Angeles Times* declaring, "'Her Sister's Secret' is surely one of the best as well as one of the most adult of these stories which the screen has shown."[91] In her column, Hollywood society reporter Louella Parsons wrote of Nancy Coleman's performance: "I wonder why some of the major companies haven't realized what a fine dramatic actress she is."[92] Yet, when the film opened in New York several months later, an unfounded rumor appears to have circulated about the film's inflated cost, something that critics in both the *New Yorker* and the *New York Times* addressed. "The message in 'Her Sister's Secret' is clear," wrote snarky *New Yorker* film critic John McCarten. "Don't go around having illegitimate babies. The lady who has one in this film passes it off as her sister's, but then she gets to feeling maternal, and after that her life is hell. It cost, I am told, a million dollars [*sic!*] to make 'Her Sister's Secret.' Maybe the money should have been donated to a home for foundlings."[93]

Though never in great supply at PRC, money soon became a far thornier issue for Ulmer. Near the end of December 1945, in a deal cut between Fromkess and former MGM producer Hunt Stromberg, who had recently established the independent Mars Film Corporation with Hedy Lamarr and Jack Chertok, Ulmer was offered $250 a week to work on loan-out with Lamarr for his next picture. Distributed by United Artists, and coproduced by Stromberg, Lamarr, and Chertok, *The Strange Woman* would in fact command a budget of more than a million dollars and allow Ulmer the chance to work on a class-A production.[94] Ulmer's longtime home studio purportedly took in six times what he was paid each week for the loan. "I made more money for PRC on *Strange Woman*," Ulmer later explained, "than they had paid me the whole time I worked there" (B 598). When he caught wind of the crooked arrangement, Ulmer broke ties with the studio for good, resigning in the final months of his last one-year contract.

ON LOAN TO LAMARR

A native of Vienna who, like Ulmer, had trained with Max Reinhardt, Hedy Lamarr (*née* Hedwig Eva Maria Kiesler) came to be known in Hollywood, where she settled in late 1937, for her intoxicating beauty and the sparkling elegance of a European diva. Having first earned notoriety for starring in Gustav Machatý's *Ekstase* (*Ecstasy*, 1933), in which she fleetingly appeared nude and offered several provocative close-ups during the film's love scenes, Lamarr was also known both onscreen and off for her coquettish behavior and for being something of a man-killer.

When the production of *The Strange Woman,* her first stint as producer and star, started in December 1945, she was on her third husband, John Loder, who had recently played Villefort in *The Wife of Monte Cristo.* Lamarr visited Loder during the shoot and was duly impressed (her marriage to Loder was over by the time *Strange Woman* was in wide release). She insisted that Ulmer be offered the opportunity to direct the film, a move that soon made headlines in a self-serving publicity item, "Film Director 'Discovered' by Hedy Lamarr," published in the *Los Angeles Times* to coincide with the film's opening.[95]

Set in nineteenth-century Bangor, Maine, *The Strange Woman,* which was based on the eponymous best-selling novel of 1941 by Ben Ames Williams, tells the story of a devilish firebrand named Jenny Hager (Lamarr). The daughter of a town drunkard whose wife ran off with another man, Jenny elicits sympathy, fear, desire, and revulsion in those who come into contact with her. "What is so beautiful as a pure woman," asks an itinerant fundamentalist preacher. "What is so vile as an evil one?" From the very first moment we see her onscreen, as a young girl who nearly drowns a boy in the river and then feigns innocence, she exudes a captivating mix of cloying sweetness and sinister calculation. (Ulmer had initially used his own daughter Arianné to play the young Jenny, but when Stromberg declared his dissatisfaction with the results—she was purportedly not nasty enough—he and Lamarr enlisted Douglas Sirk to reshoot the scenes using Jo Ann Marlowe instead.)[96] Jenny goes on to chart a path of destruction in which, as with her childhood stunt at the river, she covers up each conniving move with artificial gestures of kindness and grace; "the lips of a strange woman," so goes the biblical proverb (and the tagline of the film's poster), "drip honey."

Her first step en route to wealth and power is marrying the richest man in town, the merchant Isaiah Poster (Gene Lockhart), whose son, Ephraim, is the boy she nearly drowned. She quickly lures home the grown Ephraim (Louis Hayward), by then an architecture student at Harvard, and bewitches him with the false promise of love, while at the same time donating money to the town church and fashioning herself as a humanitarian. Much like the Woman of the City in Murnau's *Sunrise,* that early template for the femme fatale of film noir *avant la lettre,* Jenny convinces Ephraim to kill his own father—on a whitewater raft, despite his lifelong fear of water—as a means of bringing them together. Once Isaiah is out of the picture, however, Jenny turns on Ephraim, driving him to eventual suicide and running off with John Evered

(George Sanders), a man who is engaged to Jenny's only friend, Meg
Saladine (Hillary Brooke). By the time all is said and done, Jenny lies on
her back dying, having driven a carriage off a cliff in an effort to mow
down John and Meg, and utters her last duplicitous lines to John: "I
wanted the whole world. But it was really only you."

The production, which extended over several months in the winter
of 1945–46, took place on the lot of Samuel Goldwyn Studios.[97] Its
exquisite set design and lavish scenario suggest a level of financial
backing that one does not normally associate with the films of Ulmer
(as Lamarr's Jenny utters early on in the film, "Money changes everything!"). The talented Parisian-born cinematographer Lucien Andriot,
who had recently worked with Renoir on a couple of his American
pictures, offers a similar kind of painterly aesthetic as Schüfftan but
with a grander big-studio style. In collaboration with Andriot, Ulmer
returns to some of the most effective motifs explored in *Strange Illusion*, including the shimmering reflective water into which young Jenny
peers at herself near the start of the film, plotting her gilded future and
announcing her destiny to be beautiful. Andriot manipulates the rip-
pled surface to transition, via lap dissolve, from the reflection of Jenny
as a girl (Marlowe) to that of her as a young lady (Lamarr) gleefully
rising up and showing off her curves before prancing into town and
launching her merciless campaign. In the end the film forms a bridge
between such comparatively modest PRC productions as *Strange Illusion* and *Bluebeard* and the considerably glossier noir style of *Ruthless;*
similarly, Lamarr's Jenny Hager anticipates the thoroughly rotten,
devious Horace Vendig, played with equal zest by Zachary Scott, two
years later.

Although in her autobiography *Ecstasy and Me,* Lamarr claims that
she had to "hold down the pampering" on *The Strange Woman,* she
nonetheless occupies the center of attention as the magnetic current that
consistently tugs on Andriot's camera, and largely embodies the same
prima donna persona that she had in her big studio pictures (Figure 23).
During the shoot, Lamarr spent a significant amount of time with the
Ulmer family, rehearsing her lines with the director and going for long
walks with young Arianné (as a gift, Lamarr later gave her a small kitten that the young girl aptly christened Monte Cristo).[98] Ulmer had to
work hard to get the desired performance he wanted from Lamarr. Taking a page from Murnau's directing manual, he purportedly used his
baton to lash her ankles whenever she missed a cue, trying as best he
could to make her act like a tigress.[99] "We did the bedroom scene over

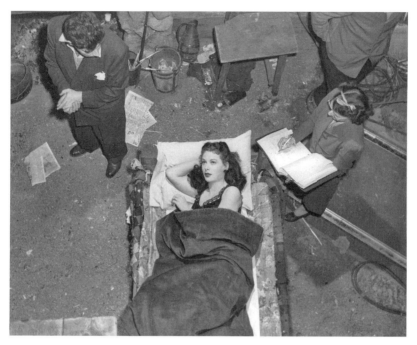

FIGURE 23. All eyes on Hedy: overhead production photo of Ulmer at work with his star, Hedy Lamarr, on *The Strange Woman* (1946), while his wife, script supervisor Shirley Ulmer, stands off to the side. Photofest.

and over so often I could do it now, twenty years later, in one 'take,'" recalled Lamarr. "Anyway, it didn't work. I just wasn't a tigress."[100] Ulmer and Lamarr are said to have had their share of tussles, not to mention romantic trysts, over the course of production. Teasingly, she and Loder wrote a satirical poem—providing their own mock credits "supervised by Hedy Lamarr, instigated by [hair stylist] Blanche Smith, written by Johannes [*sic*] Loder"—on Lamarr's stationery:

I'm quite sure that all my life
I'll envy Edgar Ulmer's wife
Her husband's always on the go
Working hard and earning dough.
He's not too busy though to think
My Shirley sweet would love a mink.[101]

Shirley Ulmer later questioned the extent if not the actuality of an affair between Lamarr and her husband, emphatically stating, "He really didn't like her."[102]

For his part, Ulmer suggested that the performance he got out of Lamarr nearly earned her an Oscar nomination, something that is corroborated in the chatter among various critics in the industry trades and the popular press. "As Jenny," wrote Philip K. Scheuer in the *Los Angeles Times,* "Hedy Lamarr slips effortlessly back into the graceful recumbent position of the heroine of 'Ecstasy'—proving that lightning can strike twice in the same place."[103] Ulmer, however, found the experience as a whole "very difficult" (B 598). He would work with Lamarr just one last time, when based in Europe in the 1950s, on *The Loves of Three Queens* (1954), the only film that he ever abandoned midproduction.

Soon after *The Strange Woman* was released, the *Los Angeles Times* contacted Ulmer to do a feature on him as someone who had made movies in Hollywood and New York and who was still shuttling back and forth between those two points. The main difference between working in the two cities, suggested Ulmer, was that in general we tend to count on New York, where he'd already begun work on *Carnegie Hall* (1947) immediately after *The Strange Woman,* more "as a location, and not as a studio setup." Ulmer suggested to journalist Philip K. Scheuer his wish as a director to depict "life as it exists in this world" and that we should not allow ourselves to forget that "the scope of motion pictures is universal and that going places is their greatest attraction. Travel is so broadening."[104] Little did he know that the remainder of his career would continue to adhere more or less to that same logic, when his *Wanderjahre,* or journey years, would begin anew. He would see none of the $2.8 million that *The Strange Woman* reportedly took in at the box office, and he was back on the road directing cheap independents almost as quickly as Jenny Hager imploded onscreen.[105]

6

Back in Black

Those guys out in Hollywood don't know the real thing
when it's right in front o' them.

—Al Roberts (Tom Neal) in *Detour*

Ever since a handful of French cineastes first wrote about American
crime pictures of the 1940s using that elusive, seductive, mildly enigmatic term *film noir,* critics and historians have been wracking their
brains to come up with an adequate working definition. For many,
these films, with their hopelessly dark, cynical outlook on the world,
their hard-boiled detectives in fedoras alongside fast-talking, dangerous
dames, shot in low-key lighting and drenched in menacing shadows,
cohere much more around a mood, a tone, or a sensibility than a bona
fide genre.[1] "It has always been easier," observes James Naremore in his
magisterial study *More Than Night,* "to recognize a film noir than to
define the term."[2] Like their forerunners in the field of crime fiction and
the *série noire* novels from which they derive their name, most if not all
of film noir seems to travel in a lurid, cheapened, morally depraved
universe.

   That is certainly true of the three best-known noirs that Ulmer
directed in the 1940s and 1950s: *Detour* (1945), *Ruthless* (1948), and
Murder Is My Beat (1955). Although not uniform in hue, budget, or
overall conception, these three pictures emerge from the strange, amor-
phous world that is film noir. They take shape during a critical phase in
Ulmer's career, one that stretches from his final year at PRC to his
protracted run as a stridently independent freelancer—well before *inde-*
pendent was a term of veneration—when he was still struggling to make
a name for himself. In examining film noir today, it's important to

recognize that there was no one singular style: "There were studio noirs and location noirs; soft-focus noirs and deep-focus noirs; gray noirs and black noirs."[3] Whereas *Detour* and *Murder Is My Beat* reflect a bare-bones rough-hewn aesthetic, *Ruthless* offers a few flickers of glamour, not to mention the acting talent that one frequently associates with more lavish productions of the period. In general, though, all three films resist standard classification. They may employ some of the formal conventions and prototypical characters of noir, but they also tend to reside in the margins separating classical film noir from what Thom Andersen has identified as the less glitzy, more politically minded *film gris*.[4] During these years Ulmer's collaborators included several writers with pronounced left-leaning tendencies—one of them, Alvah Bessie, was a member of the Hollywood Ten whose name was deliberately kept from the credits—and Ulmer himself showed genuine sympathy for those who sought to challenge the foundational myths of the American dream. There is, moreover, an altogether elemental, minimalist quality to his work during this time, due in part to the impoverished means of the productions he undertook but also to the cinematic style he managed to convey despite, or perhaps because of, this overt lack. "Unlike the polish in MGM's extravagant A production of *The Postman Always Rings Twice* or Fox's prestige Oscar contender *Laura*," avers Sheri Chinen Biesen, "Ulmer boils things down to their very essence."[5]

ON THE ROAD

Detour began its long, twisted career as a slim 1939 pulp novel by Martin Goldsmith, an aspiring New York writer still in his mid-twenties at the time of publication, who had made Hollywood his base of operation by the late 1930s. Goldsmith's only other credits were another pulp, his first, *Double Jeopardy*, which he published the previous year, and a smattering of short stories sold to such magazines as *Script* and *Cosmopolitan*. Begging comparison to James M. Cain, and crafted in the style of the grand masters (Raymond Chandler, Dashiell Hammett, Cornell Woolrich), Goldsmith's *Detour* was hailed by the *New York Times*, in the hard-boiled parlance of the day, as "a red hot, fast-stepping little number."[6] While he was still in his teens, on the eve of the Great Depression, Goldsmith had set out, much like the protagonist of his novel, to journey cross-country from New York "via the thumb-route." Several years later, he reportedly financed the writing of *Detour* by loading people into the back of his Buick station wagon and driving them, at $25 a head, from New York to Los Angeles.[7] (Ulmer himself had made the reverse commute with his wife, Shirley, slogging their way from L.A. to New York in an old beater, a few years earlier.) In October 1944, after a long dry spell with no sign of the film rights to his book ever being purchased, Goldsmith pawned them off on producer Leon Fromkess of PRC. The agreement between Goldsmith and PRC was announced by Edwin Schallert in the *Los Angeles Times*, observing a supposed affinity between Goldsmith's "murder mystery affair" and Cain's *Double Indemnity* and including a few gossipy details on the exchange: "Price is reported as $15,000, which is good for an independent."[8] Schallert notes further in his account that Martin Mooney is to supervise the project and that Tom Neal has been considered for the lead. There is no mention of Ulmer.

The principal actors selected for the film were all relatively unknown players from the B-movie circuit. Ulmer had already worked with Tom Neal on *Club Havana* (1945), whose filming ended just a couple of days before the *Detour* shoot began. With the rugged, handsome looks of an ex-boxer and a preternatural capacity for sulking, Neal was cast in the role of sad sack Al Roberts, a talented New York pianist who, in his desperate attempt to reach his fiancée in Los Angeles, gets dealt a bad hand a couple of times over. The fiancée, Sue Harvey, a nightclub singer and aspiring starlet turned hash slinger, is played by Claudia Drake, a platinum-blonde with few spoken lines and precious little time on camera. In the more critical role of Vera, Al's venomous traveling companion, a thoroughly down-and-out dame who fiendishly drops into the picture midway and keeps things in a headlock until her unceremonious departure, a feisty actress with a curiously apt *nom de guerre*, Ann Savage (*née* Bernice Maxine Lyon), was cast.[9] Savage and Neal had previously played opposite each other in a few Bs for Columbia—William Castle's *Klondike Kate* (1943), Lew Landers's *Two-Man Submarine* (1944), and Herman Rotsten's *The Unwritten Code* (1944)—and the two had an established screen chemistry and a bit of history, both onscreen and off. (While shooting their first film together in 1943, Neal purportedly wasted no time overstepping the boundaries of professionalism, making an untoward pass at Savage by burying his tongue deep in her ear; she is said to have rewarded him with a prompt grazing of her knuckles across his face.)[10] With just over a week left before the shooting of *Detour* began, Savage was brought in to see Ulmer on the set of *Club Havana;* after a quick once-over, she immediately fell into favor with the director. Finally, Edmund MacDonald, who plays the amiable, pill-popping Florida bookie Charles Haskell Jr., a man who gives Al a lift and—after revealing a few of his deepest, darkest secrets—ends up leaving him with more than just a free meal at a truck stop, was a character actor who had been around the block, earning minor roles at PRC, Columbia, Paramount, and elsewhere.

After Goldsmith and Fromkess settled the deal, a rumor circulated that John Garfield, who would soon go on to play an updated Al Roberts character in Tay Garnett's *The Postman Always Rings Twice* (1946), had read the novel and was eager to have Warner Bros. secure the rights (Ann Sheridan was considered for the role of Sue and Ida Lupino for Vera). The A-list studio reportedly made an offer to Fromkess of $25,000, but Fromkess, sensing he had his hands on a good pick, was unwilling to part with the material. Subsequent talk of having Garfield come to PRC on loan-out from Warner Bros. never amounted to anything.[11] In a serious break with Hollywood convention, Fromkess hired Goldsmith to write the screenplay from his own novel.[12] What the author produced was an elaborate, meandering text that would have required shooting a film with a running time of some two and half hours, more than twice the length of the sixty-eight minutes to which the film would finally be restricted. With seasoned input from associate producer and writer Martin Mooney, who had many PRC productions under his belt, and from Ulmer himself—who would later take much of the credit and emphatically dismiss Goldsmith's novel as "a very bad book" (B 597)—the script was pared down to a manageable length. Entire sections had to be tossed out, others radically revised, yet the threadbare quality it finally acquired, even with its intermittent reliance on the total suspension of disbelief, made for a good match with Ulmer's aesthetic.

In a considerable departure from Goldsmith's novel, the tale is told exclusively from Al Roberts's perspective. Roberts serves as the film's narrator—delivering half his lines in a pained, edgy voice-over—whose primary task, beyond recounting his life as a cursed nightclub pianist and a cursed hitchhiker, is explaining the inexplicable, proving to himself as well as to the audience that he is essentially powerless in his losing battle against fate. The story of Al Roberts begins where it ends: on the open highway. Seated at the counter of a Nevada diner, in a tableau that evokes Edward Hopper's iconic 1942 painting *Nighthawks,* Roberts whines into his coffee mug. The tale he tells, whittled down from Goldsmith's oversized script, is one of loss, whose tragic core intensifies as the human wreckage piles up all around its protagonist until he is no longer able to find a way out. Al and Sue were once happily in love. They were, in Al's words, "an ordinary healthy romance," and he was a "pretty lucky guy" (the film's theme song "I Can't Believe That You're in Love with Me," which plays a vital role in triggering Al's flashbacks, was *their* song).[13] But all this changes when Sue decides to try her luck in Hollywood—a fateful decision tantamount to jilting Al at the altar—sending things into a tailspin. Sue's sudden absence cripples Al, shatters his dreams, and breeds resentment and bitterness. Yet when the opportunity arises to reunite with Sue in Los Angeles, he leaps at it, heading off on a cross-country journey with the initial giddiness of a young boy tearing open his presents on Christmas morning. The journey, a doomed ride down a mercilessly bleak desert highway, inevitably turns sour, as Al becomes entangled in an impermeable web of lies and deception, starting with the panicked swapping of his identity for Haskell's after Haskell's mysterious death leaves Al in a fix, and ending with Vera's schemes of blackmail and extortion. By the film's denouement, Al finds himself completely unhinged with blood on his hands.

From the moment that the opening credits appear on the screen, we find ourselves tearing along the open road—a road that "lies behind us," as John Belton argues.[14] The reverse tracking shot of a desert highway, captured from the back window of a moving car, combined with the dramatic orchestral score by Erdody, immediately sets the feverish pace and the tenor of the film. We observe a single automobile, seemingly broken down on the side of the road, and nothing else but barren highway before the screen fades to black and then opens up once more on a lone figure whose silhouette can barely be made out against the inky night; the only source of illumination is the headlights of a passerby. As the figure gradually fills out the frame, traipsing along in a near somnambulant state, head tilted slightly askance and hands buried in his pockets, a quick glimpse of his unshaven face betrays a deeply distraught condition. A few paces further and the frame dissolves to a two-shot of the same figure seated, his facial expression unchanged, beside the driver of a convertible. A pithy, rather trivial exchange of words—"Well, here we are, I turn down here at the next block" and "Thanks, mister, I'll get off there"—coupled with an array of flickering neon signs ("Smokes," "News," "Bar," "Coffee Shop," and, finally, "Reno: The Biggest Little City in the World"), punctuates this atmosphere-drenched visual prologue, one that is nowhere to be found in Goldsmith's original screenplay or in his novel.

The credit sequence functions as a framing device of sorts, a means of establishing a few of the film's critical plotlines and of evoking some of the overarching themes: the lone wanderer ambles about without a clear destination on a journey that places him completely at the mercy of others, subject to chance and the contingencies of modern life; the open road, while benign and even liberating in most of American mythology, bears a distinctly gloomy quality here; the convertible sedan, a mere prop in this scene, will become one of the many confining spaces that trap the film's hero; and, in terms of the film's visual and narrative symmetry, the mood that is conveyed here will be rearticulated and amplified further in the film's epilogue, a scene that recasts the lone figure on a dark, desolate highway, only to be picked up one last time, a final bookend to the protracted flashbacks and voice-over narration that constitute the body of the film.

Here, then, is where the many changes to Goldsmith's novel begin to hatch.[15] First, there are the very basic ones: violin prodigy Alexander Roth—who wastes his talent, rejecting his years of classical training and choosing instead to play in a small-time jazz band—becomes piano virtuoso Al Roberts, who similarly squanders his talent at the Break O'Dawn Club. En route to Sue, Roth ends up serving time—"thrown in the jug," as the novel has it, "for swiping some fruit off a stand" (20)—in Dallas, an aspect of his ill-fated journey that rates a brief mention in the screenplay (where the charge is "vagrancy") but is never reflected onscreen. More substantially, the film dispenses entirely with Sue's subjective narration—over the course of the novel's seven crisp chapters, Goldsmith alternates first-person accounts by Alexander and Sue—and, in doing so, cuts out several ancillary figures who are critical to Sue's more fully developed, hard-edged character. In Goldsmith's "Extraordinary Tale," as the subtitle of his novel has it, not long after her arrival in Los Angeles, Sue gets involved with a slick bit player called Raoul Kildare, a man with a fake "Hollywood-British accent" and an "installment plan Cadillac" (46). They engage in what Sue nonchalantly refers to as "straightforward sex," which is, as she tells us, "brought about by a quantity of inferior rye which he had fed me as rapidly as I could down it" (101). The audacious Kildare stands in marked contrast to the soft, sensitive, ultimately pathetic Roth. After learning of Roth's supposed death (in a plot twist that remains undeveloped in the film, where we merely witness Al trading his clothes for Haskell's and, much later, hear from Al that Haskell's body is taken for his own), Sue entertains the fantasy of marrying Kildare and returning to New York, before she learns, in a deal-breaking turn of events, that he's already married to one of her coworkers at the hash house.

While Ulmer, in his interview with Bogdanovich, attests to his specific attachment to the character of Al Roberts ("I was always in love with the idea, and with the main character, a boy who plays piano in Greenwich Village and really wants to be a decent pianist" [B 597]), Sue's pointed commentary on Hollywood, embedded in the novel but kept from both the final screenplay and the film, would seem to speak equally well for the director. Relatively late in the extended saga, after Sue gets the official news of Roth's presumed death on his doomed highway journey, she admits to an unusually blasé attitude that has taken hold, making it possible for her to harbor a sense of cold detachment: "Hollywood is a peculiar spot. Once you're here, everything and everyone outside seems to be at the other end of the world. Live in Hollywood for a short while and then try to go home! You'll never be contented again. A week here will find you infected with that curious unrest that is so much a part of everyone in the colony" (147). Like Sue, Ulmer himself became "infected" and in due course equally alienated by that same world. "To the visitor from Mars (with permission by Orson Welles)," observes Ulmer in "The Director's Responsibility," "this fascinating place between the desert and the Pacific Ocean, which the world affectionately calls Hollywood, may seem, indeed, at the present time a sad and confused place."[16]

In Goldsmith's novel Sue admits, despite her growing pessimism, to having big dreams—the fantasy of effecting a total makeover and changing her name to Suzanne Harmony—and to having the "usual Hollywood hopes: a contract, some money, stardom and that sort of thing" (91). Sue's dreams are partly, only teasingly fulfilled in the novel, when she gets a late call from her agent Fleishmeyer who tells her he has arranged a screen test with David O. Selznick. Yet in the end the representation of Hollywood in Goldsmith's novel, as in Ulmer's film, takes on a decidedly unflattering air. Sue goes on to comment, in the penultimate chapter of the novel: "Hollywood was more sickening than ever. The studios were still impregnable fortresses, so near and yet so far beyond reach" (148). Not unlike Ulmer's own increasing sense of alienation working in the Hollywood dream factories, Sue's commentary is tinged with deep disillusionment. Similarly, Alexander Roth, who thinks that in Los Angeles he, too, might "ace [himself] into pictures" (61), makes equally dark observations once he is driving with Vera along Hollywood Boulevard: "Down the Boulevard a neon sign kept spelling: ALL ROADS LEAD TO HOLLYWOOD—AND THE PAUSE THAT REFRESHES—DRINK COCA COLA. What a joke. That sign should have read: ALL ROADS LEAD TO HOLLYWOOD—AND THE

COUNTY JAIL—DRINK POISON" (117). Elsewhere Goldsmith's novel may bear comparison to Cain, Chandler, and Hammett, but here, with the heavy dose of Hollywood cynicism, the more apt comparison is to Nathanael West (*The Day of the Locust*, 1939) or, with prescient anticipation, to Budd Schulberg (*What Makes Sammy Run*, 1941).

Finally, in the transition from novel to screenplay and to what ultimately made the cut in the film, all traces of Jewishness, rather profuse in Goldsmith's original story, are stripped. Gone with the chopping of Sue's story are Manny Fleishmeyer, her shady agent, and the heavily accented Mr. Bloomberg, her boss at the hash house. Gone, too, are Roth's Old Testament references and his sardonic questioning of whether things look "kosher." In the novel we are made privy to the otherwise useless information that Alexander Roth was born Aaron Rothenberg; that he changed his name (to aid in his professional advancement) at the suggestion of his violin instructor, Professor Puglesi; and that when he loses all ties to his identity, after Haskell's body is found and it is taken for his own, he considers the idea that, if he is ever able to marry Sue, he will take on an alias, perhaps "Israel Masseltof" (80). "Goldsmith injected such a consistent Jewish ambience into the novel," argues Robert Polito, "that it's tempting to read the Alex-Sue saga as an ethnic allegory about Jews in America."[17] Fully in keeping with the ways of the period, when assimilation, name-changing, and affecting the dominant norms of mainstream America were the order of the day, the overtly Jewish strains of Goldsmith's novel would presumably not have been considered palatable to a large filmgoing audience. The year 1945, with the horrors of World War II still fresh at the time of the film's release, was not an especially auspicious moment for such a story to hit the screen.

Yet, when examining the film in the context in which it appeared, and also in the context of an émigré director's life, there are indeed aspects that lend themselves to an allegorical reading—that is to say, to interpreting the film as an oblique commentary on the experience of exile. First and foremost is the issue of constant displacement and a severe lack of any kind of permanence. Al Roberts is "condemned to wander like the Flying Dutchman along the back roads of America," as Bill Krohn emphatically remarks.[18] Like most characters in the film, Al is constantly on the run, crossing state lines, searching for refuge in "some city," where he will be safe and anonymous. His actions mirror in certain respects the behavioral patterns of exiles, especially as Anthony Heilbut describes them in *Exiled in Paradise*: "Scurrying from place to place, 'changing one's nationality almost as often as one changed one's shoes,' they became adept at subterfuge and chicanery. Law-abiding citizens, now no longer citizens, became cunning outlaws, smuggling currency, property, and people across the borders."[19] Unlike the novel's Alexander Roth, Al Roberts is not marked as specifically Jewish. And yet he bears traits of a *luftmensch* or Wandering Jew. By the end of the film, when Al is stripped of everything, including his own name, he has become for all intents and purposes "a veritable exile."[20] There is, moreover, a pervasive sense of homelessness in all characters in the film. We see no families, no children, no other links to a larger, more stable community. In Grissemann's apt summation: "Ulmer hands over his characters to a labyrinth of bars, motel rooms and highway rest stops—to anonymous spaces that could be anywhere—or to a nowhere, a world for nothing and nobody. The locales of *Detour* are way stations, places of passage. Everything else Ulmer boldly eliminates. In contrast to Goldsmith's novel, his film noir gets by without any proper home, without living or private quarters."[21]

Ulmer's film allows for a subtle reenactment of what émigrés and exiles like him, people whose sense of belonging was significantly challenged by war and migration, were forced to face offscreen. The "contrapuntal" dimension of the exile experience, as Edward Said describes it, of coming to grips with the new and old worlds simultaneously, can be traced back to the homeless condition and what this lack of home means in the new world.[22] "The story of the German film émigrés," writes Thomas Elsaesser, "presumes a twofold estrangement: from their own home, and from the view that their American hosts had of this homeland. The consequence of this was a kind of schizophrenia, which, in turn also gave a double perspective on American society—one of admiration and the other a hyper-critical view, both perspectives vying with one another."[23] Like the two competing forms of music in the film, high and low, the Brahms and boogie-woogie that Al Roberts fuses in his well-rewarded improvisation at the Break O'Dawn, these two perspectives come into a productive conflict. The sum effect is not so much to evoke the "loneliness of man without God," as Luc Moullet once suggested as *the* overarching theme in Ulmer, but rather the loneliness of the individual—émigré, exile, and native-born alike.[24]

THE JACKPOT

Detour was budgeted at $87,579.75 and came in at $117,226.80 in the end, a figure far greater than the paltry sums often associated with the film ($30,000 in several accounts), giving it one of the smallest production budgets in the entire canon of film noir.[25] To put this into perspective, the shooting of the infamous death-house sequence in Billy Wilder's *Double Indemnity* (1944), which was bankrolled by Paramount and kept from the final cut of the picture, reportedly cost more than all of *Detour*.[26] The number of shooting days is generally given as six—most accounts, including those given by people on the set, corroborate this claim—but the final budget lists the total at fourteen in the studio, perhaps merely to allow for any extra days that might prove necessary, plus four on location. By Ulmer's own account, arguably as unreliable as Al Roberts's voice-over narration, the film was, like most of his others made for PRC, shot in six days, and he was given fifteen thousand feet of film stock and a shooting ratio of "two to one, nothing more" (B 573). Often cast in heroic terms, Ulmer was thought to possess, like the Grimm Brothers' Rumpelstilzchen, the ability to turn straw into gold, or, as John Landis puts it, to create "chicken salad out of chicken shit."[27] This meant, among other things, splicing together short ends; maximizing stock footage; borrowing sets from other directors; using his fingers, in lieu of a slate, to count off a scene; and fitting as much as he possibly could into a single take, with very few retakes. Martin Goldsmith once remarked in an interview, long after *Detour*'s release, "*Film noir*, film schnor. The whole idea was film cheap."[28] Ann Savage, for her part, claims not "even [to] recall any retakes except at the very end, when Tom apparently hadn't studied his lines too well and kept blowing it. But with Edgar, we never had retakes" (Ulmer's technique, as she tells it, was to "do a master shot and then come in and take close-ups").[29] There was in any case not a lot of room for error, or if there were errors, they had to remain buried in the final cut. As one critic argued in an early reevaluation of the picture, *Detour* "could surely be adduced as a prime exhibit in defense of André Gide's dictum that art is born of constraint and dies of freedom."[30]

Of course, certain aspects of the film's minimalist aesthetic have to do with the way in which Ulmer chose to adapt Goldsmith's story. "Ulmer's vision was to transform the rambling roadside saga into a head-trip," observes Eddie Muller. "The action is literally confined to what's roiling around in Al Roberts's mind. The bulk of screen time is consumed with tortured close-ups of Tom Neal, pondering his miserable luck in the ultimate 'why me?' voice-over."[31] In other words, Ulmer's heavy use of close-ups and voice-over, not altogether unlike his manipulation of stock footage and rear projection, was more than a mere stylistic choice or generic convention. It was what he could do to give the film a relatively stylish feel—admittedly, with plenty of glimpses of its threadbare or nonexistent sets—without breaking the bank.

The low-budget nature of *Detour,* not to mention its highly acute self-consciousness vis-à-vis money, lies at the heart of the film. We merely need to recall the pointed commentary that comes soon after Al heads out West, after he's already dismissed a ten-dollar bill as nothing but "a piece of paper crawling with germs": "Money. You know what that is. It's the stuff you never have enough of. Little green things with George Washington's picture that men slave for, commit crimes for, die for. It's the stuff that has caused more trouble in the world than anything else we ever invented, simply because there's too little of it. At least I had too little of it. So it was me for the thumb." This critical embellishment to the screenplay offers a noteworthy moment in a film by a director who once famously claimed, "I really am looking for absolution for all the things I had to do for money," and who always remained fearful of what he called "the Hollywood hash machine" (B 603, 592). In other words, Roberts's voice-over resonates powerfully both onscreen and off.

As director, by then on a one-year contract at PRC, Ulmer needed no reminding of the studio's lack of financial resources. Fittingly, a rare publicity still from the film has Al and Vera both tugging on a crumpled bill in front of a sign that reads "Money Loaned" (nowhere in the film does this actual shot appear), as if making a caustic jab at the absence of proper financial backing (Figure 24). In the case of *Detour,* as on most films he directed, Ulmer hustled to make ends meet, eking out a living by showing unremitting resourcefulness and few concerns about compensation (his director fee was a mere $750—the equivalent of less than $9,000 today—exactly half of Goldsmith's fee as screenwriter).[32] Not unlike Al Roberts, he had to thumb his way through the production, taking lifts here and there, cheating his way with an occasional shortcut when the straight and narrow just wouldn't do.

A telling example of Ulmer's attempt to employ cost-saving measures while still remaining attentive to style and atmosphere is contained in a brief sequence, not long after the film shifts into flashback at the counter of the Reno diner, when Al and Sue leave the Break O'Dawn Club and venture out into the night. Ulmer has Benny Kline's camera zero in one last time on the club's neon sign just before it blinks out—an allusion, perhaps, to the murky quality of Al's memory and a faint reminder of the indefinite location, taken in place of a more precise, more costly shot of

FIGURE 24. At the pawn shop: Al (Tom Neal) and Vera (Ann Savage) reveal their extreme codependence on capital in *Detour* (1945). Courtesy of the British Film Institute Stills Collection.

an actually existing locale. Kline then captures Al and Sue, in a fog-filled shot, on the club's steps as they begin their nocturnal stroll. When Al asks Sue if she'd like to grab a bite, she cannot hide her sense of disgust, her loss of appetite from working in a "fleabag" like the Break O' Dawn. At that same moment, filmed against a hazy background, we discern the contours of a man putting out the trash. Al and Sue continue on in what appears to be a blanket of thick fog—"the B-director's best friend," as Gregory Mank has remarked—masking the exact features of the neighborhoods they supposedly traverse, thereby sparing Ulmer and his crew the construction of an exterior set of the city.[33] It almost appears, in David Kalat's witty formulation, as if "the set designers took the week off, leaving the fog machines and back-projection screens to take up the slack."[34] As the couple strolls uptown from the club's assumed neighborhood (in Ulmer's rendition, Greenwich Village, or, as Goldsmith's novel has it, on West 57th Street "not far from Columbus Circle"), Ulmer maintains the pace by using a series of wipes and by intercutting several subtle images (a shot of horse-drawn carriages outside Central Park) and a few less-than-subtle ones (close-ups of the street signs along Riverside Drive), with the continuation of offscreen dialogue, as a means of hinting at the route they are taking.

Ulmer had already explored at great length the strategic use of the fog machine, in the absence of other means, on his other low-budget productions at PRC. As Jimmy Lydon, the lead in *Strange Illusion*, told me in an interview of 2001, "He knew what you could get without exposing a set you didn't have; he knew how to make a two-wall set look like a whole room."[35] Or, in Bogdanovich's more rhapsodic summation, "What he could do with nothing . . . remains an object lesson for those directors, myself included, who complain about tight budgets and schedules" (B 558). When Sue finally announces, in front of a building we assume is her apartment, "Well, here we are," an echo of the announcement made by the anonymous driver in the film's prologue, it is clear that another journey has been cut short. Only in this case it's a trip to the marriage altar that is rebuffed by Sue, who instead has her own plans ("I want to try my luck in Hollywood"), sans Al, mapped out for herself.

Even during a relatively cursory first viewing, and especially on closer inspection, the film is rife with basic flaws, breaks in continuity, and blemishes that were never excised or reshot. Take, for example, the scene of Roberts hitchhiking in the desert. We first see him walking along, on the right side of the road, as American traffic conventions would dictate. But then, in a twenty-second sequence, spliced in without any real recourse to continuity, we have Roberts on the left side, and traffic visibly passing as if the Mojave Desert suddenly belonged to the British Commonwealth. Ulmer presumably didn't detect this until it was too late to correct, though it might merely be evidence of a director, so some have claimed, who was willing to allow himself the leeway to sneak in a small gag here and there, especially if it would help increase the chances of keeping his budget in the black.[36] Ironically, during this same brief sequence, when the inverted negative has Roberts sticking out the wrong thumb, the voice-over, in one of its many sympathy-seeking utterances, addresses the viewer directly regarding the tortured predicament of the hitchhiker: "Ever done any hitchhiking? It's not much fun, believe me. Oh yeah, I know all about how it's an education, and how you get to meet a lot of people and all that. But me, from now on, I'll take my education in college or in P.S. 62, or I'll send a dollar ninety-eight in stamps for ten easy lessons." As if synchronized with the image, the offscreen voice ends its discourse on hitchhiking at the precise moment that Roberts resumes his act of thumbing a ride in the proper direction.

A far less detectable imperfection comes later, when Al first discovers Vera hitchhiking in front of a gas station. He addresses her with a brusque offer to give her a lift ("Hey you! Come on, if you want a ride"), and Vera approaches the car steadily and deliberately, captured in a reverse tracking shot that helps to convey her "sexual knowingness," as one critic has argued.[37] As she climbs into the car, we see, for a split second, that her sweater is noticeably pinned—a means of cinching it and thereby endowing her with considerably more sex appeal—straight up her back. Ulmer allegedly insisted that wardrobe designer Mona Barry, who worked on *Club Havana* as well, make this alteration so that the curves of Vera's figure could be accentuated, no doubt to heighten the prurient nature of the roadside pickup. We recall from Al's exchange with Haskell that the kind of girls who hitch rides are not "Sunday school teachers." As Ann Savage recalls in an interview from 1996, "He [Ulmer] took my sweater and he pulled it real tight and he had the wardrobe woman take this big lap of wool in the back and pin it from the neck down to the bottom of the sweater. And then he said, 'Don't turn around.' And as a matter of fact, when Vera starts to get into that car I caught sight of it [upon rewatching the film]. You could see a little bit of it and I knew what it was, but I'm sure it wasn't picked up by anybody else."[38]

Indeed, the tawdry, unrefined nature of the film is reflected in the characterization of its protagonists. Ann Savage's Vera ("a role as much ferally attacked as performed," in Guy Maddin's apt formulation) is unlike any other femme fatale of the era, far less polished, less beautiful, and much, much more aggressive.[39] "A sullen, dangerous, yet sympathetic figure, she leaves an indelible impression, and it is impossible to imagine any A-budget picture that would have been allowed to depict her," asserts Naremore.[40] Savage herself tells how Ulmer demanded, upon viewing the saccharine, dolled-up style that the hair and makeup artists had initially confected for her, that she have dollops of cold cream streaked through her mane to give it a grimy look and, for the same effect, plenty of dirty-brown toner applied to her face. She had to reflect the look of someone who, in Al's words, had "been thrown off the crummiest freight train in the world." Coached by Ulmer to spit out her lines with the velocity of a semiautomatic rifle—and made hoarse in the process—Vera sounds pretty much like she looks. "Her voice is shrill, harsh, punishing," notes Greil Marcus, "a complete explosion of every notion the audience of her day would have had of what a leading lady in a feature film was supposed to sound like."[41]

Rather defiantly, Ulmer chose to break with industry convention—quite severely, in this case, as Joseph I. Breen's Production Code Administration memo insisted, in no uncertain terms, that in the portrayal of Vera, "it should be established *affirmatively* that she is a crook and *not* a prostitute."[42] While Ulmer does not explicitly portray Vera as a prostitute, her putatively lascivious, transgressive behavior—"Women *never* hitchhiked rides," explains Savage in retrospect—exceeds that of her counterparts in the big-studio noirs, which were subjected to greater scrutiny, and the highly sexualized nature of her character leaves the question at the very least ambiguous.[43] Moreover, the publicity materials for the film, which feature such racy taglines as "I used my body for BLACKMAIL" and an "Adults Only" warning, have Vera leaning against a lamppost smoking and striking a pose, in a "clingy dress and ankle straps," that, as one critic has recently argued, replicates the precise body language of a lady of the night.[44] The Breen memo goes on to decry any sexual innuendo that might crop up in the film, given the fraught nature of the story: "It is essential that Alex [Al] and Vera do *not* register as man and wife, and that they be shown living in different apartments. There should be, of course, no suggestion of a sex affair between them." Of course, they *do* register as Mr. and Mrs. Haskell, they *do* share an apartment, and there are plenty of suggestions of sex—

from their fiery exchange about the folding bed to the various bits of tense chatter laced with erotic overtones—most of them emanating from Vera. As Savage has commented on her uncommonly forward advances as Vera, "That was an overt motion there, not subtle anymore. . . . When she gets up to go to bed, she's quite drunk and she reaches over to touch his shoulder and he really rejects her. It's a real rebuff and this infuriates her."[45]

While at PRC, Ulmer arguably had more directorial liberty than he would have had at a larger studio, and as a result he was in a better position to elude certain restrictions. This does not, however, mean that he was able to sidestep the dictates of the Production Code altogether. To be sure, Breen stipulates in his memo several necessary changes in order to comply with the provisions of his office. The first on his list has to do with the final scene of the film, Al walking alone on the dark highway, and the unwelcome possibility of allowing this scene to intimate, in a considerable violation of Breen's strict moral code, Al's ability to avoid punishment for his sins. "It is absolutely essential," writes Breen, "that at the end of this story Alex be in the hands of the police, possibly having been picked up by a highway police-car as he was hitch-hiking. The concluding narration by Alex's voice should be along the lines that he wonders if all the true facts concerning his troubles will come to light, and what the law will do to him."

What the film delivers in its finished form amounts, for the most part, to a seemingly reluctant acquiescence to Breen's demands. Seated at the counter of the Reno diner, shrouded once more in darkness except for the partial illumination of his eyes, and still engaged in his lengthy flashback narration, Al tells the final bit of his extended saga: "But my problems weren't solved. I had to stay away from New York—for all time—because Al Roberts was listed as dead and had to stay dead. And I could never go back to Hollywood. Someone might recognize me as Haskell. . . . Then, too, there was Sue. I could never go to her with a thing like this hanging over my head. All I could do was pray she was happy . . ." As Al expresses his wish for Sue's happiness, he gets up and leaves the diner, returning to the night. Yet for a brief moment it appears that his shaky confidence is temporarily restored. He strolls a few paces, lights up a cigarette, and resumes the voice-over narration—a monologue that Ulmer added to the screenplay—giving the fleeting impression that he might just get away with it: "I was in Bakersfield before I read that Vera's body was discovered, and that the police were looking for Haskell in connection with his wife's murder. Isn't that a laugh?

Haskell got me into this mess, and Haskell was getting me out of it. The police were searching for a dead man."

The film, however, does not end here. Instead, Al continues to walk along the highway, his thoughts shifting in tenor toward the more righteous. The shift begins with Al's return to the same impulse to forget, to "cut away a piece of your memory or blot it out," as he describes it at the start of his protracted flashback. He can't help but wonder how his life might have turned out had he never stepped into Haskell's car. But his predominant sense of uncertainty, running throughout much of the film and informing Al's many rationalizations, is countered by a sudden torrent of unequivocality: "But one thing I don't have to wonder about ... I *know* ..." The final segment of the epilogue, triggered by Al's realization that there is no way to get off scot-free, is a startling, rather inconsonant, moment of clarity that clashes with the overriding moral ambiguity of the film. Al's oft-quoted final line of voice-over narration ("Some day a car will stop to pick me up that I never thumbed. . . . Yes, fate or some mysterious force can put the finger on you or me for no good reason at all") is, in the end, a more artful way of saying that Al Roberts cannot escape the law, and Joseph I. Breen says so.

In spite of its inherently suspicious take on American capitalism and on Hollywood of the 1940s—nothing less than "an account of a country plagued by individualism and greed," as filmmaker Walter Salles later dubbed it—*Detour* received favorable reviews in the local trade papers when it was first released.[46] The *Hollywood Reporter* pronounced it "an excellent picture" and "the best film PRC has ever produced," asserting further that the overall "achievement is unmistakably attributable to Ulmer."[47] Although less effusive in its praise (calling the film "adequate as second half of a double bill"), *Variety* was quick to point out that "Director Edgar Ulmer manages to keep the show smartly paced," while a review in *Film Daily* highlighted the "suspense and vividness" that Ulmer was able to achieve with the picture and gave the direction and photography a rating of "good."[48] Finally, among the few notices in the popular press, a critic for the *Los Angeles Times* called *Detour* "one of the most poignant and disturbing stories to reach the screen in any year. . . . You're not just looking at a picture; you're right in it and suffering along with the man whose troubles are being told. . . . No mere recital of the tale can convey its painful verisimilitude. Direction is tops, with no opportunity overlooked."[49] Given Ulmer's marginal status in the world of Hollywood, and given the second-class standing of a Poverty Row studio like PRC, who could have expected more accolades? Even at the time of its release, before film noir had earned its cultural cachet and wider currency, Ulmer had to have felt a sense of achievement. As Alexander Roth remarks in Goldsmith's novel, after finally sating his famished appetite at the desert truck stop, "It tasted like the *manna* must have tasted to the starving Jews wandering around in the wilderness for God knows how long" (13).

MONEY, MONEY, MONEY

In the spring of 1948, around the time that Ulmer seemed to be hitting his stride as an independent director, he released another gritty, dark little picture called *Ruthless*. Based on a popular novel by Dayton Stoddart called *Prelude to Night* (1945), a work of somewhat greater literary ambition and historical sweep than your average dime-store pulp, *Ruthless* has come to be known as Ulmer's "*Citizen Kane* in miniature" (and like other Ulmer cheapies, this one was done, as J. Hoberman has sardonically quipped, "for the equivalent of Orson Welles's dinner allowance").[50] Framed by two low-key, brooding flashbacks typical of film noir, *Ruthless* presents a world-weary view of American capitalism and runaway greed that reflects the basic tenets of Welles's masterpiece on a considerably smaller scale. As Ulmer explained to Bogdanovich in 1970, "the complete evilness and ruthlessness about money—that's what I wanted to do" (B 601). Produced by a small outfit called Producing Artists, headed by Arthur Lyons, and released by Eagle-Lion Films, the successor company to PRC, *Ruthless* belongs to a small coterie of B noirs with uncommon flair and the production values of an A-class picture.

Featuring the big-studio talent of Zachary Scott and Sydney Greenstreet, both on loan-out from Warner Bros., the story line takes shape around the dramatic rise and fall of Horace Woodruff Vendig (Scott), a man who craves, and ultimately captures, all that others have. Born into modest means and raised by an unloving mother, Vendig systematically turns his back on his early inclinations toward benevolence, including the heroic feat of saving his childhood girlfriend, Martha Burnside, from drowning. Vendig rots from the inside out as he gains further access to the hallowed halls of affluence—first to Martha's upper-crust family, then Harvard, then other well-connected families, and on to Wall Street and beyond—acquiring a boundless appetite for power and leaving in his wake a host of jilted lovers and moneymen.

The story unfolds at a grand, formal affair inside Vendig's palatial seaside estate. There he announces, before a crowd that includes representatives from the State Department and the United Nations, his plans to establish a peace foundation. Also present is a notable contingent of people he once cheated and trampled over on his single-minded path toward financial supremacy, those who cannot help but wonder whether Vendig is merely up to a shrewd public relations stunt, a clever way to dodge taxes, or an attempt to save his soul. With the promised bequest of $25 million, along with his house and the surrounding three thousand acres, he declares his newfound devotion to the humanitarian cause. "My friends," he states, as Ulmer cuts from a long shot of the crowd standing in rapt attention to a medium close-up of Vendig, "I have enjoyed the battle of life, yet I have tasted defeat. I have enjoyed the fruits of victory to the full. But after the dreaded lesson of the last few years, I think that all of us are a little weary of victories and battles, whether great or small. We *want* peace." The assembly also marks the arrival of Vendig's estranged best friend, Vic Lambdin (Louis Hayward), and Vic's girlfriend, Mallory Flagg (Diana Lynn)—engaged in a dramatic exchange with Vic in the film's brief prologue—whose mesmerizing beauty bears a striking resemblance to the mature Martha Burnside (also played by Lynn), one of Vendig's first victims. Mallory's appearance provokes a sudden surge of Vendig's tormented memories. As he observes, just seconds before sending the story into prolonged retrospection, "I do a great deal of remembering myself—I rarely ever talk about it."

In the first of two flashbacks, into which Ulmer stylishly transitions by way of Vendig's languid movements as he attempts to light his cigarette, Bert Glennon's subjective camera tracks forward, training our deep-focus gaze on Mallory's glowing face (the flashback will end with Mallory blowing out Vendig's match, before he's managed to light the cigarette himself, and in turn lighting it for him). Ulmer seizes the opportunity of shifting into the past tense as a means of introducing the audience to the *ur*-scenes of Vendig's childhood: first, as Mallory's face dissolves to the face of young Martha Burnside (Ann Carter), singing in a canoe together with young Vendig (Bob Anderson) and Vic (Arthur Stone), we observe a joyful sequence cut short by Horace's heroic rescue of Martha after the boat capsizes; we then cut to the home of Horace's abusive, shrewish mother (Joyce Arling)—"You're a Vendig alright," she snaps at her son, "not caring that I work my fingers to the bones, teaching brats, whose mothers I wouldn't let take in my washing as a girl"; this is immediately contrasted with sudden intervention by Mrs. Burnside (Edith Barrett), who offers nothing but affection for Horace ("you brave, wonderful boy") and who, together with her husband, takes him in and nurtures him only to be left behind when he climbs the next rung of the social ladder.

In the same flashback, as Horace and Vic venture to the town's seedy waterfront, we're introduced to Vendig's otherwise absent father, Pete Vendig (Raymond Burr), a compulsive gambler and financial deadbeat, who offers his son a formative piece of advice and a few dollars. "Opportunity knocks on every man's door once, just once," he avers, as if divulging one of life's most precious secrets. "Well, go after it, grab it with both hands. Don't let nothin' stand in your way. Yes sir, all you gotta do is find out what the common people gotta have and grab it tight."

Horace Vendig heeds his father's words, destroying families and marriages, inciting suicide, and showing no human emotion in the process. ("I am an adding machine," he declares in a critical moment. "What other people have, I *want!*" he exclaims in another.) This is, perhaps, what makes him the consummate *homme fatal*, mirroring the countless female counterparts who populated the screen during the peak of film noir.[51] Among his prey is Susan Doane (Martha Vickers, who played Carmen Sternwood, that sly, seductive femme fatale, in Howard Hawks's *The Big Sleep* a couple of years before). A fetching young woman of considerable wealth and sophistication, she hails from a prominent line of bankers, but, like Martha, she is a mere stepping-stone in Vendig's larger quest for wealth and power. Susan provides Horace with the fast track to Wall Street ("You've arrived, Mr. Vendig," she tells him at a Duane family soiree, shortly before ushering him into a circle of well-connected businessmen). Vendig trades his women the way he trades commodities: upgrading from Martha to Susan, Susan to Christa, and ultimately, albeit unsuccessfully, to Mallory. He exudes nothing but frosty indifference as he moves from one venture to the next. As he puts it in one of his many breakups, "I'm going far, Martha, and fast, and alone."

Vendig ultimately meets his match in Buck Mansfield (Greenstreet), the CEO of Delta Bond and Share, an equally thick-skinned industrialist who, after losing his wife, Christa (Lucille Bremer), and his riches to Vendig, can think only of payback ("We kill for profit," he barks near the close of the film, "for the taste of victory, for revenge"). While other guests at Vendig's seaside gathering may not wish to recall the past, Mansfield doesn't flinch in its face. A few moments before returning to flashback narration, Greenstreet utters the seemingly pregnant words:

FIGURE 25. Love triangle *(left to right)*: Vic (Louis Hayward), Mallory (Diana Lynn), and Horace (Zachary Scott) in *Ruthless* (1948). Photofest.

"What else are we here for, but to remember?" In the film's climactic scene, Mallory forces Vic to countenance the prospect of losing her to Vendig the same way he lost Martha years ago (Figure 25).

Glennon's camera then follows the couple strolling ominously along the estate's docks toward the end of the pier, when Vendig intervenes in the hopes that Mallory might finally succumb to his overtures. A drunk and angry Buck Mansfield ambushes Vendig on the dock, bringing the two of them crashing down into the water below. "There seems to be an almost Freudian attachment to water," remarks Paul Schrader in his "Notes on Film Noir." "Docks and piers are second only to alleyways as the most popular rendezvous points."[52] This particular rendezvous, shot on Catalina Island, off the coast of Los Angeles, turns out to be the final test for Horace Woodruff Vendig's crass sink-or-swim attitude toward life; he and Mansfield drown each other in a nonredemptive counterbalance to his schoolboy bravery with Martha. "He wasn't a man," Mallory explains to Vic in the final line of the film, serving as an epitaph of sorts; "he was a way of life" (a quip that seems to get reworked, if only obliquely, by Marlene Dietrich, as Tanya, in Orson Welles's *Touch of Evil* a decade later).

Though more of a bildungsroman, tracking the rise and fall of Horace Vendig against an expansive historical backdrop, than a snappy pulp à la *Detour,* Stoddart's *Prelude to Night* showcases all the core ingredients: vice, trickery, sex, and the full catalogue of human vulnerabilities. Stories of this kind, observes Geoffrey O'Brien in his *Hardboiled America,* "tell of a dark world below the placid surface, a world whose inhabitants tend to be grasping, dissatisfied, emotionally twisted creatures. . . . This other America, when it is not a bleak rural wasteland inhabited by murderous primitives, is a glittering hell ruled by money and violence, flaunting images of beauty that are either deceptive or unobtainable."[53] Like their cinematic counterparts, these novels frequently plumb the depths of America's underbelly; cheap, sensational, and devoid of scruples, they are meant for consumption while "on the move."[54]

Unsurprisingly, *Prelude to Night* is shot through with allusions to wealth and power. This aspect gets compounded by the extreme class-consciousness of young Vendig, who is born into the rough proletarian quarters of immigrant South Boston yet disavows his lot in life as only a true arriviste might do (the inscription on a coat of arms, kept by Vendig late in the novel, says it all: "'Tis not the birth, 'tis money makes the lord").[55] Already in the first chapter, Horace's father, Frank Vendig, whose twenty-five-dollar-a-week salary as a clerk leaves him hustling to get by, poses the fundamental question: "But without capital, where are you? A slave to money, somebody else's money" (12). He reiterates the point a couple of chapters later: "Where am I without capital? Nowheres [*sic*]. And I should be a millionaire" (44). As in the film, Stoddart's Horace—often referred to as "Horrors" by his friend Vic Lambdin—steamrolls all who stand in his way, exploiting each relationship until there is nothing left to be used or abused for his own personal gain. Even as a boy, when Horace's aspirations of financial greatness are first made transparent, his neighbor Mrs. Burnside sees a Rockefeller in the making, calling him "young John D." (35).

Ulmer's film proves to be a generally faithful adaptation of Vendig's calculated moves: from South Boston to Cambridge, to Wall Street, to cutthroat entrepreneurship and Ponzi schemes on a global scale. His daily routine revolves around a question that he pursues with unremitting zeal: "How [to amass] more power and money for Vendig?" (189). The novel contains, however, in its portrayal of some thirty years in the life of Horace Woodruff Vendig, a strand that is kept from the film, one that links it more directly to Goldsmith's *Detour:* a subtle critique of the movie industry. In his boundless quest for dominion, Vendig tries his hand producing in the factory of dreams—the novel features brief cameos by Jack Warner, Carl Laemmle, and Irving Thalberg—establishing a company called Pan-American Pictures (which almost sounds like the name of a company we might find listed on Ulmer's employment history), and pursuing his newest hope "to be even a bigger fellow in Hollywood" (196). It also shares with Goldsmith's novel an unabashed depiction of Jewish characters who inhabit the same world as Vendig, some of them, such as his business partner at Pan-American Pictures, Sanford Lott, and his dentist, Sol Neff, quite close to him, despite their distinct ethnic mannerisms (both pepper their speech with Yiddish and exhibit none of the refinement that Vendig otherwise prizes). Vendig also has an affair with a local seductress named Shirley Green, who is happy to maintain their physical relationship until it is time for a more ethnically and socially appropriate match—the novel mentions the use of a "schadchen" (122), or matchmaker, for such purposes—to be made. (*Prelude to Night* also features a Dresden-born psychoanalyst named Dr. Farbex, whom Vendig visits on a regular basis to discuss his dreams, and a number of other colorful characters absent from the film.)

Like the adaptation of *Detour,* which required the taming of some of the less restrained depictions of vice, *Ruthless* similarly had to make changes with respect to the steamier passages of Stoddart's novel, rendering them less objectionable on the big screen. One character in particular, Christa Mansfield, who is depicted in the novel as a woman who exudes unbridled sexuality, had to be tamped down in the film. Though not generally beholden to the hard-boiled idiom of the day, Stoddart relents in his depiction of Christa: "She could undress faster than a fireman could slide down a pole at the old engine house around the corner" (231). In Ulmer's rendition, Lucille Bremer, a former contract actor at MGM, who played opposite Judy Garland in *Meet Me in St. Louis* and who, during her teens, danced as a Radio City Rockette, endows Christa with notable sex appeal but also with greater subtlety and without the nudity suggested in the novel. Given the Code restrictions, that would not have been possible. In fact, as Joseph Breen puts it, in his memorandum of October 23, 1947, in a canned line he'd use again in his response to *Murder Is My Beat,* "The Production Code makes it mandatory that the intimate parts of the body—specifically, the breasts of women—be fully covered at all times. Any compromise with this regulation will compel us to withhold approval of your picture."[56] Bremer's Christa has some of the same sexual knowingness of

Ann Savage's Vera in *Detour,* but as in the case of Vera, her eroticism tends to percolate beneath the surface. Similarly, she possesses an uncanny ability to see through the sexual schemes of others: "From the first day, you weren't kissing me," she tells Vendig; "you were kissing 48 percent of Delta Bond and Share."

As in *Detour,* there are several understated aspects of the production that seem to have a more personal bearing on the director. The orchestral score by Werner Janssen, for instance, played by the Janssen Symphony Orchestra of Los Angeles and supervised by German émigré composer Paul Dessau, who had scored Ulmer's *Wife of Monte Cristo* two years earlier, allows the picture to luxuriate in the sounds of Old Europe, even a generic Viennese-style waltz at the critical moment in which Vendig invites Mallory to indulge him in a first dance. This helps not only to characterize the film's protagonist and his chosen milieu but also to showcase the taste of the director. (Mallory, as we learn, is a professional classical pianist.) There are, in addition, a few autobiographical affinities, conscious or unconscious, buried in the film's narrative. Early on, after Horace is forced to flee his father's rundown restaurant, he returns home one last time only to discover, through the crack of the door, his mother in the arms of her lover—a German-accented man named Alfred (Fred Nurney, *né* Fritz Nuernberger)—who wishes to take her away. Ulmer's own return to Vienna, after living in foster care in Sweden in the wake of the First World War, entailed a similar confrontation, recognizing that his mother had a new man in her life and that he was no longer completely at home in the family apartment in Vienna.[57] To be sure, the basic homelessness of young Horace makes him one in a string of refugees, social outcasts, and orphans (whether Fishke and Hodel in *The Light Ahead,* Peter in *Jive Junction,* or Paul in *Strange Illusion*) that Ulmer affectionately depicted in his films of the 1930s and 1940s.

In the end, however, the existential strain evidenced in the film may merely be a residual feature of Stoddart's novel. "Everybody was in the same boat in this struggle of existence," observes the narrator early on in *Prelude to Night,* "and a leaky scow it was, all bailing furiously with sieves, not hoping to free the boat of water so much as trying not to be swamped altogether" (7). In the film, of course, all paths lead to Vendig's inexorable decline, alluded to at the outset, when the guests gathered at Vendig's assembly speak of him "as though he just died." Ulmer skillfully teases out the tensions, building them to a crescendo in the final scene, with Scott and Greenstreet killing each other off. It is an appreciably more tragic, if less ironic, finish than in Stoddart's work, where after the news of Vendig's death hits the papers ("WOODRUFF VENDIG DROWNS"), his "Algerlike career" becomes a cause célèbre among the ruling elite: "His career will be an inspiration," so read the final lines of the novel, "to those who believe in the American system of free enterprise" (435).

Not long after the film's theatrical release, in mid-April 1948, critics from the industry's trade papers and the popular press were divided over its message and over the portrayal of its unsavory protagonist. In an advance review in the *Hollywood Reporter,* an unnamed critic praised the vérité qualities of the film, suggesting it had "borrowed its plot freely from Wall Street history and the events depicted [had] been plucked from yesteryear's headlines."[58] Several months later, Philip K. Scheuer of the *Los Angeles Times* highlighted "the strong and effective climaxes" of the film that "Edgar G. Ulmer, in his old-fashioned but all-out direction, has dealt with tellingly" (Scheuer also paid special tribute to the performances of the three female characters, from whom "Ulmer has drawn emotional responses . . . unsuspected until now").[59] In marked contrast, the *New York Times* called the film "[a] long, tedious recital about how a poor lad worked his way up the Wall Street ladder in the fabulous Twenties, brutally trampling over friend and foe." The main fault of the film, the reviewer argued, lay in the problem that "it is impossible to become concerned about a character so patently fabricated," a character "so cruelly cold and inhuman that he assumes a degree of monstrousness unrelated to reality."[60]

What the critic from the *New York Times* was presumably unaware of at the time of his writing was that the film's viciously anticapitalist narrative, adapted from Stoddart's novel, had been cowritten by two blacklisted screenwriters, Alvah Bessie (uncredited at the time) and Hungarian-born Gordon Kahn, both of whom had been summoned to testify before Congress the same year that the film was in production (a veteran of the Spanish Civil War, Bessie was forced to serve time in prison for refusing to confirm or deny party membership, while Kahn eventually fled to Mexico).[61] No doubt to Bessie and Kahn, and to their left-leaning writing partner S. K. Lauren, the charges of monstrousness and cruelty seemed like an accurate representation of the byways of money and power. "*Ruthless* is less concerned with the portrait of an unscrupulous megalomaniac," contends Reynold Humphries, "than with the portrayal of a system where money is paramount and people irrelevant except as pawns to move around the board to win ever more (financial) games in the name of ever-increasing profit."[62] Owing to its subversive undercurrent, the film belongs to "the neglected gems of the Hollywood Left" with its politically savvy "script full of Abraham Polonsky-style bon mots."[63] Indeed, Stoddart's novel has its own share of bon mots: the narrator remarks at the close of a central chapter, "A dollar is, as everyone knows, the scariest thing on earth" (125); or, even more self-consciously, Vendig's partner at Pan-American Sanford Lott talks about his "writers trying to slip in a Russian angle" (265).

Ulmer's own brand of politics—he was a lifelong Democrat, an ardent supporter of FDR and the New Deal—was considerably less radical, or less overtly radical, than those of his collaborators in the writing department. Yet both he and Shirley continued to maintain lifelong friendships with several of those who were called in to testify. "By 1947," writes Kenneth Anger in *Hollywood Babylon*, "the anti-Communist campaign led by Congressman J. Parnell Thomas had cast a pall over Hollywood as insidious as the newly-pervasive Los Angeles smog. With the House Un-American Activities Committee granting them open season, Movieland's fanatical right wingers emerged from the woodwork, wrapped themselves in the flag and came out punching—generally below the belt."[64] As Shirley Ulmer explained in 1996, in conversation with filmmaker Michael Henry Wilson, "Edgar was not a joiner, so they couldn't do anything with him." In the same interview, however, she relays a chilling anecdote, possibly embellished, about a couple of G-men who paid them a visit at their home on King's Road soon after *Ruthless* was released:

> I remember two FBI agents knocked on our door one evening and came in as we were getting ready to go to Europe, and they asked me to leave the room and talked to Edgar at length. Afterward, when they left, they gave him a sealed envelope, which I saw him put in his pocket. When I questioned him afterward, he said, "now that was [one] of the most difficult moments of my life. They wanted me to squeal on friends. They gave me this envelope, which had a special address on it, and I was not to lose this, but was to send it to them with names of anybody that I found suspicious living abroad while I was there." He took the envelope and tore it in half.[65]

There is no record contained in the FBI's extensive files made available to the public through the Freedom of Information Act, nor is there any other concrete evidence of Ulmer's political engagement.[66] Yet in his films—those made before, during, and after the McCarthy era—Ulmer never shied away from pitting venal money worship against higher moral and aesthetic choices.

What Ulmer sought to achieve in *Ruthless* was, by his own account, a twentieth-century rendition of a morality play, a kind of allegory of good and evil. In choosing a venerated European literary model that harkens back to the late Middle Ages—and which tends to subordinate individual character to the purposes of reflecting larger moral choices—he was once again drawing on his cultural lineage, even if pursuing such ambitions in Hollywood might be perceived as misguided or inappropriately high-minded.[67] As a means of explaining this unusual undercurrent, the film's press kit announced, in its section devoted to "Feature Material," extra information on the director: "Probably the only movie director in the business who can boast a Master of Philosophy degree is Edgar G. Ulmer."[68] Needless to say, Ulmer had not earned a Master of Philosophy—unless such degrees were granted on the basis of life experience—but he did have a recurrent tendency to pad his credentials. (A "Ph.D." mysteriously appears next to his name on the script for *Diagnostic Procedures in Tuberculosis,* one of the shorts he made for the National Tuberculosis Association in the late 1930s, and later, while working as a producer at Eichberg-Film in Munich in the mid-1950s, he rather boastfully, if disingenuously, lists the academic title "dr. phil." on his personal letter head.)[69] Regardless of his academic pedigree, Ulmer was fully aware of the philosophical and, indeed, political critique that comes across in the film. He insisted to Bogdanovich that, for him, it amounted to "a very bad indictment against 100 percent Americanism—as Upton Sinclair saw it" (601). As director, he took aim at the utter lack of morality that crippled an American character type like Vendig. Along these lines we might think of Vendig as somewhat akin to the gangster figure that Robert Warshow fashioned in his classic essay, "The Gangster as Tragic Hero," published in *Partisan Review* the same year that *Ruthless* was released. As Warshow puts it, the gangster "is what we want to be and what we are afraid we may become . . . [and as if paraphrasing the final line of the film] not a man, but a style of life."[70] Like other such characters, whether gangsters or *hommes fatales,* Zachary Scott's Horace Vendig is by turns deeply alluring and more than a little terrifying.

Over the years *Ruthless* has not lost its timeliness. Indeed, the core issues that Ulmer tackles have not disappeared in our age, nor have such characters as Vendig. Writing on his "Talking Pictures" blog, *Chicago Tribune* film critic Michael Phillips devoted a series of poignant reflections to the newly restored print of *Ruthless* touring the country as part of UCLA's 2009 Festival of Preservation. With the Madoff scandal, the financial meltdown, and Michael Moore's latest filmic intervention still fresh in our memory, Phillips writes, "Ulmer may as well have titled his 1948 opus 'Capitalism: A Love Story.' It is no less than a stinging critique of unchecked American greed and the rapaciousness of a personality type very much in our collective experience today."[71] It is almost too darkly ironic, too prescient in the wake of the colossal bank bailout of 2009, that a line from Stoddart's novel, when Vendig and a business partner are trying to secure venture capital, reads, "Try Goldman Sachs. They'll try almost anything" (195). *Ruthless* may have never had as much piercing resonance, even during its own day.

A LAST GASP OF STALE AIR

Somehow even mediocrity can become majestic when it is coupled with death.

—Andrew Sarris

After directing a few generally unnoticed pictures abroad, including the Italian production *I pirati di Capri* (*Pirates of Capri*, 1949) and the Spanish-English coproduction *Muchachas de Bagdad* (*Babes in Bagdad*, 1952), and continuing to work as a freelancer, Ulmer returned to the terrain of American hard-boiled noir one last time. His agent and friend Ilse Lahn, a transplant from Vienna who worked for the Paul Kohner Agency—which represented among other émigré filmmakers Billy Wilder, William Wyler, and Erich von Stroheim—came to him with a project called "The Long Chance" (what would ultimately acquire the release title *Murder Is My Beat*). In a letter of February 14, 1954, soon after the script had been vetted and approved by Joseph I. Breen's office, Ulmer informed his daughter Arianné that he was busy scouting locations for the production, which was scheduled to begin shooting that April.[72] At the time, he and Shirley were living in a rental apartment on Fountain Avenue in Hollywood, not terribly far from the studios for which he'd once worked. It had been a welcome return for both of them, having bounced around Europe for several years battling recurrent loneliness and feelings of marginalization.[73] Ulmer especially embraced the opportunity to work again in America, which by then, despite some of the recent political turmoil, he regarded as his true home.

Scripted by the British writer Aubrey Wisberg, who had cowritten Ulmer's *Man from Planet X* with Jack Pollexfen a few years before, and coproduced by Lahn and Wisberg for Masthead Productions as an Allied Artists release, *Murder Is My Beat* represents another instance in Ulmer's career of work done on the fly.[74] Owing in part to the vertiginous nature of the story confected by Wisberg and Martin Field and to the elliptical editing undertaken by Ulmer and Fred Feitshans Jr. (who, like Wisberg, had worked with him on *The Man from Planet X*), the film often feels unmoored, almost unfinished, given over more to atmosphere and emotion than to narrative coherence. "Ulmer introduces us to situations and characters without warning," observes John Belton. "The frequency and consistency of his narrative lapses give them thematic significance: whether it is intentional or not, Ulmer's narrative discontinuity becomes symbolic of the forces of disorder and destruction that dominate his artistic universe."[75] Like *Detour*, the film exudes an air of rawness, its players and settings notably gruff and downtrodden, a relatively accurate reflection of the bargain-basement production.

As in the case of his other two noirs, *Murder Is My Beat* takes shape more or less via flashback narration. The film opens with a sedan careening down a California highway bathed in sunlight, the man at the wheel exhibiting a look of dogged determination—the strains of Al Glasser's modest score helping to highlight the initial suspense—as he turns into a roadside motel. He exits the car and snakes his way around several motel cabins before sidling up to the one he's looking for, ducking under the window to make sure he's not noticed. Inside, viewed furtively through the cabin window shot from outside, Detective Ray Patrick (Paul Langton) lies on his back, eyes glazed over in a state of apparent resignation, staring up at the ceiling. The pose he strikes vaguely recalls the one struck by Burt Lancaster's Ole "Swede" Andersen near the start of Robert Siodmak's *The Killers* (1946), moments before his door is kicked in, which is precisely what occurs here.[76] Instead of being gunned down, though, Patrick leaps up and tackles his assailant, who after a few awkward, clumsy blows is recognizable as his boss in the Los Angeles Homicide Division, Captain Bert Rawley (Robert Shayne). As it turns out, Rawley has been chasing down Patrick ever since he and Eden Lane (Barbara Payton) jumped from the train that was to bring Lane to a prison upstate. There she was to serve a sentence for the murder of a man known as Frank Dean, a man with whom she allegedly had been having an adulterous affair and who was found lying headfirst in his own fireplace, face and hands charred beyond recognition.

Despite Rawley's insistence on taking Patrick back with him to Los Angeles in cuffs, and despite his firm belief that one of his "best men" was played for a sucker, Patrick manages to persuade his boss to listen to his story, which, unsurprisingly, is when Ulmer rolls out his flashback told in voice-over narration. Detective Patrick explains things from the very beginning, from the first moment that he showed up at the scene of the crime (i.e., when he was still the "level-headed, on-the-job, no-fancy-frills, straight-shooting cop" that Rawley took him to be when he assigned him to the case) to the burgeoning sense of doubt with respect to Lane's supposed guilt (i.e., when Patrick begins to feel as if he were "coming apart at the seams") and his ultimate decision to take "the long chance" of the film's working title—which is to say, to take the law into his own hands.

Along the way, we are given a tour of the inscrutable world of Eden Lane: we meet Patsy Flint (Tracy Roberts), Lane's shifty, tight-lipped roommate at "The Spotlight" nightclub, where Lane sings and where Flint works as a "picture snatcher" (her chief occupation, we later learn, is blackmail); we get a quick look at Flint and Lane's cluttered apartment and a few clues suggesting Lane's hurried departure on a Greyhound bus bound for Northern California; we then follow Detective Patrick, who, after trudging up a snow-covered mountain, finds his catch holed up in a chalet in the Sierras, on the lam but looking deceptively innocent ("all sweetness," as he puts it, "but the most dangerous type at that"); and finally, we witness Patrick becoming more and more smitten with the very woman he's sent to arrest for murder, from their first cigarette to their dramatic leap from the moving train, after Lane claims to have seen Frank Dean on the platform of a station they passed (Figure 26). Viewed in the wider context of film noir, Patrick shares some of the same susceptibilities that undercut the otherwise steely, rugged exterior of Detective Mark McPherson (Dana Andrews) in Otto Preminger's far more polished and generously bankrolled *Laura* (1944). They both exhibit a near-pathological faith in the innocence of a woman who is taken, at least fleetingly, to be a murderess. Moreover, they both show a willingness to ignore the rule of law in favor of their own vigilante pursuit of love.

At the very moment that Patrick has his story loop back to the original point at which Rawley entered the scene, Ulmer returns things to the present. With some additional coaxing, Patrick convinces his boss to give him another twenty-four hours and to lend a hand in finding the true murderer. Working as a team, they discover that Frank Dean was merely an alias for a married man named Abbott (Roy Gordon), the owner of a ceramics factory in the small Northern California town in which Patrick and Lane fatefully find themselves after jumping from the prison-bound train. Rawley and Patrick hunt down Abbott, squeezing

FIGURE 26. Partners in crime: Eden Lane (Barbara Payton) with Detective Ray Patrick (Paul Langton), holed up in a roadside motel, in *Murder Is My Beat* (1955). Photofest.

a confession out of him. In the film's penultimate scene, caught on a train leaving town with his wife, Abbott admits that while having an affair with Lane, he was blackmailed by a private investigator, the man he killed and whose body he left in his fireplace (the investigator, we learn, was romantically involved with Patsy Flint, who continues the extortion efforts). By the close, all loose ends are essentially tied up, and Patrick, in the ill-conceived, incommensurately sentimental final scene of the film, is free to marry Eden Lane, now proven innocent, with Rawley as his best man.

In terms of its generic trappings, *Murder Is My Beat* oscillates between noir, the police procedural and, as one critic has recently put it, a "rather ordinary whodunit."[77] Given its limited means, it isn't long on style, has minimal camera work, and essentially gets by on its canny use of mirrors, stock footage, and rear projection. But the basic mood of the film conveys the same social disillusionment encountered in other bleak pictures of the period. The specter of war, though slowly beginning to recede on the horizon by the mid-1950s, is still eminently palpable in *Murder Is My Beat*. Detective Patrick's moral compass, which we know from the world of noir is always in danger of being compromised, is guided by his wartime experience. "I'd seen too much killing in the Pacific," he announces while wading through the deep snowbanks in pursuit of Lane. Much like Al Roberts—and countless other noir anti-heroes—he is adrift in the world, taking each blow as it's dealt. And like Roberts, he ultimately accepts his fate, inauspicious as it may be. The final line of his flashback narration evokes a similar sense of ensnarement: "Now I knew I was licked." Similarly, Ulmer takes up the vexed issue of class—those who have it and those who don't—once more with this film. Indeed, Abbott's extramarital affair with the much younger nightclub singer Eden Lane is a form of social slumming for the factory owner, a way for him to indulge anonymously in the vices of big-city life. And as we observe further in the plot's unfolding, Mrs. Abbott (Selena Royle) comes from an unusually affluent, well-established family—the ceramics factory belongs to her—which makes the final charges of blackmail, those leveled against her and her husband by the conniving, déclassé Patsy Flint, all the more menacing. Mrs. Abbott would rather commit suicide, as she does in the end, than have her family name dragged through the mud.

If there is one thing that elevates the film, however, it's Barbara Payton's performance as Eden Lane. Having reached the pinnacle of her career playing opposite James Cagney in *Kiss Tomorrow Goodbye* (1950), only to then suffer from a pileup of scandals onscreen and off, Payton brought a degree of human vulnerability to the lead part, her last. Even if she's missing the high-octane verve of Ann Savage's Vera, Payton's Eden Lane, dressed in her formfitting sweaters, with her platinum blonde hair and thick, glistening lipstick of a 1950s pinup girl, helps get the film up on its feet. "It may lack the classic dimensions of . . . *Detour*," suggest film noir historians Bob Porfirio and Alain Silver, "but benefits from the presence of Barbara Payton as an ambiguous *femme fatale*. Ulmer extracts the maximum narrative tension from the viewer's uncertainty over Eden Lane's guilt, an uncertainty reinforced by Payton's portrayal of Eden in a 'neutral' manner."[78] From the moment we first meet her, sequestered in the mountain chalet looking pouty and forlorn but not entirely culpable, there is a magnetism that draws the viewer in and drives the film. It doesn't take long for Ray Patrick, and the audience with him, to fall for Eden, to believe her sighting of Frank Dean—what initially seems sure to be a mere MacGuffin—and to maintain an abiding faith in the distraught nightclub singer. Playing against type, she'd rather turn herself in for a crime she didn't commit than to have Detective Patrick jeopardize his career for his indiscretions.

Although review attention at the time of the film's release, in the final days of February 1955, was scant—and what did appear was uneven at best, with Ulmer's direction called "well-paced" in one trade paper but considered run of the mill elsewhere, i.e., "[direction of a] standard thriller in standard style"—Milton Luban's evaluation in the *Hollywood Reporter* declared, "Miss Payton is excellent as the wrongfully convicted girl."[79] As a side note, Luban found it fully within his rights as critic to offer his view of Payton's putatively expanding figure: "she is getting a bit too buxom." Of course, the film—from the script to casting to wardrobe, lighting, cinematography, and direction—no doubt played up this aspect, following the logic of exploitation, in the hope of box-office appeal. Early in Patrick's flashback, after arriving at the crime scene, Frank Dean's neighbor Miss Sparrow (Kate McKenna) recounts that Miss Lane "wore tight clothes [that] in an indecent way showed her shape" and that even her name "reminded you of original sin." When coproducer Ilse Lahn first supplied Joseph Breen with a copy of the script in January 1954, he flagged any and all suggestive bits (repeating the same canned language on the need to cover all body parts, specifically in the case of "the negligee worn by Eden").[80] It had to be clear, moreover, that Eden was not a prostitute. This was true of Patsy Flint as well. In the film she is referred to as a "picture snatcher," not to be confused with "middle-aged hustler," as the stage directions of the script initially had it—a red flag for Breen's office—but whose wardrobe, body movements, and gestures, after the shooting was complete, might suggest otherwise. As in *Detour,* Ulmer ultimately appears to have had a fair degree of wiggle room when it came to sexually charged banter (e.g., the flirtatious exchange between Patsy and Detective Patrick in her apartment) and racy innuendo.

Part of the attraction of a film like *Murder Is My Beat*—not altogether unlike that of *Detour*—is the visual pleasure taken in its imperfections and its flagrant violations of Hollywood studio conventions. It requires a certain appreciation of the so-called spirit of poverty, or what Antoine Rakovsky calls "l'esthétique du 'cheap,'" of underbudgeted, minimalist filmmaking in extremis.[81] By the time the initial enthusiasm for film noir, expressed by French cineastes and the auteur-focused critics of *Cahiers du cinéma,* had made its way across the Atlantic, such films as *Detour, Ruthless,* and *Murder Is My Beat* had found a new audience. Replicating the efforts of the French *Cahiers* crowd, American art-house moviegoers and critics of the late 1960s and 1970s took great pains to find virtues, even poetry, in the neglected, depraved, misunderstood independent pictures made on the fringes of Hollywood. Following such an approach, it was now possible, to paraphrase Andrew Sarris, to perceive the "mediocrity" of a second-bill crime picture as something truly "majestic." James Naremore describes the American film scene at the time in his history of film noir: "Critical commentary circulated through alternative newspapers and campus journals, and from the beginning, aficionados lavished special praise on B movies or slightly pulpish genre films. It was hip, for instance, to prefer *Murder Is My Beat* over *The Maltese Falcon,* or to argue that *Touch of Evil* was a better movie than *Citizen Kane.*"[82] In this cultural climate, driven at the beginning, perhaps, merely by a compensatory or contrarian impulse toward hipness, a director like Ulmer would achieve a new wave of recognition, one that was built in no small measure around the appreciation of his work in film noir.

+ + +

While there never was much media buzz around Ulmer's three films noirs, there was plenty swirling around his actors, whose career paths and personal lives seemed to become entangled in the most unimaginable ways. What occurred in real life, it turns out, far exceeded what was performed onscreen. "If Ulmer's best films deal with the plight of the misguided loser who strays from a righteous path to find comfort in the shadowy fringes," writes Payton biographer John O'Dowd, "he found just the right actress for the role of *Murder*'s troubled and ambiguous *femme fatale*—a character Barbara may have seen as a kindred spirit to her own jaded soul."[83] Over the years, Payton had been made the target of unforgiving Hollywood gossip, especially for her tempestuous relationship to *Detour*'s Tom Neal. She and Neal caused major headlines in September 1951, when Neal, in a jealous fit of rage, beat the actor Franchot Tone—to whom Payton was then formally engaged (they would eventually marry and divorce, Hollywood-style, within a matter of seven short weeks)—to a bloody pulp. The *Los Angeles Herald-Express* announced in extra-large, boldface type, "TOM NEAL KNOCKS OUT TONE IN LOVE FIST FIGHT!"[84] Payton did her best to deflect charges of two-timing (she was spotted cavorting with Neal throughout Tone's courtship), though she later admitted her incurable, near visceral weakness for Neal: "He had a chemical buzz for me that sent red peppers down my thighs."[85] Neal for his part defended his actions by invoking the red-baiting rhetoric of the day: "I didn't do anything wrong like being named a Communist. I just fought for the woman I love."[86]

A couple of years after the scandal, Payton and Neal would play opposite each other in Reginald Le Borg's B western *The Great Jesse James Raid* (1953), and with their romance still smoldering, they would go on to tour the Midwest together in a road-show theatrical adaptation of Cain's *The Postman Always Rings Twice* (with Neal picking up where John Garfield left off and Payton standing in for Lana Turner). A sensationalized advertisement for the production announced in tabloid fashion: "See Barbara and Tom Enact Torrid Love Affair Nightly in a Powerful Blend of Homicide and Passion."[87] By the time that *Murder Is My Beat* was released, it appeared that things had cooled off between them. Yet for Neal, who retreated from the industry by the mid-1950s, his role in generating headlines was not quite over. In what has to be one of the more bizarre cases of life imitating art, on the evening of April 1, 1965, Neal, by then working as a gardener in Palm Springs, walked into the Tyrol, an Alpine restaurant in the neighboring town of Idyllwild, where he was a regular, and announced to the owners that he had killed his wife. Despite Neal's infamous past, often presented as his given reason for fleeing to the desert, the owners of the Tyrol expressed incredulity when hearing what he had to say that night. "This is not an April Fool's joke," Neal insisted; "it's true."[88]

Early the next morning, the police entered Neal's home and found Gail Neal (*née* Kloke) dead on the couch, shot in the head with a .45 automatic. The story behind her murder, as it seeped into the courtroom later that autumn, included Gail's rumored plans for divorce and, from Tom's side, allegations of her multiple affairs and threats to kill him. For weeks on end the drama maintained a cheap air of celebrity, Barbara Payton consistently seated among the spectators, wearing dark sunglasses, all eyes focused on Tom Neal. Arthur Lyons claims that in the courtroom the cursed B actor managed to achieve "what had escaped him in his film career—top billing."[89] Most astounding was Neal's defense, which could have been borrowed almost directly from the script of *Detour*: a mere accident, "the gun went off." The pathologist who conducted the autopsy called his account "unlikely," but Neal's version held up before the jury. He was charged with involuntary manslaughter and served six years of a maximum fifteen-year sentence before being released. As he told a reporter at his sentencing, as if offering a new publicity tagline for Ulmer's picture in which he starred: "It's been a long, tough road."[90]

7

Independence Days

The final arc of Ulmer's career, especially after his years at PRC, is that of a director whose professional path was anything but straight. On a practical level this meant going wherever work took him, whether in the United States or abroad, and adjusting to the ebb and flow of an erratic and rapidly changing industry. Despite some initial discussion in the immediate wake of *The Strange Woman* that Ulmer might work once more with Hedy Lamarr and John Loder on the Hunt Stromberg production of *Dishonored Lady* (1947), he left Los Angeles for New York to prepare *Carnegie Hall,* a film that would allow him yet again to step outside the narrow world of Hollywood and to immerse himself in the broader realm of music. This move signaled the beginning of a protracted final phase for Ulmer, in which he directed stridently independent productions for generally small outfits and, as at the start of his career, trafficked in a number of different genres, styles, and national settings. From the late 1940s onward, he would make movies in New York City *(Carnegie Hall* and *St. Benny the Dip),* in far-flung corners of Europe *(Pirates of Capri, Babes in Bagdad, Hannibal, Journey beneath the Desert, The Cavern),* and in Hollywood's independent underground *(The Naked Dawn, The Daughter of Dr. Jekyll).* He would explore what was for him the uncharted world of science fiction *(The Man from Planet X, The Amazing Transparent Man, Beyond the Time Barrier),* and he would even release, under a pseudonym, a 1950s "nudie" *(The Naked Venus).* Thus, he returned to the well-trodden ground of the western, film noir, and horror, finally finishing his directorial career with a highly claustrophobic, existential war drama shot in the mountains of Yugoslavia in 1964.

As a testimony to Ulmer's versatility, but also his limits, a note on his service record at the Paul Kohner Agency, where he was a client throughout the final phase of his film career, reads: "Good film technician, capable production man, resourceful, fast worker, hard worker, invaluable for independent producer, good man for budget-wise studio such as U-I [Universal International], AA [Allied Artists], etc."[1] In other words, Ulmer's apprehensions vis-à-vis B-movie production, and his fear of being forever tagged a B director, were justified; he continued to make B-grade pictures into the 1950s and early 1960s, even after that niche within the industry had lost much of its initial market demand. If the first years of his career often forced him to the margins, both formally and financially, these final years were filled with a kind of marginal cinema *in extremis*, an unusually colorful string of ragtag productions—some of them surprisingly lovely, others eminently forgettable—that are long neither on coherence nor on consistency. Paradoxically enough, however, several of these films are no less personal than the work with which he is most commonly and deeply identified, including his earlier noirs and such formative films as *People on Sunday* and *The Black Cat*.

Because Ulmer crossed the Atlantic with such dizzying frequency during this time, and because the work that he completed was so spectacularly diverse, it makes much more sense to think of these films as organized—if they are organized at all—around thematic categories and geographic locations rather than approaching them in strict chronological order. Similarly, because of the extreme range in quality, from dross to minor wonders of ingenuity, some of the films made during this phase in Ulmer's career demand considerably more attention than others. Finally, given the unusually extensive, lively correspondence—letters to and from his wife, Shirley; his agent, Ilse Lahn; his publicity man, Wilson Heller; and others—that Ulmer maintained throughout the 1940s, 1950s, and 1960s, this period affords personal insights that some of the earlier periods, when Ulmer did not reflect on his work as a director, set designer, writer, and artist with as much zeal, do not.

MANHATTAN TRANSFER

Months before *The Strange Woman* enjoyed its premiere, in October 1946, Ulmer was already hard at work on his next film, *Carnegie Hall,* a semidocumentary tribute to musical virtuosity and its most cherished American shrine. The Ulmer family took a short-term leave from their home on Kings Road in late summer 1946, moving back East where they lived in rented rooms at the St. Moritz Hotel, just a couple of blocks from Carnegie Hall, on Central Park South. They remained in Manhattan for the full duration of the production, which entailed more than sixty days of shooting. Almost from the very start, and certainly since *The Black Cat,* Ulmer's unwavering commitment to classical music had impacted his career as a director and influenced nearly every facet of his private life. In conversation with Tag Gallagher, Ulmer's daughter, Arianné, observed how as a young girl she and her father would habitually listen on Saturday mornings to the radio broadcasts of the Metropolitan Opera; they took piano lessons together around this same time and frequently played their favorite compositions, including Mozart's *Well-Tempered Clavier,* as a four-hander.[2] In a similar vein, Arianné relates a story that her mother liked to tell of their earliest days, strapped for cash, living as a young family in New York in the late 1930s: "Mother once sent him out with our last five, six dollars to go shopping for food for the family, and he came home with a bag of oranges and two tickets to the Ninth Symphony."[3] In Ulmer's eyes personal sacrifice, if not outright starvation, was a supremely fair exchange for art.

While first living with Shirley in New York, a full decade before *Carnegie Hall,* Ulmer had spent a great deal of time with the Budapest-born conductor Fritz Reiner (whom he originally knew from his youth in Vienna and whom he would name as Arianné's godfather), who was then teaching at the Curtis Institute of Music in Philadelphia. Near the end of his life, Ulmer occasionally spoke of his own teaching stint at Curtis, and his work on several cherished musical recordings—Toscanini, in particular—for the Philadelphia-based Philco Program, though the full extent of that work is largely unverifiable and may be another instance of embroidered memory (B 599). What we do know, more or less, is that Reiner put Ulmer in touch with the music impresario Sol Hurok, a Russian-born agent who represented a talented list of European and American performing artists, and who in turn introduced him to the great virtuoso performers Jascha Heifetz and Artur Rubinstein and to the opera stars Lily Pons, Risë Stevens, and Ezio Pinza, all of whom are featured in *Carnegie Hall.*

Shot on location, in the late summer and early fall of 1946, with limited interior photography done at Fox Movietone News studio, the film was produced by Boris Morros and William LeBaron, both formerly of Paramount (where Morros had served as a musical director and producer, LeBaron as a lead producer), who established a small independent company, Federal Films, for the production. (Morros also had the dubious distinction of being a former Soviet spy and double agent for the FBI during the McCarthy years, beginning his stint as a counterspy just after the release of *Carnegie Hall,* his last film produced in America.)[4] During the casting of the film, a short notice, "One-Named Baton Waver Achieves Aim," appeared in the *Los Angeles Times.* The report tells how Morros and LeBaron, together with Ulmer, managed to find their ideal stand-in for Tchaikovsky for an early scene depicting the hall's opening week in 1891. During the early days of principal photography, Ulmer had been quick to recognize in conductor Alfonso D'Artega, a native of Mexico known professionally only by his last name, a striking resemblance to the Russian maestro. He thus approached D'Artega, the article recounts, and asked him, "Can you act?" "No," he responded, "but I can conduct an orchestra." The final line of the notice, as if relaying Ulmer's own indifferent stance toward the level of acting required by the film, reads matter-of-factly: "That was enough."[5]

What Ulmer faced as director of *Carnegie Hall* was the task of blending two rather incompatible parts: the part he cared about in the tribute to the world's greatest artists, on the one hand, and the part he would have been happy to scrap altogether, the inconsonant yarn spun by screenwriters Karl Kamb and Seena Owen, on the other. "It was impossible to tell a story after Wagner's *Meistersinger,*" he later insisted to Bogdanovich. "I had wanted to do a documentary, which they wouldn't let me do: I wanted the hall to speak, and have the experience of the music." In the end, though, he "had to have that silly story," as he pronounced it. "What are you going to do after Rubinstein plays Chopin? You're going to have a scene where *actors talk?* It's impossible" (B 599). Ulmer had worked with Leopold Stokowski, or "Stokie," as he liked to call him, several years before, purportedly helping him with recordings made for *Fantasia* (1940), and the charismatic British conductor appears here in dignified, even heroic form. Throughout the film Ulmer and his cameraman, William Miller, who had shot several of Ulmer's ethnic features, including *Green Fields, The Singing Blacksmith,* and *Cossacks in Exile,* took great pains to capture the almost superhuman quality of his subjects—Stokowski, Bruno Walter, Artur Rubinstein, and others— frequently shooting them from an extreme low tilt with the hall's ornate interior and ceiling lights forming a resplendent backdrop. As before at

FIGURE 27. Virtuosity: Ulmer *(right)* with Jascha Heifetz *(far left)* and Fritz Reiner on the set of *Carnegie Hall* (1947). Courtesy of the Academy of Motion Picture Arts and Sciences.

PRC, Ulmer also had the great cinematographer Eugen Schüfftan at his side, credited here as responsible for "production technique," to provide additional aesthetic input.

During the shoot, the performers, nearly all of them from overseas, formed a kind of émigré colony at the grand auditorium in midtown Manhattan. Several production photos taken on location document the close interaction between Ulmer and the star musicians, not to mention the striking harmony on the set, making rather clear where his own personal allegiances lay and the extent of his identification with the artists (Figure 27). Where aesthetics did not matter, where the focus was simply on story, Ulmer seems to have allowed things to work their way through—or not. Much of the contrived narrative centers on a music-loving cleaning woman named Nora (Marsha Hunt), an Irish immigrant who, in 1891, as an orphaned little girl fresh off the boat, visits the hall and sees "Tschaikowski" (D'Artega) conduct. In an early flashback we see the enraptured young girl, with Shirley Temple locks and dimples, looking on from backstage, seated in the private box opened to her by conductor Walter Damrosch (Harold Dyrenforth). There she takes in one of the legendary performances during the hall's first week, the dramatic first movement of Tchaikovsky's Piano Concerto in B-flat Minor, and is forever changed.

The actual present tense in which the film opens is a full eighteen years later, in 1909. We first enter the hall—still listening to the strains of the second movement of Beethoven's Fifth Symphony played during the credit sequence—to find the musicians onstage tuning their instruments for a rehearsal. Miller's camera tracks outward to capture the full accompaniment of the strings and brass sections flanked by an army of cleaners preparing the auditorium for the next performance. Wending her way to the orchestral level, Nora, by now a young woman, dusts while listening attentively. At this same moment the fictional Tony Salerno Sr., played by the Austrian actor Hans Jaray (here credited as "Yaray"), sits in for pianist Ignacy Jan Paderewski (ironically, the same figure that the frustrated piano prodigy Al Roberts is compared to in *Detour*) to play a piano concerto by Tchaikovsky.

The telling of Nora's story encompasses, and to a great extent embodies, the story of the hall ("But Nora," insists Jascha Heifetz late in the film, in one of his few onscreen lines, "you *are* Carnegie Hall"), chronicling its first six decades of existence. This is indeed the same place where "millions of people have listened to the world's greatest music," as an opening intertitle superimposed over a shot of the building's majestic facade tells us. We follow Nora as she falls in love with the temperamental European artist Salerno—who from his first appearance onstage, arguing with Damrosch about the proper way to interpret Tchaikovsky, shows himself to be something of a hotheaded rebel with a distinct Viennese lilt, two attributes he shares with the film's director—and gives birth to a boy, Tony Jr., during the hall's 1915–16 season. But even before that, during his initial courting of Nora, Tony Sr. ushers us into a familiar world for Ulmer and for viewers of Ulmer's films. We see the young couple as they visit with other musicians at the home of Anton Tribik (played by veteran Yiddish stage actor Joseph Buloff), eating sausages and drinking beer, surrounded by the Middle European accoutrements of a faux *Bierstube*, before breaking into an impromptu version of Schumann's Quintet in E-flat Major, the favored second movement we know so well from *Jive Junction* and *The Black Cat*. The romantic composition serenades the young lovers, Tony Sr. clutching Nora's hand to his breast, as the onlooking

Tribik announces to his wife that they should be playing Mendelssohn's Wedding March instead—which is precisely what we hear, after the fade-out transition, when the couple enters the apartment vestibule in the musicians' residences.

Meanwhile, the honeymooners' bliss doesn't last, as a drunken Tony soon returns home from rehearsal to announce that he's quit his job. "I'm sick of Carnegie Hall," remarks the defiant, self-righteous pianist, seemingly channeling the tortured soul of *Detour*'s Al Roberts. "I'd rather play in a saloon." And as if to dramatize his tragic descent from Olympian heights, he immediately falls to his death, plunging down the apartment stairs. But Salerno's musical legacy, and the trajectory from concert pianist to saloon-playing jazzman, similarly explored by Ulmer in *Jive Junction* and *Detour,* continues in Tony Jr. (William Prince). Despite all of Nora's efforts to instill in her son the very finest of classical music—paraphrased in the scattered scenes of mother-son outings to Carnegie Hall to see, among others, Bruno Walter conducting *Die Meistersinger,* Lily Pons singing an aria from *Lakmé,* and Artur Rodzinski conducting Beethoven's Fifth Symphony—Tony cannot control the urge to play more modern, improvisational music. We witness him, in a telling scene about halfway through the film, playing a jazz-inspired variation of Chopin's Waltz in C-sharp Minor, op. 64, no. 2, in which he pounds the keys with a frenzied velocity similar to Roberts's in Ulmer's earlier film. Nora enters the room and, after pausing to look at snapshots of her unruly late husband on the sideboard, brings Tony sheet music given to him by Rubinstein with the exhortation to study hard ("You must practice Bach, Bach, and Bach again"). As a means of appeasing his mother, Tony offers to play one of Chopin's nocturnes, to which she sternly responds, "Let's just make sure that it's Chopin, and *not* Tin Pan Alley."

Later in the film, after a number of set pieces used for the sole purpose of showcasing more musical performances (Jan Peerce doing "O sole mio" on a rehearsal stage or Ezio Pinza singing "Il lacerato spirito" offstage), Nora berates her son for focusing his energies on playing big-band jazz on tour with the Vaughn Monroe Orchestra. "You're *not* an entertainer," she snaps at him, "you're a musician!" Tony realizes at this point that his classical training has been to satisfy his mother and runs off to pursue fulfillment in the jazz world. The film, and its painfully trite story line, comes to resolution in the closing scene (almost a rehash of Friedrich Feher's maestro watching the Clinton High School band performance in *Jive Junction*), when Tony gets his chance to redeem himself at Carnegie Hall. He performs "57th Street Rhapsody," a composition attributed to him, featuring a solo by jazz trumpeter Harry James, with his mother looking on in approval. For optimal contrast, this is preceded by a scene of Stokowski conducting the second movement from Tschaikovsky's Fifth Symphony, captured in a series of dramatic low-angle shots of his famously wild mane looking virtually electrified. "Ulmer borrows the modernist tools of cinematic spectacle," *New Yorker* film critic Richard Brody has recently observed, "to unify space with a classical poise and to replicate the melodic swirl of the music itself."[6] Tony is thus finally accorded the same status as the great conductors who have come before him. American popular music, embodied in Tony, is shown to advance and reconfigure European classical music for the future, much as real-life composers like George Gershwin had done with such celebrated compositions as *Rhapsody in Blue* decades before.

Working together with Danish-born costume designer and set director Max Rée, whose previous screen credits include the William Dieterle– Max Reinhardt collaboration on *A Midsummer Night's Dream* (1935), Ulmer captured not merely the spirit of the hall and its evocative grandeur but the international spirit of American musical culture of the late nineteenth and early twentieth century. Of the some eighteen featured performers in the film, only two had been born in the United States. Similarly, the dominant music that the film champions—and for which Ulmer shows his biases—hails from the world that the musicians, vocalists, and assorted crewmembers once called home (musical adviser Sigmund Krumgold helped Ulmer with his expert selections). Indeed, as the film's pressbook makes clear, the story of immigration lay at the heart of the production and the institution it celebrates: "To the great foreign artists, Carnegie Hall is the official gate to America."[7] Perhaps the true sign of acculturation and popular acceptance comes in a fleeting scene, toward the end of the film, in which Margaret, the black cleaning woman (uncredited) who works for Nora, is seen furtively dancing to one of Tony Jr.'s jazz records, the aptly titled "American Rhythms." She and her girlfriends, she later confesses to Nora, have established a "Tony Salerno Fan Club," the ultimate stamp of approval.

Just as Bill Krohn claims that we might understand Ulmer's Yiddish comedy *American Matchmaker* as a kind of cinematic epilogue to his drama *The Light Ahead*, so, too, we may consider *Carnegie Hall* a happy-ending sequel to *Detour*. In other words this is the story of what could have happened to Al Roberts, had he made it to the big leagues.

Tony Jr. pursues a path similar to Al's, moving freely in the world of urban musical culture from classical to jazz, but unlike Al he manages to triumph in the end. "Again, it is tempting to read Ulmer's own situation into these films," remarks musicologist Erik Ulman, "as an artist who descended from Murnau and Reinhardt to the depths of PRC, with Tony as a kind of wish fulfillment of finding artistic validity . . . in commercial culture."[8] To Ulmer, Carnegie Hall represented a mythical place, a sacred shrine or golden temple, embodying the best that high culture could offer. Soon after the production wrapped, Ulmer told a reporter from the *Hollywood Citizen-News* that there was "magic" in the hall throughout the production: "I just sat back and listened to that glorious music day after day."[9] Like the name Max Reinhardt, Carnegie Hall possessed wide recognition; it was a name to be venerated, one that carried considerable cultural cachet, and like Reinhardt a name with which Ulmer was all too happy to be associated. Ulmer had long portrayed the place as a proper point of aspiration in his films. Most memorably, *Detour* glosses it as the pinnacle of cultural legitimacy, the kind of venue that a doomed nightclub pianist like Al Roberts will never play. When little Billy Jr., in *Her Sister's Secret,* is seen banging away on his toy music box near the close of that film, his father comments: "Skipper, we have a long way to go before we're ready for Carnegie Hall."

As much as Ulmer would have preferred to scrap the fictional story line of the film, it allowed *Carnegie Hall* to reach audiences beyond the committed music aficionados. "You should have seen it as this reporter did, in the company of bobby-soxers," notes one critic in an advance review, as if describing the cast of *Jive Junction,* "and hear these kids cheer for Pons, Rubinstein and Peerce even louder than they did for Vaughn Monroe and Harry James. It was a thrilling experience."[10] Members of the cultural elite were slightly less charitable. Film critic Bosley Crowther of the *New York Times,* in his review the day after the film's New York premiere on May 2, 1947, at the Winter Garden on Park Avenue, dismissed the story with a stroke of the pen "as hackneyed and maudlin a 'hanger' as ever dripped from a screenwriter's pen." After pointing to some of the notable performances (Rubinstein on the piano, Heifetz on violin), he suggests, "the conventional pictorial presentation is generally monotonous." Yet he reserves the bulk of his ire for the finale (the "57th Street Rhapsody"), which he brands "a pretentious piece of musical claptrap," contending more damningly, "It is as brash and artificial as the story and staging of 'Carnegie Hall'—which leaves us back on the curbstone."[11]

In a similar vein, writing in *The Nation,* James Agee fulminated, "*Carnegie Hall* is about the sickest and sourest mess of musical mulligatawny I have yet had to sit down to, a sort of aural compromise between the Johnstown flood and the Black Hole of Calcutta." But he also felt, on balance, that "as a record of what various prominent musicians look like under strange professional circumstances, it is a permanently fascinating and valuable show."[12] Compelled to offer a rejoinder, *New York Times* music critic Olin Downes, who is treated to a brief cameo in the film and who is mocked in Crowther's review, published a piece under the apologetic subtitle "'Carnegie Hall' May Be Milestone Despite Story." For Downes, who considered the film "a sensation of thrilling intensity—nothing less," the production afforded a chance for classical music to be rendered in a new light, thereby reaching a wider audience; he notes further in his defense that the screenings he attended were not only sold out but that audiences remained in their seats, hoping to sit through the two-hour show twice.[13]

The original 140-minute version that Ulmer submitted to producers Morros and LeBaron, and that allegedly bore a price tag of $1.7 million, had to be trimmed somewhat. "You don't even see the Toscanini sequence I made," Ulmer bemoaned to Bogdanovich, "which was cut out because the producer failed to pay [for the rights]" (B 599). In his probing analysis of the director, Michael Henry Wilson underscores Ulmer's dogged pursuit of aesthetic greatness and the perennial clash between art and commerce, a tribute, perhaps, to his European training:

> In America, however, the artist cannot survive if he doesn't yield to popular tastes. This very personal dichotomy may account for a recurrent lament: to survive, Ulmer's characters have to rein in their ambition and give up classical music (the mystical legacy bestowed by their dead fathers) on behalf of jazz or swing. Dick Moore switches from Schumann to jive, while Frederick Feher lends his instruments to a band playing for GIs in a junior canteen *(Jive Junction).* Tom Neal would rather play boogie-woogie in the Break O'Dawn nightclub than end up as Carnegie Hall's janitor *(Detour).* A year and four films later, we find William Prince "betraying" the classic tradition he has been raised into when he joins a modern orchestra and creates Harry James' 57th Street Rhapsody *(Carnegie Hall).* In *St. Benny the Dip,* Nina Foch, herself a failed opera singer, explains her cellist father's decline: "Too much bebop, not enough Beethoven!"[14]

Wilson astutely recognizes the recurrent frustrations that someone like Ulmer must have felt, churning out cheap entertainment at PRC and later for other independent companies. "When Ulmer was hailed as 'the Capra of PRC,'" he concludes, "it probably struck him as a bitter joke, for this was a man who knew he was an artist, not a mere entertainer. The maestro toiled at Club Havana, but really belonged in Carnegie Hall."[15]

+ + +

Ulmer would direct once more in New York, just a few years after *Carnegie Hall,* and after he'd completed *Ruthless* and *Pirates of Capri.* He returned, in the spring of 1950, to make his low-budget comedy *St. Benny the Dip* for Danziger Productions. The independent company, run by brothers Edward and Harry Lee Danziger (sometimes jokingly referred to by Ulmer as "the brothers Karamazov"), London-based American hoteliers, produced B movies in Europe and America. Ulmer's first stint with the Danzigers was assisting them on *So Young, So Bad* (1949), a reform-school drama (with a significantly higher budget than Ulmer's PRC quickie *Girls in Chains*) directed by Bernard Vorhaus and starring Paul Henreid. (Ulmer is said to have filled in for Vorhaus in the final phase of the shoot, but he receives no credit on the print.) *Benny* represented Ulmer's first return to comedy—and also his last—since *My Son, the Hero* at PRC. Like that earlier film, he attempted, in collaboration with scriptwriter John Roeburt, to give a wink to Damon Runyon, a writer Ulmer admired and allegedly befriended while in New York. In so doing, he hoped to create something "that was quintessentially American."[16] But, as in *My Son, the Hero,* comedy was not Ulmer's strong suit.

Opening with exterior shots of the city at night, vaguely evocative of those used at the start of both *Moon over Harlem* and *American Matchmaker,* the camera soon tracks in on a hotel where a card game is under way. Tough guy Monk Williams (Lionel Stander), who has a gravelly voice and the comic air of a strongman prancing around in ballet tights, fixes a round of drinks for his two partners in crime, Benny (Dick Haymes) and Matthew (Roland Young), and their unknowing guest, whom Monk coyly slips a mickey. The three crooks soon fleece their guest and frame it to look like he was robbed during a visit from a call girl—lipstick traces, lingerie, and all. Someone tips off the cops, sending the three crooks on the run. As they cut through the dark corners of the city, initially seeking refuge in a Greenwich Village cathedral—identified as the Episcopalian Grace Church in the correspondence between censorship czar Joseph I. Breen and Ulmer (which articulates the Production Code's concerns about any possible defamation)—they don priests' garb and disappear into the night, marching right by the unsuspecting police.[17]

As long as they remain in disguise, the three crooks, holed up in a vacant former church mission on skid row, in the shadows of Lower Manhattan's waterfront, can live without fear of imprisonment.

Like *My Son*, the thrust of the comedy in *Benny* comes from the struggle to keep up appearances, including Marx Brothers–style hat routines and plenty of slapstick, in this case acting like holy men and doing the good deeds expected of them. Benny escorts home the drunken cellist Mr. Kovacs (played by the Austrian-born theater and film actor Oskar Karlweis), who takes to drink to help inoculate his senses against the music he has to play for a living in the New World ("too many saxophones, too many terrible saxophones"), and meets his attractive daughter, Linda (Nina Foch), in the process. With an implicit nod to *Carnegie Hall*, Linda confesses her unrealized dream, "I wanted to be a great operatic star," while her father unhappily sets aside his classical training to play bebop. Benny spends much of the film trying to woo Linda without blowing his cover (his only fears in life, as he tells us, are "old age, the atom bomb, and inquisitive dames"), while the others, too, find themselves exploiting their disguise and becoming more like the people they are impersonating. Matthew eventually believes the sermons he gives ("Let there be light!"), and Monk attempts rather clumsily and endearingly to follow the righteous path.

By no means Ulmer's best work, though certainly not his worst, the film was completed at Eastern Service Studios in June 1950 (Shirley Ulmer celebrated her thirty-sixth birthday on the set, with the full cast and crew in attendance) and went on to receive modest review attention in the trade papers the following summer.[18] (After Ulmer made his way back to Europe, where he'd begun making pictures the year before *Benny*, he complained to his agent about the stingy publicity budget for the film.) "*St. Benny the Dip* may be a sleeper and turn in profitable results at the box office," forecasted *Variety*. "This crook-saint yarn has Dick Haymes, Nina Foch, Roland Young, Lionel Stander and Freddie Bartholomew to brighten the marquee, and word-of-mouth should help it in many locations." The same unnamed reviewer goes on to suggest: "The Danziger (Edward J. and Harry Lee) production sets a high standard for their future pictures. It has the necessary values, including a nice directorial job by Edgar Ulmer, a tight script by John Roeburt from the smooth-rolling original by George Auerbach, and a well-chosen cast."[19] The next time that Ulmer would reconnect with the Danzigers would be in Europe, as he began crossing the Atlantic during the final phase of his career with the frequency of an international businessman or, perhaps, of someone who was still trying to figure out where exactly he belonged.

WANDERLUST

Ulmer's final years as a director ended just as they had begun: in a state of seemingly constant motion. As fellow Austrian émigré screenwriter Salka Viertel, a collaborator of Ulmer's in the 1950s and a close family friend since their early years in Los Angeles, writes in her memoir, *The Kindness of Strangers:* "In those first years in California, I don't think I met anyone who had been born or raised there. The actors and writers, especially those from the East, were transitory, having come to make money and to get out as soon as possible. I also was counting the days till our return to Europe."[20] Ulmer, too, appears to have harbored a strong desire to revisit the continent that he had left behind almost two decades before. While the embers of World War II still burned, the conditions of McCarthy-era America made his adopted home less palatable than it had once been. Like many others in his cohort of émigré actors and filmmakers who retraced their steps across the Atlantic soon after the war ended, including Robert Siodmak, Peter Lorre, Fritz Kortner, and Otto Preminger, he hoped he might be greeted with a warm embrace, an attitude resembling that of Karl Rossmann, the protagonist of Kafka's unfinished novel *Amerika: The Man Who Disappeared.* "We've lost touch now of course," notes the unmoored Rossmann, "but if I ever return to Europe, they'll be glad to see me, and we'll be friends again right away."[21]

Toward the end of the 1940s, finding it increasingly difficult to land work, Ulmer left behind the moribund American B-movie industry for Europe, where he soon became involved in a variety of offbeat productions. Starting with the Italian-American coproduction *I pirati di Capri* (*The Pirates of Capri,* 1949), a swashbuckler starring Ulmer's dear friend and standby actor Louis Hayward, and leading up through the Danziger brothers' Spanish coproduction *Muchachas de Bagdad* (*Babes in Bagdad,* 1951), his aborted directorial efforts in the French-Italian Hedy Lamarr vehicle *The Loves of Three Queens* (1954), and the codirected epic costume dramas *Annibale* (*Hannibal,* 1960) and *L'Atlantide,* a.k.a. *Antinea* (*Journey beneath the Desert,* 1961), Ulmer churned out a string of movies that have largely been ignored—some for good reason—by film history. His concerted efforts to reinvent himself while in Europe, where among other things he acquired the self-appointed title of "Dr." Edgar Ulmer while working at Eichberg-Film in Munich in the 1950s, resemble to a large extent what he had already done decades before in the United States. But they also represent a redoubled attempt to achieve a new kind of aesthetic freedom and the financial stability he'd long yearned for in Hollywood. In spite of his renegade status and his reputation for turning his nose up at commercial success, his private writings—notes and letters to his agent, various collaborators, and to his family—convey lingering hopes of returning to Hollywood and experiencing that ever-elusive breakthrough and the kind of fame that never came during his lifetime. "Independence can hurt," observes Grissemann in his chronicle of the director's life.[22]

After pursuing several untenable ideas, including a remake of Leni Riefenstahl's Alpine drama *Das blaue Licht* (*The Blue Light*, 1932)—optioned by his agent Ilse Lahn at the Paul Kohner Office, with Ulmer in mind to direct, and whose original producer, Henry Sokal, had hoped to make it in Switzerland with Louis Hayward as his leading man—Ulmer committed to producer Victor Pahlen, electing to direct *Pirates* in early fall 1948.[23] Like many of the European productions with which he became involved, *Pirates* was shot simultaneously in two languages: Italian and English. A couple of months in advance of the shoot, which took place on location in southern Italy and in and around Rome throughout the winter and spring of 1949, Ulmer traveled on his own to scout locations and to secure a suitable ship on which to photograph key scenes in the film. From Italy he cabled Shirley and Arianné in California, who were living once more on Kings Road, urging them to join him. The call to work on *Pirates,* as Shirley later remembered, marked a significant change for her and her husband, one in which they "started [to pursue] a Gypsy-like livelihood." As she notes further, commenting on their seemingly nomadic lifestyle, "I became an expert packer and I know how to—or I tried to—make a hotel room homey. He [Ulmer] used to laugh, and say, 'we were wandering Jews now,' that's the way it was going to be because he was going to make these films."[24]

Soon after receiving the telegram, sometime in late fall 1948, Ulmer's ever-faithful script supervisor and their eleven-year-old daughter, who plays a small part in *Pirates,* traveled overnight from Los Angeles to New York, where they caught a flight to Rome. There they had just enough time for a quick shower and dinner before catching a midnight train to Taranto, a coastal town and major naval seaport in the boot heel of Italy, where filming was set to begin. Upon their arrival at Ciampino Airport in Rome, Shirley immediately noticed the postwar deprivation. "The city was in shambles," she later recalled, almost as if describing the backdrop of Vittorio De Sica's *Ladri di biciclette* (*Bicycle Thieves*, 1948) made in the Italian capital that same year. "We arrived in Rome, there was no airport, there was nothing. We arrived on dirt ground."[25]

Shirley relates another story of how upon their arrival, exhausted, shivering, and possibly a bit delirious from their back-to-back flights, they were greeted by swarms of Italian children in tattered clothing. The children insisted on following her and her daughter as they lugged heavy suitcases—filled with clothes, hair spray, makeup, and other supplies for the shoot—across the cold dirt, shouting what sounded like "Bastard, Jew! Bastard, Jew!" With the horrors of the fascist past and Italy's alliance to Nazi Germany still on her mind, Shirley, on her first-ever trip to Europe, imagined the worst: "I thought, oh, my God, you mean we've got another Hitler situation here, what the hell have I gotten into?" Only later did she realize that in Italian what these children were really saying was "basta" (enough) and "giù" (down), asking them to put down their luggage so they could help carry it for them—for a small gratuity, of course.

The saga was not yet over, however; a final surprise awaited them in Taranto. There they were met at the train station by Russian-born actor Michael Rasumny, who plays the puckish pirate jester Pepino in the film, and who explained that Edgar—preoccupied with running tests on the ship—was eagerly expecting them. In his absence Rasumny showed Shirley and Arianné to their new living quarters. It was the only building, in Shirley's recollection, that was left standing, windows still boarded up, after the heavy British bombardment during the war. "In that building there were a lot of servants, girls wearing potato sacks tied around them, no clothes. And there was a woman who sat in the middle of the place, she had a coffee maker going with hot water."[26] If filming her husband's ethnic pictures in late-1930s rural New Jersey—on that legendary farm sandwiched between a nudist colony and a pro-Nazi training camp—had been an adventure for Shirley, this was something of an entirely different magnitude. It turned out that the woman with the coffeemaker, affectionately known as *Animale*, was the madam of the brothel in which they were now all suddenly living. As Ulmer later liked to joke, "I'll bet you I'm the only man who took his wife and daughter to live in a whorehouse."[27]

The state of affairs on the set was not much better. Shooting had to be postponed owing to the film's missing lead, who in late fall 1948 was still in Los Angeles recovering from a driving accident and a nasty bout of pneumonia. "Hayward thought he might have to give up his engagement in 'Pirates of Capri' in Italy," announced *Los Angeles Times* reporter Edwin Schallert, whose actor son William Schallert would soon play the lead in Ulmer's *Man from Planet X*, "but present plans call for him to leave Dec. 2 to start work on Dec. 6. It seems Producer-Director Edgar Ulmer has been able to rearrange the shooting schedule to accommodate the situation."[28] What Hayward encountered upon his arrival couldn't have helped his health. The coastal climate of Taranto in winter was bitter cold (the still recovering Hayward purportedly had to keep a makeshift heating pad—a rubber douche hidden beneath his gauzy pirate shirt).[29] As a former U.S. Marine in the war, Hayward was not thrilled about performing on an old Italian navy ship, even one christened *Cristoforo Columbo,* nor acting opposite Mariella Lotti, who plays Countess Mercedes de Lopez in the film and was known to have been one of Mussolini's many lovers.

Language problems, the handling of an unusually large cast of extras, recurrent financial setbacks, and chronic illness comprised just some of the challenges that Ulmer and company faced on the shoot. According to Shirley, her husband, who never flinched in the face of adversity, spoke of such productions as "wars." In his roman à clef, *The Celluloid Asylum, Pirates* scriptwriter Sidney Alexander portrays a German-accented director named Sigmund Melson, who, in the process of making his movie *I briganti di Napoli,* drives his cast and crew to the brink of insanity. The maniacal, workaholic director of Alexander's novel aspires to make his dialogue "more Mozartian, you know the Minuetto of the *C Major* . . . with just a trace of Handel's fanfare."[30] The director's wife is left to suffer the fate of living with a mad genius.

On the actual set there was plenty of suffering, too. "All of us were deathly sick with colds and dysentery," reported Shirley to agent Ilse Lahn back in Hollywood.[31] Because of insufficient payment from Pahlen, Ulmer and company had to borrow money from Hayward to cover expenses in Taranto before departing for Amalfi—a fourteen-hour drive in a tiny Italian car stuffed with passengers, their stacks of luggage piled on top—where the shoot continued. In the same letter to Lahn, Shirley urged her to help hawk their Buick for much-needed cash and shared with her a few juicy anecdotes from the shoot. "It was a strange sight," she recounted, "to see Rasumny's costume catch fire in a vital frontal spot from a flare he was carrying in a scene. He finished the take on fire and won not only Edgar's cheers but those of the whole

Italian navy."[32] In subsequent letters Shirley told Lahn of widespread poverty, the deep misery and bands of naked children in Salerno, and the dangers of shooting all night in a grotto cave near Amalfi. She also conveyed another moment of levity and mutual understanding among members of the Italian crew, when, on the occasion of the Ulmers' fourteenth wedding anniversary, the hotel orchestra dressed in costumes pilfered from the *Pirates* wardrobe and serenaded Shirley, Edgar, and the entire cast and crew during a sumptuous meal, with vast quantities of wine and dancing into the early hours.[33]

In the finished film, released in the United States on Christmas Day 1949, the myriad problems Ulmer had faced offscreen are virtually undetectable. Compared to *The Wife of Monte Cristo*, Ulmer's swashbuckler made for PRC three years earlier, *Pirates* has much more fluidity in its long tracking shots, more dramatic flair, and considerably higher production values. "I hear it will be superb," wrote Ilse Lahn to producer Pahlen in late January 1949. "Someone who saw the rushes [i.e., Shirley Ulmer] recently writes me that it has an 'Eisenstein quality' which, to my way of thinking, is about the highest praise that can be given to any picture."[34] Like the earlier film for PRC, *Pirates* deals with a masked count who aids a revolutionary underclass in the battle against a tyrannical regime. In this case, however, the film is set in the immediate wake of the bloody French Revolution, with the execution of Marie Antoinette, sister of Queen Carolina Maria (Binnie Barnes) of Naples, providing an ominous specter of what "the people" are capable of perpetrating against an oppressive ruling class. From start to finish, *Pirates* portrays the pitched battles between the pirate-led masses, with the masked Sirocco (Hayward) at the helm, and the uncaring and corrupt Neapolitan court embodied in the figures of Baron von Holstein (Rudolph Serato), a man who is "rotten with power" and who still has blood on his hands from the murder of Count Amalfi's brother, and his equally conniving colleague Commodore Van Diel (Alan Curtis).

Hayward earns the most screen time, moving back and forth between his roles as the charismatic, sword-wielding, masked pirate captain Sirocco (a man of many talents, Hayward does all his own fencing) and the scarf-waving, foppish dandy Count Amalfi. In the opening scene, as Sirocco, he helps his men take over a ship bound for Naples transporting munitions and the lovely Countess Mercedes de Lopez, who has been summoned by the queen to marry Count Amalfi. The rugged Sirocco relishes taunting the countess ("You're even more beautiful when you're angry"), whom he proceeds to woo in his dual roles, sneaking into her sleeping chamber in a later scene, and marching off with her—after she finally realizes that Sirocco and Amalfi are one and the same—in the film's climax. Sirocco and his comedic sidekick Pepino, who provides a heavy dose of vaudeville shtick, manage to plot their way into a palace ball reenacting, much like Ulmer's play-within-a-play *Faust* episode in *Bluebeard,* a circus-like performance of the count triumphing over Baron von Holstein. Leading up to this, Hayward hams it up as Amalfi, seizing the opportunity to ingratiate himself into the queen's inner circle, and ultimately saving her life ("Better she lose the crown than her head," he remarks early on), with the sort of contrived laughter, impish wit, and rhetorical innuendo that anticipate Tom Hulce's shrill portrayal of the title role in *Amadeus* (1984).

Although the film's story line follows a relatively predictable course, its performances are strikingly uneven and its dialogue—a good chunk of it dubbed—rather stilted, *Pirates* includes a few graceful moments. Thanks in no small measure to cinematographer Anchise Brizzi, who had photographed De Sica's *Shoeshine* (1946) just a few years earlier and who would soon serve as cameraman on Orson Welles's *Othello* (1952), the film enjoys an unexpected touch of realism in the handsome exterior shots of the rocky Amalfi coast. Similarly, Brizzi's filming of the nighttime battle between the Neapolitan loyalists and Sirocco's men, including a dramatic rooftop escape by the disguised count, proves equally effective. Another standout scene comes near the end, in the shadow-drenched sword fight between Sirocco and Holstein—shot by Ulmer, Brizzi, and their crew inside the Palazzo Brancaccio in Rome—after the queen's ball has been stormed by the rebelling masses; the flickering candles left over from the ball and the blazing torches held by the revolutionaries allow Brizzi to bathe the scene in rich chiaroscuro lighting. Enhancing the dramatic thrust of the film is Nino Rota's subtle, romantic score (even if it isn't of the same strength and international renown as the Italian composer's subsequent work with Fellini, Visconti, and Scorsese).

During the film's final phase of production and postproduction, in spring 1949, Ulmer remained in Rome, where he worked day and night shooting the last scenes, recording the soundtrack, and continuing to await payment from "that S.O.B." Pahlen. "Whatever you lived through in money worries during the making of the picture," he reported back to Shirley, who by then had returned to California with Arianné, "is child's play [compared] to what goes on now." By his own bitter calculation, he was owed five weeks of back pay and, adding insult to injury, was left to countenance the poor behavior of the actors, Hayward among them, whom he later compared to prima donna Hedy Lamarr. Yet in the same letter he boasts that Pahlen had screened an early cut of the film for the European heads of MGM, Paramount, Columbia, and Warner Bros. at the Excelsior Hotel. After the screening, while seated at the bar with Brizzi, Ulmer purportedly received a visit from a Mr. Levy from Paramount, who marched up to him and announced ("so that everybody could hear it"): "That the picture was a triumph for one Edgar Ulmer, that I was [a] genius and more ad nauseam. Arthur Loew of Metro chimed in that nobody of the actors could live up to my job."[35]

In truth, *Pirates* was neither comparable to Eisenstein, as Lahn had optimistically suggested to Pahlen, nor a particular triumph for Ulmer, whose cinematic achievements in the eyes of high-power studio heads were fleeting at best. Both the advance press and the reviews that followed the film's American release on Christmas Day 1949 were mixed with an occasional nasty barb here and there, especially concerning the story. "Here's a good, old-fashioned, swashbuckling adventure drama shot against authentic Italian backgrounds," wrote industry critic Fred Hift in the *Motion Picture Herald,* "full of fine costumes, clashing swords and roaring mob. . . . Directed by Edgar Ulmer with a sensitive regard for the real needs of pictures of this kind, the pirates plot, ride and fight with vigor and courage sufficient to appeal to any fan."[36] Writing in *Variety,* an unnamed critic observed on balance: "Edgar Ulmer's direction injects a number of rough-and-tumble sequences that give the film its best chance for a payoff, but neither he nor the players can do much with the script's lines."[37] A far less charitable critic in the *New York Times* inveighed: "Stuffy and obvious are the adjectives that best describe 'The Pirates of Capri.'"[38] Finally, a critic in *Films in Review,* writing a decade later, when the film was limited to the occasional airing on television, summed it up: "Louis Hayward as Errol Flynn imitating John Gilbert burlesquing Doug Fairbanks."[39]

Indeed, in the wake of *Pirates,* left behind in Rome, Ulmer's continued loneliness, intermittent depression ("in the darkest pit of my life," he wrote Shirley), and fears of getting stuck in an unsatisfying rut of offbeat productions soon set in. "Darling, I am very tired," he confided to his wife. "I am not as young as I used to be. I want to live. . . . I do not want to be the most successful director in Forrest Lawn Memorial Park."[40] During this period he found himself prone to introspection. He wrote Shirley long letters in which he reflects on their marriage, invoking Freud, ruminating on his love-hate relationship with his mother, and introducing various lofty and abstract categories that represent life ("ambition equals subjugation of sex and character," "self-willed lone-liness," "Karfreitagszauber—Good Friday Magic").[41] In another letter from the same cycle, after underscoring once more his lonesome condi-tion, he compares himself to the great German composers: "You see Ulmer is not Wagner and not Bach, but Beethoven. Deaf to everything but his love and beauty. Forbidding, cruel to himself and the ones he loved. Because to love means to know the weaknesses and strengths inherent in a human being."[42] A few weeks later, still in Rome, Ulmer trains his focus on mortality and his European lineage: "I have been thinking that I should take a quick trip to Vienna to see my father's grave, before I return home. But I'm such a coward. I couldn't take the emotional upset of seeing the town destroyed and talk to people who undoubtedly must have murdered scores of our kind. So I think I [will] just skip it, and the Lord will have to forgive me."[43]

After such an unusually long and trying production, *Pirates* left the émigré director temporarily untethered in Europe. Professionally speak-ing, his career was no better off than when he'd taken on the project, and financially—after a terribly expensive emergency appendix opera-tion for Arianné, in Rome, almost a repeat of the operation that Shirley had endured during the final days of work on *From Nine to Nine* in Montreal more than a decade earlier—no ground had been gained. He wrote to Shirley that he often found himself humming Cole Porter (doing a George and Ira Gershwin tune from *Girl Crazy*), "Just biding my time." However, much like the mad director in Sidney Alexander's fictionalized account of *Pirates,* who responds nonchalantly to the wor-ries of his current picture with the quip, "I always have another picture already planned," Ulmer was soon chasing other projects.[44] By April 1949, before *Pirates* was in the can, plans were afoot to have Ulmer work with Italian producer Dario Sabatello on another film slated to be made in Italy later that year (*Shadow of the Eagle*, 1950). Ulmer pre-pared an abundance of material, traveled with the producer to Venice, and naively entered into contract negotiations—something that got him into hot water with his agents at the Kohner Office on Sunset Boule-vard—later referring to his squandered efforts as "the Dario disaster."[45] At this same juncture Ulmer quarreled repeatedly with his agents, threatening to sever ties for their lack of proper procurement of work, while Kohner himself promised to pursue leads at Fox and Universal, urging patience and good humor in his client.[46]

Throughout the waiting, Ulmer continued to hope for better projects to materialize in America. His letters reiterate and amplify his deep yearnings for serious, well-paying productions, a fleeting and unrealized chance to direct for RKO or, as he put it, simply to "work on a Hollywood lot again."[47] Yet he remained in Europe (with a few return trips to the States to make such low-budget quickies as *Benny* and *The Man from Planet X*) into the 1950s. Soon after *Benny*, the Danziger brothers had Ulmer hammering away on a new idea, a film that bore the working title "The Queen's Mark," which they hoped to shoot in the Belgian Congo. Despite several protracted efforts, it never made its way into production. What did get off the ground instead, relocating Edgar and Shirley to Barcelona in 1951, was a Spanish-American coproduction known as *Muchachas de Bagdad* or *Babes in Bagdad,* an exotic costume drama set in the fantasy world of a Middle Eastern harem and shot in lurid Cinecolor (a primitive two-strip color process sometimes called "Exoticolor," as befits the film's subject), costarring Paulette Goddard and Gypsy Rose Lee.

The idea for the picture, in Goddard's telling, was as simple as the Danzigers' asking the former Ziegfeld girl and Chaplin muse, "What do you look best in?" Her tart reply: "A bathtub, bath towel and tights, in that order."[48] They purportedly devised the entire script to showcase the costumes worn by her and ex-stripper Lee; they even tossed in a "Milk and Lotus Bath" as a set piece to tempt viewers (something that unnerved the censors, prompting them to insist that "the intimate parts of their persons . . . be properly covered at all times," and that served up obvious exploitation value in the film's pressbook—"SEE THE SPECTACULAR MILK-AND-LOTUS BATH OF THE HAREM QUEENS IN *BABES IN BAGDAD*").[49] By pairing Goddard and Lee, even if they were both on the other side of the hump in their respective movie careers, the Danzigers hoped—in vain, as it turned out—to drive audiences to the box office (Figure 28).

Edgar, Shirley, and Arianné set sail on the *Liberté,* departing from New York soon after they had completed *Benny,* and reached France sometime in winter 1951. The Ulmers stayed in Paris for several months, cooking up new ideas in dialogue with the Danzigers, before eventually making their way to Spain, where they would connect with Goddard, Lee, and the extended cast and crew. "I am working 14 hrs. a day and love it of course," Ulmer reported back to Lahn in Hollywood with the optimism that frequently accompanied the start of a new project. "I am very confident of turning out a very good picture. The set-up is very substantial and the boys [the Danzigers] are treating me financially so good and so correctly that I have to pinch myself to believe it."[50]

FIGURE 28. Arabian Nights: Ezar (Richard Ney), Zohara (Gypsy Rose Lee), and Kyra (Paulette Goddard) in *Babes in Bagdad* (1952). Courtesy of Edgar G. Ulmer Preservation Corp.

That optimism, however, was short-lived, if not grossly misplaced. The film suffered from a basic lack of support in terms of technical crew and studio facilities, as well as from the same kinds of challenges Ulmer had faced on *Pirates*. (The initial shipment of equipment and canisters of film was impounded by Spanish customs—in a preproduction interview, Ulmer had referred to Franco as "the butcher of Europe," and he worried there might be retribution—but Goddard charmed the officials into releasing the goods.)[51] "I cannot tell you how lonesome I am for Hollywood," he wrote to Lahn just a couple of months into the shoot, "and if it would not be for Shirley and Arianné I surely would have chucked the whole think [*sic*] and be on my way home. I can only repeat again and again 'You can only make pictures in Hollywood and nowhere else.' By that I mean make them and don't work yourself into a state where everything borders on heart failure. Undoubtedly we are spoiled. . . . Equipment has given me sleepless nights."[52]

The film's two stars were no less disillusioned by their experiences. "Whatever I am doing here," wrote Goddard from Spain to her then husband, writer Erich Maria Remarque, "is certainly the wrong way to live. Picture making is for another kind of 'mensch.' It's nice to be a movie star & collect the dough, but the actual making of the film is a horrible experience." Describing the motley bunch involved in the production, she continued: "Everyone connected with this epic is an outcast—either blacklisted in England or have-beens in America, so everyone is completely off-center."[53] Lee was equally unimpressed. According to her biographer, Noralee Frankel, "Gypsy found the plot silly." She purportedly never even watched the finished film after returning to New York, mocking the hokey exoticism, and the costumes she and Goddard were required to wear, as "made strictly for Muncie, Indiana."[54]

And for good reason. The film's main conceit is a kind of cheap orientalism, a lowbrow *Arabian Nights* concocted by scriptwriters Joe Ansen and Felix Feist (who would direct the cult horror film *Donovan's Brain* the following year), that didn't get much better with the additional dialogue provided by John Roeburt, who penned the script for *Benny*. In a nutshell—and there isn't much more than that—the story revolves around a powerful ruler named Hassan (John Boles); his favored wife, Zohara (Lee), in a harem of twelve beauties; a troublemaking newbie to the harem called Kyra (Goddard), who voices loud opposition to being subjected to polygamy; and a sympathetic upstart in the Caliph's godson, Ezar (Richard Ney). The main plot twist has Zohara, Kyra, and Ezar conspiring to have Hassan drugged, kidnapped, and made temporarily into a beggar, before Zohara rescues him, schools him (and the audience) on the virtues of monogamy, and holds up newlyweds Kyra and Ezar as the great modern example.

Visually, there's not much to recommend the film. British-born cinematographer Jack Cox, who began his career working with Hitchcock, confines the main filmic space to a lifeless chamber drama (the only vitality coming fleetingly and haltingly in an inconsonant pageant of harem showgirls performing, as if Busby Berkeley had been airdropped in for a quick laugh, for Hassan and his court). When the film was released in midsummer 1952, critics tended to agree with Lee's gut feelings. "Rarely has there been so much promise of sex high-jinks with so little performance," remarked *Motion Picture Herald*, while the *Hollywood Reporter* simply tagged it "a slapdash production." "Is it just a bad film on a routine subject," asked another critic, "or is it a reasonably clever takeoff on the long string of Arabian Nights tales?"[55] (Many decades later, another critic would suggest: "It feels like an experimental film testing the limits of abstraction and artifice.")[56] In an interview conducted in 1991, the film's codirector, Jerónimo Mihura, who was responsible for the Spanish-language version shot simultaneously with the English, had few kind words for his directorial counterpart: "Ulmer was really awful, he did not know a single word of Spanish and I think he was a very bad director. He shot it that way that they had to bring an editor from England to see if he could put sense into what Ulmer had shot. . . . It was a disaster."[57]

In the years since its release, *Babes* has found a few admirers, or at least people willing to give it the benefit of the doubt. Filmmaker Bertrand Tavernier, who in an interview from the late 1990s initially branded the picture "very, very, very bad," suggests that there are also a few moments "of poetry, imagination, and charm" when the focus shifts to the morality tale of the ruler-turned-beggar (Tavernier's former colleague François Truffaut once hailed it as "a Voltairean tease").[58] Critic Dave Kehr has more recently observed: "If, on close inspection, *Babes in Bagdad* turns out to be less momentous than *Ulysses* or *The Rite of Spring*, it remains a strange, sympathetic little film, poignantly illustrative of the lengths to which its doomed director would go in his determination to pursue art against all odds."[59] In a *New York Times* profile that Kehr published on Christopher Lee, who has a bit part in *Babes*, one gains further insight into Ulmer's pursuit of art during the production: "I played some sort of awful slave trader in a black silk dress, or that's what it looked like. The director was Edgar Ulmer, and we had a shared passion for opera. We went to see 'Tristan' in Barcelona, and he kept making comments about how little he thought of it all the way through."[60] If he could only have known how little critics would think of the film he was then finishing.

Like *Pirates* before it, *Babes* would leave Ulmer tired and dispirited after having spent many months invested in what turned out to be another misguided venture. Nevertheless, his seeming susceptibility to such ventures—bad business instincts or a romantic faith in his ability to redeem the irredeemable—soon had him back in Italy, tied to one last production with screen diva Hedy Lamarr and shifty producer Victor Pahlen (Ulmer would later refer to himself as "Victim Pahlen").[61] The project, another star vehicle for Lamarr, had begun as a planned television series, *The Great Loves of History,* cowritten by Salka Viertel and Aeneas MacKenzie (whom Ulmer liked to refer to as "Kafka" in his letters), to be shot in Acapulco. In early June 1952, syndicated

Hollywood columnist Louella Parsons announced the production: "Victor Pahlen, the producer who signed the American beauty, is giving Hedy a good director, Edgar Ulmer, who will direct the series."[62] But what started as a television idea—with an initial segment to be shot in London—eventually morphed into a convoluted patchwork known as *The Loves of Three Queens*, a high melodrama starring Lamarr as Geneviève of Brabant, Helen of Troy, and Empress Josephine, filmed in Rome in fall 1953. Given the intense friction that Ulmer had already experienced working with Lamarr on *The Strange Woman*, less than a decade before, it must have been sheer desperation that put him back in the director's chair. Even Ulmer's daughter felt the residual tensions; after a small spat with Lamarr on the set, Arianné was off in England, under the care of Romanian-born producer Marcel Hellman and his wife, Ellie, studying acting at the Royal Academy of Dramatic Arts.

Whatever his motive, Ulmer and Lamarr picked up where they'd left off, sparring from the very start. The Scottish-born actor John Fraser, who plays opposite Lamarr in the first part of *Three Queens*, recalls experiencing the fiery interaction between the star actress and Ulmer on the set. Prior to shooting, Fraser had managed to offend Lamarr—who purportedly brought with her not only her own personal assistant but also a full-time psychiatrist—by offering unsolicited advice. "Our scenes together were not easy since she refused to talk to me; all communications were therefore through the director, Edgar Ulmer, who was Austrian by birth and Jewish, like Hedy, which might have led one to expect a warmth of feeling between them based on shared history and tribal loyalty, but this was far from the case. Their relationship was bitter and hate-filled and spectacularly stormy." The real drama ensued when Hedy, not especially eager to share the spotlight with anyone, let alone with a young no-name actor like Fraser, grabbed hold of his head— ignoring the script altogether in a way that only an egomaniacal, and self-consciously aging, star might do—removed his wig and planted his face "deep in the cleft between her breasts" (as Fraser dryly quips, "Most men would willingly give up all thoughts of a career in the cinema to have this experience no fewer than ten times before Edgar's patience broke").

Each time this occurred, Ulmer interrupted Lamarr's machinations, yelling at the top of his lungs, "Cut!" (allegedly biting into his arm to keep from having an apoplectic fit). The resulting clash, recounted by Fraser, accent and all, deserves full citation:

"Mees Lamarr!" he groaned, when he had removed his savaged limb from between his teeth. "Ze vay you turn ze boy's head—we cannot tell if she iss a man, or he iss a vooman. Ve cannot tell if ziss hairy zing you hold in your hendz is an Animal or a Shooman Beenz. Ve cannot tell if ziss Shooman Beenz or ziss Zinamal iss alive or dead! Und, vot iss more, if ve cannot see his VACE, vee don't CARE! . . . Mees Lamarr! I am zee Director of ziss Fucking Rabbish, unt you vill do vot I say! Ve vil chute ze scen mit a DUB-BEL eff you vill not letus ZEE ZE BOY'S VACE."[63]

This final boiling point was reached sometime in early October, just weeks into the shoot, when a red-faced Ulmer marched out the door never to return again (Lamarr, who had personally invested £50,000 in the production, claims to have fired her director).[64] "Hedy unfortunately is completely out of hand and I am unable to cope with her," wrote Ulmer to Lahn. "She refuses direction. Therefore to avoid another 'Babes in Bagdad' I have resigned from the picture. I have finished 'Genevieve,' but 'Helen' and 'Josephine' must be done by somebody else. The little self-respect I still have I cannot and will not lose. On top of her behavior, she photographs badly. Age is showing and with a vengeance. So I am at liberty and willing to make a picture from the first of November on. But only in Hollywood. I've got my free [sic] of wandering."[65]

After director Marc Allégret stepped in for Ulmer, and finished a film that, as Ruth Barton has observed, "verges on a Monty Pythonesque parody of the historical epic," Ulmer continued a minor campaign to restore his standing while lambasting Lamarr.[66] In a piece that ran in the *London Sunday Pictorial,* under the unambiguous title "Hedy's Glittering Too Much for Ulmer," he fumed to a reporter: "Miss Lamarr is no Academy award winner," while an interview with him after returning to Los Angeles by ship a couple of weeks later gave him yet another opportunity to settle the score. "I had hoped," he said of Lamarr, "she would approach these three classical parts with sincerity, if not actual humility. Instead, we got what I can only call the typical Hollywood cover girl attitude. . . . Miss Lamarr wished to be dolled up like a fugitive from the *Ziegfeld Follies.* I just couldn't go on seeing the film being ruined by the caprice of one human being."[67] If the old Hollywood adage, that you're only as good as your last movie, had any validity, then Ulmer's professional stock—especially after *Babes* and *Three Queens*—was not exactly on the rise. "Surely no acting or production personality connected with films," asserted publicity agent Wilson Heller in the puffed-up press bio he prepared for Ulmer in April 1953, "has had a more varied or colorful career."[68]

OTHER SHORES

Lack of success abroad did not keep Ulmer from trying his hand once more in independent cinema on the fringes of Hollywood. "Believe it or not," he wrote to his daughter in mid-February 1954, "mother and I are getting ready to move again. I feel like a dog who is trying out hundreds of places in the year, circles around, scratches. Well, we hope this time is it."[69] In the same letter he mentioned that he was on the hunt for locations for a film that, although made in this country, would lift Ulmer's reputation in Europe. Based on a script by blacklisted writer Julian Zimet, alias Halevy, who had left McCarthy-era America for Mexico, *The Naked Dawn*, a lyrical western shot in Technicolor, would find its most ardent following in France. There it was shown, under the title *Le bandit*, after it was made a late addition (as a "Spanish" film not requiring subtitles) to the 1955 Venice Film Festival.[70] At the behest of independent producer Josef Shaftel, Ulmer shot the film, initially known only by its original title, "The Bandit," just outside of Los Angeles County—not, as the pressbook would have it, on location in Mexico—at the Corriganville Movie Ranch, the same location used in John Ford's *Fort Apache* (1948), over a couple of weeks in the spring of 1954. (Ilse Lahn sent Ulmer a telegram on March 24, wishing him "Hals und Beinbruch," or "break a leg," assuring him, "I know it will be a great picture and we'll bask in its reflected glory.")[71] When Shaftel could no longer come up with the required capital for distribution, producer James O. Radford acquired the film on a pickup deal for Universal and premiered it domestically, to lackluster box office and anemic reviews, on Halloween 1955.[72]

What originated for the exiled screenwriter Zimet as a loose adaptation of Maxim Gorky's "Chelkash," a short story about an aging Russian thief, had evolved into a screenplay bearing the name "Tierra." In the eyes of its leftist creator the story, concerning a "disillusioned ex-revolutionary who survives as a rural bandit," hinges on the twice-repeated line, an ode to those betrayed by greed and oppression, "Here is your land!"[73] Unable to receive credit under his true name, Zimet used his sister and brother-in-law, Nina and Herman Schneider, as a front (Ulmer never had any direct contact with either Zimet or the Schneiders). After Shaftel sold the negative to Universal, the final title was imposed. Included on the long list of prospective titles, kept among the studio's files, is "He Rides Alone," an apt encapsulation of the renegade spirit embodied in the film's outlaw hero Santiago (Arthur Kennedy) and, indeed, evocative of the director's loner status (Figure 29).

FIGURE 29. The lonely hero: Santiago (Arthur Kennedy) and Maria (Betta St. John) in *The Naked Dawn* (1955). Courtesy of USC Cinematic Arts Library.

The film opens with a botched heist at the Matamoros train station—depicted in Ulmer's finely crafted, suspenseful credit sequence—and the tragic shooting of Santiago's partner, Vicente (Tony Martinez), as the barefooted bandit rides off with the stolen goods, pulling his mortally wounded comrade with him. As a surrogate priest of sorts, Santiago soon delivers a eulogy to his friend on his deathbed, recounting their difficult past as revolutionaries, later as prisoners, and assuring him that San Pedro will open his gates for him. In his telling, Vicente will ultimately be granted the land, the "tierra" of Zimet's original title, long his due (Ulmer tacks on the same sermon, unscripted and given in voice-over, in the film's last moments, with Santiago then at death's door). After burying his fallen comrade in a makeshift grave, he dons his boots and hat and continues the struggle alone, following his own path, a point that the film continues to underscore, both visually and in its dialogue, from beginning to end ("My road lies in another direction" and "My road is not for you" fill out Santiago's final lines).

Bearing recognizable affinities with the *folksmentsh* and raconteur Mendele in Ulmer's Yiddish feature *The Light Ahead*, Santiago is a man of the people, a philosophizing vagabond who operates beyond social norms (sleeping among the coyotes under the stars) and observes things with the acuity of an outsider. As the plot unfolds, he soon encounters the beautiful Maria Lopez (Betta St. John) singing and daydreaming by a secluded pond—we later see her bathing al fresco, in one of the film's most suggestive sequences—her reflection glistening with the same allure as Hedy Lamarr's in *The Strange Woman*. He cannot take his eyes off Maria, leering at her as he helps himself to a drink, then accompanying her partway back to her home. He expresses his regrets on learning she is married ("the young bird with its wings clipped even before it learns to fly," in Zimet's lyrical formulation) and announces his joy at being alive, at worldly pleasures, attributing all joys to God. Sensing the predatory nature of Santiago's advances, and the heaviness of his gaze, Maria retorts that perhaps the devil has sent him. When she next sees him, inside her home, she offers a devilish grin of her own, as she furiously makes fresh tortillas, pounding at them as if beating at the depths of her repression.

Before we reach this point, however, Santiago meets Maria's husband, Manuel Lopez (Eugene Iglesias), a young *Indio* digging a well outside their home. Santiago gains entry to the Lopez home by propositioning Manuel, offering to hire him and his truck with "dirty money," a term that *Detour*'s Al Roberts or a Marxist bandito are equally apt to utter, to take him back to Matamoros to collect what is owed to him for the earlier heist. Manuel agrees, but only after insisting that they first have dinner together with his wife. Ulmer's fondness for the dramatic tension of a love triangle—in this particular instance, inspiring François Truffaut, who saw the film in 1956, to undertake his screen adaptation of *Jules et Jim*—comes to passionate articulation. Santiago's worldliness, his libertine attitudes and his penchant for wandering, serve as a sharp contrast to Manuel's seeming desire for bourgeois conventionality, respectability, and rootedness, making him a gradual source of attraction for the shackled Maria.

Yet Iglesias's portrayal of Manuel, as a man who is not without human vulnerability and contradiction, adds to the moral ambiguity otherwise reserved for Santiago, a true "Westerner" ("lonely and to some degree melancholy," representative of "the moral 'openness' of the West") in the definition that Robert Warshow laid out in the pages of *Partisan Review* the year the film was made.[74] As they travel together to the Mexican border town, their roles evolve, allowing Manuel to show hints of Pancho Villa and Santiago to serve as a mentor, even a father figure, who guides his young disciple to taste life as never before. Their journey reaches a high point in a scene—one of the very few in the film that prompted Ulmer to deviate a bit from his otherwise faithful adherence to Zimet's script—that takes place in a cantina, after Santiago and Manuel have collected their money from a crooked border official named Guntz (Roy Engel).

Ulmer initially sticks to the basic scenario described by Zimet ("a smoky dive, half filled with cowboys and oil workers from both sides of the border, sporting gunbelts and fancy sombreros . . . a couple of U.S. sailors, and B girls with flowers and combs in their hair and wearing flamboyant costumes"). But once Santiago and "Manuelito," as Iglesias is now called, take their seats at a table, and Santiago exhorts the mariachi to play its own songs instead of American covers, things take a slight detour. The cantina songstress, Tita (Charlita), performs a torrid number called "Ai hombre," written by composer Herschel Burke Gilbert, and, as if channeling the Weimar spirit of Marlene Dietrich's Lola Lola from *The Blue Angel,* she stuns her male audience. Like Dietrich's performance in that venerated earlier film—one that Ulmer had once hoped, in a flight of fancy, to remake with Veronica Lake—Tita's dance reflects a charged eroticism that radiates from the screen.

To stoke the fire, Ulmer has cameraman Frederick Gately offer a high-angle tilt of Tita's fishnet-covered legs ("selling her number with a little dance step," the script reads), intercutting shots of the male guitarist, whose strumming invites more of the syncopated dance, and more discrete shots of Tita's legs. This finally builds up to the sensual song and dance, a Latin take on Dietrich's "Falling in Love Again," with Tita interacting with the crowd of male spectators in a similarly flirtatious, playful, and assertive fashion. All warnings by censorship boss Joseph Breen—who dispatched a sternly worded memo to Ulmer and Shaftel in late January 1954 insisting, "Tita's dance in the cantina must contain no bumps, grinds, or other sex suggestive movements"—were summarily ignored.[75] Ulmer and Shaftel opted likewise to ignore all other warnings about the sexually or morally subversive nature of Zimet's script (whether in the staging of Maria's outdoor shower, with a rooster placed in a naughty vantage point, or the tense dialogue between Maria and Santiago, in the film's most elongated and theatrical take, about running away together to Veracruz).

This scene is followed by another in which Santiago and Tita do a dance of their own. When the band begins a melancholy orchestral prelude, Santiago leaps to his feet, taunting the mariachi musicians with the question, "Who are we burying? Faster! Faster!" He then abruptly approaches Tita, pulling the tablecloth from where she's seated and, before beginning their fiery dance, turns to Manuel for a small, unscripted dedication: "Manuelito, para ti!" Santiago uses the cloth as a torero's cape, provoking Tita to charge, and then performs his own dance step, shot with the same compositional flair as Tita's earlier number. Zimet suggests in his script that Santiago and Tita "do their dance as if spitting in the face of death," and indeed, in Ulmer's interpretation this scene stands out as a moment of remarkably high artistic and emotional intensity. "This is the most elaborately lit and edited sequence in the film," observes Bill Krohn, "shots of feet, and shots of feet framed by other feet (repeated from details in other parts of Zimet's script)— pink lights, yellow lights, fast cutting, pounding boot heels on the soundtrack."[76] In a similar vein, focusing on Ulmer's aesthetic, Tavernier regards this particular scene as "very German . . . the way it is shot, the use of the light."[77] He likens the film more to Nicholas Ray's iconoclastic *Johnny Guitar* (1954), a film that Truffaut also rated highly, than to classic American westerns. It should perhaps come as little surprise that the film, with its continental pacing, long takes, and unconventional visual style, would not have much commercial appeal with mainstream American audiences.

After advance screenings were held in Hollywood in late July 1955, the review attention in the trade papers could not have been less encouraging. The *Hollywood Reporter*'s Jack Moffitt began his review on a savage note: "'The Naked Dawn' would look a lot better if [it] were clothed in a few box-office values." He went on to characterize it as "the type of film that will discourage the average movie fan from continuing his habit of seeking entertainment at the theatres" and, still further, as "exactly what legitimate audiences raved over and movie audiences couldn't get in the days of World War I. It's a great pity that we do not possess a time machine by which we could send it back to them." *Variety* was no less impressed: "Its tempo is much too slow for popular taste, and there will be little patience with the many long speeches." The same reviewer added, "Edgar G. Ulmer's direction is too deliberate for popular consumption, but is effective in establishing mood and most certainly rates credit for the fine performances."[78] When the film later received reviews in the popular press, mainly in small regional or middlebrow newspapers, the prognosis remained relatively grim. "'The Naked Dawn' is a Western," remarked a movie reviewer in *Stars and Stripes,* "that could easily go down as the weirdest movie of the year," while Marjorie Barrett of the *Denver Post* pronounced "the off-beat melodrama . . . slower than some action fans may like."[79]

Far more appreciative of the style and sensibility of Ulmer's film were audiences on the other side of the Atlantic. Most famously, the young critic and aspiring filmmaker Truffaut offered a paean to the film, and to its director, in *Arts-Lettres-Spectacles* magazine in 1956. With a nod of approval to the prized notion that Luc Moullet introduced in *Cahiers du cinéma* that same year, branding Ulmer "le plus maudit des cinéastes," the twenty-four-year-old Truffaut suggests, "Edgar Ulmer is undoubtedly the least-known American filmmaker. Few of my colleagues are able to boast of having seen the few films of his that have made it to France, all of which are surprisingly fresh, sincere, and inventive."[80] He continues to follow this line of inquiry, speculating that Ulmer "hasn't had much luck in Hollywood, probably because he doesn't know how to fit into the system. His carefree humor and pleasant manner, his tenderness toward the characters he depicts remind us inevitably of Jean Renoir and Max Ophüls." Such comparisons put Ulmer in good company, staking a claim to his European lineage. The film had made its way into Parisian theaters after being screened in Venice, where, among others, Robert Aldrich's latest feature, *The Big Knife,* was also shown (in a letter to his agent, Ilse Lahn, Ulmer insisted that his film "came close enough to beat out 'The Big Knife'") and where *The Naked Dawn* allegedly enjoyed "a great success."[81] In Paris, as Truffaut reports in his review, "the public on the Champs-Elysées took to this film, as they did a few months ago to Robert Aldrich's *Kiss Me Deadly*" (156).

Truffaut's final summation is written with all the rhetorical bravado of the auteurist critics of his day:

Talking about *The Naked Dawn* is equivalent to drawing a portrait of its author, because we see him behind every image and feel we know him intimately when the lights go back on. Wise and indulgent, playful and serene, vital and clear, in short, a good man like the ones I've compared him to.

The Naked Dawn is one of those movies we know was made with joy; every shot shows a love of cinema, and pleasure in working in it. It is also a pleasure to see it again and to talk to friends about it. A small gift from Hollywood. (156)

For Truffaut and his like-minded colleagues, it was as if they had suddenly discovered greatness lurking on the margins of the American dream factories. The impulse, often contrarian if not cultist, spurred a generation of critics and cinephiles to lionize the work of directors like Ulmer. "I remember when Truffaut came to New York," Luc Moullet recounted. "There was a question, 'who are the best American directors?' And he said Edgar Ulmer and Samuel Fuller! Which in '59 was rather provocative since the critic who asked the question may not have known Ulmer and saw very little of Fuller. At the time, people said Kazan, or Stevens, or Zinnemann."[82] As a counterbalance, however, Jean-Luc Godard, who went on to dedicate his film *Détective* (*The Detective*, 1985) to Ulmer, John Cassavetes, and Clint Eastwood, warned of the potential hagiography espoused by the *politique des auteurs*. "It was difficult enough," he remarked in 1962, "getting them [i.e., readers of *Cahiers du cinéma*] to see that people like Ray and Aldrich had genius, but when they find interviews with directors like Ulmer, they give up. I am for the *politique des auteurs,* but not just anybody. Opening the door to absolutely everyone is very dangerous. Inflation threatens."[83]

+ + +

Soon after filming *The Naked Dawn,* Edgar and Shirley Ulmer made their way back East once more, where they lived temporarily in Greenwich Village, in the Brittany Hotel on East 10th Street. In a letter to Ilse Lahn, written in mid-June 1955, Shirley tells of taking creative writing classes at the New School and of a recent meeting with old friend and cameraman Eugen Schüfftan ("full of ideas for Europe").[84] As it turns out, both Schüfftan and Ulmer had been tapped to work with producer Joseph Kaufman on the *Ivanhoe* television series. Although that project never panned out—despite Ulmer's having prepared three scripts—within weeks of arriving in New York, Ulmer was back in Europe on what was initially thought to be a short trip with Kaufman, scouting locations and discussing other television ideas. Yet instead of limiting himself to the collaboration with Kaufman, which eventually petered out, he found additional employment at Munich-based Eichberg-Film, a company run by executive producer Carol Hellman, brother of Marcel, where he was hired on a one-year contract as head of production in the fall of 1955.

As she had many times before, Shirley followed her husband across the Atlantic, setting up shop in Munich, living once again out of hotel rooms. The pair went frequently to the theater and opera. After seeing a Munich production of *Der gute Mensch von Szezuan (The Good Person of Szechwan)*, by Bertolt Brecht, whom Ulmer regarded as "undoubtedly the most important figure in world theater today," he expressed in a letter to Arianné his dream of directing a Brecht play on Broadway. (Half a decade later, Edgar and Shirley would travel to Zurich to meet Brecht's daughter, and soon after to East Berlin to reconnect with their friend and longtime Brecht collaborator Paul Dessau, who, in Shirley's words, "conducts magnificently in his rubbled-out Opera House.")[85] On their very first day together in Germany, at a local restaurant, Edgar and Shirley bumped into old friends, screenwriter Hans Jacoby and actor Fritz Kortner, both of whom, like Ulmer, had spent the Nazi years in California and returned to Europe after the war. Despite Shirley's initial apprehensions about living in Munich ("a frightening city," she writes Lahn), she recognized the step up it represented in terms of the financial compensation from Eichberg, not to mention the rich cultural offerings that her husband prized, and she learned to approach things with a sense of humor. As she impishly reported to Lahn, a month after relocating to Bavaria, by then living in Munich's Hotel Stachus: "Edgar says he's thinking of doing a TV series entitled 'My meshugineh American Wife in Europe.'"[86]

Among the initial projects Ulmer began to work on was something called "Volga Boatman"—in his letters to Lahn he sometimes refers to it as "Wolgaschlepper"—a project scripted by Salka Viertel and attached to producer Nat Wachsberger. Viertel and the Belgian-born Wachsberger joined Ulmer in Munich that winter, hoping to develop the project. In a missive to Lahn on the progress of the script, Viertel wrote in mid-February 1956: "Ilselein, dearest, I'm writing in German, because I spent the whole day arguing with Edgar in German. Not quarreled *for heaven's sake* [English in original], just story conference. Wachsberger is also here and our work is going *full blast* [in original] from morning to night." She explains in the same letter that they all share great enthusiasm about the first part of the script, which was finished, but that the second part had prompted Ulmer and Wachsberger to lock horns ("screaming and laughter"). Of Ulmer specifically, Viertel writes: "He's charming and very pleasant. Please convey this to Paul [Kohner], too. . . . We've already gotten used to each other. He is extremely talented, only occasionally one has to cut some of what he comes up with in his effervescent way." Kohner later penciled in a handwritten comment on Viertel's letter: "All I see is lots of charm—but no dough."[87]

Like many other projects Ulmer had a hand in developing while at Eichberg (including "Dark Wings" and "Casino de Paris"), this one got away from him—after he'd invested close to a year of his time, had chosen locations in Yugoslavia, and even brought Arianné, then studying acting with Stella Adler in New York, to Munich to play a small part in the production. He'd also lobbied his agent to cast the enormously famous singer and dancer Caterina Valente as the lead and to have star composer Dimitri Tiomkin score the film.[88] After it was finally yanked from his hands for reasons that have been lost to time ("torn out from under us," as Shirley told Lahn), sometime in late July 1956, the film, or a reworked version of it, with Viertel's name still listed among the screenwriters, was eventually released; as an international coproduction, under the direction of Russian-born director Viktor Tourjansky, it bore the titles *I battellieri del Volga, Les bateliers de la Volga,* and *Wolgaschiffer* (1959). Despite the unfortunate outcome, Ulmer and Wachsberger continued intermittent collaboration, and several years later they would work together again on *L'Atlantide.*

Ulmer's chief accomplishment at Eichberg, in addition to helping to establish the film studio—perhaps prompting him to adopt the "Dr." title on his stationery letterhead (a source of great ridicule at the Kohner Office)—was serving as producer of Rudolf Jugert's *Der Meineidbauer* (*The Perjurer,* 1956), a relatively renowned *Heimatfilm,* or German pastoral drama, billed in the film's original pressbook as "Eine Edgar-George-Ulmer-Produktion." The picture was shot in the Alps, near Brenner Pass, over the early summer months of 1956; by the end of October it enjoyed wide release in West Germany. As the producer, Ulmer held 25 percent interest, and even a mild heart attack, the first of many, in the run-up to the shoot didn't keep him from finishing the film or from considering taking on German citizenship pending his signing of a long-term contract with the company ("Nicht für mir [*sic*], danke!" wrote Shirley to Ilse). But in the wake of *l'affaire Wachsberger,* as Ulmer called the "Volga Boatman" fiasco, and after *Meineidbauer* was done,

Ulmer harbored doubts about remaining in Munich. "I am afraid I am no judge of German-speaking pictures. The language startles me, the dramatic delivery of it frightens me. Believe it or not, I have much more relationship to an Italian picture than to a German one."[89] A couple of weeks later, he wrote again to Lahn, expressing misgivings about the lack of vision of the other producers he was then working with (who, in his witty formulation, "would be just as happy selling herrings as selling motion pictures"). He thus confided in Lahn: "I am torn between these two alternatives [staying in Europe and coming back to Hollywood], but in my methodical, logical alter ego I have booked passage on September 25, out of Genoa. So I am whispering, not saying it loud yet, 'Get me my boots and saddle; California here I come!'"[90]

Ulmer returned to California several times during the 1950s. There he worked on such independent productions as *The Naked Dawn,* and in late fall of 1957, just a year after writing to Lahn in the voice of a California-bound cowboy, became involved in developing the *Swiss Family Robinson* television series. Coproduced with his old friend Louis Hayward, and shot on location south of Acapulco (and in the Churubusco Studios in Mexico City), the series was conceived as having Hayward and Ulmer alternate directing its half-hour episodes.[91] The show's main story of a shipwrecked family and an orphan, surviving on a desert island, would seem to have held a certain topical appeal to Ulmer, especially after spending so many years bouncing around Europe (the very name of the production company, Trans-World Artists—not to mention the title of the pilot he directed, "Lost in the Jungle"—have a peculiar resonance). What is notable in the single pilot episode, which is all that survives, is a basic late-1950s TV aesthetic—with corny dialogue, poor acting, and repeated invocations of the Lord—that is not all that far removed from the two costume dramas that Ulmer went on to make in Europe in the ensuing years.

Having first visited Yugoslavia on his trip to Munich in the mid-1950s, when he scouted locations with Joe Kaufman—and signed a postcard to his daughter, from Belgrade, "The Wandering Minstrel"— Ulmer returned in the early fall of 1959 to direct a historical epic, *Annibale (Hannibal, 1960)*, shot simultaneously in Italian and English. Producer Ottavio Poggi hired Ulmer to direct the picture, filmed on location in the Yugoslavian countryside, the Abruzzo Mountains of Italy, and in and around Rome. In October 1959, by then in Italy, Shirley wrote to publicity agent Wilson Heller to convey a few highlights from the production: "A fast line to report we just returned from Yugoslavia where we shot scenes with three and four thousand men on horseback—whole cavalries."[92] The film, which is set in 218 BC, during the Second Punic War, and chronicles the exploits of the Carthaginian general Hannibal (Victor Mature)—beginning with his triumphant crossing of the Alps en route to Rome—entailed a massive number of extras, thousands of horses, and six very talented elephants. "It was a very tough picture to make," recalled Shirley many years later, explaining how when crossing the mountains the elephants' feet got sore and the crew had to use felt booties on their feet "so they [i.e., the elephants] could stop complaining."[93] Not unlike shooting on *Pirates,* the conditions on the set were cold and austere, and lead actor Mature, who was prone to all manner of superstition, had an incapacitating fear of elephants. (He later remarked, rather heroically if disingenuously, of the production: "I got headaches and nausea from riding elephants.")[94]

Ulmer's claim to fame on the picture was that he shot the great Battle of Cannae, almost like one of his legendary PRC quickies, in just five days instead of the twenty-three days that the shooting schedule had called for. To do this, he purportedly deployed six different cameramen moving from one marker to the next, locating the numbered stakes that he and his crew had driven into the ground during preparation. "Everybody said it was impossible," he boasted to Bogdanovich. "My nicest scene, they cut out" (B 574). Yet even Ulmer recognized in the end, all claims of technical bravado aside, the film was nothing more than a "typical costume picture." Mature, who was known for his suitability for the "sword and sandal" genre, lumbers his way through the film, sporting an eye patch, a wild assortment of flashy body armor, and his own air of gladiator machismo (his glistening black pompadour and bronzed face make him appear as though he's just returned from a weekend of sunbathing in Vegas with the Rat Pack), while Rita Gam, who plays his forbidden love interest, the Roman Sylvia, basically pouts and slips in and out of sheer outfits (vaguely reminiscent of *Babes in Bagdad*). The endless battle scenes, by turns gruesome and soporific, the stilted dialogue (largely dubbed), and the garish color, photographed by Raffaele Masciocchi in Supercinemascope, do little to animate the picture. Regrettably, Italian actor Gabriele Ferzetti, who plays the Roman senator Fabius Maximus, the powerful uncle of Silvia—and who would star in Antonioni's *L'avventura* a year later—never has the chance to avail himself of his talents.

Although the film did not receive much attention in the trade press ("it contains enough sheer spectacle, gore and quasi-historical action to excite those still willing to meet such films on their own primitive level," offered *Variety*), it somehow managed to garner a review in the newspaper of record, the *New York Times,* soon after its U.S. release by Warner Bros. in summer 1960. "Rome would have been a pushover for Hannibal, according to 'Hannibal,' if the Carthaginian conqueror hadn't scooped up a senator's pretty niece on the road," wrote critic Howard Thompson. "This seems to be the real message of the old-fashioned historical saga, in color . . . complete with Victor Mature, hordes of battling legionnaires, dubbed English and some extremely capable elephants." Commenting specifically on the film's direction, Thompson adds, "Edgar G. Ulmer does quite well with the small knots of snarling warriors."[95]

Not more than a month after the *Times* review had appeared, in September 1960, Ulmer signed a deal to produce *L'Atlantide (Journey beneath the Desert)*, another costume drama, for the Rome-based independent company Titanus (it was ultimately released by Compagnia Cinematografica Mondiale), with principal photography to begin in early October. Ulmer was assigned to former collaborator and money-man Nat Wachsberger to help get the project on its feet, while the two of them worked on another picture, *Mata Hari,* which they hoped to make in Paris later that year. Based on Pierre Benoît's influential 1919 novel of the same name—a late-Weimar screen adaptation, G.W. Pabst's *Die Herrin von Atlantis* (1932), had been made by Ulmer cronies Seymour Nebenzal and Eugen Schüfftan—*Journey* was slated for director Frank Borzage, with Ulmer on board to produce. Ulmer considered Borzage "one of the giants of the industry," as his daughter, Arianné, who served as dialogue coach on the film, explained years later.[96] He was thrilled that he'd managed to convince Wachsberger to import a Hollywood professional of his stature for the picture. As he wrote to his agent, announcing the minor coup he'd achieved with Wachsberger, "on my insistence, he signed Frank Borzage as director for the new picture. Dorothy Dandridge will play the leading part."[97] (In the same letter he dispelled the rumor he was next going to do a picture in Pakistan with producer Jack Dietz, who had helped finance *Hannibal:* "I think I am a little bit too tired and too old for adventures like Pakistan.")

As with other projects in Europe, the initial excitement concerning the film didn't last. Soon after shooting began, Shirley dashed off a note to publicity agent Heller to inform him that Borzage, sixty-seven years old and in declining health—he would die of cancer a year and half later—

had "conked out" on the second day, and Ulmer had to step in for him. "It's too bad, really. We don't want to say anything to hurt the guy, but he sure didn't know what to do—strange language and customs, perhaps."[98] Shirley also relayed the news that in the place of Dorothy Dandridge, the Israeli actress Haya Harareet, who had played Esther in *Ben Hur* (1959), had been cast as Queen Antinea. She also mentions the casting of Georges Revière and Jean-Louis Trintignant. ("This boy is really big," she writes of him, as if anticipating his starring roles in films by Costa-Gavras and Michael Haneke. "If he ever hits America, there'll be no holding him.") Ulmer had to struggle somewhat with his actors, notably the young American Rad Fulton (a.k.a. James Westmoreland), who plays Robert and who was unresponsive to his direction (to coax an emotional response out of him, Ulmer purportedly used some of the same tactics, including a tap or two from his beloved baton, he'd used on Hedy Lamarr in *The Strange Woman*). Italian actor Amedeo Nazzari, who plays Tamal, the evil leader of Atlantis, had to leave the production midway due to a kidney stone operation. In the end Ulmer had to share a codirector credit with Italian director Giuseppe Masini, who is said never to have set foot on the film locations, ostensibly to appease the Italian government, which had helped subsidize the multinational coproduction.

The film centers on the titular journey, highlighted in the English release, to the lost city of Atlantis. Initially set in the present, with three men (Revière, Trintignant, and Fulton) in a helicopter surveying an atomic energy testing zone—like Ulmer's science fiction pictures from the same period, *Journey* is steeped in cold war paranoia—the story quickly brings us into the mythical, ancient city of Atlantis. There the three outsiders, after a crash landing in a massive storm, are held hostage by Tamal and his henchmen. (The primitive use of miniatures in the crash recalls the toy diver in a fish tank used in *Isle of Forgotten Sins*.) The men soon fall under the spell of Queen Antinea, a kind of warrior sex kitten with the same anatomical strengths as Raquel Welch and Ursula Andress, who promptly informs them, lest they have hopes of escape: "No man has ever left Atlantis alive." Robert is the first to sneak out of the chamber where all three are kept, catching glimpses of a sacrificial ceremony before he's caught, tortured, and sent to the work camp where he helps lead a revolt. Thanks to the arrival of the benevolent Zinah (Giulia Rubini), who was herself kidnapped and brought to Atlantis against her will, Pierre (Trintignant) is finally able to escape, the two of them barely eluding the apocalyptic blast and mushroom cloud as the ancient city walls crumble.

Ulmer worked not only on the English script for the film, in conversation with executive producer Wachsberger, but was also largely responsible for the film's set design, showcasing monumental artifice and grand spaces for pageantry—when Antinea is introduced, after the guests in Tamal's court watch an incendiary female snake dancer, she emerges like the evil Maria in Fritz Lang's *Metropolis* (Lang had directed his own *Journey to the Lost City* just before Ulmer's film), on an ornately sparkling stage, and the enslaved workers in the bowels of Atlantis bear further affinities to Lang's epic. Critic Bret Wood likens the film to "a low-budget *She,* complete with an immortal goddess and subterranean pagan ceremonies, which likewise demonstrates Ulmer's fascination with production design."[99] This did not, however, mean that the experience of the production offered any pleasure. "The making of this picture," wrote Ulmer to Lahn after the film was finished and had been released, "as you undoubtedly know, was a nightmare. He [Wachsberger] positively miscast the picture, and after two days of work by Borzage, the whole thing fell apart and I inherited the grand melange. There was nothing I could do about it."[100]

In his eyes the projects he made in Europe—including those he wasn't ever able to bring to fruition—never really managed to advance his career. And many of them, like *Journey,* were ultimately beyond his control. In the end, then, Ulmer's extended stint of directing movies in Europe only made him even more aware of his lack of big success on the other side of the Atlantic and his increasing alienation from Hollywood. At times he may have thought of himself as a cosmopolitan citizen of the world, but he also felt an increasing sense of rootlessness while living in Europe. As Curt Siodmak has said of his brother Robert, who like Ulmer returned to Europe in the 1950s, he remained "in limbo, in a constant Diaspora . . . a perambulating motion picture director."[101] When, in *The Naked Dawn,* Santiago is asked where his home is, he replies, as if speaking for the director and others like him who have lost their way: "Quién sabe? Who knows?" The near-nomadism of his later years in Europe ultimately left Ulmer distraught and eager to return to the United States. Writing to his agent from Paris in autumn 1961, when his *Mata Hari* project had fizzled and he was flirting with the idea of returning to Vienna to help stage and design a new production of *Boris Godunov,* with Herbert von Karajan conducting, he noted in a wistful key: "Shirley and I are desperately lonely and very, very homesick. It has been a long haul in Europe for both of us."[102]

OTHER WORLDS

Running parallel to the films Ulmer was making in Europe in the 1950s—resulting in a spate of transatlantic passages and a passport littered with entry and exit stamps—were several offbeat American productions, the kinds of movies that would later be released on DVD from companies like Something Weird Video or Sinister Cinema. They encompass three science fiction features, a last return to horror, and an especially outré nudist film. All of these pictures depict a recurrent yearning for an alternative universe. Indeed, at around this same time, in the early 1950s, Ulmer wrote a short piece called "The Director's Responsibility," in which he not only called the mainstream film industry "a sad and confused place" but suggested it had "lost the markets of the world" (markets into which he had hoped to make a few minor incursions). And yet, as he also observes somewhat later in the same piece, "Hollywood is the city of 1,000 dreams in the public's eyes."[103] An inveterate dreamer, Ulmer never gave up on the idea of making movies in Southern California's factories—he simply adjusted. As B-movie specialist Tom Weaver has noted, Ulmer's U.S.-based projects from this period were all essentially work for hire, odd jobs that he picked up here and there during fallow periods when his income sources were limited.

The first of these assorted projects, *The Man from Planet X* (1951), came to Ulmer through his agent, Ilse Lahn, who also served as associate producer of the film. It was made for Mid Century Films, a company run by writer-producers Jack Pollexfen and Aubrey Wisberg, and later released by United Artists. Like much of his work at PRC in the early to mid-1940s, *Planet X* was shot in less than a week, in mid-December 1950, and had almost no budget to speak of (when a car pulls into the frame, in two separate shots in the film, it has to back out as there's simply no set beyond what's captured in the frame); the final line on the budget was a meager $41,000. "I think Edgar could get more on the screen, with less time and money," commented Pollexfen in retrospect, "than any other director I worked with. [He] could get more values than any of the B-budget specialists."[104] Ulmer shot the film on location, at the Griffith Park Observatory in Los Angeles, just north of Los Feliz, and on the Hal Roach lot in Culver City, where, as he'd done in the past, he made clever use of leftover sets—in this case, from Victor Fleming's *Joan of Arc* (1948). Ulmer designed many of the additional sets himself, painting the glass backdrops and working together with art director Angelo Scibetta, who had previously had a hand in such matters on *Isle of Forgotten Sins*.

The film takes place largely within the half-lit interior of an observatory setting on what's to be taken first for a California college campus and later for a remote island off the coast of Scotland, which Ulmer conveys by way of hand-painted backdrops, a miniature castle nestled in the highland marshes, loads of thick fog created from Nu-Gel and tetrachloride (causing everyone on the set to become ill), and a few stock shots of cliffs and crashing surf. The opening sequence has hardboiled American reporter John Lawrence (Robert Clarke) giving a tense voice-over account, in flashback, of the sensational events that he himself has just witnessed ("the strangest story a newspaperman has ever covered") while visiting the amiable Professor Elliot (Raymond Bond) in Scotland. A former wartime meteorologist responsible for observing bomber raids, Elliot had been tracking the orbit of the unknown Planet X, when, in Lawrence's ominous telling, science fiction and film noir became odd bedfellows.

Lawrence is not the only one visiting Professor Elliot at the time his story takes place. An unsavory, shifty former student, Dr. Mears (William Schallert), is also present, as is Elliot's doting young daughter, Enid (Margaret Field, mother of Sally), when a spaceship from Planet X carrying an alien robot suddenly arrives on the scene. Invasion fantasies were, as David Skal points out, not at all uncommon in Hollywood films from the early 1950s.[105] (Ulmer himself began "The Director's Responsibility" with the image of a "visitor from Mars.") Yet the real threat in Ulmer's film, hailed in the trade press as "one of the first out in the new cycle dealing with space visitors from other planets," is not so much invasion of the kind seen in other Red Scare films of the period but rather Mears's misguided attempt—pinning the alien to the ground and turning off his life-support valve—to exploit the creature from Planet X in the service of greed and his personal quest for power.[106]

The alien creature, played by a small Russian-born former vaudeville actor known for his slow-motion routine, eventually turns on Dr. Mears, much like the Golem in Paul Wegener's seminal film, causing him to become enslaved by the same inexplicable, mesmeric ray that has nearly the entire population in a zombielike state. The "terror of a split society," as Franco Moretti once dubbed it, and the need to heal that split, is the driving force of the remainder of the film. After the creature from Planet X turns on the villagers, there is a gulf between those who are enslaved to the alien and those who, like John Lawrence and a local constable (Roy Engel), as well as the detectives from Scotland Yard who soon descend upon the town, are able to keep from being enlisted in the army of zombies. By the end of the film, Mears and the alien are both killed off, while the professor, Enid, and the villagers are mercifully spared.

Like other Ulmer films from the period, the mise-en-scène is rather spare, even bleak, with few technical embellishments (in an early scene at the college observatory, Lawrence is told "the world is now experiencing strange astronomical phenomena," and thus the scene is shot entirely in the dark). Even the alien's mask is quite primitive with "eyes of a dead cod fish," as one of the spooked villagers comments in the film (Ulmer is said to have referred to the mask, while on the set, as "the douche bag from space").[107] Given the film's reliance on such simple, inexpensive aesthetic touches as hiding a small light inside the alien's helmet and some minor shadow play, what might be considered part of Ulmer's Weimar-era bag of tricks—the painted sets, the seemingly static focus on inanimate objects, a fog-drenched atmosphere, artful lighting and composition—it almost seems, as writer Jay Bonansinga has suggested, "as if the gods of German [silent] cinema had come down and breathed fiery life into this cartoonish UFO film."[108] Pollexfen himself spoke of the film, and in particular of Ulmer, in a similar vein: "His flair was mood. I think if silent films had lasted, he could have become one of the greats." He elaborated on this fundamental point: "Ulmer was [an] extremely good director for a *fast* picture. . . . When he had to turn out the best possible film he could with his back to the wall, he was marvelous."[109] The film's lead actor, Robert Clarke, who would go on to star in Ulmer's *Beyond the Time Barrier* years later, explains things somewhat differently, once more emphasizing the fate of the B-movie director: "He was never given the kind of opportunity he really deserved, because he could make pictures so inexpensively that's about all he ever got to do!"[110]

In early March 1951, independent exhibitor Sherrill Corwin, who by then had purchased the finished film of *Planet X* (Pollexfen and Wisberg retained 25 percent), arranged a test screening at San Francisco's Paramount Theatre. It was an apparent success, and the film soon opened across the country. Exhibitors and merchandisers were quick to seize on the exploitation value of the film (the tagline used on the poster art made this plain: "The Weirdest Visitor the Earth Has Ever Seen!"), helping to lure audiences to the box office. Ulmer, however, would see none of the profits, none of the "excellent returns in the ballyhoo market" that *Variety* correctly forecasted.[111] Finally, in the popular press, the review that the film received in the *New York Times,* soon after opening at the Mayfair, did not mince words: "one of the most excruciating bores ever to emerge from the pinpoint on this planet known as Hollywood. Before handing out raspberries, it might be fair to suggest that buried in this pitifully low-budget goo is the germ for a compact, spine-tingling little fantasy."[112] Instead of experiencing a boost, work of this kind, even if it anticipated, on a much smaller scale, such cult classics as Nicolas Roeg's *The Man Who Fell to Earth* (1976), continued to push him further to the periphery, away from the mainstream and away from the spotlight. This may explain in part why Ulmer, along with several other European-born émigré filmmakers of his generation, including André de Toth, Robert Siodmak, and Jacques Tourneur, would later be thought of chiefly as purveyors of "expressive esoterica" ("unsung directors with difficult styles or unfashionable genres or both," as Andrew Sarris fashioned the category in his influential *American Cinema).*[113] The movies Ulmer made in the United States during the 1950s, especially the more outlandish productions, continued to take him in this direction.

Sandwiched between his science fiction films made in California and, somewhat later, in Texas were two other cheapies, a fly-by-night horror film and a Z-budget nudie. Like *Planet X,* neither of these films ran much more than seventy minutes, and neither was apt to enhance the director's reputation. On *Daughter of Dr. Jekyll,* his horror quickie of 1957, released by Allied Artists that summer as the lower half of a double bill with Bert Gordon's *The Cyclops,* Ulmer worked again with producer Pollexfen and agent-producer Lahn. They shot on location in the Hancock Park section of Los Angeles ("the Beverly Hills of seventy years ago," as lead actress Gloria Talbott recalls) in an old mansion; made in less than a week, it was, in Talbott's words, "one of those 'wham-bam-thank-you-ma'am' shoots."[114] Pollexfen supplied the script, a confection of horror motifs built much more around atmosphere than narrative, and veteran horror and sci-fi actor John Agar played opposite Talbott in the lead.

Following a voice-over prelude, cuing the viewer to the long terror-filled history of Dr. Jekyll, a car drives up to a mysterious estate somewhere in England, filmed in miniature and enshrouded in billowy fog, indicating the arrival of Janet Smith (Talbott) and her fiancé, George Hastings (Agar), at the home of Dr. Lomas (Arthur Shields), a scientist who moonlights as a werewolf. Janet and George function in the film more or less as do the naive American couple Peter and Joan Alison in Ulmer's earlier entry to the genre, *The Black Cat,* uncovering and eventually escaping the depths of horror. Something of a Poelzig-like figure from that earlier film, Dr. Lomas serves as Janet's legal guardian yet has obvious designs on her—not, perhaps, to embalm her body behind glass, as in *The Black Cat,* but to help guide her toward the demonic world of the werewolf. As he soon explains to Janet that she carries with her the legacy of her late father Dr. Henry Jekyll ("May his tortured soul rest in peace"), we see her, in a pair of hallucinatory nightmare sequences, transforming herself into a ghoulish doppelgänger (played by an actual body double for Talbott)—talons, fangs, and all—and leaving victims in her wake. Undeterred by Janet's condition, George sets out to solve the mystery, much like Peter Alison, with the same doe-eyed expressions of a Boy Scout, eventually saving Janet and killing off the werewolf-possessed Dr. Lomas.

As in *Planet X,* Ulmer's principal strength in *Dr. Jekyll* is in mood and atmosphere. It may not have the dynamism of *Bluebeard* or the full-blown campiness of *The Black Cat,* but it does show a flair for illusion, for getting the most out of smoke pots and miniatures, and for working with actors. (As Sarris wrote, perhaps half in jest, "anyone who loves cinema must be moved by *Daughter of Dr. Jekyll.*")[115] Talbott, especially, who would soon after star in a seeming mash-up of *Planet X* and *Dr. Jekyll, I Married a Monster from Outer Space* (1958), shows notable strength in playing the tormented heir to her father's condition, and she later credited Ulmer for her portrayal. "He just was easy to work with," she told Tom Weaver. "He was not Douglas Sirk, who thinks he can get a performance out of somebody by scaring them to death. He was affable and fun—a pixie, sort of."[116] Unlike some of the more trying of Ulmer's later films, *Daughter of Dr. Jekyll* seems to have allowed him a little levity. One scene in particular, an otherwise fleeting and inconsequential interlude near the close, granted him the occasion to toy with the viewers' voyeuristic impulses: Ulmer has cinematographer John F. Warren place the camera outside the window of an unsuspecting woman (Marjorie Stapp), a Barbara Payton–style platinum blonde dressed in nothing but a black bustier, putting on her stockings and sheer negligee while a jazz record plays on a phonograph and the werewolf lingers lasciviously outside her window. He ogles her in an obvious state of intoxicated delight, as she takes a call from an operator warning her that the werewolf is on the loose. The werewolf finally enters the room, his menacing shadow cast on the wall behind her, and kills her amid shrieks while the jazz record and the operator's panicked voice trail off. A mere flash in the film, a chance to emphasize vulnerability and complicity—perhaps causing the Legion of Decency to give the film a B rating—the scene forms an unexpected link to the next feature Ulmer would make, in September 1958, under the pseudonym Ove H. Sehested.

Shot over a couple of weeks on location in Los Angeles County, and partly set in Paris (by way of stock footage of the Arc de Triomphe, the Champs-Élysées, the Moulin Rouge, and Orly Airport, as well as a few apartment interiors and painted backdrops), *The Naked Venus* was prompted by Ulmer's desire to work with French producer Gaston Hakim. He hoped that by agreeing to direct a nudie, coscripted and produced by Hakim, he might later be given more prestigious projects to complete on the other side of the Atlantic. Although those projects never materialized, *The Naked Venus,* released the third week of April 1959 by Gaston Hakim International, was not merely a curio on the director's résumé (in fact, it was often kept from his past service records) but a throwback to Weimar-era free body culture, an update to the beach scenes in *Menschen am Sonntag* sans swimsuits, couched in the post-McCarthy climate and puritanical social mores of the United States.

The story, cowritten by Hakim and an unknown writer named Gabriel Gort (quite possibly a front for Ulmer), chronicles the unhappy return of American Bob Dixon (Don Roberts), a decorated war veteran and aspiring painter living in Paris with his French wife, Yvonne (Patricia Conelle), and their small daughter, Sherie (Sherie Elms), to his childhood home. At the urging of his domineering mother, Bob and his family leave Paris, where they once enjoyed a bohemian lifestyle among expats, artists, jazz fans, and other eccentrics, and come to California and the conservative home of Mrs. Dixon (Wynn Gregory). A woman of considerable wealth and respectability, Bob's mother uses all means at her disposal to drive a wedge between her son and Yvonne. She impugns Yvonne's character, as an artist's model and practicing nudist, hiring a private detective to document her morally dubious behavior; she accelerates divorce proceedings, manipulating evidence against Yvonne in an attempt to gain custody of her granddaughter; and she keeps her son in her clutches, nearly destroying all remnants of his past life in the process.

With an eye toward the same kind of prurient voyeurism addressed in *Daughter of Dr. Jekyll, The Naked Venus* opens with a prologue showing two men with cameras and binoculars draped around their necks and tripods in their hands, winding their way down a mountainous path to an alpine lake. What could at first easily be mistaken for a naturalist expedition soon reveals itself as something altogether different. As the men look through their binoculars, and soon through the lens of a Bolex 16 mm camera, we see the object of their study is not birds, bears, or mountain lions but rather two nude women swimming and frolicking about—the one woman, who we later learn is Yvonne, stretches out, performing Mary Wigman–style dance movements in the sun, nothing but classical music playing in the background, and looking vaguely like a nude athlete from Leni Riefenstahl's *Olympia* (1938). Only after watching the entire movie do we realize that the man looking into the viewfinder and grinning with intense self-satisfaction (he lets out: "Oh, Mrs. Dixon is gonna *like* this!") is the private investigator (Allan Singer) hired by Mrs. Dixon to besmirch the reputation of Yvonne and help build a case for divorce.

Although the film is classified as a "nudie," very little of it depicts actual nudity—apart from a few scattered scenes at the lake and within the Royal Palms Nudist Park, where Yvonne seeks refuge when she and her daughter flee the home of Mrs. Dixon. Even then, the nudism, nothing that would warrant above a PG rating today, is more in keeping with the *Freikörperkultur* (free body culture), the German naturist movement that Ulmer knew well from Europe—and to which he and Shirley are said to have shown great sympathy in their private lives ("the practice of nudism is anyone's private business," asserts Dr. Hewitt in the film)—than with the grindhouse pictures of the 1950s and 1960s. Its main emphasis lies instead in the courtroom drama that occurs a little less than halfway through, when we witness the divorce proceedings. Yvonne receives legal representation by a young, independent-minded female litigator named Lynn Wingate, played with remarkable dexterity by Arianne Arden (Ulmer). The daughter of a powerful judge, Wingate seizes the opportunity to demonstrate her rhetorical skills, exposing the moral hypocrisy in the tactics used by Mrs. Dixon and her private investigator. She eventually calls as her star witness Dr. Hewitt (Harry Lovejoy), director of the contemporary art museum in Paris, where Bob's paintings, among them the so-called *Naked Venus*, hang. "Ignorance and prejudice have always been civilization's archenemies," Dr. Hewitt tells the court.

The film may be best understood as Ulmer's take on the so-called *Auflärungsfilme*, or enlightenment films, of the 1920s aimed at reforming the public's views of taboo topics. In that vein the courtroom drama serves a subtle commentary on the McCarthy-era witch hunts, the House Un-American Activities Committee interrogations, and the discrimination against those thought to be political subversives. It was not at all uncommon at the time to lump nudism together with other un-American activities. "Non-nudists seem convinced that nudists are 'freaks,'" noted one contemporary testimonial. "They believe that nudists go to nudist camps merely to satisfy their warped sexual, animalistic urges. . . . They usually consider nudists to be acute exhibitionists. Some consider them to be a 'Communistic tactic.'"[117] Finally, the film's sharp critique of puritanical morality, especially as it impinges on artistic expression, further anticipates the incendiary debate, some three decades later, concerning Robert Mapplethorpe's photography and the support it received from the National Endowment for the Arts.

+ + +

Faced with another girdle-tight schedule of little more than fourteen days, in April 1959, Ulmer shot two independent sci-fi flicks back-to-back in Dallas, Texas. The first of these, *Beyond the Time Barrier,* was made with a budget of $125,000 and photographed at an abandoned hangar from the 1936 Centennial Fairgrounds and at Carswell Air Force Base in Fort Worth. The production manager, Lester Guthrie, whose father, W.L. "Pop" Guthrie, served as the location coordinator, knew Ulmer from *Planet X,* on which the younger Guthrie had been assistant director. Sometime in the fall of 1958, after reading the apocalyptic script by Arthur C. Pierce, a former naval photographer, Guthrie approached Robert Clarke, who played John Lawrence in *Planet X* and who had purchased the rights to Pierce's script. "If you want to get the most out of this picture," Guthrie told Clarke, "I would highly recommend Ulmer."[118] Ostensibly drawn to the visual possibilities of the script, Ulmer quickly threw himself into the project, working together with the experienced German-born art director Ernst Fegté, who helped transform the drab interiors of the Centennial Building into a dynamic and visually striking space—a world in which Russian constructivism and German expressionism merge.

Ulmer chose to shoot in a semidocumentary style reminiscent of the Turbocharger shorts he directed for the air force during the war. The basic story line is cast against a tense political backdrop in which the arms race and the threat of nuclear disaster loom large. U.S. Air Force major William Allison (Clarke) embarks on a mission to explore the limits of speed travel in space, and in the process, breaking the time barrier, he is catapulted forward from the year 1960 to the year 2024. Allison lands his aircraft at a long-abandoned air base (in reality, Carswell Field in Fort Worth), which now serves as a deserted no-man's-land shared by an angry, oppressed group of mutants (an unruly group of male extras dressed in tattered clothes and ill-fitting swim caps) and The Supreme (Vladimir Sokoloff) and his loyalists. Cosmic plague has devastated the planet, and the future appears nothing but grim. Allison becomes a prisoner of The Supreme, but manages to form an alliance with three other fellow time-travelers, similarly stranded in the citadel: Dr. Bourman (John Van Dreelen); General Karl Kruse (Stephen Bekassy), known with wicked irony as "Karl Kraus," the sharp-tongued critic from the Vienna of Ulmer's childhood; and Captain Markova (named after the British ballerina Alicia Markova, in whose New York apartment the Ulmers had once lived), played by Ulmer's daughter Arianné (credited as Arianne Arden) (Figure 30).

The scheme that finally gets hatched, and is aided by The Supreme's granddaughter, the deaf-mute Princess Trirene (Darlene Tompkins), is to send Allison back to the year 1960 with the hope that he might prevent "cosmic plague" from ever occurring (in the story, the plague arrived in 1971, so Allison, in traveling back to 1960, offers the only hope of reversing history).

One by one, each of these scientists betrays the other, revealing the inexorable madness lurking beneath their scientific knowledge. Each is out for him- or herself, desirous of harnessing the power of science to go back in time, leaving the others behind. Allison functions merely as a pawn in their power struggle; he is the only one who knows how to operate the aircraft that will transport him back to 1960. In the end, when he finally does return home alone, he is debriefed, now looking six decades older than when he embarked on his mission, by officials flown in from Washington (Ulmer uses his old visual shorthand showing a couple of quick stock shots of the Pentagon). Allison begs them to end their own version of mad science—nuclear proliferation and such policies as Mutually Assured Destruction. After he explains his experiences, the head of the questioning team, in the movie's final line, says, with the camera resting on Allison's haggard, shell-shocked face: "Gentlemen, we've got a lot to think about." This rather heavy-handed finale reflects Ulmer's own deeper skepticism about the path modern science and the arms race were then taking. As his daughter, Arianné, has said: "The pessimism of these films was the result of the fear of

FIGURE 30. All in the family: Shirley *(left)*, Edgar, and Arianné Ulmer (as Captain Markova), on the set of *Beyond the Time Barrier* (1960). Courtesy of the Academy of Motion Picture Arts and Sciences.

nuclear catastrophe which we all felt at the time. . . . Ulmer's fear was even greater than ours, as he had experienced things during the First World War, which he did not wish to witness again. He was sure that World War III stood before us."[119]

The second of these films, *The Amazing Transparent Man,* treats the fantasy of a top-secret experiment in rendering human life invisible. Famed safe-cracker Joey Faust (Douglas Kennedy)—*yes,* Faust—is assisted in a prison break only to be used by evil-minded Major Paul Krenner (James Griffith)—not quite Mephisto but not a far cry from him either—a former military man who suffers from delusions of grandeur in the form of a scheme to assemble an invisible army. Faust doesn't exactly sell his soul, but he does become a part of the ongoing experiment conducted by Dr. Peter Ulof (Ivan Triesault), a man who has, as he tells us, had his "soul," which is to say his daughter, taken from him and therefore has no choice but to perform his function in Krenner's experiment. As long as his daughter is held hostage, he has no freedom to disengage himself from the morally dubious and highly dangerous project. Underpinning the larger drama that ensues in the act of becoming invisible—and the break-in at a local power plant made possible only because of the invisibility—is the gathering threat of nuclear disaster. Several years before the release of Ulmer's film, an article in the *New York Times* spoke of "an age of A-Bombs, B-pictures, cold wars and science fiction," almost anticipating a picture like *The Amazing Transparent Man.*[120] The fear of scientific secrets landing in the wrong hands was widespread—this was, after all, the immediate wake of the highly publicized Rosenberg execution. In her essay of 1965 "The Imagination of Disaster," Susan Sontag makes the trenchant point that in American science fiction films of this period there often "lurk the deepest anxieties about [our] contemporary existence." As she puts it further in the same essay, "I don't mean only the very real trauma of the Bomb—that it has been used, that there are enough now to kill everyone on earth many times over, that those new bombs may very well be used. Besides these new anxieties about physical disaster, the prospect of universal mutilation and even annihilation, the science fiction films reflect powerful anxieties about the condition of the individual psyche."[121]

Ulmer's film ends with a tense battle between Faust and Krenner, a battle in which the mad scientist (Krenner) and his disobedient assistant are decimated, together with the laboratory, in a massive nuclear mushroom cloud. Thanks to the help of a reformed Faust, the good Dr. Ulof manages to escape with his daughter. And in the final scenes, as he watches the explosion from afar in the company of a pair of G-men, Ulof explains that the CIA is considering exploring such experiments—with the idea of creating an invisible army to fight against national threats. Ulof looks directly into the camera, with a kind of Brechtian self-awareness, and says, "It's a serious problem. What would *you* do?"

GRAND ILLUSIONS

The 1960s offered little reprieve for Ulmer. Beleaguered by innumerable financial setbacks and unable to finish many of the projects he'd started in Europe, he and Shirley were again on the hunt for work. They retreated temporarily to the desert, to La Quinta, just south of Palm Springs, where Ulmer had bought a small piece of land in the 1940s with longtime collaborator Louis Hayward. Eager for any kind of freelance job he could get, he served briefly as a cameraman, using the same pseudonym he'd used on *The Naked Venus,* on Timothy Carey's *The World's Greatest Sinner* (1962), a low-budget comedy with a musical score by Frank Zappa. In the summer of 1961 the Ulmers returned once more to Europe, subletting an apartment in Paris, where Edgar continued to chase a few of the projects conceived with Nat Wachsberger that were still in play. Another reworking of "Mata Hari" occupied him at the start of July (he sent a copy of the script to Lahn, asking her to resubmit it to Geoffrey Shurlock of the "vicious Production Code for independents"); he also flirted with the idea of a coproduction known as "Corsican Brothers" and was "trying very hard to sell Nat" on a project called "Caravan to Samarkand."[122] Later that summer he commenced work on another script, a musical known as "Manon of Montparnasse" ("for a popular singer called Dalida," Ulmer wrote to Lahn, "the female Elvis Presley of France"). Producer Carol Hellman, formerly of Eichberg-Film, tried to entice Ulmer with a project, another costume drama, called "Nefertite," to be made in London.[123] Ulmer would never make any of these films.

Yet, while in France that summer, soon after *L'Atlantide* had opened in Parisian theaters, Ulmer was approached by young cineastes Luc Moullet and Bertrand Tavernier, who were hoping to conduct one of the first substantial interviews with the director. He agreed, and the printed text of their conversation took up more than a dozen pages in the August 1961 issue of *Cahiers du cinéma.* Among the things that Tavernier most recalled, many years later, was a discovery made in the interview and then clarified in subsequent research: "I explained to him [Ulmer] that we wanted to know who wrote *The Naked Dawn*. And he gave us about seven wrong leads! He said: 'It was the guy who was the gardener of Tennessee Williams.' I mean, forget it! Then he says: 'Oh, my frrrriend—it was Dalton Trrrrumbo!' When I worked with Trumbo, I asked him. He said: 'No, I did not write *The Naked Dawn*—but I wrote *The Cavern!*'"[124] As fate would have it, *The Cavern*, with a script that was at least partly, if not entirely, written by the blacklisted Trumbo (with credits officially given to British screenwriters Jack Davies and Michael Pertwee), would be the next—and, indeed, the *last*—feature film that Ulmer would complete.

A short notice in *Variety*, published just a few months after the *Cahiers* interview, announced with all the trademark hyperbole: "Edgar Ullmer [*sic*] has been signed by Martin Melcher to corporate and direct six features under Melcher and Doris Day's Arwin banner. Pix will be shot with exteriors abroad."[125] The first of these planned pictures, and the only one to get made, bore the working title "Search for the Sun" (ultimately released by 20th Century–Fox as *The Cavern*), and was scheduled to start shooting "in the border area of Italy, Yugoslavia and Austria" in January 1963. The piece mentions, further, that Ulmer, known to have been "working abroad [the] past three years," was now said to be negotiating with Swiss playwright Friedrich Dürrenmatt for another project and to have a commitment from Jeanne Moreau for still one of the others (Moreau would in fact star in the 1964 French production of *Mata Hari, Agent H21*, directed by Jean-Louis Richard for Truffaut's production company and made from a script by Richard and Truffaut that bore an all-too-close resemblance to what Ulmer had written, prompting a lawsuit in 1965).[126] The *Variety* notice also announced that Ulmer and Melcher were searching to cast appropriate players but not only big stars: "Let all the actors in Hollywood know this," Ulmer is quoted as saying. "I want them all knocking at my doorstep."

One of the actors to come knocking was a young Peter Marshall, who plays the witty Tyrolean-outfitted Canadian Lt. Peter Carter in the film. Sometime after the piece in *Variety* had been published, Marshall was given a tip by his friend, actor Larry Hagman, who had already been cast as the alcoholic Capt. Wilson. "I'm going to be doing a picture in Yugoslavia," Hagman told him. "It's a really good script, and there's a wonderful part for an English guy. Why don't I set an interview up for you?" Marshall met with Ulmer in an office in Beverly Hills to discuss the part. "My English accent isn't the greatest," he told the director. "Why don't we make the character Canadian?" Ulmer required no convincing; such minor tweaks to a script never fazed the director. "The money was lousy," Marshall admits decades after the production, "but, as Hagman said, it *was* a good part."[127]

British actor Brian Aherne, who was selected to play the old-school, stuffy English Gen. Braithwaite in the film, writes at length of the production in his memoir *A Dreadful Man:* "It seemed that Martin Melcher, the husband of Doris Day, had made a handsome profit from the exhibition of her pictures abroad and sought a way of repatriating it, or secreting it, without attracting the attention of the U.S. Internal Revenue Service—no easy trick. He bought a good script, *The Cavern,* written by one of the famous 'Hollywood Ten' Communist sympathizers who had been disbarred from the screen but still wrote, when occasion offered, under assumed names." Aherne's recollections match Tavernier's account, making it plausible that British screenwriters Davies and Pertwee were merely a front for Trumbo (like Herman and Nina Schneider on *The Naked Dawn*). "As director," adds Aherne, "we had Edgar Ulmer, a rather florid, temperamental character who had much experience and some talent but so far not much success." Ulmer would have chafed at such unflattering pronouncements. But his reputation was not especially strong, and among cast members Aherne's views were not unique. Morale on the set was, by all accounts, unusually low. Not only did the jolting news of John F. Kennedy's assassination, in late November 1963, cast a pall over filming, which had begun just weeks before, but the financial backing of the film seems to have fallen apart midway. "Melcher had flown back to Hollywood," Aherne adds, "leaving poor Ulmer with total responsibility for everything and—as we were to find later—barely half the money necessary to shoot the picture. Ulmer and his loyal, overworked wife, who acted as assistant producer, script girl, wardrobe mistress, secretary, cashier, and everything else necessary, plunged into their tasks and scarcely slept for many weeks."[128]

Having sketched the basic idea for the film already in the mid-1950s, Ulmer, along with his cast and crew, began shooting sometime in early fall of 1963. Several cast members, including Hagman, Marshall, Aherne, and John Saxon (who plays the hotheaded Pvt. Joe Carter), met the Ulmers in Rome and from there took the train together to Belgrade. Melcher had purportedly deposited money for the production in a Yugoslavian bank in Belgrade. Yet, like other European productions that Edgar and Shirley had experienced in the years before, this one included plenty of mishaps, beginning with lost luggage upon their arrival in Yugoslavia. "We had *nothing* with us but the clothes on our back," recalls Shirley. "And we were all pretty hysterical and angry at Edgar about this!"[129] Without their possessions, they checked into the large, unfinished Hotel Metropol—it'd be hard to invent a better-named hotel for a multinational Ulmer production—in Belgrade, where they met up with other members of the cast and crew.

Among the remaining members of the international ensemble cast are two Italians, Rosanna Schiaffino, who plays the feisty Anna, the only woman, and Nino Castelnuovo, who plays Mario, a man plagued by his unrequited love for Anna; an Austrian, the Viennese actor Hans von Borsody, whom Ulmer knew from his work on *Der Meineidbauer* and who gives a fine performance as German first lieutenant Hans Beck; and a German, Joachim Hansen, who is killed off in the explosion near the start of the film. Hungarian cameraman Gábor Pogány rounded out the polyglot Middle European flavor of the film and endured with the cast the frigid conditions of filming inside the renowned caves at Postojna, in the Yugoslavian mountains (now Slovenia), near the Italian border. When money suddenly ran low in Yugoslavia, the cast and crew crossed the border ("Like thieves in the night!" in Marshall's recollection) into Italy, continuing the production in Trieste, where on a shoestring they built makeshift caves at a municipal swimming pool.

The story of the film is quite simple yet in many ways advances the core themes that Ulmer pursued in his late work—the long-term reckoning with war, the consequences of national and ethnic chauvinism, oppression, and various threats to freedom. Set in Italy in September of 1944, when World War II had not quite yet run its course and when, as the opening scenes have it, soldiers can still be captured for crossing enemy lines, the plot pivots on the device of a bomb explosion that unwittingly traps seven people of different nationalities and political stripes inside a mountain cavern. (Before the plot unfolds, during the opening credits, Bobby Bare's country-and-western theme song adds a little Americana to the mix.) With limited food options, no natural light, and no apparent way out, the characters are suddenly "all prisoners," as von Borsody announces early on. The moral imperative, then, is cooperation, despite any mitigating animosities harbored in the outside world. "We shall all work together, and absolutely forget about nationalities," insists Gen. Braithwaite, speaking for the group. From their very first evening together, after a few minor spats, the seven refugees express their shared commitment to mutual understanding, bidding good night to each other in their respective languages: *good night, gute Nacht, buona notte.*

As the prisoners search for a way out, testing the various schemes they cook up (digging tunnels, setting off dynamite, attempting a doomed waterway escape), they face the equally profound human challenges of getting along. We see by turns petty bickering, romance, collaboration and deception, communal rituals, and all manner of alienation. In one of the film's obvious high points we hear Aherne's voice reading aloud from the *Book of Genesis* ("Let there be light!" a prized scriptural citation we recognize from Ulmer's use of it in *St. Benny the Dip*). It reverberates throughout the labyrinthine passages—and returns later, in a similar fashion to *The Naked Dawn*, as a voice-over recitation in the film's final moments—while Pogány's camera travels through the Postojna caves, surveying the crevasses and shadow-laden corners, and intercutting with a tight close-up of Joe and Anna in a loving embrace with the glistening waterfalls in the background. This scene leads to a poignant monologue by John Saxon, delivered with considerable swagger and early Brandoesque intensity, to his fellow refugees: "All a man ever did want on this earth is a little love and a way to show it." Finally, the story arrives at a joyful celebration, all seven characters seated around a table, exchanging gifts and toasting to peace, on Christmas Eve (Figure 31). This final flicker of hope, however, cannot sustain itself as the film—announcing the steady passage of time by way of intertitles ("96 days later," "152 days later")—soon shows Gen. Braithwaite coming apart at the seams, suffering from acute delusions, while Capt. Wilson, in a drunken stupor, plunges to his death. In an equally forceful, emotional scene, we observe Hans's miraculous climb to freedom, into the blinding daylight, only to watch him be shot by armed Partisans patrolling the mountains, when they recognize the swastika still affixed to his uniform.

In Germany, where the film was misleadingly known as *Neunzig Nächte und ein Tag* (*Ninety Nights and a Day*), and where it reached perhaps its widest audience and earned more accolades than elsewhere, the pressbook included a special tribute under the banner "Das Hohe Lied der Kameradschaft" (The great ballad of comradeship): "The war ended almost twenty years ago, but the peace is still far in the distance. We have proclaimed international friendship, treaties and alliances exist and are celebrated, but the comradeship among human beings unfortunately has not yet overcome hidden ethnic hatred and resentments. Just as G. W. Pabst in his 1931 film *Kameradschaft (Comradeship)* appealed to humanity on all sides of the borders, so too decrees director Dr. [*sic*] Edgar Ulmer with the suspenseful, almost scorching

FIGURE 31. Peace on Earth: the ensemble cast of *The Cavern* (1964), celebrating Christmas. *Left to right:* Nino Castelnuovo, Peter Marshall, John Saxon, Rosanna Schiaffino, Brian Aherne, Larry Hagman, Hans von Borsody. Courtesy of the Deutsche Kinemathek—Museum für Film und Fernsehen, Berlin.

plot of his film *Neunzig Nächte und ein Tag.*"[130] An accompanying essay, "Einst 'Menschen am Sonntag' nun 'Menschen in Not'" (Once "People on Sunday" now "People in Crisis"), also included in the German pressbook, likened the universality of Ulmer's directorial debut in Weimar Germany to the universal embrace of humanity in *The Cavern*. (Just a couple of years before, in conversation with Luc Moullet, Ulmer had suggested a remake of *Menschen am Sonntag* using young French actors.) Yet perhaps even more influential for Ulmer than Pabst was the work of the great cinematic humanist Jean Renoir, especially *La grande illusion* (*Grand Illusion*, 1937), which conveyed an uncompromising antiwar sensibility and a passionate appeal to humanity.

The circumstances surrounding the completion of *The Cavern* were quite different from those other storied productions. As was the case with most of Ulmer's late pictures made in Europe, the financial backing was tenuous at best. As Peter Marshall remembers it, "I guess he was doing *The Cavern* on a budget and Marty Melcher wasn't sending him the money, and the poor guy was scrambling—he scrambled through the whole film." Already in his early sixties at the time, and having endured a mild heart attack several years earlier, Ulmer suffered both physically and emotionally. He was known to respond poorly to working in confined spaces—his wife recalled several bouts of claustrophobia—yet he never slowed down. When the cast and crew relocated to Italy, he collapsed while aboard the night train out of Yugoslavia. "We just thought that he had been overstressed," remembers Shirley. "But in retrospect, I believe that was the beginning of all the strokes that happened thereafter."[131] Ulmer finished the film, which reached the screens in West Germany by summer 1964, followed by Italy in December of that year, and the United States a full year later. The press the film received in the Hollywood trade papers was negligible ("Producer-director Edgar G. Ulmer's biggest problem is to keep the confirmed action from becoming static," wrote *Variety*), and on Christmas Day 1965, the *New York Times* ran a review in which critic Howard Thompson called the film "only so-so," suggesting that "Mr. Ulmer, as director, perks up the final stretch" but that the picture as a whole was "small, respectable and forgettable."[132] These no doubt were not the kind of words that Ulmer envisioned for his epitaph.

While his work on *The Cavern* certainly affected his health, and possibly his professional standing, something else happened that brought about a significant change in Ulmer's personal life. During a visit to the Munich offices of Ernst Neubach, executive producer of the film, he met a young woman, Irmgard Kornauth, a classically trained Viennese actress and singer twenty-four years his junior, who was responsible for dubbing Rosanna Schiaffino's lines into German and doing vocals for her, when Schiaffino, half-naked and her back to the camera, sings while bathing. Although Ulmer was known over the years to have had a few on-set crushes, even minor flings or short affairs, the relationship that he started with Irmgard was different. Ulmer invited her to the United States in December 1965, under the pretense that he would eventually leave Shirley. In August 1966 a pregnant Irmgard moved to Las Vegas, where Shirley's brother, Fred Kassler (unbeknownst to his older sister), helped find her living quarters with his girlfriend, Barbara. In December of that year Irmgard gave birth to a daughter, Carola Angela, at Sunrise Hospital in Las Vegas (on the hospital papers, Kassler vouched for his brother-in-law that he was the true father). Although Edgar did his best to keep the entire affair hush-hush, Shirley found out—one day a real estate agent named Mr. Fink knocked at the door of Edgar and Shirley's home and announced to Shirley that he had found a nice apartment for Mrs. Ulmer and the new baby—and threatened divorce.[133] The Ulmers remained married, but tensions persisted until Edgar's health eventually gave out. (Edgar continued, furtively, to send letters and postcards to his infant daughter, Carola. From the Hotel Geneve in Mexico City, in September 1967, he wrote, in German, how he thinks about his baby daughter every minute of the day, telling her of the great love between fathers and daughters, reaching back to the ancient Greeks: "You will one day go to school and read these great immortal works and see them performed in the theater, tragedies like: *Oedipus at Colonus, Antigone, Electra, Iphigenia in Aulis,* and many others.")[134]

+ + +

After returning from Europe following *The Cavern,* and regaining some of his energy, Ulmer began to focus his attention more exclusively on the little screen, thinking up ideas for television and looking for a new audience, especially among young people. One of the few English-language profiles devoted to Ulmer during his lifetime was published in the *New York Times* in 1966, just a few months after the *Cavern* review. It appeared under the apt title "How to Be a Loner in Hollywood," and in it Peter Bart, who went on to become the legendary editor of *Variety,* suggests that Ulmer managed throughout his career to distinguish himself, almost defiantly, as one of the great "professional loners" ("men who finance their own pictures, sign their own players and arrange distribution of their films, often through haphazard channels"), separate in kind from the "proficient organization men" who dominated the industry. "To true film buffs," writes Bart, "the very mention of Ulmer's name is guaranteed to trigger an argument. To some, he is the father of the 'new wave.' To others, he is the dubious master of 'cheapie' exploitation pictures."[135] Bart rehearses segments of Ulmer's career, declaring him, at different phases, the "master of the ethnic picture" and "the man who ground out pot-boilers." Despite his unusually prolific, varied career, asserts Bart, Ulmer has remained "an 'outsider' in his trade." As he puts it, "Today, while most filmmakers focus on multi-million dollar epics financed by the big studios, Ulmer continues to turn out $150,000 films on money raised from private angels."

He notes further in the same piece that Ulmer was presently working on a new TV project, "Body on the Beach," a title that vaguely evokes a darker *Gidget* (created by agent Paul Kohner's brother Frederick), which the director describes as "a dramatic documentary of today's youth" and which he was hoping to sell to a "new TV art circuit" aimed at "a more literate audience." Ulmer tells Bart, with seemingly misplaced optimism: "I think it can be done. . . . We shall keep costs down. We shall use unknown actors. We shall establish a profit-sharing pool as an incentive to the technicians." In terms of exhibition and distribution Ulmer hoped that after first airing on television the films could be shown on the art-house circuit and in Europe ("where, as he freely admits, his reputation far surpasses his renown in this country"). Bart notes more generally how Ulmer's "cinema style" appealed more to the *Cahiers* critics, who were less concerned with plot or coherence than was mainstream America, and how a film like *The Naked Dawn* became a veritable "hit in Paris but aroused little excitement in Hollywood." He later quotes Ulmer, comparing the fate of the director in Europe versus America: "In Europe, no one can be a 'loner,' an outsider in his own profession. There are always eager young critics and filmmakers who are studying your films and who regard you as their teacher. But here things are different." Ulmer suggests to Bart that his proposed model for an art-house television market—decades before such programming would be developed on cable—could provide an alternative to Hollywood's penchant for massive budgets, megastars, and a surplus of special effects. Bart gives Ulmer the final word: "Perhaps we can find a way for better films to reach a wide audience. Moviemaking means much too much to me to turn out imitation James Bond pictures."

Later that same year, in an interview with *Modern Monsters* magazine, Ulmer responded once more to the question of why so many people think of him as a "loner": "'Loner' could only come from the fact that I have never been 'married' to any one studio, or producer who could ever make me do something I felt I couldn't. I usually speak my mind, and in such cases I have either won the battle, been asked for my resignation, or quit. If I do not believe completely in a project, have complete faith in it and in my co-workers on it, I can't do it. It's that simple."[136] The attitude that Ulmer expressed in 1966—for which he had ostensibly been recognized already in 1929, when he was branded a *Betriebshasser,* or business hater, in one of the publicity pieces published during the production of *Menschen am Sonntag*—is arguably what kept him from becoming one of the successful "organization men," as Bart called them. Although "Body on the Beach" never came to fruition, Ulmer continued his efforts in television. In early 1967, in a deal between Associated Film Artists Productions and CBS, he and Louis Hayward proposed to create an action-adventure series consisting of thirteen feature-length movies made for television (for CBS and their five stations, the *Los Angeles Times* reported in March 1967).[137] As with "Body on the Beach," however, nothing came of this. Undeterred, Ulmer finished work on yet another TV project, "Danger: Children at Play," again unproduced. In collaboration once more with Martin Melcher's Arwin Productions—despite his experience on *The Cavern*—he wrote some thirteen scripts for the *Doris Day Show*. After Melcher's death in 1968, Ulmer's hopes of employment on the show, like all of his other TV projects, were dashed.

Ironically, it was also around this time that Ulmer decided to rewrite *Detour*—or "The Loser," as he called it, set in bohemian Greenwich Village and the flower-power world of San Francisco in the late 1960s, and whose alternate title, appropriately enough, was "The Loner." Up until the end of his life, Ulmer maintained a profound identification with the plight of the hero from his best-known movie ("the idea to get involved on that road of Fate—where he's an absolute loser—fascinated me," as he told Bogdanovich [B 597]), his inability to follow the straight and narrow, his unrecognized talent and dedication, his seemingly innate ability to fall into life's traps and be led astray. The script, registered with the Screen Writers Guild in 1969, aimed at reaching the hippie generation (down-and-out pianist Al Roberts becomes Steve Bryan, Julliard-educated guitarist for The Ghouls, who hitches to the coast in a 1969 Cadillac convertible, only to get tripped up by the ghost of Vera in Chris Logan, "a helluva good looking bitch") and of course at granting Ulmer a final chance at a comeback. Yet as Hollywood lore and such cynical pictures as Nicholas Ray's *In a Lonely Place* (1950) tell us, it's much harder to come back than to arrive. Ulmer would struggle with both.

Monetary woes continued to dog Ulmer throughout his final years. Shirley not only had to reckon with her husband's recent infidelity but also had to figure a way to keep afloat financially, especially when he failed to collect on payment owed to him and when he was no longer able to work after the first of several major heart attacks in 1968. "I do not approve of what your Dad has done business wise," Shirley confided in a letter to Arianné after a string of his European projects fizzled.[138] Continuing to work as a script supervisor on such film projects as Jacques Demy's *Model Shop* (1969), Shirley returned home one evening to find her husband lying unconscious on the floor. As she tells it:

Edgar had a *very* rough ending. For four years, one stroke after the other. He was unable to move, unable to talk. We communicated by my giving him an ink pad and holding his hand, and he would scrawl with the little movement he had in the hand—*very* little. He couldn't even raise his head, had to be fed intravenously. It was four years of this agony. And I didn't like being in the hospital—he was at Cedars [Sinai], and when the insurance people cut us off, I didn't know what to do. I went to the Motion Picture Home, and they said they would take him in for $400 a month if I would sign off all my belongings—car, jewelry, *everything* you have to sign.off. We got him set up in a nice private room and they were good to him and took care of him. I took him home every weekend.[139]

After liquidating her possessions and moving into a small apartment, Shirley continued working on commercials and doing all that she could to support her ailing husband. To help defray the high costs of his care, in November 1969 she and Edgar hired a Los Angeles attorney, Jerome Rosenthal, to apply for a pension from the Screen Directors Guild (as testimony of his services to the industry, past collaborators—from Leon Fromkess, Jack Chertok, and Ilse Lahn through Robert Clarke, Aubrey Wisberg, William Wyler, and Carl Laemmle Jr.—wrote letters in his behalf). Having never been a contract director at a major studio, securing such a pension was no easy matter, and what Ulmer ultimately received was not sufficient to pay for the costs of long-term care.

Indeed, Ulmer never appeared more *maudit*, as the French critics liked to call him, than in the very final phase of his life. "The horror of the last five, ten years of Hollywood," he told Bogdanovich in 1970, "is most debased—and I say now objectively. I lived through the birth and growth of this town, but we have no spirit here now." Gone in Ulmer's eyes was a time of "men who built the business brick by brick, and each brick was an idea of love, of how to do it better, how to do it finer. This has all been lost" (B 570). A photograph of Ulmer, shot sometime in 1970, before paralysis had fully set in, conveys a certain melancholy self-awareness. He's seated behind a blue Madonna statuette (Figure 32).

Despite the great stories that Shirley Ulmer liked to tell of the statuette—that it had been given to him by producer Ottavio Poggi's wife while filming *Hannibal* and that the six-hundred-year-old object came from a church in Trastevere—it had, as Arianné explains today, really come from the Porta Portese flea market in Rome, acquired during the ill-fated production of Hedy Lamarr's *Loves of Three Queens*. Her father saw the striking blue Madonna lying on the ground at one of the stands and decided to buy it (it was, perhaps for him, like the famed talisman in John Huston's *The Maltese Falcon,* "the stuff that dreams

FIGURE 32. Salvation: Ulmer posing in 1966 with a Madonna statuette he bought at a Roman flea market while filming in Europe. Courtesy of John Belton.

are made of").[140] In the photo, rendered half in shadow, half in light, Ulmer looks into the camera, with the Madonna offering a universal gesture of forgiveness.

As it turns out, the published interview with Bogdanovich ends with Ulmer's claim that he's "looking for absolution for all the things I had to do for money's sake." In the actual recording and the printed type-script, however, Ulmer counters Bogdanovich's follow-up remark ("You made some good pictures") with one last burst of optimism. "I'm *going* to make some good pictures," he retorts. "I want kids around me . . . really." According to his daughter Arianné, "he always (even in the latter stages of his illness) thought he was going to come back. He said, 'They'll put me in a wheelchair and I'll *work,* I'll make good things, I'll work with young people. They'll help me.' He was still dreaming, and not until the last three, four months of his life did he ever even contemplate that this was the end of the line."[141] Likewise, Taver-nier talks about the tireless zeal of the maverick American directors of Ulmer's ilk: "I mean they are always full of projects—they more often live in a dream world where they are even inventing themselves the projects. I mean Fuller was like that. Ulmer was like that. He was always going to do the greatest super production. The most important film of his life which was going to win twenty-five Oscars."[142]

All dreams came to an end at the Motion Picture Home, in Wood-land Hills, on the afternoon of September 30, 1972—not quite two weeks after Ulmer's sixty-eighth birthday. Earlier that same day, his breathing having become noticeably labored, he began gasping for air. The caregivers at the facility were no longer able to marshal life-support, and Arianné, who happened to be at her father's side, en route with her family to Montecito, recognized that her father was in his last hours. She quickly called Shirley and told her to come at once. By the time she arrived, taking the first taxi she could get, Edgar's legs had already turned black and blue, all circulation having given out, and it was then merely a matter of hours. Shirley climbed into her husband's hospital bed, embraced him one final time beneath the blankets, and he died in her arms. Shirley and Arianné were both present, showing their resilience, as they had done at so many other important junctures in their personal and professional lives. They were the very first to bid farewell.

Days later, on October 3, at the memorial service at Beth Olam Mau-soleum, located inside the Hollywood Forever Cemetery on Santa Monica Boulevard, a rabbi was brought in to deliver a eulogy. "After sixty-eight years of dynamic creative living on this plane," his speech begins, "Edgar Ulmer folds his hands in eternal sleep." He then continued, placing Ulmer in the kind of company that he surely wouldn't have minded: "Edgar, like Stroheim, Sternberg, Lang, Wilder, and Preminger, was born in Vienna of the turn of the century."[143] In the remaining sections of his ten-page hand-written text, the rabbi celebrates the great highlights of Ulmer's life and career (138 films, by his generous estimation) before calling on the actor Fritz Feld to offer a tribute of his own. Feld, who had previously appeared in *The Wife of Monte Cristo* and *Her Sister's Secret*, and who also had acted in the New York production of Reinhardt's *The Miracle*, notes in rueful key: "When we think of a departed friend, we try to visualize once more, what attracted us to seek his friendship. To me it was this very fact of having found a man whose life was dedicated to literature, to music, to painting, to dance, to sculpture and most of all to theatre." He proceeds to quote, in the final lines of his text, from the Hungarian-born "Viennese playwright" Franz (Ferenc) Molnár's famous turn-of-the-century play *Liliom* (performed on Broadway in the early 1920s with Ulmer's child-hood friend Joseph Schildkraut in the title role and later adapted for the screen by Fritz Lang in French exile). Liliom's wife, Julie, is speaking, in the play, after her husband has died: "Good Bye!—Dear boy—sleep—peacefully—they can't understand how I feel. I can't even explain how I feel—You'd only laugh at me. But you can't hear me any more.—I LOVE YOU." As actor Jimmy Lydon, from *Strange Illusion*, remarked many years later, "You could have all the talent in the world and starve to death, as Edgar almost did, or you can have no talent and work all the time."[144] The strangely resonant, if also tragic, words written on Ulmer's gravestone read: "TALENT OBLIGES."[145]

Postscript

When Ulmer passed away in September 1972, the prevailing fear among family members was that his work would be forgotten forever—something he himself had articulated near the end of his life—that it would slowly, inexorably drift into oblivion. Although his departure did not go entirely unnoticed, with obituaries published in *Variety,* the *Los Angeles Times,* and the *New York Times,* the legacy of his life and career was surely in jeopardy. Because of the irreversible decline in his health, he was never able to finish the multisession interview with Bogdanovich that he began in February 1970, after the initial strokes had already left him partially paralyzed (the recordings essentially trail off after the two men discussed *Ruthless* and *Carnegie Hall,* with only passing mention of the films he made in the 1950s and 1960s). By the time the interview was published, in Jonas Mekas's *Film Culture* magazine in 1974, Ulmer was already an obscure figure, someone who was recognized if at all only by fringe cinephiles, devotees of the *Cahiers* circle, of film societies and the art-house circuit, and of the film pages of the independent weeklies like the *Village Voice,* the *Chicago Reader,* and the *Boston Phoenix.* That same year, in his composite study of Hawks, Borzage, and Ulmer, John Belton remarked without exaggeration: "Edgar G. Ulmer, one of the least known, least seen and least appreciated of American directors, remains one of the greatest filmmakers to emerge from the shadowy lower depths of Hollywood's 'B' feature production industry in the Forties. One of the era's bleakest artists and one of film noir's blackest visionaries, Ulmer today is all but forgotten, except for a handful of admirers and a score of detractors."[1]

The 1970s were largely a decade of underground appreciation of Ulmer's work. In 1975, a year after Belton's monograph and Bogdanovich's interview were both published, Todd McCarthy and Charles Flynn coedited their pioneering *Kings of the Bs: Working within the Hollywood System,* in which Ulmer (along with Sam Fuller, Joseph H. Lewis, Val Lewton, and several others) attained a crown. "Edgar G. Ulmer is the ultimate proof," McCarthy insists in his introduction to the anthology, "that distinctive and personal direction can emerge at any level of filmmaking."[2] The volume features Andrew Sarris's essay "Beatitudes and the Bs," in which Sarris hails *Detour* as a "poetic conceit from Poverty Row," as well as a reprint of the Bogdanovich interview and Myron Meisel's paean to Ulmer, "The Primacy of the Visual," originally published in the *Boston Phoenix* a month after Ulmer's passing. Much like Sarris before him, Meisel, a critic and contributing editor at the *Chicago Reader,* speaks of a certain poetry, attributing to the director an almost mystical ability to leave an artistic stamp on all that he touched. "Ulmer transformed his camera into a precise instrument of feeling," he asserts early on in the piece, "and his convulsive abstractions of screen space intensify that feeling by investing it with particular gestures of light, shadow, form, and motion that define his own director's soul, and none other." For Meisel and others of his ilk, despite the impoverished conditions under which he operated—or rather *because* of them—Ulmer was to be held in the same high esteem as the other great visionaries of American and European cinema. As he notes in the closing lines of his tribute: "For a long time Ulmer cultists like myself enjoyed using him as a club to demonstrate to the unbelieving that art can indeed thrive in even the least fertile soil. But Ulmer's work needs no polemic to defend its glories. Ulmer made no excuses and his work stands as it is—intransigent in its disregard for the normal niceties of conventional aesthetics."[3]

One of the critical reflexes among Ulmer's champions, especially in America of the 1970s, was to align his work with other prized aesthetic achievements of the twentieth century. In a 1978 program note for a screening series at the University of Texas, for instance, David Rodowick writes: "*Detour* may be one of the great unrecognized works in the absurdist style, rivaling even Kafka in its determination to strip life of logic and stability."[4] Other critics likened Ulmer's sensibility to Gide and Sartre (Ulmer himself, who always looked to the great literary sources for inspiration and who until his final years was hoping to do an adaptation of one of Arthur Schnitzler's works, once suggested in an interview that his work "veers between Kafka and Camus"). Similarly, filmic comparisons tended toward the directors already firmly ensconced in the canon of Western cinema, much as critics like Jacques Rivette had likened him to Nicholas Ray and Anthony Mann in *Cahiers du cinéma* decades before.

A watershed moment in Ulmer's afterlife came in October 1983, when UCLA's Melnitz Theatre hosted a two-month Ulmer retrospective, declaring him the true "King of the Bs" (a title etched further into memory by Bill Krohn's eponymous profile of the director that same year in *Film Comment*). The inaugural event of the retrospective, a screening of *Detour,* was announced in the arts section of the *Los Angeles Times,* which saw fit to eulogize the picture as "one of the most relentlessly intense psychological thrillers anyone has ever filmed." As the reporter for the *Times,* Kevin Thomas, added: "For the past 20 years the reputation of Ulmer, widely crowned the King of the Bs, has grown steadily as a virtuoso stylist who could turn out highly personal films in any genre on minuscule budgets."[5]

The "King of the Bs" retrospective traveled onward, under the auspices of the German cultural and educational forum, the Goethe-Institut, to less film-saturated American cities like Houston and Atlanta (and later to such remote corners of the world as Nairobi, Kenya), where it was greeted with considerable praise and a touch of bafflement. The *Houston Chronicle* ran an article titled "Edgar G. Who?" in which the author, invoking America's oft-forgotten thirteenth president, declared Ulmer "the Millard Fillmore of film directors," who was "at last getting respect."[6] In a piece published in the *Atlanta Constitution,* the author quotes Shirley Ulmer, who remarked of her husband's talent as a director of minor independent films: "Today, they're called art pictures. That's the switch. He had to use these artistic means to cover up a small budget. He had to have lots of imagination."[7]

Much of the attention that initially came to Ulmer was indeed due to the tireless efforts of Shirley, who, in addition to fighting court battles to secure the various forms of back payment and royalties still owed to her late husband—from the *Doris Day Show,* among others—fought to promote his work. She helped arrange festival screenings, hunted down stray prints, advocated for preservation and for video (and later DVD) production, while continuing to earn her own livelihood as a freelance script supervisor; she worked throughout the 1970s on such successful television series as *Little House on the Prairie, S.W.A.T.,* and *CHiPs.* In

1986 she published the first-ever guide to script supervision, *The Role of Script Supervision in Film and Television,* in which she drew chiefly on her experience collaborating with her husband and with their mutual friends and colleagues. In it she includes such anecdotes as how on *Carnegie Hall,* as a matter of professionalism, she insisted on addressing the director as "Mr. Ulmer," keeping all personal matters off the set.[8] Shirley's commitment to her profession was, of course, rivaled only by her commitment to the legacy of her husband, which she, together with her daughter, Arianné, helped to secure.

By the 1990s, a formerly neglected movie like *Detour* was no longer merely the darling of the subterranean cultists, or exclusively the subject of rarefied academic conversation, but had entered into the mainstream. In 1992 it received approval for inclusion in the National Film Registry at the Library of Congress, the first B picture to have earned the honor (it had been nominated just a few years earlier to be considered among the twenty-five foremost national film treasures), and was released in wide circulation on VHS (and later DVD).[9] Not long after, in summer 1997 and fall 1998, respectively, full-scale Ulmer retrospectives took place at the Edinburgh International Film Festival, curated by Lizzie Francke, and at Film Forum in New York, curated by Bruce Goldstein, both generating greater interest and a broader reception (an earlier such series, curated by Emanuela Martini in conjunction with Arianné Ulmer Cipes, had been organized in 1989 at the Bergamo Film Meeting in Italy). After Shirley's death, in 2000, Arianné picked up where her mother left off, establishing the Edgar G. Ulmer Preservation Corp. and laboring assiduously to promote the work of her father, to acquire additional prints and oversee new restorations. She mounted further efforts in the area of DVD production, working with David Kalat and All-Day Entertainment to produce the Edgar G. Ulmer Collection, the first in a string of DVD releases, and continued collaboration with archivists Michael Friend and Michael Pogorzelski at the Academy of Motion Picture Arts and Sciences, Alan Howden of the British Film Institute, D. J. Turner of the National Archives of Canada, and Sharon Pucker Rivo of the National Center for Jewish Film. She later worked with Austrian filmmaker Michael Palm to produce a feature-length documentary, *Edgar G. Ulmer: The Man Off-Screen,* which played at numerous festivals and was released on DVD by KINO International in 2006.

Although for significant stretches of time it may have appeared as though the memory of Ulmer's career would inevitably find its way into the dustbin of history, the past decade or so has been unusually kind to the émigré filmmaker. There have been numerous large retrospectives of his work: "Edgar G. Ulmer: Le bandit démasqué," at the International Film Festival in Amiens, France, in fall 2002; another equally ambitious series at the Austrian Film Museum in Vienna, in spring 2003, to coincide with the publication of Stefan Grissemann's German-language biography, *Mann im Schatten: Der Filmemacher Edgar G. Ulmer* (Man in the shadows: The filmmaker Edgar G. Ulmer); and most recently, in summer 2012, to commemorate the fortieth anniversary of Ulmer's death, at the Cinémathèque française in Paris. Moreover, there have been multiday symposia held on two continents: the first, sponsored by the National Endowment for the Humanities and hosted by the New School and Anthology Film Archives in New York City, in October 2002; and the second, a so-called *Ulmerfest*, sponsored by the German Research Foundation, the Jewish Museum, and the Goethe-Institut in Prague, convened in the city of his birth, at the Palacký University of Olomouc (Olmütz) in the Czech Republic, in September 2006 (yielding two separate critical anthologies). In a similar trend the number of DVD releases and the general availability of Ulmer's work continue to rise. From the 2005 release, by the National Center for Jewish Film, of Ulmer's four Yiddish features and the Criterion Collection's 2011 release of *People on Sunday* up to Warner Archive's release of *Murder Is My Beat* and Olive Films' release of *Ruthless*, both in 2013, a large number of Ulmer's films are now in circulation.

On a more subtle level we can also observe the journeys of certain Ulmer films as they travel across time and continue to reverberate. There are notable traces, for instance, of *The Black Cat* in *The Rocky Horror Picture Show* (1975) and of *Detour* in David Lynch's *Lost Highway* (1997).[10] These days, it's safe to say, there may be an Ulmer film lurking in the shadows, even in places where one might not think to look. As Luc Moullet has recently said of Ulmer's enduring influence:

When [Bertrand] Tavernier and I interviewed Ulmer in 1961, he suggested we make a film together. He was obviously in need of a project. He wanted to remake *Menschen am Sonntag* with young French actors. He wanted me and Bertrand and a few other people to write some scenes for that film. But he was not a sure producer. He couldn't even produce his own films! He made just one more film after 1961. So our project didn't come off the ground, but 48 years later I took some of what I had written then—on madness—and used it in a documentary way, as a starting point for my own *La terre de la folie* (*Land of Madness*, 2009).[11]

Some three decades after interviewing Ulmer, when the forum had changed from printed text to movie blog, Peter Bogdanovich offered a bold reappraisal tucked into a review of the recent DVD release of *Bluebeard*. "The career of director Edgar G. Ulmer," he observes, "one of the diehard film buff's major cult favorites, is an object lesson in the triumph of talent, courage, ingenuity and passion over time and money." He compares his observations of the film from more than forty years ago, when he first saw it, to those after screening the DVD. His final assessment underscores Ulmer's long-term significance: "That so much good work could be accomplished with so little encouragement and so few means makes our current situation—much money, little talent—all the more distressing, and Ulmer's achievement all the more impressive."[12] Ulmer's life and career still have much to say to a new generation of movie fans and aspiring filmmakers, working in a DIY digital era, when minimalism and independent production are experiencing yet another new wave. It's hard not to wonder what Ulmer might have pulled off with little more than an iPhone and his boundless imagination.

Filmography

The Border Sheriff (US 1926) [Universal, b/w, 50 min.]

Director: Robert N. Bradbury, Edgar G. Ulmer (uncredited)

Screenplay: Robert N. Bradbury

Story: W. C. Tuttle

Producer: N/A

Cinematography: Harry Mason, William Nobles

Cast: Jack Hoxie (Cultus Collins), Olive Hasbrouck (Joan Belden), S. E. Jennings (Carter Brace), Gilbert "Pee Wee" Holmes (Tater-Bug), Buck Moulton (Limpy Peel), Tom Lingham (Henry Belden), Bert De Marc (Joe Martinez), Frank Rice (Marsh Hewitt)

DVD: Loving the Classics

Menschen am Sonntag / People on Sunday (Germany 1930) [Filmstudio 1929, b/w, 73 min.]

Directors: Robert Siodmak, Edgar G. Ulmer

Screenplay: Billie Wilder, Kurt Siodmak

Producer: Moriz Seeler, Heinrich Nebenzahl

Cinematography: Eugen Schüfftan

Cinematography Assistance: Fred Zinnemann

Editor: Robert Siodmak (uncredited); Eugen Schüfftan (uncredited)

Music: Otto Stenzeel

Art Direction: Moritz Seeler

Cast: Erwin Splettstößer (Taxi Driver), Brigitte Borchert (Record Seller), Wolfgang von Waltershausen (Wine Seller), Christl Ehlers (Extra in films), Annie Schreyer (Model), Kurt Gerron (Himself), Valeska Gert (Herself), Heinrich Gretler (Himself), Ernö Verebes (Himself)

DVD: Criterion Collection

Damaged Lives (Canada/US 1933) [Weldon Pictures Corporation, b/w, 69 min.]

Director: Edgar G. Ulmer

Screenplay: Donald Davis, Edgar G. Ulmer

Producer: Max Cohn

Cinematography: Al Siegler

Editor: Otto Meyer

Sound: Glenn Rominger

Cast: Diane Sinclair (Joan), Lyman Williams (Donald Bradley), George Irving (Mr. Bradley), Almeda Fowler (Mrs. Bradley), Jason Robards (Dr. Bill Hall), Marceline Day (Laura Hall), Charlotte Merriam (Elise Cooper), Murray Kinnell (Dr. Vincent Leonard), Harry Myers (Nat Franklin), Vic Potel (Captain Olaf Jensen)

DVD: Grapevine Video

The Black Cat (US 1934) [Universal Pictures, b/w, 67 min.]

Director: Edgar G. Ulmer

Screenplay: Peter Ruric

Story: Edgar G. Ulmer, Peter Ruric

Producer: Carl Laemmle, Carl Laemmle Jr. (uncredited)

Supervising Producer: E. M. Asher (uncredited)

Cinematography: John J. Mescall

Editor: Ray Curtiss

Music: Heinz Roemheld

Art Direction: Charles D. Hall

Costumes: Vera West, Ed Ware

Makeup: Jack P. Pierce (uncredited)

Script Supervisor: Moree Herring (uncredited)

Assistant Script Supervisor: Shirley Alexander (uncredited)

Cast: Boris Karloff (Hjalmar Poelzig), Bela Lugosi (Dr. Vitus Werdegast), David Manners (Peter Alison), Jacqueline Wells (Joan Alison), Lucille Lund (Karen), Egon Brecher (The Majordomo), Harry Cording (Thamal), Henry Armetta (The Sergeant), Albert Conti (The Lieutenant)

DVD: Universal Home Entertainment

Thunder over Texas (US 1934) [Beacon Productions, b/w, 51 min.]

Director: Edgar G. Ulmer (as Joen Warner)

Screenplay: Eddie Granemann, Shirley Ulmer (as Sherle Castle)

Producer: Max Alexander

Production Manager: Arthur Alexander

Technical Director: Fred Preble

Cinematography: Harry Forbes

Editor: George Merrick

Sound: Frank McKenzie

Cast: Guinn "Big Boy" Williams (Ted Wright), Marion Shilling (Helen Mason), Helen Westcott (Betty "Tiny" Norton), Philo McCullough (Sheriff Tom Collier), Vic Potel (Dick), Benny Corbett (Harry), Tiny Skelton (Tom), Claude Payton (Bruce Laird), Bob McKenzie (Judge Blake), Dick Botiller (Gonzalez)

DVD: Alpha Video

From Nine to Nine (Canada 1936) [Coronet Pictures, Ltd., b/w, 75 min.]

Director: Edgar G. Ulmer

Screenplay: Edgar G. Ulmer, Shirley Ulmer (as Sherle Castle), Kenneth Duncan

Producer: William Steiner

Cinematography: Alfred Jacquemin

Art Director: Fred Govan (as Donald Govan)

Editor: Ross Philip-Taylor (as Phillip Taylor)

Sound: Maurice Metzger

Cast: Ruth Roland (Cornelia Du Play), Roland Drew (Inspector Vernon), Doris Covert (Yvonne Balsac), Kenneth Duncan (John Sommerset), Eugene Sigaloff (Schubin), Mariam Battista (Toinette), Arthur Stenning (Williams), Alexander Frazer (Louis Mentone), Julian Gray (Balsac), George A. Temple (Ivanov)

DVD: Grapevine Video

Natalka Poltavka/The Girl from Poltava (US 1937) [Avramenko Film Productions, Inc., b/w, 93 min.]

Director: Vasile Avramenko, M. J. Gann, Edgar G. Ulmer

Screenplay: Vasile Avramenko, M. J. Gann

Producer: Vasile Avramenko

Music: Mykola Vitaliyovych Lysenko

Script Supervisor: Shirley Ulmer (uncredited)

Cast: Thalia Sabanieeva (Natalka), Dimitri Creona (Petro), Olena Dibrova (Terplykha), Michael Shvetz (Vyborny), Lydia Berezovska (Mariyka), Fedir Braznick (Peasant), Maria Lavryk (Peasant wife), Peter Kushabsky (Terpylo), Mykola Novak (Landlord), Michael Skorobohach (Office Clerk), Andrew Stanislavsky (Lirnyk), Theodore Swystun (Mykola), Mathew Vodiany (Vozny), Vladimir Zelitsky (Palamar), Shirley Ulmer (Peasant Girl, uncredited)

DVD: N/A

Grine felder/Green Fields (US 1937) [Collective Film Producers/Kinotrade, b/w, 97 min.]

Director: Jacob Ben-Ami, Edgar G. Ulmer

Screenplay: Peretz Hirschbein, George G. Moscov

Producer: Roman Rebush, Ludwig Landy, Edgar G. Ulmer

Cinematography: William Miller, J. Burgi Contner

Editor: Jack Kemp

Music: Vladimir Heifetz

Art Direction: Steve Goulding

Script Supervisor: Shirley Ulmer (uncredited)

Cast: Michael Goldstein (Levi Yitskhok), Helen Beverley (Tsine), Izidor Casher (Dovid-Noich), Anna Appel (Rokhl), Max Vodnoy (Elkone), Lea Noemi (Gitl), Dena Drute (Stera), Saul Levine (Hersh-Ber), Hershel Bernardi (Avrom-Yankov), Aron Ben-Ami (Yeshiva Boy)

DVD: National Center for Jewish Film

Let My People Live (US 1938) [Motion Picture Service Corporation, b/w, 13 min.]

Director: Edgar G. Ulmer

Dramatic Assistants: S. E. Walker, Edward Lawson

Screenplay: N/A

Producer: Motion Picture Camera Service

Cinematography: William Miller

Sound: Nelson Minnerly

Script Supervisor: Shirley Ulmer (uncredited)

Cast: Rex Ingram (Dr. Gordon), Peggy Howard (Mary), Merritt Smith (George), Erostine Coles (Minister)

DVD: Grapevine Video

Diagnostic Procedures in Tuberculosis (US 1938) [Motion Picture Service Corporation, b/w, 13min.]

Director: Edgar Ulmer, Ph.D. [*sic*]

Cinematography: William Miller

Supervisor: J. Burgi Contner

DVD: N/A

Yankel der schmid/The Singing Blacksmith: (US 1938) [Collective Film Producers, b/w, 105 min.]

Director: Edgar G. Ulmer

Screenplay: Ben-Zvi Baratoff, Ossip Dymow, David Pinski

Executive Producer: Roman Rebush

Production Supervisor: Ludwig Landy

Cinematography: William Miller

Editor: Jack Kemp

Music: Edward Fenton, Edwin Schabbehar

Script Supervisor: Shirley Ulmer (uncredited)

Cast: Moishe Oysher (Yankel), Miriam Riselle (Tamara), Florence Weiss (Rivke), Anna Appel (Chaye-Peshe), Ben-Zvi Baratoff (Bendet), Michael Goldstein (Raffuel), Lea Noemi (Mariashe), Max Vodnoy (Simche), Luba Wesoly (Frumeh), Yudel Dubinsky (Reb Aaron), Luba Rymer (Sprintz-Gnesye), Benjamin Fishbein (Frolke), Rubin Wendroff (Elia), Ray Schneier (Chaika–Rivke's mother), R. Shanock (Leah), Hershel Bernardi (Young Yankel), Arianné Ulmer (Baby in Crib, uncredited)

DVD: National Center for Jewish Film

Zaporozhets za Dunayem/Cossacks in Exile (Canada 1939) [Avramenko Film Company, Ltd., b/w, 84 min.]

Director: Edgar G. Ulmer

Screenplay: Vasile Avramenko

Producer: Vasile Avramenko, Michael J. Gann

Cinematography: William J. Miller, Leo Lipp

Editor: Jack Kemp

Music: Antin Rudnytsky

Costumes: Fedir Braznick

Script Supervisor: Shirley Ulmer (uncredited)

Cast: Maria Sokil (Odarka), Michael Shvetz (Ivan Karas), Nicholas Karlash (Sultan), Alexis Tcherkassky (Andrii), Helen Orlenko (Pxana), Dimitri Creona (Kobzar), Vladimir Zelitsky (Selih-Agha), General Vladimir Kikevitch (Kalnyshewsky), S. Mostowy (Prokip), L. Biberowich (Catherine II), N. Mandryka (General Tekely), Jean Harasymyk (Hassan), Anna Mushinsky (Neboha), Fedir Braznick (Old Cossack), Vasyl Yatsyna (Solo Dancer)

DVD: Grapevine Video

Moon over Harlem (US 1939) [Meteor Productions, Inc., b/w, 69 min.]

Director: Edgar G. Ulmer

Assistant Director: Fred Kassler, Gustav Heimo

Screenplay: Shirley Ulmer (as Sherle Castle), original story by Mathew Mathews

Producer: Edgar G. Ulmer

Associate Producer: Peter E. Kassler

Cinematography: J. Burgi Contner, Edward Hyland

Editor: Jack Kemp

Music: Donald Heywood

Art Direction: Eugene Wolk

Script Supervisor: Shirley Ulmer (uncredited)

Cast: Bud Harris (Dollar Bill), Cora Green (Minnie), Izinetta Wilcox (Sue), Earl Gough (Bob), Zerita Stepeau (Jackie), Petrina Moore (Alice), Daphne Fray (Pat), Mercedes Gilbert (Jackie's mother), Frances Harrod (Maud), Alec Lovejoy (Fats), Walter Richardson (Brother Hornsby), Slim Thompson (Long-Boy), Freddie Robinson (Half-Pint), John Bunn (Wallstreet), Marieluise Bechet (Nina Mae Brown), John Fortune (Jamaica), Audrey Talbird (Connie), Marie Young (Jean), Christopher Columbus and His Swing Crew (Themselves), Sidney Bechet and His Clarinet (Himself)

DVD: All-Day Entertainment

Fishke der krumer/Di klyatshe/The Light Ahead (US 1939) [Collective Film Producers, b/w, 94 min.]

Director: Edgar G. Ulmer

Screenplay: Chaver Paver, Mendele Moykher Sforim, Edgar G. Ulmer, Shirley Ulmer

Producer: Edgar G. Ulmer, Peter E. Kassler

Cinematography: J. Burgi Contner, Edward Hyland

Editor: Jack Kemp

Sound: Dean Cole

Art Direction: Robert Benny, Edgar G. Ulmer

Cast: David Opatoshu (Fishke), Helen Beverley (Hodel), Isidore Cashier (Mendele Mokher Sforim), Rosetta Bialis (Dropke), Anna Guskin (Gitel), Wolf Mercur (Getzel the Thief), Jenny Cashier (Dobe the Hunchback), Yudel Dubinsky (Isaak the Stutterer), Leon Seidenberg (Reb Alter); Arianné Ulmer (Yentele, uncredited)

DVD: National Center For Jewish Film

Nube en el cielo/Cloud in the Sky (US 1940) [Sponsor: National Tuberculosis Association, b/w, 19 min.]

Director: Edgar G. Ulmer

Screenplay: Harry E. Kleinschmidt

Cinematography: J. Burgi Contner

Sound: Dean Cole

Editor: Marc C. Asch

Script Supervisor: Shirley Ulmer (uncredited)

Cast: Rosario de la Vega (Consuelo), F. L. Tafolla (Doctor), Frederick J. Mann (Padre), R. C. Ortega (Lopez), R. Trevino Jr. (Pedro)

DVD: Grapevine Video

Goodbye Mr. Germ (US 1940) [De Frenes & Company, b/w, 14 min.]

Director: Edgar G. Ulmer

Cinematography: Joseph Noble

Animation: H. L. Roberts

Settings: Stanley Levick

Editor: Hans Mandl

Cast: James Kirkwood (Dad)

DVD: All-Day Entertainment

They Do Come Back (US 1940) [De Frenes & Company, b/w, 16 min.]

Director: Edgar G. Ulmer

Cinematography: Joseph Noble

Editor: Hans Mandl

Narrator: Alois Havrilla

Cast: Wilma Caspar, Edward Mulhern

DVD: Grapevine Video

Amerikaner shadkhn/American Matchmaker (US 1940) [Fame Films Inc., b/w, 87 min.]

Director: Edgar G. Ulmer

Screenplay: Gustav H. Heimo, Shirley Ulmer (as Sherle Castle), B. Ressler

Producer: Edgar G. Ulmer

Cinematography: J. Burgi Contner, Edward Hyland

Sound: Dean Cole

Editor: Hans E. Mandl

Music: Sam Morgenstern

Art Direction: William Saulter, W. Mack

Script Supervisor: Shirley Ulmer (uncredited)

Cast: Leo Fuchs (Nat Silver/Uncle Shya), Judith Abarbanel (Judith Aarons), Yudel Dubinsky (Maurice), Anna Guskin (Elvie Silver), Celia Boodkin (Nat's Mother), Rosetta Bialis (Mrs. Aarons), Abraham Lax (Simon P. Schwalbenrock), Arianné Ulmer (uncredited)

DVD: National Center For Jewish Film

Another to Conquer (US 1941) [Springer Pictures Inc., b/w, 22 min.]

Director: Edgar G. Ulmer

Screenplay: Harry E. Kleinschmidt

Cinematography: Robert Cline

Sound: Clarence Townsend

Editor: Hans E. Mandl

Script Supervisor: Shirley Ulmer (uncredited)

Cast: Howard Gorman (Slow-Talker), Sammy Day (Don), Geraldine H. Birdsbill (Nema), Richard Hogner (Robert), W. W. Peter, M.D. (Doctor)

DVD: Grapevine Video

Prisoner of Japan (US 1942) [Atlantis Pictures Corporation, Producers Releasing Corporation, b/w, 64 min.]

Director: Arthur Ripley, Edgar G. Ulmer (uncredited)

Screenplay: Arthur Ripley, Edgar G. Ulmer (uncredited)

Producer: Leon Fromkess, Seymour Nebenzal, Edgar G. Ulmer (uncredited)

Cinematography: Jack Greenhalgh

Editor: Holbrook N. Todd

Music: Leo Erdody

Art: Fred Preble

Script Supervisor: Shirley Ulmer (uncredited)

Cast: Alan Baxter (David Bowman), Gertrude Michael (Toni Chase), Ernest Dorian [Ernst Deutsch] (Matsuru), Corinna Mura (Loti), Tom Seidel (Ensign Bailey), Billy Moya (Maui), Ray Bennett (Lieutenant Morgan), Ann Staunton (Edie)

DVD: N/A

Tomorrow We Live (US 1942) [Atlantis Pictures Corporation, Producers Releasing Corporation, b/w, 63 min.]

Director: Edgar G. Ulmer

Screenplay: Bart Lytton

Producer: Leon Fromkess, Seymour Nebenzal

Cinematography: Jack Greenhalgh

Editor: Dan Milner

Music: Leo Erdody

Art Direction: Fred Preble

Script Supervisor: Shirley Ulmer (uncredited)

Cast: Ricardo Cortez (The Ghost), Jean Parker (Julie Bronson), Emmett Lynn (Pop Bronson), William Marshall (Lt. Bob Lord), Roseanne Stevens (Melba), Ray Miller (Chick), Frank S. Hagney (Kohler), Rex Lease (Shorty), Jack Ingram (Steve), The Blonde (Barbara Slater), The Dancer (Jane Hale)

DVD: Alpha Video

Corregidor (US 1943) [Atlantis Pictures Corporation, Producers Releasing Corporation, b/w, 73 min.]

Director: William Nigh

Screenplay: Doris Malloy, Edgar G. Ulmer

Producer: Edwin Finney, Dixon Harwin, Peter R. Van Duinen

Cinematography: Ira H. Morgan

Editor: Charles Henkel Jr.

Music: Leo Erdody

Art Direction: Frank Paul Sylos

Cast: Otto Kruger (Dr. Jan Stockman), Elissa Landi (Dr. Lee Royce Stockman), Donal Woods (Dr. Michael), Frank Jenks (Sgt. Mahoney), Rick Vallin (Cpl. Pinky Mason), Wanda McKay (Nurse Jane Van Dornen), Ian Keith (Capt. Morris), Ted Hecht (Platoon Lieutenant), Charles Jordon (Bronx), Frank Jacquet (Priest), Alfred Noyes (Narrator)

DVD: N/A

My Son, the Hero (US 1943) [Atlantis Pictures Corporation, Producers Releasing Corporation, b/w, 65 min.]

Director: Edgar G. Ulmer

Screenplay: Doris Malloy, Sam Newfield, Edgar G. Ulmer

Producer: Leon Fromkess, Peter R. Van Duinen

Cinematography: Robert E. Cline, Jack Greenhalgh

Editor: Charles Henkel Jr.

Music: Leo Erdody

Art Direction: Fred Preble

Script Supervisor: Shirley Ulmer (uncredited)

Cast: Patsy Kelly (Gerty Rosenthal), Roscoe Karns (Big Time Morgan), Joan Blair (Cynthia Morgan), Carol Hughes (Linda Duncan), Maxie Rosenbloom (Kid Slug Rosenthal), Luis Alberni (Tony), Joseph Allen Jr. (Michael Morgan), Lois Collier (Nancy Cavanaugh), Jenny Le Gon (Lambie), Nick Stewart (Nicodemus), Hal Price (Fight Manager), Al St. John (Gus the Night Clerk), Elvira Curcy (Rosita), Isabel La Mel (Mrs. Olmstead), Maxine Leslie (Girl Reporter)

DVD: Alpha Video

Hitler's Madman (US 1943) [Angelus Pictures Inc., Metro-Goldwyn-Mayer Corporation, b/w, 84 min.]

Director: Douglas Sirk

Second Unit Director: Edgar G. Ulmer (uncredited)

Screenplay: Emil Ludwig, Bart Lytton, Peretz Hirschbein, Melvin Levy, Doris Malloy, Edgar G. Ulmer (uncredited)

Producer: Seymour Nebenzal

Cinematography: Jack Greenhalgh, Eugen Schüfftan (uncredited)

Editor: Dan Milner

Music: Karl Hajos

Art Direction: Fred Preble

Cast: John Carradine (Heydrich), Patricia Morison (Jarmila), Alan Curtis (Karel), Howard Freeman (Himmler), Ralph Morgan (Jan), Ludwig Stössel (Mayor Bauer), Edgar Kennedy (Nepomuk), Al Shean (Father Semlanik), Elizabeth Russell (Maria), Jimmy Conlin (Dvorak), Blanche Yurka (Mrs. Hanka), Jorja Rollins (Clara Janek), Victor Kilian (Janek), Johanna Hofer (Mrs. Bauer), Wolfgang Zilzer (Colonel), Tully Marshall (Professor)

DVD: N/A

Girls in Chains (US 1943) [Atlantis Pictures Corporation, Producers Releasing Corporation, b/w, 75 min.]

Director: Edgar G. Ulmer

Screenplay: Albert Beich, Edgar G. Ulmer

Producer: Leon Fromkess, Peter R. Van Duinen

Cinematography: Ira H. Morgan

Editor: Charles Henkel Jr.

Music: Leo Erdody

Art Direction: Fred Preble

Set Decoration: Harry Reif

Script Supervisor: Shirley Ulmer (uncredited)

Cast: Arline Judge (Helen Martin), Roger Clark (Frank Donovan), Robin Raymond (Rita Randall), Barbara Pepper (Ruth), Dorothy Burgess (Mrs. Peters), Clancy Cooper (Mr. Marcus), Allan Byron (Johnny Moon), Patricia Knox (Jean Moon), Sidney Melton (Pinkhead), Russell Gaige (Dalvers), Emmett Lynn (Lionel Cleeter)

DVD: Something Weird Video

Isle of Forgotten Sins/Monsoon (US 1943) [Atlantis Pictures Corporation, Producers Releasing Corporation, b/w, 82 min.]

Director: Edgar G. Ulmer

Screenplay: Raymond L. Schrock, Edgar G. Ulmer

Producer: Peter R. Van Duinen

Cinematography: Ira H. Morgan

Editor: Charles Henkel Jr.

Music: Leo Erdody (as Erdody)

Art Direction: Fred Preble

Art Department: Harry Reif, Angelo Scibetta

Script Supervisor: Shirley Ulmer (uncredited)

Cast: John Carradine (Mike Clancy), Gale Sondergaard (Marge Williams), Sidney Toler (Carruthers/Captain Krogan), Frank Fenton (Jack Burke), Veda Ann Borg (Luana), Rita Quigley (Diane), Rick Vallin (Johnny Pacific), Tala Birell (Christine), Patti McCarty (Bobbie Nelson), Betty Amann (Olga), Marian Colby (Mimi), William Edmonds (Noah)

DVD: Alpha Video

Jive Junction/Swing High (US 1943) [Producers Releasing Corporation, b/w, 63 min.]

Director: Edgar G. Ulmer

Screenplay: Irving Wallace, Walter Doniger, Malvin Wald

Producer: Leon Fromkess

Cinematography: Ira H. Morgan

Editor: Robert O. Crandall

Music: Leo Erdody (as Erdody)

Art Direction: Frank Paul Sylos

Script Supervisor: Shirley Ulmer (uncredited)

Cast: Dickie Moore (Peter Crane), Tina Thayer (Claire Emerson), Gerra Young (Gerra), Johnny Michaels (Jimmy Emerson), Jack Wagner (Grant Saunders), Jan Wiley (Miss Forbes), Beverly Boyd (Cubby), Bill Halligan (Mr. Maglodian), Johnny Duncan (Frank), Johnny Clark (Chick), Friedrich Feher (Frederick Feher), Caral Ashley (Mary), Bob McKenzie (Sheriff)

DVD: N/A

The Turbosupercharger: Master of the Skies (US 1943) [Raphael G. Wolff Studios Inc., b/w, 23 min.]

Director: Edgar G. Ulmer

Script Supervisor: Shirley Ulmer (uncredited)

Cast: O.P. Echols, Sanford A. Moss

DVD: N/A

The Turbosupercharger: Flight Operation (US 1943) [Raphael G. Wolff Studios Inc., b/w, runtime N/A]

Director: Edgar G. Ulmer

Script Supervisor: Shirley Ulmer (uncredited)

Cast: N/A

DVD: N/A

Bluebeard (US 1944) [Producers Releasing Corporation, b/w, 73 min.]

Director: Edgar G. Ulmer

Screenplay: Pierre Gendron, Arnold Phillips, Werner H. Furst

Producer: Leon Fromkess, Martin Mooney

Cinematography: Jockey Arthur Feindel, Eugen Schüfftan (uncredited)

Production Designer: Eugen Schüfftan (as Eugen Schufftan)

Editor: Carl Pierson

Music: Leo Erdody (as Erdody)

Art Direction: Paul Palmentola, Angelo Scibetta

Set Decoration: Glenn P. Thompson

Script Supervisor: Shirley Ulmer (uncredited)

Cast: John Carradine (Gaston Morrell), Jean Parker (Lucille), Nils Asther (Inspector Lefevre), Ludwig Stössel (Jean Lamarté), George Pembroke (Inspector Renard), Teala Loring (Francine), Sonia Sorel (Renee), Henry Kolker (Deschamps), Emmett Lynn (Le Soldat), Iris Adrian (Mimi), Patti McCarthy (Babette), Carrie Devan (Constance), Anne Sterling (Jeanette Le Beau)

DVD: All-Day Entertainment

Strange Illusion / Out of the Night (US 1945) [Producers Releasing Corporation, b/w, 85 min.]

Director: Edgar G. Ulmer

Screenplay: Adele Comandini, Fritz Rotter

Producer: Leon Fromkess

Cinematography: Philip Tannura, Benjamin H. Kline (uncredited), Eugen Schüfftan (uncredited)

Editor: Carl Pierson

Music: Leo Erdody (as Erdody)

Art Direction: Paul Palmentola

Set Decoration: E. H. Reif

Script Supervisor: Shirley Ulmer (uncredited)

Cast: Jimmy Lydon (Paul Cartwright), Warren William (Brett Curtis/Claude Barrington), Sally Eilers (Virginia Cartwright), Regis Toomey (Dr. Vincent), Charles Arnt (Professor Muhlbach), George H. Reed (Benjamin), Jayne Hazard (Dorothy Cartwright), Jimmy Clark (George), Mary McLeod (Lydia), Pierre Watkin (Armstrong), Sonia Sorel (Miss Farber), Vic Potel (Mac), George Sherwood (Langdon), Gene Stutenroth (Sparky), John Hamilton (Mr. Allen)

DVD: All-Day Entertainment

Club Havana (US 1945) [Producers Releasing Corporation, b/w, 62 min.]

Director: Edgar G. Ulmer

Screenplay: Raymond L. Schrock

Story: Fred L. Jackson

Producer: Leon Fromkess, Martin Mooney

Cinematography: Benjamin H. Kline, Eugen Schüfftan (uncredited)

Production Supervisor: Eugen Schüfftan (as Eugen Schuftan)

Editor: Carl Pierson

Music: Howard Jackson

Art Direction: Edward C. Jewell

Set Decoration: Glenn P. Thompson

Script Supervisor: Shirley Ulmer (uncredited)

Cast: Tom Neal (Bill Porter), Margaret Lindsay (Rosalind), Don Douglas (Johnny Norton), Lita Baron (Isabelita), Sonia Sorel (Myrtle), Dorothy Morris (Lucy), Renie Riano (Mrs. Cavendish), Ernest Truex (Willy Kingston), Gertrude Michael (Hetty), Eric Sinclair (Jimmy Medford), Paul Cavanagh (Clifton Rogers), Marc Lawrence (Joe Reed), Pedro de Cordoba (Charles), Carlos Molina and His Music of the Americas (Themselves), Eddie Hall (Ace, uncredited), Frank Fenton (Detective Lieutenant, uncredited), Helen Heigh (Susan, uncredited)

DVD: Mr. Fat-W Video

Detour (US 1945) [Producers Releasing Corporation, b/w, 67 min.]

Director: Edgar G. Ulmer

Screenplay: Martin Goldsmith

Producer: Leon Fromkess, Martin Mooney

Cinematography: Benjamin H. Kline

Editor: George McGuire

Music: Leo Erdody (as Erdody)

Art Direction: Edward C. Jewell

Set Decoration: Glenn P. Thompson

Script Supervisor: Shirley Ulmer (uncredited)

Cast: Tom Neal (Al Roberts), Ann Savage (Vera), Claudia Drake (Sue Harvey), Edmund MacDonald (Charles Haskell Jr.), Tim Ryan (Gus), Esther Howard (Hedy), Pat Gleason (Joe)

DVD: Alpha Video

The Wife of Monte Cristo (US 1946) [Producers Releasing Corporation, b/w, 79 min.]

Director: Edgar G. Ulmer

Screenplay: Dorcas Cochran, Edgar G. Ulmer, Franz Rosenwald

Producer: Leon Fromkess

Cinematography: Edward A. Kull, Eugen Schüfftan (uncredited)

Editor: Douglas Bagier

Music: Paul Dessau

Art Direction: Edward C. Jewell

Set Decoration: Glenn P. Thompson

Script Supervisor: Shirley Ulmer (uncredited)

Cast: John Loder (De Villefort), Lenore Aubert (Haydée), Fritz Kortner (Maillard), Charles Dingle (Danglars), Eduardo Ciannelli (Antoine), Martin Kosleck (Count of Monte Cristo), Fritz Feld (Bonnett), Eva Gabor (Lucille), Clancy Cooper (Baptiste), John Bleifer (Louis), Egon Brecher (Proprietor), Anthony Warde (Captain Benoit), Colin Campbell (Abbe Farria), Crane Whitley (Officer in Charge)

DVD: N/A

Her Sister's Secret (US 1946) [Producers Releasing Corporation, b/w, 83 min.]

Director: Edgar G. Ulmer

Screenplay: Anne Green

Producer: Heinz Brasch (as Henry Brash)
Cinematography: Frank Planer
Editor: Jack W. Ogilvie
Music: Hans Sommer
Art Direction: Edward C. Jewell
Set Decoration: Glenn P. Thompson
Script Supervisor: Shirley Ulmer (uncredited)
Cast: Nancy Coleman (Antoinette "Toni" DuBois), Margaret Lindsay (Renée DuBois Gordon), Philip Reed (Dick Connolly), Felix Bressart (Pepé), Regis Toomey (Bill Gordon), Henry Stephenson (Mr. DuBois), Fritz Feld (Wine Salesman), Winston Severn (Billy Jr.), George Meeker (Guy), Helene Heigh (Etta), Frances E. Williams (Mathilda), Rudolph Anders (Birdman)
DVD: Mr. Fat-W Video

The Strange Woman (US 1946) [Hunt Stromberg Productions, Mars Film Corporation, b/w, 99 min.]

Director: Edgar G. Ulmer, Douglas Sirk (uncredited)
Screenplay: Herb Meadow
Producer: Jack Chertok, Hunt Stromberg, Hedy Lamarr
Cinematography: Lucien Andriot
Editor: John M. Foley, Richard G. Wray
Music: Carmen Dragon
Art Direction: Nicolai Remisoff
Script Supervisor: Shirley Ulmer (uncredited)
Cast: Hedy Lamarr (Jenny Hager), George Sanders (John Evered), Louis Hayward (Ephraim Poster), Gene Lockhart (Isaiah Poster), Hillary Brooke (Meg Saladine), Rhys Williams (Deacon Adams), June Storey (Lena Tempest), Moroni Olsen (Rev. Thatcher), Olive Blakeney (Mrs. Hollis), Alan Napier (Judge Henry Saladine), Dennis Hoey (Tim Hager)
DVD: All-Day Entertainment

Carnegie Hall (US 1947) [Federal Films, b/w, 136 min.]

Director: Edgar G. Ulmer
Screenplay: Karl Kamb, Seena Owen
Producer: William LeBaron, Boris Morros
Cinematography: William Miller, Eugen Schüfftan (uncredited)

Editor: Fred R. Feitshans Jr.

Music: Sigmund Krumgold (musical advisor)

Art Direction: Max Rée

Production Technique: Eugen Schüfftan (as Eugene Shuftan)

Script Supervisor: Shirley Ulmer (uncredited)

Cast: Marsha Hunt (Nora Ryan), William Prince (Tony Salerno Jr.), Frank McHugh (John Donovan), Martha O'Driscoll (Ruth Haines), Hans Yaray (Tony Salerno Sr.), Olin Downes (Himself), Joseph Buloff (Anton Tribik), Walter Damrosch (Himself), Bruno Walter (Himself), Lily Pons (Herself), Gregor Piatigorsky (Himself), Risë Stevens (Herself), Artur Rodzinski (Himself), Artur Rubinstein (Himself), Jan Peerce (Himself), Ezio Pinza (Himself), Jascha Heifetz (Himself), Fritz Reiner (Himself), Leopold Stokowski (Himself), Harry James (Himself), Emile Boreo (Himself), Vaughn Monroe (Himself), Alphonso D'Artega (Tschaikowski)

DVD: Kino International

Ruthless (US 1948) [Producing Artists Inc., b/w, 105 min.]

Director: Edgar G. Ulmer

Screenplay: Alvah Bessie (uncredited), Gordon Kahn, S.K. Lauren

Producer: Joseph Justman, Arthur S. Lyons

Cinematography: Bert Glennon

Editor: Francis D. Lyon

Music: Werner Janssen

Art Direction: Frank Sylos

Set Decoration: Ray Robinson

Script Supervisor: Shirley Ulmer (uncredited)

Cast: Zachary Scott (Horace Woodruff Vendig), Louis Hayward (Vic Lambdin), Diana Lynn (Martha Burnside/Mallory Flagg), Sydney Greenstreet (Buck Mansfield), Lucille Bremer (Christa Mansfield), Martha Vickers (Susan Duane), Edith Barrett (Mrs. Burnside), Dennis Hoey (Mr. Burnside), Raymond Burr (Pete Vendig), Joyce Arling (Kate Vendig), Charles Evans (Bruce Endicott McDonald), Bob Anderson (Horace Vendig, as child), Arthur Stone (Vic Lambdin, as child), Ann Carter (Martha Burnside, as child), Edna Holland (Libby Sims), Fred Worlock (J. Norton Sims), John Good (Bradford Duane), Claire Carleton (Bella)

DVD: Olive Films

I pirati di Capri / The Pirates of Capri (Italy/US 1949) [Industrie Cinematografiche Sociali S.r.l. (ICS), AFA Film S.r.l., Film Classics, b/w, 95 min.]

Director: Edgar G. Ulmer, Giuseppe Maria Scotese (uncredited in US version)

Screenplay: Sidney Alexander, Golfiero Colonna, Giorgio Moser

Producer: Rudolph Monter (uncredited in US version),Victor Pahlen, Niccolò Theodoli

Cinematography: Anchise Brizzi

Editor: Renzo Lucidi

Music: Nino Rota (credited as "Nina")

Art Direction: Guido Fiorini

Script Supervisor: Shirley Ulmer (uncredited)

Cast: Louis Hayward (Count di Amalfi, alias Capt. Sirocco), Binnie Barnes (Queen Carolina Maria), Mariella Lotti (Countess Mercedes de Lopez), Massimo Serato (Baron von Holstein), Alan Curtis (Commodore Van Diel), Michael Rasumny (Pepino), Virginia Belmont (Annette), Franca Marzi (Carla), William Tubbs (Pignatelli), Arianné Ulmer (uncredited)

DVD: Image Entertainment

St. Benny the Dip (US 1951) [Danziger Productions Ltd., b/w, 82 min.]

Director: Edgar G. Ulmer

Screenplay: George Auerbach, John Roeburt

Producer: Edward J. Danziger, Harry Lee Danziger (credited as "The Danzigers")

Cinematography: Don Malkames

Music: Robert W. Stringer

Script Supervisor: Shirley Ulmer (uncredited)

Cast: Dick Haymes (Benny), Nina Foch (Linda Kovacs), Roland Young (Matthew), Lionel Stander (Monk Williams), Freddie Bartholomew (Reverend Wilbur), Oscar Karlweis (Mr. Kovacs), William A. Lee (Police Sergeant Monahan), Richard Gordon (Rev. Miles), Jean Casto (Mrs. Mary Williams), Eddie Wells (Patrolman McAvoy), James Bender (House Detective)

DVD: Alpha Video

The Man from Planet X (US 1951) [Mid Century Films Inc., b/w, 71 min.]

Director: Edgar G. Ulmer

Screenplay: Jack Pollexfen, Aubrey Wisberg

Producer: Jack Pollexfen, Aubrey Wisberg

Associate Producer: Ilse Lahn (uncredited)

Cinematography: John L. Russell

Editor: Fred R. Feitshans Jr.

Music: Charles Koff

Art Direction: Angelo Scibetta, Byron Vreeland

Assistant Director: Les Guthrie

Script Supervisor: Shirley Ulmer (uncredited)

Cast: Robert Clarke (John Lawrence), Margaret Field (Enid Elliot), Raymond Bond (Professor Elliot), William Schallert (Dr. Mears), Roy Engel (Tommy the Constable), David Ormont (Inspector Porter), Gilbert Fallman (Dr. Robert Blane)

DVD: MGM Home Video

Muchachas de Bagdad/Babes in Bagdad (Spain/US/Great Britain 1952) [Danziger Productions Ltd., color, 80 min.]

Director: Jerónimo Mihura (Spanish Version), Edgar G. Ulmer (English Version)

Screenplay: Joe Ansen, Felix E. Feist, Reuben Levy, John Roeburt

Producer: Daniel Aronés (Spanish Version), Edward J. Danziger (English Version), Harry Lee Danziger (English Version), Antonio Pujol (Spanish Version)

Cinematography: Jack E. Cox (English Version), Georges Périnal (Spanish Version), José Luis Pérez de Rozas (Spanish Version)

Editor: Teresa Alcocer, Edith Lenny (English Version), Angeles Pruña

Music: Jesús García Leoz

Art Direction: Enrique Bronchalo, Juan Frexe

Script Supervisor: Shirley Ulmer (uncredited)

Cast: Paulette Goddard (Kyra), Gypsy Rose Lee (Zohara), Richard Ney (Ezar), John Boles (Hassan), Thomas Gallagher (Sharkhan), Sebastian Cabot (Sinbad), MacDonald Parke (Caliph), Natalie Benesh (Zelika), Hugh Dempster (Omar), Peter Bathurst (Officer)

DVD: N/A

The Loves of Three Queens (Italy/France 1954) [Cino Del Duca Produzioni, Produzioni Cenmatografiche Europee (P.C.E.), Lamarr Productions Inc., color, 90 min.]

Director: Marc Allégret, Edgar G. Ulmer

Screenplay: Marc Allégret, Vittorio Nino Novarese, Roger Vadim, Salka Viertel

Producer: Hedy Lamarr, Victor Pahlen

Cinematography: John Allen, Desmond Dickinson, Guglielmo Lombardi, Fernando Risi

Editor: Manuel del Campo

Music: Nino Rota

Art Direction: Mario Chiari, Virgilio Marchi

Script Supervisor: Shirley Ulmer (uncredited)

Cast: Hedy Lamarr (Hedy Windsor/Helen of Troy/Empress Joséphine/Geneviève de Brabant), Massimo Serato (Paris), Cathy O'Donnell (Oenone), Anna Amendola (Minerva), Robert Beatty (Menelaus), Alba Arnova (Venus), Elli Parvo (Giunone), Guido Celano (Giove), Enrico Glori (Priamo), John Fraser (Drago), Serena Michelotti (Cassandra), Gérard Oury (Napoleon Bonaparte), Piero Pastore (Simone)

DVD: N/A

Murder Is My Beat (US 1955) [Masthead Productions, b/w, 77 min.]

Director: Edgar G. Ulmer

Screenplay: Aubrey Wisberg

Producer: Ilse Lahn, Aubrey Wisberg

Cinematography: Harold E. Wellman

Editor: Fred R. Feitshans Jr.

Music: Al Glasser

Art Direction: James Sullivan, Harry H. Reif

Script Supervisor: Shirley Ulmer (uncredited)

Cast: Paul Langton (Ray Patrick), Barbara Payton (Eden Lane), Robert Shayne (Police Captain Bert Rawley), Selena Royle (Beatrice Abbott), Roy Gordon (Abbott), Tracy Roberts (Patsy Flint)

DVD: Warner Archive

The Naked Dawn (US 1955) [Josef Shaftel Company Inc., color, 82 min.]

Director: Edgar G. Ulmer

Screenplay: Julian Zimet (a.k.a. Julian Halevy) [credited as Herman and Nina Schneider]

Producer: James O. Radford, Josef Shaftel

Cinematography: Frederick Gately

Editor: Dan Milner

Music: Herschel Burke Gilbert

Art Direction: Martin Lencer

Set Decoration. Harry Reif

Script Supervisor: Shirley Ulmer (uncredited)

Cast: Arthur Kennedy (Santiago), Betta St. John (Maria Lopez), Eugene Iglesias (Manuel Lopez), Charlita (Tita, entertainer), Roy Engel (Guntz), Tony Martinez (Vicente)

DVD: N/A

Der Meineidbauer/Die Sünderin vom Fernerhof/The Perjurer (Germany 1956) [Eichberg-Film GmbH, color, 104 min.]

Director: Rudolf Jugert

Screenplay: Erna Fentsch

Producer: Edgar G. Ulmer

Cinematography: Roger Hubert

Editor: Lilian Seng

Music: Friedrich Meyer

Art Direction: Wolf Englert, Max Mellin

Cast: Heidemarie Hatheyer (Paula Roth), Carl Wery (Matthias Ferner), Hans von Borsody (Franz Ferner), Christiane Hörbiger (Marie Roth), Attila Hörbiger (Pichler), Joseph Offenbach (Christoph Demuth), Bobby Todd (Pedro)

DVD: N/A

Daughter of Dr. Jekyll (US 1957) [Film Ventures Inc., b/w, 71 min.]

Director: Edgar G. Ulmer

Screenplay: Jack Pollexfen

Producer: Ilse Lahn, Jack Pollexfen

Cinematography: John F. Warren

Editor: Holbrook N. Todd

Music: Melvyn Lenard

Art Direction: Theobald Holsopple

Set Decoration: Mowbray Berkeley

Script Supervisor: Shirley Ulmer (uncredited)

Cast: John Agar (George Hastings), Gloria Talbott (Janet Smith), Arthur Shields (Dr. Lomas), John Dierkes (Jacob), Mollie McCard (Maid Maggie),

Marjorie Stapp (Woman Getting Dressed)
DVD: All-Day Entertainment

Swiss Family Robinson (TV Pilot: "Lost in the Jungle") (US 1958) [Trans-World Artists Inc., color, 26 min.]

Director: Edgar G. Ulmer

Screenplay: Harold Jacob Smith

Producer: Edgar G. Ulmer, Henry F. Ehrlich

Cinematography: J: Charles Carbajal

Editor: Charles Savage

Music: Lan Adomian

Art Direction: Edward Fitzgerald

Dialogue Director: Arianné Ulmer

Script Supervisor: Shirley Ulmer (as Shirley K. Ulmer)

Cast: William Vann Rogers, Casey Rogers Williams, Reba Waters, et al.

DVD: All-Day Entertainment

The Naked Venus (US 1959) [Beaux Arts Films Inc., Europa G.H.P., b/w, 74 min.]

Director: Edgar G. Ulmer [as Ove H. Sehested]

Screenplay: Gabriel Gort, Gaston Hakim

Producer: Gaston Hakim

Cinematography: Jacques Sheldon

Editor: Ronald V. Ashcroft (as Ronny Ashcroft)

Music: Arne Hasse

Cast: Patricia Conelle (Yvonne Duval Dixon), Don Roberts (Bob Dixon), Arianné Ulmer [as Arianne Arden] (Lynn Wingate), Wynn Gregory (Mrs. Dixon), Douglas McCairn (John Rutledge), Doris Shriver (Laura Dixon), Allan Singer (Charles Becker), Harry Lovejoy (Dr. Hewitt), Louis Bertrand (Insp. Merchant), Sherie Elms (Sherie), Bill Lough (The Judge)

DVD: Something Weird Video

Beyond the Time Barrier (US 1960) [Miller-Consolidated Pictures, b/w, 75 min.]

Director: Edgar G. Ulmer

Screenplay: Arthur C. Pierce

Producer: Robert Clarke, Robert L. Madden, John Miller

Cinematography: Meredith M. Nicholson

Editor: Jack Ruggiero

Music: Darrell Calker

Art Direction: Ernst Fegté

Production Manager: Lester Guthrie

Location Coordinator: W. L. "Pop" Guthrie

Script Supervisor: Shirley Ulmer

Cast: Robert Clarke (Major William Allison), Darlene Tompkins (Princess Trirene), Vladimir Sokoloff (The Supreme), Boyd 'Red' Morgan (Captain), Stephen Bekassy (Gen. Karl Kruse), Arianné Ulmer [as Arianne Arden] (Capt. Markova), John Van Dreelen (Dr. Bourman), Ken Knox (Col. Marty Martin), Jack Herman (Dr. Richman)

DVD: Sinister Cinema

The Amazing Transparent Man (US 1960) [Miller-Consolidated Pictures, b/w, 57 min.]

Director: Edgar G. Ulmer

Screenplay: Jack Lewis

Producer: Lester D. Guthrie, Robert L. Madden, John Miller

Cinematography: Meredith M. Nicholson

Editor: Jack Ruggiero

Music: Darrell Calker

Art Direction: Ernst Fegté

Set Decoration: Louise Caldwell

Script Supervisor: Shirley Ulmer

Cast: Marguerite Chapman (Laura Matson), Douglas Kennedy (Joey Faust), James Griffith (Major Paul Krenner), Ivan Triesault (Dr. Peter Ulof), Red Morgan (Julian), Cormel Daniel (Maria Ulof), Edward Erwin (Drake), Jonathan Ledford (Smith)

DVD: Alpha Video

Annibale/Hannibal (Italy/US 1960) [Liber Films, Chefordi, color, 100 min.]

Director: Carlo Ludovico Bragaglia, Edgar G. Ulmer

Screenplay: Mortimer Braus, Allesandro Continenza, Edgar G. Ulmer

Producer: Ottavio Poggi

Cinematography: Raffaele Masciocchi

Editor: Renato Cinquini

Music: Carlo Rustichelli

Art Direction: Ernest Kromberg

Set Decoration: Amedeo Mellone

Script Supervisor: Shirley Ulmer (uncredited)

Cast: Victor Mature (Hannibal), Gabriele Ferzetti (Fabius Maximus), Rita Gam (Sylvia), Bud Spencer [as Carlo Pedersoli] (Rutario), Terrence Hill [as Mario Girotti] (Quintilius), Milly Vitale (Danila), Rik Battaglia (Hasdrubal), Franco Silva (Maharbal), Mirko Ellis (Mago), Andrea Aurei (Gajus Terentius Varro), Andrea Fantasia (Consul Paulus Emilius)

DVD: VCI Entertainment

L'Atlantide/Antinea l'amante della città sepolta/Journey beneath the Desert (Italy/France/US 1961) [Compagnia Cinematografica Mondiale, Fidès Film, Transmonde Film, color, 105 min.]

Director: Giuseppe Masini, Edgar G. Ulmer

Screenplay: Remigio Del Grosso, Ugo Liberatore, André Tabet, Edgar G. Ulmer

Producer: Luigi Nannerini

Executive Producer: Nat Wachsberger

Cinematography: Enzo Serafin

Editor: Renato Cinquini

Music: Carlo Rustichelli

Art Direction: Piero Filippone

Set Design: Edgar G. Ulmer

Script Supervisor: Shirley Ulmer (uncredited)

Dialogue Coach and Translation Supervisor: Arianné Ulmer (uncredited)

Cast: Jean-Louis Trintignant (Pierre), Haya Harareet (Queen Antinea), Georges Rivière (John), Rad Fulton (Robert), Amedeo Nazzari (Tamal), Giulia Rubini (Zinah), Gabriele Tinti (Max), Gian Maria Volonté (Tarath)

DVD: Something Weird Video

Sette contro la morte/Neunzig Nächte und ein Tag/The Cavern (Italy/Germany/US 1964) [Cinedoris S.p.A., Ernst Neubach Filmproduktion GmbH, Arwin Productions, Inc., b/w, 94 min.]

Director: Edgar G. Ulmer

Screenplay: Dalton Trumbo (uncredited), Jack Davies, Michael Pertwee

Producer: Ernst Neubach, Edgar G. Ulmer

Cinematography: Gábor Pogány

Editor: Renato Cinquini

Music: Carlo Rustichelli, Franco Ferrara

Theme Song sung by: Bobby Bare

Script Supervisor: Shirley Ulmer (uncredited)

Cast: John Saxon (Pvt. Joe Cramer), Rosanna Schiaffino (Anna), Larry Hagman (Capt. Wilson), Peter L. Marshall (Lt. Peter Carter), Nino Castelnuovo (Mario Sconamiglio), Brian Aherne (Gen. Braithwaite), Hans von Borsody (Oberlt. Hans Beck), Joachim Hansen (German Sergeant)

DVD: N/A

Notes

PREFACE

1. Ed Sikov, *On Sunset Boulevard: The Life and Times of Billy Wilder* (New York: Hyperion, 1998), viii.

2. George Lipsitz, "The New York Intellectuals: Samuel Fuller and Edgar Ulmer," in *Time Passages: Collective Memory and American Popular Culture* (Minneapolis: University of Minnesota Press, 1990), 195.

3. Bert Rebhandl, "Lauter Umwege zum Ruhm," *Frankfurter Allgemeine Zeitung*, April 10, 2003.

CHAPTER 1. TRACES OF A VIENNESE YOUTH

Epigraph: Correspondence between Frieda Grafe and Josef von Sternberg, cited in English translation in Alexander Horwath, "Working with Spirits—Traces of Sternberg: A Lost Film about the 'City of My Dreams,'" trans. Peter Waugh, in *Josef von Sternberg: The Case of Lena Smith,* ed. Alexander Horwath and Michael Omasta (Vienna: Synema, 2007), 42.

1. On the various claims that Ulmer made during his lifetime, see Stefan Grissemann, *Mann im Schatten: Der Filmemacher Edgar G. Ulmer* (Vienna: Zsolnay, 2003). See also Peter Bogdanovich, "Edgar G. Ulmer: An Interview," *Film Culture* 58–60 (1974): 189–238; repr. in *Who the Devil Made It: Conversations with Legendary Film Directors* (New York: Ballantine, 1998), 558–604; all subsequent references, unless otherwise noted, refer to the Ballantine (B) edition of the interview and are cited parenthetically in the text: (B 558–604). The claim about Fellini's *La dolce vita* comes from the unpublished, unabridged transcript of the interviews conducted by Bogdanovich, included among the papers of the Edgar G. Ulmer Collection, Margaret Herrick Library, Academy of Motion Picture Arts and Sciences, Los Angeles (hereafter cited as EGUC-

AMPAS). The claim about *Gone with the Wind* comes from Bertrand Tavernier, interview by Michael Henry Wilson, Nov. 7, 1997, Paris, EGUC-AMPAS.

2. Cited in Deborah Lazaroff Alpi, *Robert Siodmak* (Jefferson, NC: McFarland, 1998), 20.

3. John Belton has provided a thorough elaboration of the term, and its application to Ulmer; see John Belton, "Edgar G. Ulmer (1900[sic]–1972)," in *American Directors*, ed. Jean-Pierre Coursodon with Pierre Sauvage (New York: McGraw-Hill, 1983), 1:340. See also Luc Moullet, "Présentation Edgar G. Ulmer," *Cahiers du cinéma*, no. 58 (April 1956): 55–57; and François Truffaut, *The Films in My Life*, trans. Leonard Mayhew (1975; New York: Da Capo, 1994), 155–56.

4. Manny Farber, "White Elephant Art vs. Termite Art," *Film Culture* (1962), repr. in *Farber on Film: The Complete Writings of Manny Farber*, ed. Robert Polito (New York: Library of America, 2009), 535.

5. John Belton, "Cinema Maudit," in *Retrospective* catalogue (Edinburgh: Edinburgh Film Festival, 1997), 150.

6. See Luc Moullet and Bertrand Tavernier, "Entretien avec Edgar G. Ulmer," *Cahiers du cinéma*, no. 122 (August 1961): 1–16; and Bogdanovich, "Edgar G. Ulmer."

7. Rudolf Ulrich, *Österreicher in Hollywood* (Vienna: Edition S, 1993), 325.

8. Grissemann, *Mann im Schatten*, 9. Unless otherwise noted, all translations are my own.

9. Tavernier, Wilson interview.

10. Ibid. See also Bertrand Tavernier, interview by Stefan Grissemann, Feb. 9, 2009, Berlin, author's personal collection.

11. See the official documents printed in Bernd Herzogenrath, "Introduction: The Return of Edgar G. Ulmer," in *Edgar G. Ulmer: Essays on the King of the B's*, ed. Bernd Herzogenrath (Jefferson, NC: McFarland, 2009), 8.

12. Grissemann describes the birth in greater detail in *Mann im Schatten*, 21.

13. Ibid., 28.

14. See Shirley Ulmer, interview by Michael Henry Wilson, May 7, 1996, Los Angeles, EGUC-AMPAS. Arianné Ulmer Cipes similarly notes, in an unpublished letter to Paul Mandell from Oct. 18, 1984: "The true picture of her was that she was desperate, cold, ungiving and certainly not what we today consider an ideal mother. . . . If anything [she was] a great source of pain and confusion to my father."

15. Shirley Ulmer to Arianné Ulmer, June [n.d.] 1939, EGUC-AMPAS.

16. Stefan Zweig, *The World of Yesterday* (Lincoln: University of Nebraska Press, 1964), 1, 6, and passim. The citation from Josef von Sternberg comes from Horwath, "Working with Spirits—Traces of Sternberg," 11. See also, more generally, Carl Schorske, *Fin-de-siècle Vienna: Politics and Culture* (New York: Pantheon, 1980), 116–80.

17. See Steven Beller, *Vienna and the Jews, 1867–1938: A Cultural History* (New York: Cambridge University Press, 1991).

18. Tavernier, Wilson interview.

19. Fritz Göttler, "King Edgar," *Süddeutsche Zeitung*, March 27, 2003, 16.

20. Shirley Ulmer refers to this incident in her interview with Michael Henry Wilson. See also Grissemann, *Mann im Schatten*, 22.

21. Shirley Ulmer, interview.

22. Edgar G. Ulmer, "Beyond the Boundary," EGUC-AMPAS. All subsequent citations from Ulmer's unpublished novel refer to this source.

23. Shirley Ulmer, interview.

24. Shirley Ulmer, interview.

25. Edgar G. Ulmer to Shirley Ulmer, April 25, 1949, EGUC-AMPAS.

26. Edgar G. Ulmer to Arianné Ulmer, Dec. 27, 1955, EGUC-AMPAS.

27. Herzogenrath, "Introduction," 6.

28. Cited in Frederic Morton, *Thunder at Twilight: Vienna, 1913/1914* (New York: Da Capo, 2001), 185–86.

29. See Daniela Sannwald, "Metropolis: Die Wien-Berlin-Achse im deutschen Film der 10er und 20er Jahre," in *Elektrische Schatten: Beiträge zur Österreichischen Stummfilmgeschichte,* ed. Francesco Bono, Paolo Caneppele, and Günter Krenn (Vienna: Filmarchiv Austria, 1999), 139–48.

30. Frieda Grafe, "Wiener Beiträge zu einer wahren Geschichte des Kinos," in *Aufbruch ins Ungewisse: Österreichische Filmschaffende in der Emigration vor 1945,* ed. Christian Cargnelli and Michael Omasta (Vienna: Wespennest, 1993), 227.

31. Schorske, *Fin-de-siècle Vienna,* 129.

32. Robert Horton, *Billy Wilder: Interviews* (Jackson: University Press of Mississippi, 2002), 27.

33. Grissemann, *Mann im Schatten,* 66.

34. In the unabridged, unpublished transcript Ulmer follows up his remark with a statement on the contradictory character of Stroheim: "a very illiterate man who did a tremendous amount of reading." On the process of self-reinvention among exile (or émigré) directors see Stuart Klawans's illuminating discussion of the case of Erich von Stroheim, "The Politics of Authorship," in *Film Follies: The Cinema Out of Order* (New York: Cassell, 1999), 41–68.

35. Quoted in Göttler, "King Edgar," 16.

36. Thomas Elsaesser, "Ethnicity, Authenticity, and Exile: A Counterfeit Trade? German Filmmakers in Hollywood," in *Home, Exile, Homeland: Film, Media, and the Politics of Place,* ed. Hamid Naficy (New York: Routledge, 1999), 112.

37. Grissemann, *Mann im Schatten,* 26.

38. Eric Kronning (*né* Katz) to Edgar G. Ulmer, May 4, 1947, EGUC-AMPAS. "He always spoke of Sweden with great affection," explains Arianné Ulmer Cipes. See Tag Gallagher, "All Lost in Wonder: Edgar G. Ulmer," *Screening the Past* 12 (March 2001): http://tlweb.latrobe.edu.au/humanities/screeningthepast /firstrelease/fr0301/tgafr12a.htm

39. Neil Sinyard, *Fred Zinnemann: Films of Character and Conscience* (Jefferson, NC: McFarland, 2003), 9–10.

40. On his alleged study with Alfred Roller see Grissemann, *Mann im Schatten,* 26.

41. Shirley Ulmer to Arianné Ulmer, June [n.d.] 1939, courtesy of Arianné Ulmer Cipes. In this letter Shirley attempts to provide an account of Ulmer's background so that their daughter will later have the opportunity to understand

more about her family lineage and, in particular, about her father's upbringing and cultural heritage.

42. Tom Weaver, "Her Father's Keeper: Arianné Ulmer Cipes," *Video Watchdog* 41 (1997): 35–36.

43. Julius Bab, *Schauspieler und Schauspielkunst* (Berlin: Oesterheld, 1926), 181–82.

44. Egon Dietrichstein, *Die Berühmten* (Vienna: Wiener Literarische Anstalt, 1920), 148.

45. Joseph Schildkraut, *My Father and I* (New York: Viking, 1959), 4.

46. Ibid., 81.

47. Otto Preminger, "Otto Preminger: An Interview," in *Max Reinhardt, 1873–1973,* ed. George Wellwarth and Alfred Brooks (Binghamton, NY: Max Reinhardt Archive, 1973), 109, 111. On Preminger's training with Reinhardt see also Foster Hirsch, *Otto Preminger: The Man Who Would Be King* (New York: Knopf, 2007), 23–29. Reinhardt's authority was so great at this time that Lotte Eisner, in her magisterial study of Weimar cinema, highlighted this key facet in the extended subtitle of her book, *The Haunted Screen: Expressionism in the German Cinema and the Influence of Max Reinhardt,* trans. Roger Greaves (Berkeley: University of California Press, 1969).

48. See Claude Bragdon, "A Theatre Transformed," *Architectural Record* (April 1924): 388–97.

49. On the statistics and overview of the play's significance see Gottfried Reinhardt, *The Genius: A Memoir of Max Reinhardt* (New York: Knopf, 1979), 36–47.

50. Fritz Feld, "In Memoriam of Edgar Ulmer" (unpublished ms.), Oct. 3, 1972, EGUC-AMPAS.

51. The database available at www.ellisisland.org contains Ulmer's passenger record from April 12, 1924, his place of residence given as "Wein [*sic*], Austria," and his ethnicity as "Austria Hebrew." A reproduction of the ship manifest of the SS *President Roosevelt,* listing Ulmer as an actor and giving Vienna as his proper home, is also included in Herzogenrath, "Introduction," 7.

52. Stark Young, "The New and the Old," *New York Times,* Nov. 9, 1924.

53. See Heinrich Huesmann, *Welttheater Reinhardt* (Munich: Prestel, 1983), n.p. The catalogue of performances does not give page numbers, but the entry on *Die Verbrecher* is numbered 1941.

54. Shirley Ulmer, interview.

55. See "Professor Reinhardt Proves He Is Fully as Great an Artist as Herald," *New York Journal,* Jan. 16, 1924. For Atkinson's commentary see Reinhardt, *The Genius,* 38.

56. See Gerd Gemünden's illuminating discussion of the concept of an "accented cinema," as it applies to such German-speaking émigré directors as Wilder, in *A Foreign Affair: Billy Wilder's American Films* (New York: Berghahn, 2008), 6–29.

57. Cited in the revised and expanded German version of Bogdanovich's interview in *Filmhefte* 1 (Summer 1975): 36.

58. Andrew Sarris, *The American Cinema* (New York: Dutton, 1968), 143.

59. Dale Thomajan, "Ready When You Are, Mr. Ulmer," *Film Comment* 26, no. 3 (March-April 1990): 67–68.

60. Oscar Wilde, "The Decay of Lying," in *The Complete Writings of Oscar Wilde,* vol. 7 (New York: Nottingham Society, 1909), 56.

61. Bogdanovich, "Edgar G. Ulmer," 560.

62. Tavernier, Wilson interview.

CHAPTER 2. TOWARD A CINEMA AT THE MARGINS

1. Grissemann, *Mann im Schatten,* 38.

2. See also Shirley Ulmer to Arianné Ulmer, June [n.d.] 1939, EGUC-AMPAS.

3. Schildkraut, *My Father and I,* 114.

4. See Elsaesser, "Ethnicity, Authenticity, and Exile," 97–123. The term "phantom Europe" comes from J. Hoberman, *Bridge of Light: Yiddish Film between Two Worlds* (New York: Museum of Modern Art/Schocken, 1991).

5. Frederick Kohner, *The Magician of Sunset Boulevard: The Improbable Life of Paul Kohner, Hollywood Agent* (Palos Verdes, CA: Morgan Press, 1977), 17–19.

6. Cited in Helmut G. Asper, *Filmexilanten im Universal Studio* (Berlin: Bertz and Fischer, 2005), 14.

7. Grissemann, *Mann im Schatten,* 38–39.

8. See Neal Gabler, *An Empire of Their Own: How the Jews Invented Hollywood* (New York: Crown, 1988).

9. Fred Zinnemann to Herbert Rappaport, Dec. 10, 1929, Paul Kohner Archive, Deutsche Kinemathek Museum für Film und Fernsehen, Berlin (hereafter cited as PKA-DKMFF). For this reference I wish to thank Imme Klages, of the University of Frankfurt, whose doctoral research on Fred Zinnemann has provided several useful insights into Ulmer's life and career.

10. See Grissemann, *Mann im Schatten,* 40.

11. "Edgar G. Ulmer, Movie Producer: Low-Budget Specialist Dies—Made 128 Pictures," *New York Times,* Oct. 2, 1972.

12. Philip Kemp, "Ulmer, Edgar G(eorg)," in John Wakeman, *World Film Directors,* vol. 1, *1890–1945* (New York: H.W. Wilson, 1987), 1108. See also Axel Madsen, *William Wyler* (New York: Crowell, 1973), 52–53.

13. Tom Weaver, "Shirley Ulmer," *Cult Movies* 25 (1998): 52. The complete interview, originally conducted in January 1998, has since been reprinted in *The Films of Edgar G. Ulmer,* ed. Bernd Herzogenrath (Lanham, MD: Scarecrow, 2009), 265–87.

14. Carl Laemmle Jr. to "To Whom It May Concern," Sept. 4, 1969, EGUC-AMPAS.

15. On the evening of July 17, 2003, in the Sherman Oaks home of Arianné Ulmer Cipes, I had the pleasure of watching an ultragrainy, weathered 16 mm print of *The Border Sheriff* projected onto a dining room wall. Among the few notes I jotted down during the screening were references to the primitive use of corny, dialogue-driven intertitles throughout, the endless string of chase scenes on horseback, and the unsurprising lack of a director's credit for either Ulmer

or Bradbury. A DVD has since been made available through a company called Loving the Classics.

16. Madsen, *William Wyler*, 52.

17. Edgar G. Ulmer, "The Director's Responsibility," unsourced document dated "ca. 1950s," EGUC-AMPAS.

18. Henriette Ulmer to Edgar G. Ulmer, May 10, 1927, EGUC-AMPAS.

19. For a brief personal account of Joen Warner by her daughter Joen Mitchell (born to Ulmer and Warner in Los Angeles on Dec. 15, 1929), see Gregory William Mank, "The Black Cat," in Herzogenrath, *Edgar G. Ulmer*, 94. See also Grissemann, *Mann im Schatten*, 46.

20. See Lotte Eisner, *Murnau* (Berkeley: University of California Press, 1973), 86. See also the audio commentary by David Kalat, who addresses the issue of Ulmer's ostensible contribution, on the 2009 KINO International release of the restored DVD.

21. Cited in Michael Omasta, "Eine Filmschau und eine Biografie präsentieren Leben und Werk des in Wien aufgewachsenen und in die USA emigrierten B-Movie-Regisseurs Edgar G. Ulmer," *Falter*, Feb. 26, 2002, 62.

22. "Studio Flashes: Fox Builds 'City' Mile and a Half Wide for Film," *New York Times*, Feb. 13, 1927.

23. See Mank, "The Black Cat," 94.

24. Eisner, *Murnau*, 180.

25. Monroe Lathrop, "'Sunrise,' New Masterpiece, Evokes Gasps," *Los Angeles Evening Express*, Nov. 30, 1927. Lathrop also praises producer William Fox, who, by his count, "placed more than $1,000,000 at Murnau's disposal for the making of this work of art."

26. Eisner, *Murnau*, 87–88.

27. Sarris, *The American Cinema*, 143.

28. Belton, "Edgar G. Ulmer (1900[*sic*]–1972)," 342.

29. See Huesmann, *Welttheater Reinhardt*, n.p.

30. The credits are listed in Gerhard Lamprecht, *Deutsche Stummfilme, 1927–1931* (Berlin: Deutsche Kinemathek, 1967–70), 520, 634. See also the German online resource www.filmportal.de.

31. Billie Wilder, "Wie wir unseren Studio Film drehten," *Der Montag Morgen*, Feb. 10, 1930.

32. As Neil Sinyard has noted of the production, "none of the young hopefuls who made it had any idea that a little piece of screen history was being made and that all of their careers were pointing in the direction of Hollywood." See Sinyard, *Fred Zinnemann*, 10.

33. Robert Siodmak, interview of Dec. 26, 1970, *Filmkundliche Hefte* 1–2 (1973): 11. Cited in Guntram Vogt, *Die Stadt im Film: Deutsche Spielfilme, 1900–2000* (Marburg: Schüren, 2001), 226. See also Günther Elbin's account in *Am Sonntag in die Matinee: Moriz Seeler und die Junge Bühne* (Mannheim: Persona, 1998), 85–92; and Curt Siodmak, *Wolf Man's Maker: Memoir of a Hollywood Writer*, rev. ed. (Lanham, MD: Scarecrow, 2001), 97–98.

34. Robert Siodmak, *Zwischen Berlin und Hollywood: Erinnerungen eines großen Filmregisseurs*, ed. Hans C. Blumenberg (Munich: Herbig, 1980), 168.

35. Moullet and Tavernier, "Entretien avec Edgar G. Ulmer," 5. A decade later, in conversation with Bogdanovich, Ulmer would take more credit. "I organized it," he insists, and goes on to claim that he backed the picture with $5,000 dollars he brought over from America. See Bogdanovich, "Edgar G. Ulmer," 565.

36. *Weekend am Wannsee* (*Weekend at the Wannsee*, 2000), directed by Gerald Koll and coproduced by ZDF and Arte. This documentary is included on the 2011 DVD release of *People on Sunday* from the Criterion Collection.

37. Delia Arndt-Steinitz, "Filmstudio 1929," *Berliner Tageblatt*, July 25, 1929.

38. Pem, "Film mit Dilettanten," *12 Uhr Blatt*, July 30, 1929.

39. Ibid.

40. Elbin, *Am Sonntag in die Matinee*, 88. See also the voice-over narration of *Weekend am Wannsee*, which credits Seeler with having discovered Borchert at the shop.

41. Cited in Elbin, *Am Sonntag in die Matinee*, 92.

42. Billie Wilder, "Wir vom Filmstudio 1929," *Tempo*, July 23, 1929, cited in Vogt, *Die Stadt im Film*, 226.

43. The film was hailed as a "grand success" by Herbert Ihering, among others, in his review in the *Berliner Börsen-Courier*, Feb. 5, 1930; called "magnificent" in the *Licht-Bild-Bühne*, Feb. 5, 1930; and "a delightful film" by the *12 Uhr Blatt*, Feb. 5, 1930.

44. "So ist es und nicht anders! Der Sieg des Filmstudios und die Entlarvung der Konjunkturindustrie," *Berliner Herold*, Feb. 9, 1930.

45. Kurt Mühsam, "Junge Leute machen einen Film," *Berliner Zeitung*, Feb. 5, 1930.

46. "*Menschen am Sonntag*: Filmstudio im Ufa-Theater Kurfürstendamm," *12 Uhr Blatt*, Feb. 5, 1930.

47. Lutz Koepnick, "The Bearable Lightness of Being: *People on Sunday* (1930)," in *Weimar Cinema: An Essential Guide to Classic Films of the Era*, ed. Noah Isenberg (New York: Columbia University Press, 2009), 239.

48. See Petra Löffler, "The Ordinary Life of Ordinary People: *Menschen am Sonntag*," in Herzogenrath, *Edgar G. Ulmer*, 49–62.

49. Eugen Szatmari, "Junges Blut verfilmt Berlin," *Berliner Tageblatt*, Feb. 6, 1930. Another critic expressed a similar degree of *Schadenfreude*, suggesting that the unconventional production "hit the film industry smack in [the] middle of its heart." See "*Menschen am Sonntag*: Filmstudio im Ufa-Theater Kurfürstendamm," *12 Uhr Blatt*, Feb. 5, 1930.

50. Luc Moullet, interview by Stefan Grissemann, Jan. 17, 2010, Paris, author's personal collection.

51. See Grissemann, *Mann im Schatten*, 46.

52. In his unpublished letter of December 26, 1969, actor Fritz Feld attests to Ulmer's direction of the German-language version of *Anna Christie*. See also Edgar G. Ulmer, "Past Service Record," EGUC-AMPAS. In the Paul Kohner Archives at the Deutsche Kinemathek—Museum für Film und Fernsehen, Berlin, there is also a handwritten draft of the same record, dated May 17, 1959, which alleges, among other things, work as an art director for Cecil B. DeMille

in 1928 (repeated later in typescript). The printed versions also list Ulmer as assistant director of Albert S. Rogell's *Aloha* (1931), a credit that is confirmed by Rogell in an unpublished letter of December 19, 1969, EGUC-AMPAS.

53. See Grissemann, *Mann im Schatten*, 56–57. According to Kenneth Anger's gossipy account, "Only eleven brave souls (Garbo was there) showed up for the funeral." See Kenneth Anger, *Hollywood Babylon* (New York: Dell, 1975), 246. On Ulmer's role in arranging for the proper embalming of Murnau's body and its return to Germany for burial in Berlin, see Eisner, *Murnau*, 224–25.

54. (Helen) Joen Mitchell, interview by the author, August 4, 2009. See also Grissemann, *Mann im Schatten*, 244.

55. "Ulmer Joins Peerless in Charge of Production," *Film Daily*, Feb. 16, 1932, 2.

56. Richard Koszarski, *Hollywood on the Hudson: Film and Television in New York from Griffith to Sarnoff* (New Brunswick, NJ: Rutgers University Press, 2008), 306. For an additional account of Ulmer's involvement in *Mr. Broadway* see James McGuire, *Impresario: The Life and Times of Ed Sullivan* (New York: Random House, 2006), 68–69.

57. A letter contained in the Production Code file on the film, dated August 22, 1933 (the day of a prescreening of the film at the Little Carnegie Playhouse in New York), and addressed to Mr. McKenzie and Mr. Wilstach, makes plain that Weldon Pictures is a separate venture from Columbia: "George Brown of Columbia Pictures tells that he knows nothing of the picture and that it would not be handled by the Columbia Company so far as he knows. In point of fact, he says that he never heard of the picture before I told him about it and he is quite certain that if Columbia was to have anything to do with it, he would be informed." See F. J. W. to Mr. McKenzie and Mr. Wilstach, August 22, 1933, PCA file on *Damaged Lives*, Special Collections, Martha Herrick Library, Academy of Motion Picture Arts and Sciences, Los Angeles (hereafter cited as PCA-AMPAS). In his interview with Bogdanovich, Ulmer claims—seemingly mistakenly—that Weldon Pictures was a Jamaican corporation.

58. Bogdanovich, "Edgar G. Ulmer," 572.

59. Grissemann notes this feature in *Mann im Schatten*, 62. In his more thorough account of the film's production history and reception—and the intriguing course of its subsequent adaptation as a novel—the Czech scholar Marcel Arbeit covers the same ground as Grissemann but then offers additional insight into the film and its larger path of development. See his "Ulmer's Anti-syphilis Film: *Damaged Lives* and Its Novelization," in Herzogenrath, *Edgar G. Ulmer*, 63–88. I am indebted to Arbeit's research.

60. Harleigh Schultz, "Bold Stroke in Movie Proves Keen Drama," *Boston Globe*, Sept. 18, 1933, 10. Cited in Arbeit, "Ulmer's Anti-syphilis Film," 66.

61. The letter from the Production Code file, recounting a prescreening of the film in New York, underscores some of the concern regarding advertising: "Among other things, he [Dr. William F. Snow of the American Social Hygiene Association] stated that it was the intention of the owners of this film, the Weldon Company, that the picture should not be advertised in a salacious manner."

See F. J. W. to Mr. McKenzie and Mr. Wilstach, August 22, 1933, PCA file on *Damaged Lives*, PCA-AMPAS.

62. Eric Schaefer, *"Bold! Daring! Shocking! True!" A History of Exploitation Films, 1919–1959* (Durham, NC: Duke University Press, 1999), 121.

63. This figure is given in J. Hoberman, "Low and Behold," *Village Voice,* Nov. 17, 1998. Ulmer, for his part, claims the film "made a fortune" and that 10 percent due as his earnings, money he never saw, would have amounted to $180,000—which is to say, the film, by his own calculation, made $1.8 million (B 572–73). In his extensive research on the film, combing through the original correspondence of the Canadian Social Hygiene Council, Canadian archivist D. J. Turner reports that upwards of five million tickets were sold to screenings in the United Kingdom alone (personal email correspondence with the author, June 13, 2011).

64. See Salka Viertel, *The Kindness of Strangers* (New York: Holt, Rinehart and Winston, 1969), 61.

65. During the Weimar years the so-called *Aufklärungsfilme* (enlightenment or educational films), dealing with such taboo subjects as homosexuality, similarly offered a precedent for films like *Damaged Lives*. On the *Aufklärungsfilme* of Richard Oswald see Jill Suzanne Smith, "Richard Oswald and the Social Hygiene Film: Promoting Public Health," in *The Many Faces of Weimar Cinema: Rediscovering Germany's Filmic Legacy,* ed. Christian Rogowski (Rochester, NY: Camden House, 2010), 13–30.

66. See Grissemann, *Mann im Schatten,* 62. On the precise nature of Donald's downfall in *Damaged Lives* see Arbeit, "Ulmer's Anti-syphilis Film," 70.

67. Owing to the radical cuts made to the film—i.e., for the 1937 release and for the 1958 rerelease—the version in circulation today and available on DVD from Alpha Video is regrettably far more elliptical than either the original 1933 film or the restored 35 mm print produced by the joint preservation efforts undertaken in 1990 by D. J. Turner, senior film archivist and restorationist at the National Archives of Canada, and UCLA's Robert Gitt. The differences between the DVD and the preserved film are too numerous to list here. Fortunately, I had the opportunity to view the restored print, introduced by D. J. Turner, in November 2002, shown as part of a three-day Ulmer symposium I co-organized with my New School colleague Robert Polito, at New York's Anthology Film Archives. For more on the various discrepancies in the different versions, as well as the details surrounding the story's strange course of development into a novel, see Arbeit, "Ulmer's Anti-syphilis Film."

68. Both Grissemann and Arbeit take up this angle—that is, seeing the tour of syphilitic patients as a freak show—in their respective critiques. The phrases "shock treatment" and "sideshow attraction" come from Arbeit, "Ulmer's Anti-syphilis Film," 74. A contemporary review of the film highlights this aspect as well: "There is, of course, the possible temptation of capitalizing on the forbidden angle." See "Damaged Lives," *Motion Picture Daily,* June 17, 1937. By contrast, a reviewer for *Variety* dismissed the issue out of hand: "Hard to see why anyone should object to the film as shown, particularly in view of the current tendency toward public education on the whole subject of social diseases. Certainly there is nothing obscene [about it]." See "Damaged Lives," *Variety,* June 16, 1937.

69. Sarris, *The American Cinema,* 143.

70. See Geoff Andrew, *The Director's Vision: A Concise Guide to the Art of 250 Filmmakers* (Chicago: Chicago Review, 1999), 224.

71. "Damaged Lives," *Motion Picture Daily,* June 17, 1937.

72. Grissemann, *Mann im Schatten,* 61.

73. The first quote comes from the *Boston Globe* review by Harleigh Schultz cited in note 64 above; the second is from an unnamed review in the *Times* of London, "The Coliseum—'Damaged Lives,'" *Times,* August 21, 1933, 8 (cited in Arbeit, "Ulmer's Anti-syphilis Film," 66–67).

74. J. T. M., "The Cinema Joins an Important Campaign with the Central's 'Damaged Lives,'" *New York Times,* June 14, 1937, 26.

75. Bogdanovich, "Edgar G. Ulmer," 573.

76. Arbeit, "Ulmer's Anti-syphilis Film," 66.

77. Theodor W. Adorno, *Minima Moralia: Reflections from Damaged Life,* trans. E. F. N. Jephcott (London: Verso, 1974), 33 (trans. mod.). On Adorno's struggle with exile see also Nico Israel, *Outlandish: Writing between Exile and Diaspora* (Stanford, CA: Stanford University Press, 2000), 75–122.

78. John Belton, *Howard Hawks, Frank Borzage, Edgar G. Ulmer* (New York: A. S. Barnes, 1974), 156. See also Belton's more recent reflections on the subject, "The Search for Community," in Herzogenrath, *The Films of Edgar G. Ulmer,* 21–37.

79. See Shirley Ulmer, interview by Michael Henry Wilson, May 7, 1996, Los Angeles, EGUC-AMPAS.

80. Michael Henry Wilson, "Edgar G. Ulmer: 'Let There Be Light!'" in *Divini Apparizioni: Edgar G. Ulmer, Joseph Losey, Leonid Trauberg* (Milan: Transeuropa, 1999), 249.

Epigraph: Ed Wood Jr., *Hollywood Rat Race* (New York: Four Walls Eight Windows, 1998), 73.

1. See Gregory William Mank's account of the birthday festivities in his "The Black Cat," in Herzogenrath, *Edgar G. Ulmer,* 92. See also Mank's more detailed discussion "'Improper Faces'—*The Black Cat,*" in his *Bela Lugosi and Boris Karloff: The Expanded Story of a Haunting Collaboration* (Jefferson, NC: McFarland, 2009), 153–200. In the analysis that follows, I am greatly indebted to Mank's work on the film.

2. See Gregory William Mank, "When the Black Cat Crossed Her Path," *The Bloody Best of Fangoria* 12 (June 1993): 65. See also Mank, "The Black Cat," 91–92. In his biography of Irving Thalberg, who began at Universal, Mark Vieira puts it more bluntly: "Uncle Carl had a penchant for hiring relatives; his California studio was a nepotistic nest." See Vieira, *Irving Thalberg: Boy Wonder to Producer Prince* (Berkeley: University of California Press, 2009), 6.

3. See Paul Mandell, "Edgar Ulmer and *The Black Cat,*" *American Cinematographer,* Oct. 1984, 36.

4. As she puts it in the same interview, "He [Junior] was a hypochondriac—he was always fighting some illness, some of them real and some of them, I

think, imaginary. He wore Kotex to keep from catching cold on his penis—*that* I remember!" (Weaver, "Shirley Ulmer," 53–54).

5. See Mandell, "Edgar Ulmer and *The Black Cat*," 38. According to Shirley Ulmer, "*The Black Cat* would never have been made if Uncle Carl had not gone to Europe, that I *know*" (Weaver, "Shirley Ulmer," 54).

6. Quoted in Mank, "The Black Cat," 95.

7. See the Production Estimate (March 2, 1934) and the Picture Costs in *The Black Cat* files (Box 277/8314), Universal Archives, Cinematic Arts Library, University of Southern California (hereafter cited as CAL-USC). See also Mank, "Improper Faces," 193.

8. Hall was nominated for an Oscar for Best Art Direction on a couple of otherwise obscure pictures made for Hal Roach Studios, *Merrily We Live* (1938) and *Captain Fury* (1939).

9. Donald Albrecht, *Designing Dreams: Modern Architecture and the* Movies (New York: Harper and Row, 1986), 100–101.

10. See William H. Rosar, "Music for the Monsters: Universal Pictures' Horror Film Scores of the Thirties," *Quarterly Journal of the Library of Congress* 40, no. 4 (1983): 391–421.

11. *Hollywood Reporter,* April 13, 1934, cited in Mank, "'Improper Faces'—*The Black Cat*," 403. See also Rosar, "Music for the Monsters," 403.

12. See Mandell, "Edgar Ulmer and *The Black Cat*," 36. Mandell suggests further that the two mystery titles glossed in the film's final scene, *The 69th Crime* and *The Purple Spot,* may actually have been Paul Cain titles.

13. See Weaver, "Shirley Ulmer," 54. As Shirley Ulmer says of Ruric, "He was brilliant, really, but *cuckoo*. He wasn't like any ordinary person I'd ever met. But very, very brilliant—Edgar adored him, they were very close."

14. See Mandell, "Edgar Ulmer and *The Black Cat*," 35. Mandell calls it "a banal fusion of Poe and *Frankenstein*." See also Michael Brunas, John Brunas, and Tom Weaver, "The Black Cat," in *Universal Horrors: The Studio's Classic Films, 1931–1946* (Jefferson, NC: McFarland, 1990), 78–87, esp. 81.

15. "M.M. interviews Edgar Ulmer," *Modern Monsters,* August 1966, 19.

16. "Who's Who in Pictures: Boris Karloff's Career as a Monster in the Films," *New York Times,* Jan. 28, 1934.

17. Cited in Grissemann, *Mann im Schatten,* 84.

18. For whatever reason, the emphatic statement "Lugosi nearly ate my set up!" is only included in the unabridged typescript of the interview (EGUC-AMPAS), not in the published text (cf. B 577).

19. Cited in David J. Skal, *The Monster Show: A Cultural History of Horror,* rev. ed. (New York: Faber and Faber, 2001), 178.

20. Greg Mank, "Julie Bishop Remembers *The Black Cat*," *Movie Club* 12 (Autumn 1997): 44; Mank, "When the Black Cat Crossed Her Path," 64. In her 1993 interview with Mank, Lund offers a revealing comparison to her treatment on the set: "I laugh at the Clarence Thomas case, the Supreme Court controversy, because the stuff that came out in that was *nothing* compared to the harassment that went on in the studios" (Mank, "When the Black Cat Crossed Her Path," 65).

21. Joseph I. Breen to Harry Zehner, Feb. 26, 1934, PCA file on *The Black Cat,* AMPAS. Unless otherwise noted, all subsequent references to Breen's

response come from this document. On Breen's intervention see also Mark A. Vieira, *Sin in Soft Focus: Pre-Code Hollywood* (New York: Harry N. Abrams, 1999), 175; and Mank, "The Black Cat," 96.

22. Joseph I. Breen to Henry [*sic*] Zehner, April 2, 1934, PCA-AMPAS.

23. While Mandell claims that "the depot set had been specifically built for *The Black Cat*," Mank contends that the "atmospheric depot opening actually comes from the British film *Rome Express* (1932)." See Mandell, "Edgar Ulmer and *The Black Cat*," 38; and Mank, "Improper Faces," 166.

24. Otto Friedrich, *City of Nets: A Portrait of Hollywood in the 1940's* (Berkeley: University of California Press, 1997), 198.

25. All citations from the pressbook are cited in Mank, "'Improper Faces'— *The Black Cat*," 153, 166, 183.

26. In March 2007, a vintage poster of *The Black Cat* sold at an art auction for a record-breaking $286,800—more than three times the original budget of the film. See "Big Day for 'Black Cat,'" *Heritage Magazine*, Fall 2007, 14.

27. Review of *The Black Cat, Variety*, May 22, 1934. On the contemporary reception of the film see Gary D. Rhodes, "'Tremendous' Hopes and 'Oke' Results: The 1934 Reception of *The Black Cat*," in *Edgar G. Ulmer: Detour on Poverty Row*, ed. Gary D. Rhodes (Lanham, MD: Lexington Books, 2008), 301–22.

28. Review of *House of Doom* [i.e., *The Black Cat*], *Film Pictorial*, March 1935, 19–20.

29. Jerry Hoffman, "*Frankenstein* Meets *Dracula* in *The Black Cat*," *Los Angeles Examiner*, May 4, 1934.

30. Bernard Eisenschitz and Jean-Claude Rohmer, "Entretien avec Edgar G. Ulmer," *Midi-Minuit fantastique* 13 (Nov. 1965): 4.

31. "*Black Cat* Proves Most Educated of Horror Films," *San Francisco Examiner*, May 12, 1934 (cited in Rhodes, "'Tremendous' Hopes and 'Oke' Results," 313).

32. A.D.S., "Not Related to Poe," *New York Times*, May 19, 1934. The two subsequent citations come from the same review.

33. See William K. Everson, "Horror Films," *Films in Review* 5, no. 1 (Jan. 1954): 12–23; see also Robert C. Roman, "Poe on the Screen," *Films in Review* 12, no. 8 (Oct. 1961): 462–73.

34. Asper, *Filmexilanten im Universal Studio*, 35. Though he similarly notes that *The Black Cat* was Universal's "top grosser" in 1934, Paul Mandell gives the more modest figure of $140,000 profit. See Mandell, "Edgar Ulmer and *The Black Cat*," 47.

35. Mandell, "Edgar Ulmer and *The Black Cat*," 45.

36. Ibid., 35.

37. J. Hoberman, "Low and Behold," 135.

38. David Robinson, *Das Cabinet des Dr. Caligari* (London: BFI Film Classics, 1998), 7.

39. On the greater thrust of the European-American tensions of the film see Paul A. Cantor, "The Fall of the House of Ulmer: Europe vs. America in the Gothic Vision of *The Black Cat*," in *The Philosophy of Horror*, ed. Thomas Fahy (Lexington: University Press of Kentucky, 2010), 137–60.

40. Mandell, "Edgar Ulmer and *The Black Cat*," 36. For his part Ulmer declares in his interview with Bogdanovich, "On the set he [Lang] was the incarnation of the Austrian who became a Prussian general—a sadist of the worst order you can imagine" (B 563).

41. Quoted in Mandell, "Edgar Ulmer and *The Black Cat*," 39.

42. Mank, "When the Black Cat Crossed Her Path," 67.

43. Belton, "Edgar G. Ulmer (1900[sic]–1972)," 344–45.

44. Cited in Mandell, "Edgar Ulmer and *The Black Cat*," 38.

45. Grissemann, *Mann im Schatten,* 67. According to Grissemann, the film is peppered with references to old Austria, from the chords of Schubert's *Unfinished Symphony* coming from the radio in Poelzig's study to the actual sites in which the film takes place.

46. Mandell, "Edgar Ulmer and *The Black Cat*," 37.

47. Herbert Schwaab, "On the Graveyards of Europe: The Horror of Modernism in *The Black Cat*," in Herzogenrath, *The Films of Edgar G. Ulmer,* 46.

48. See Mank, "Improper Faces," 168.

49. Rosar, "Music for the Monsters," 396. As Paul Mandell asserts, "With the exception of *Fantasia, 2001,* and *A Clockwork Orange,* no other sound film embraced the classics from head to tail [as robustly as *The Black Cat*]." See Mandell, "Edgar Ulmer and *The Black Cat*," 46.

50. Rosar, "Music for the Monsters," 403.

51. Ibid., 404.

52. Calvin Thomas Beck, *Heroes of the Horrors* (New York: Collier, 1975), 128.

53. Skal, *The Monster Show,* 177.

54. Ibid., 179–80.

55. Cited in Mandell, "Edgar Ulmer and *The Black Cat*," 44.

56. Gerd Gemünden, "A History of Horror," in *Continental Strangers: German Exile Cinema, 1933–1951* (New York: Columbia University Press, 2014), 46.

57. Cited in Mandell, "Edgar Ulmer and *The Black Cat*," 44.

58. "Austria Bans Film Based on Poe Story," *New York Herald Tribune,* August 22, 1935, PCA file on *The Black Cat,* AMPAS.

59. Joseph I. Breen, memorandum, Nov. 12, 1935, PCA file on *The Black Cat,* AMPAS.

60. Cited in Mandell, "Edgar Ulmer and *The Black Cat*," 45.

61. William K. Everson, *Classics of the Horror Film* (Secaucus, NJ: Citadel, 1974), 122.

62. Quoted in Mandell, "Edgar Ulmer and *The Black Cat*," 47.

63. See Mank, "The Black Cat," 101.

64. Pem, "Film mit Dilettanten," *12 Uhr Blatt,* July 30, 1929.

65. Shirley Ulmer, interview by Michael Henry Wilson, May 7, 1996, EGUC-AMPAS.

66. Weaver, "Shirley Ulmer," 52.

67. Ibid.

68. See Sherle Alexander (i.e., Shirley Ulmer), *Sinners in Sight* (New York: Empire, 1934). The publicity material for the novel—alas, the novel itself is

unobtainable—offers the following gloss: "The book is a tribute to the father of that ancient axiom: 'Only a woman can know a woman.' Her subtle and piercing treatment of feminine psychology exploits a field which hitherto has been either crudely handled or entirely ignored by most authors."

69. Weaver, "Shirley Ulmer," 53. In 1935, on stationery from The Fenmore Hotel in Hollywood, Shirley composed a love poem that begins with the following lines:

I walked upon the yellow waves of moonlight
And there meeting God, that Great Artisan
Asked him in accents hushed by the night
Of what my Lover was made . . . my beautiful man.
(Shirley Ulmer, unpublished poem, EGUC-AMPAS)

70. According to Shirley, Uncle Carl would solicit her thoughts on current actors. "I remember one opinion I gave," she observes. "I told him how I had seen Margaret Sullavan in a play in New York, I've forgotten which one, and I thought she was a great actress. He turned to Junior and he said, 'You hear what Shirley said? Find out more about Margaret Sullavan!' And he later hired her! So *that* was my contribution to the industry" (Weaver, "Shirley Ulmer," 53).

71. Ibid., 53, 56.

72. See Shirley Ulmer, interview. Here Shirley reiterates her point: "He [Uncle Carl] was angry that I would dare to leave his favorite nephew."

73. Carl Laemmle Jr. to "To Whom It May Concern," Sept. 4, 1969, EGUC-AMPAS.

74. It's unclear whether the title was an ironic allusion to or a shameless repurposing of Sergei Eisenstein's *Thunder over Mexico* (1933), his documentary on the Mexican people.

75. See Arthur Alexander to "To Whom It May Concern," Oct. 1, 1969, EGUC-AMPAS.

76. Bill Krohn, "King of the B's," *Film Comment* 19, no. 4 (July-August 1983): 61.

77. Grissemann, *Mann im Schatten,* 84–85.

78. Ibid., 86.

79. In conversation with Bogdanovich, Ulmer insists on having worked on Garbo's first picture, *The Gösta Berling Saga* (1924), with Mauritz Stiller (see B 561), and also on the German-language version of *Anna Christie* (1931).

80. See D.J. Turner, "*From Nine to Nine,*" in Herzogenrath, *The Films of Edgar G. Ulmer,* 53. Further clarification provided in personal email communication from Turner, May 21, 2011.

81. Grissemann, *Mann im Schatten,* 90.

82. Turner, "*From Nine to Nine,*" 55–56.

83. On February 18, 1936, a *Montreal Daily Star* reporter quoted Ruth Roland as saying, "We hope to create a character that I can keep using in other motion pictures to be made here." I am grateful to D.J. Turner for this reference.

84. Krohn, "King of the B's," 62.

85. Turner, *"From Nine to Nine,"* 58–59.

86. Shirley Ulmer, interview.

CHAPTER 4. SONGS OF EXILE

1. In a letter dated November 16, 1969, Joseph Steiner (whose relation to Canadian producer William Steiner, of *From Nine to Nine*, remains unclear) recounts, "In March 1936 I was instrumental in bringing Director Edgar G. Ulmer to New York City from Hollywood to direct the feature film *Natalka Poltafka* [*sic*] which was done in the Ukrainian language. The producing company was Avramenko Film Corporation. Ulmer was on this job from April 1936 to February 1937." He continues, "In 1938, Ulmer was rehired by Avramenko to direct *Cossacks Across the Don* [i.e., *Cossacks in Exile*]—to the best of my knowledge, this assignment lasted twenty weeks." See Joseph Steiner to "To Whom It May Concern," Nov. 16, 1969, EGUC-AMPAS.

2. See Myron B. Kuropas, *The Ukrainian Americans: Roots and Aspirations, 1884–1954* (Toronto: University of Toronto Press, 1991), 344.

3. On Avramenko's life and career see ibid., 341–46. See also Bohdan Y. Nebesio, *"Zaporozhets za Dunaiem* (1938): The Production of the First Ukrainian-Language Feature Film in Canada," *Journal of Ukrainian Studies* 16, no. 1–2 (Summer-Winter 1991): 117–19.

4. Kuropas, *The Ukrainian Americans,* 343–44.

5. "6 Ukrainian Musicals for Prod'n at Biograph," *Hollywood Reporter,* Sept. 14, 1936.

6. See Nebesio, *"Zaporozhets za Dunaiem,"* 121; Kuropas, *The Ukrainian Americans,* 344; and the entry contained in the American Film Institute catalogue *Within Our Gates: Ethnicity in American Feature Films, 1911–1960*, ed. Alan Gevinson (Berkeley: University of California Press, 1997), 701.

7. Shirley Ulmer, interview by Michael Henry Wilson, May 7, 1996, Los Angeles, EGUC-AMPAS.

8. Krohn, "King of the B's," 62.

9. The review of *Natalka* in *Variety* lists Ulmer and M. J. Gann as directors and Avramenko as "Ukrainian director." See review of "Girl from Poltava," *Variety,* Feb. 17, 1937. On Gann see also Hoberman, *Bridge of Light,* 255n7.

10. This quote is inexplicably absent from the reprint of Bogdanovich's interview in *Who the Devil Made It* but appears in the version included in Todd McCarthy and Charles Flynn, eds., *Kings of the Bs: Working within the Hollywood System* (New York: E. P. Dutton, 1975), 393.

11. Mary Ann Herman, "Vasyl [*sic*] Avramenko as I Knew Him," *Trident Quarterly* (Summer 1962), cited in Kuropas, *The Ukrainian Americans,* 343.

12. See Koszarski, *Hollywood on the Hudson,* 381. In his interview with Bogdanovich, Ulmer refers to the Edison studios in the Bronx.

13. Shirley Ulmer, interview.

14. George Lipsitz, "The New York Intellectuals: Samuel Fuller and Edgar Ulmer," in *Time Passages: Collective Memory and American Popular Culture* (Minneapolis: University of Minnesota Press, 1990), 198.

15. Shirley Ulmer, interview.

16. Koszarski, *Hollywood on the Hudson*, 381.
17. Ibid.
18. "The Screen" (review of *Natalka Poltavka*), *New York Times*, Dec. 25, 1936.
19. Grissemann, *Mann im Schatten*, 101.
20. See the listings in the *New York Times*, July 11, 1937.
21. "The Screen" (review of *Girl from Poltava*), *New York Times*, Feb. 15, 1937. The one notable complaint that the *Times* review of the Soviet film voiced was that "the photography in general is indifferent." Cf. "The Screen" (review of *Natalka Poltavka*), *New York Times*, Dec. 25, 1936. On the impact of U.S.-Soviet relations on the film see Brian D. Harvey, "Soviet-American 'Cinematic Diplomacy': Could the Russians Really Have Infiltrated Hollywood?" *Screen* 46, no. 4 (Winter 2005): 487–98.
22. Review of *Girl from Poltava*, *Variety*, Feb. 17, 1937.
23. Review of *Natalka Poltavka*, *Film Daily*, Feb. 18, 1937.
24. David Platt, "An Émigré Produces Operetta of 19th Century Ukrainia," *Daily Worker*, Dec. 27, 1936.
25. "To Produce at Monastery," *Motion Picture Daily*, July 8, 1938.
26. Nebesio, "*Zaporozhets za Dunaiem* (1938)," 121–22. The financial data is given on page 127. Nebesio considers the film, especially in light of the financial backers, to be a veritable Canadian production.
27. A reproduction of the article from the September 18, 1938, edition of the *New York Mirror* can be found in J. Hoberman and Jeffrey Shandler, *Entertaining America: Jews, Movies, and Broadcasting* (Princeton, NJ: Princeton University Press, 2003), 106.
28. Nebesio, "*Zaporozhets za Dunaiem* (1938)," 123.
29. Review of *Cossacks in Exile*, *Variety*, Feb. 15, 1939. See also Grissemann, *Mann im Schatten*, 117.
30. Review of *Cossacks in Exile*, *Variety*, Feb. 15, 1939.
31. "The Screen" (review of *Cossacks in Exile*), *New York Times*, Jan. 28, 1939.
32. Review of *Cossacks in Exile*, *New York Herald Tribune*, Jan. 30, 1939.
33. See Koszarski, *Hollywood on the Hudson*, 383.
34. Nebesio, "*Zaporozhets za Dunaiem* (1938)," 116–17, 127. See also Claudia Pummer, "At the Border: Edgar G. Ulmer's Foreign Language Productions," in Rhodes, *Edgar G. Ulmer*, 41–57.
35. Krohn, "King of the B's," 64.
36. Pressbook for *Green Fields*, AMPAS. In his groundbreaking history of Yiddish cinema, *Bridge of Light*, J. Hoberman suggests that Ulmer, soon after arriving in America, may have attended the Vilna Troupe's 1924 stage production of *Green Fields* at one of New York's many Yiddish theaters along Second Avenue, the same theaters he mentions with great reverence in his interview with Bogdanovich. See Hoberman, *Bridge of Light*, 247.
37. Hirschbein would later serve as screenwriter for *Hitler's Madman*, the 1943 wartime drama for PRC on which Ulmer would serve as second unit director and which would mark Douglas Sirk's American directorial debut.

38. "Jacob Ben Ami with New Co-op Film Outfit," *Hollywood Reporter,* July 12, 1937.

39. Sharon Pucker Rivo, "In Search of Jewish Identity," in Herzogenrath, *Edgar G. Ulmer,* 109.

40. Hoberman, *Bridge of Light,* 248.

41. Helen Beverley, interview by Michael Henry Wilson, May 8, 1996, Los Angeles, EGUC-AMPAS. See also Beverley's account given in Stefan Kanfer, *Stardust Lost: The Triumph, Tragedy, and Mishugas of the Yiddish Theater in America* (New York: Knopf, 2006), 201.

42. Cited in Kanfer, *Stardust Lost,* 201.

43. Beverley, interview.

44. "'Greene Felder' to Start," *Film Daily,* July 29, 1937.

45. Koszarski, *Hollywood on the Hudson,* 382.

46. Bogdanovich, "Edgar G. Ulmer," 587–88. See the account provided in Hoberman, *Bridge of Light,* 249; see also Gevinson, *Within Our Gates,* 417–18.

47. See John Belton, "The Search for Community," in Herzogenrath, *The Films of Edgar G. Ulmer,* 28.

48. Beverley, interview.

49. Ibid.

50. Ibid.

51. Hoberman, *Bridge of Light,* 250–51; see also Koszarski, *Hollywood on the Hudson,* 382.

52. Cited in Hoberman, *Bridge of Light,* 249.

53. N. Buchvald, "Yidishe film in amerike" (Yiddish film in America), *Yidishe kultur,* March 1940, 28. English translation by Sonia Beth Gollance.

54. Nakhman Meisel, "Perets Hirshbayns 'Grine felder' in film" (Peretz Hirschbein's 'Green Fields' as a film), *Literarishe bleter,* Feb. 25, 1938, 143. English translation by Sonia Beth Gollance.

55. Ibid., 144.

56. Helen Beverley's account matches Ulmer's: "People came and they were so enchanted, they didn't want to leave. They wanted to see it again, so they just sat there, and they had to be forcibly removed" (Beverley, interview).

57. Pressbook for *Green Fields;* see also Hoberman, *Bridge of Light,* 248.

58. "*Green Fields,*" *Motion Picture Daily,* Oct. 15, 1937.

59. Review of *Green Fields, Film Daily,* Oct. 20, 1937.

60. Frank S. Nugent, "The Screen" (review of *Green Fields*), *New York Times,* Oct. 12, 1937.

61. Meisel, "Perets Hirshbayns 'Grine felder' in film," 145.

62. Hoberman, *Bridge of Light,* 252; Koszarski, *Hollywood on the Hudson,* 383.

63. Grissemann suggests that Ulmer even taught a class in music theory and music history at the Curtis Institute in Philadelphia around the same time that he was working on his ethnic pictures. See Grissemann, *Mann im Schatten,* 145.

64. Beverley, interview. Shirley Ulmer explains that her husband received "his favorite baton," originally in the possession of Franz Liszt, as a gift from

Leo Erdody, his loyal musical collaborator, who scored the bulk of Ulmer's PRC productions from the 1940s. "And that's the baton he used, I think, with Helen and he also used it at home a lot" (Shirley Ulmer, interview).

65. Review of *The Singing Blacksmith, Variety,* Nov. 9, 1938.

66. See Pummer, "At the Border," 52–53.

67. Ber Green, "Dort vu men makht dem film 'yankl der shmid'" (There where the film 'The Singing Blacksmith' is made), *Morgn frayhayt* (New York), July 11, 1938. English translation by Sonia Beth Gollance. See also Hoberman, *Bridge of Light,* 268.

68. Hoberman, *Bridge of Light,* 265.

69. Ibid., 266.

70. Pummer, "At the Border," 55.

71. "New Jewish Film Opening Tuesday," *Sunday Worker,* Oct. 30, 1938. The parenthetical account on the opening is from the *Brooklyn Eagle,* cited in Hoberman, *Bridge of Light,* 268.

72. David Platt, "'Blacksmith' Fine Film," *Daily Worker,* Nov. 5, 1938.

73. Carrie Rickey, review of *The Light Ahead, Village Voice,* Oct. 19, 1982. The film was originally released in late September 1939 under the title *Di klyatshe* but was known at the time as both *Fishke der krumer* and by the English title *The Light Ahead.*

74. Dan Miron, "Introduction," in *Tales of Mendele the Book Peddler,* ed. Dan Miron and Ken Frieden (New York: Schocken, 1996), viii.

75. Hoberman, *Bridge of Light,* 302.

76. Grissemann, *Mann im Schatten,* 133–38.

77. Cited in Kanfer, *Stardust Lost,* 216.

78. See Rickey, review of *The Light Ahead.*

79. Shirley Ulmer, interview.

80. Hoberman, *Bridge of Light,* 303; see also Grissemann, *Mann im Schatten,* 135.

81. Arianné Ulmer Cipes, "Foreword," in *When Joseph Met Molly: A Reader on Yiddish Film,* ed. Sylvia Paskin (Nottingham, UK: Five Leaves, 1999), 2.

82. "Light Ahead," *Exhibitor,* Oct. 4, 1939.

83. William Edlin, "Der nayer yiddisher film 'di kliatshe'" (The new Yiddish film 'A Light Ahead'), *Der Tog* (New York), Sept. 28, 1939. English translation by Sonia Beth Gollance.

84. Frank S. Nugent, "The Screen" (review of *The Light Ahead*), *New York Times,* Sept. 23, 1939.

85. "Yiddish Picture a Sensation in K.C.," *Hollywood Reporter,* Dec. 20, 1939.

86. In addition to his three ethnic-oriented shorts, Ulmer directed three other TB shorts, likewise under the auspices of the National Tuberculosis Association, aimed at a predominantly white audience: *Goodbye Mr. Germ* (1940), *Diagnostic Procedures in Tuberculosis* (1940), and *They Do Come Back* (1940). For a more detailed discussion of Ulmer's educational shorts see Devin Orgeron, "Spreading the Word: Race, Religion, and the Rhetoric of Contagion in Edgar G. Ulmer's TB Films," in *Learning with the Lights*

Off: Educational Film in the United States, ed. Devin Orgeron, Marsha Orgeron, and Dan Streible (New York: Oxford University Press, 2012), 295–315.

87. See Grissemann, *Mann im Schatten*, 149; and D. J. Turner, unpublished Ulmer filmography, author's personal collection.

88. See David Cantor, "Seeking to Live: Cancer Education, Movies, and the Conversion Narrative in America, 1921–1960," *Literature and Medicine* 28, no. 2 (Fall 2009): 291.

89. Krohn, "King of the B's," 63.

90. See Lipsitz, "The New York Intellectuals," 200; see also "Dorothee Codozoe Selected to Head New Harlem Film," *Chicago Defender*, Nov. 13, 1937, cited in Jonathan Skolnik, "Exile on 125th Street: African Americans, Germans, and Jews in *Moon over Harlem*," in Herzogenrath, *The Films of Edgar G. Ulmer*, 63.

91. Frank Mehring, "Moon of Alabama/*Moon over Harlem*: African American Culture and German Imaginations from Brecht to Ulmer," in Herzogenrath, *Edgar G. Ulmer*, 133.

92. Thanks to the primary research conducted by D. J. Turner, it is possible to piece together some of the finer details of the historical record concerning the preview screenings, the premiere, and final release of *Moon over Harlem*. Personal email from Turner, Nov. 21, 2011.

93. Production Code Administration (unsigned) to G. Garris, secretary of Mercury Film Laboratories, June 1, 1939, PCA file on *Moon over Harlem*, AMPAS.

94. Review of *Moon over Harlem*, *Exhibitor*, July 26, 1939.

95. Hoberman, *Bridge of Light*, 312; Koszarski, *Hollywood on the Hudson*, 387.

96. Hoberman, *Bridge of Light*, 316.

97. William Edlin, "'Der amerikaner shadkhn'—naye yidishe film-komedie, in neshonal teater" ("The American Matchmaker"—New Yiddish Comedy Film, at the National Theatre), *Der Tog* (New York), May 8, 1940. English translation by Sonia Beth Gollance.

98. Krohn, "King of the B's," 64.

99. Cited in Hoberman, *Bridge of Light*, 318.

100. See Judith N. Goldberg, *Laughter through Tears: The Yiddish Cinema* (East Brunswick, NJ: Farleigh Dickinson University Press, 1983).

101. Interview included as a supplement on the DVD release.

102. Grissemann, *Mann im Schatten*, 144.

103. Kanfer, *Stardust Lost*, 230.

104. Review of *American Matchmaker*, *New York Times*, May 7, 1940.

105. Edlin, "'Der amerikaner shadkhn.'"

106. Gallagher, "All Lost in Wonder," par. 9.

107. Krohn, "King of the B's," 64.

108. Maurice Schwartz, *Shylock and His Daughter* (New York: Yiddish Art Theatre, 1947). The inscribed copy is part of the personal collection of Arianné Ulmer Cipes.

109. Beverley, interview.

110. Tom Weaver, "Arianné Ulmer," in *Science Fiction and Fantasy Film Flashbacks: Conversations with 24 Actors, Writers, Producers and Directors from the Golden Age* (Jefferson, NC: McFarland, 1998), 317.

CHAPTER 5. CAPRA OF PRC

Epigraph: Jon Halliday, ed., *Sirk on Sirk* (London: Faber and Faber, 1997), 71.

1. Edgar G. Ulmer to Shirley Ulmer, n.d. ["Saturday Night," i.e., June 28, 1941], EGUC-AMPAS.

2. Edgar G. Ulmer to Shirley Ulmer, July 1, 1941, EGUC-AMPAS.

3. Myron Meisel essentially confirms the suspicion held by Sirk, when he writes: "Once Ulmer was typed as a cheapie director, it became nearly impossible for him to command any budget whatever." See Myron Meisel, "Edgar G. Ulmer: The Primacy of the Visual," in McCarthy and Flynn, *Kings of the Bs*, 149.

4. See Blair Davis, *The Battle for the Bs: 1950s Hollywood and the Rebirth of Low-Budget Cinema* (New Brunswick, NJ: Rutgers University Press, 2012), 5–6.

5. Charles Flynn and Todd McCarthy, "The Economic Imperative: Why Was the B Movie Necessary?" in McCarthy and Flynn, *Kings of the Bs*, 13–43. See also Richard Combs, "Edgar G. Ulmer and PRC: A Detour Down Poverty Row," *Monthly Film Bulletin* 49, no. 582 (July 1982): 152; and Wheeler W. Dixon, ed., *Producers Releasing Corporation: A Comprehensive Filmography and History* (Jefferson, NC: McFarland, 1986).

6. The first quote comes from Arthur Lyons, *Death on the Cheap: The Lost B Movies of Film Noir* (New York: Da Capo, 2000), 48; the second from Greil Marcus, *The Shape of Things to Come: Prophecy and the American Voice* (New York: Farrar, Straus and Giroux, 2006), 130.

7. See Don Miller, "A Brief History of Producers Releasing Corporation," in Dixon, *Producers Releasing Corporation*, 9–34.

8. Weaver, "Arianné Ulmer," 317, 322. Arianné Ulmer uses the term "Mortgage Hill" in conversation with film historian David Kalat in his essay "The True Story behind Edgar G. Ulmer's *Bluebeard*," *FILMFAX* 77 (Feb./March 2000): 92.

9. Grissemann, *Mann im Schatten*, 158.

10. See Erika Wottrich, ed., *M wie Nebenzahl: Nero-Filmproduktion zwischen Europa und Hollywood* (Hamburg: CineGraph, 2002).

11. Shirley Ulmer, interview by Michael Henry Wilson, May 7, 1996, Los Angeles, EGUC-AMPAS.

12. Edgar G. Ulmer to Shirley Ulmer, August 15, 1940, EGUC-AMPAS.

13. This comment by Ulmer is on the audiocassette of the interview with Bogdanovich and is recorded in Michael Palm's documentary *Edgar G. Ulmer: The Man Off-Screen* (2004).

14. Arianné Ulmer Cipes, interview by Bob Baker, June 15, 1998, Los Angeles, EGUC-AMPAS.

15. Leon Fromkess to "To Whom It May Concern," Dec. 5, 1969, EGUC-AMPAS.

16. To put Ulmer's director's fee in perspective: in February 1942 at Warner Bros., Michael Curtiz received $3,600 per week as director. See Aljean Harmetz,

The Making of "Casablanca": Bogart, Bergman, and World War II (New York: Hyperion, 2002), 76.

17. See the unpublished production budgets from Ulmer's PRC years, EGUC-AMPAS. An illustrative table on the "Budget Range of Studio Features, 1944," included in Thomas Schatz's study of Hollywood cinema of the 1940s, lists PRC at the very bottom, beneath Republic and Monogram. See Schatz, *Boom and Bust: American Cinema in the 1940s* (Berkeley: University of California Press, 1997), 173.

18. Jimmy Lydon, interview by the author, Dec. 16, 2001, Bonita, CA.

19. Grissemann, *Mann im Schatten,* 165–66.

20. In a German interview from 1973 Douglas Sirk gave a more affirmative take on his B movies. "I had more freedom," he said of his collaborations with Nebenzal, "from the OK to the story to the release." Cited in Saverio Giovacchini, *Hollywood Modernism: Film and Politics in the Age of the New Deal* (Philadelphia: Temple University Press, 2001), 55.

21. See, for example, the review published in the *Hollywood Reporter,* July 10, 1942, and the assorted clippings contained in the PCA files at AMPAS. See also Clayton R. Koppes and Gregory D. Black, *Hollywood Goes to War: How Politics, Profits, and Propaganda Shaped World War II Movies* (New York: Free Press, 1987), 61.

22. In his final film released by PRC during the war, in late March 1945, *Strange Illusion* includes a similar announcement tacked on after the film's end credit: "LET'S ALL BACK THE ATTACK! BUY AN EXTRA WAR BOND TODAY."

23. Grissemann, *Mann im Schatten,* 178.

24. See, e.g., "Start Shooting before Invaded: President Roosevelt's Advice," *Australian Associate Press,* Oct. 6, 1941.

25. Edgar G. Ulmer, unpublished poem "on the 21st day of the Second World War," EGUC-AMPAS.

26. See Joseph I. Breen to Semon Nebenzall [*sic*], June 24, 1942, PCA-AMPAS.

27. Cited in Gallagher, "All Lost in Wonder." According to his daughter, Ulmer stopped speaking German altogether soon after he learned the news of *Kristallnacht,* the anti-Jewish pogrom that took place across Germany and Austria on the night of November 9, 1938. Email communication from Arianné Ulmer Cipes, May 31, 2012.

28. Friedrich, *City of Nets,* 106.

29. Review of *Tomorrow We Live, Daily Variety,* Sept. 17, 1942.

30. Cited in Paul Vangelisti, ed., *L.A. Exile: A Guide to Los Angeles Writing, 1932–1998* (New York: Marsilio, 1999), 37.

31. Eugen Schüfftan to Siegfried Kracauer, Jan. 17, 1942, in Helmut G. Asper, ed., *Nachrichten aus Hollywood, New York und anderswo: Der Briefwechsel Eugene und Marlies Schüfftans mit Siegfried und Lili Kracauer* (Trier: Wissenschaftlicher Verlag, 2003), 33.

32. See "Kurt Weill Now a Citizen," *New York Times,* August 28, 1943. Ulmer's naturalization ceremony took place in Los Angeles on August 13, 1943. Email communication from Arianné Ulmer Cipes, May 31, 2012.

33. David Thomson, *The New Biographical Dictionary of Film* (New York: Knopf, 2002), 888.

34. Review of *My Son, the Hero, Daily Variety*, Jan. 17, 1943. The critic for the *Hollywood Reporter* was less generous ("direction by Edgar G. Ulmer muffs the few fresh opportunities the yarn might have contained"). See "Tests PRC Market on Wacky Comedies," *Hollywood Reporter*, Jan. 18, 1943.

35. Flynn and McCarthy, "The Economic Imperative," 23.

36. Review of *Girls in Chains, Daily Variety*, April 1, 1943. The *Hollywood Reporter* published its review under the damning title "Below Standard of Usual PRC Output," April 1, 1943.

37. J. Hoberman, "Bad Movies," *Film Comment* 16, no. 4 (July/August 1980): 12.

38. Bret Wood, "Edgar G. Ulmer: Visions from the Second Kingdom," *Video Watchdog* 41 (Sept./Oct. 1997): 30.

39. Ibid.

40. All quotes in this paragraph are from Baker's interview with Arianné Ulmer Cipes (see note 15 above).

41. See Weaver, "Arianné Ulmer," 320; Shirley Ulmer, interview; Grissemann, *Mann im Schatten*, 193–95.

42. See Grissemann, *Mann im Schatten*, 180, 183.

43. "'Forgotten Sins' Better Forgotten," *Hollywood Reporter*, June 29, 1943.

44. For reasons unknown to me, this passage, included in the original interview (in the typescript, in its initial publication in 1974 in *Film Culture* and its reprint in *Kings of the Bs* a year later), is excised, without comment, from the reprint in *Who the Devil Made It*. See Bogdanovich, "Edgar G. Ulmer," *Film Culture* 58 (1974): 226; see also Bogdanovich, "Edgar G. Ulmer," in McCarthy and Flynn, *Kings of the Bs*, 400.

45. I thank my colleague Ivan Raykoff for this idea and also for helping me to identify the diverse musical sources that Ulmer draws from in his collaborations with Erdody.

46. Dick Moore, interview by the author, June 12, 2012, New York.

47. Ulmer's daughter, Arianné Ulmer Cipes, points this out; See *"Detour* (VII): Q&A," *LIT* 13 (Fall 2007): 143.

48. Weaver, "Shirley Ulmer," 57.

49. Shirley Ulmer, interview.

50. Grissemann, *Mann im Schatten*, 187.

51. Alexander Horwath, "Das Shining: *Strange Illusion* von Edgar G. Ulmer (1945)," in *Schatten. Exil: Europäische Emigranten im Film Noir*, ed. Christian Cargnelli and Michael Omasta (Vienna: PVS, 1997), 299.

52. "PRC's 'Jive Junction' Has Pep, Youth, Topical Value," *Hollywood Reporter*, Nov. 12, 1943.

53. Grissemann, *Mann im Schatten*, 28.

54. Arianné Ulmer Cipes, email communication with the author, June 27, 2012.

55. Eugen Schüfftan to Paul Kohner, June 30, 1941, in Asper, *Nachrichten aus Hollywood*, 126.

56. See Robert Müller, "Zwischen Licht und Schatten: Eugen Schüfftan im Hollywood der vierziger Jahre," in Asper, *Nachrichten aus Hollywood*, 127–47.

57. See Belton, *Howard Hawks, Frank Borzage, Edgar G. Ulmer*, 158–60. See also Steffen Hantke, "Puppets and Paintings: Authorship and Artistry in Edgar G. Ulmer's *Bluebeard*," in Rhodes, *Edgar G. Ulmer*, 181–94.

58. Müller, "Zwischen Licht und Schatten," 139.

59. Bertolt Brecht, *Poems, 1913–1956*, ed. John Willett and Ralph Manheim (New York: Methuen, 1976), 382.

60. Grissemann, *Mann im Schatten*, 197.

61. *Hollywood Reporter*, April 12, 1934, cited in Mank, "'Improper Faces'—*The Black Cat*," 193.

62. Ulmer Cipes, interview.

63. Kalat, "The True Story," 39.

64. "PRC 'Bluebeard' Excellent, Distinctive Class Film," *Hollywood Reporter*, Oct. 9, 1944. The review in *Daily Variety* (Oct. 9, 1944) was similarly effusive: "Producer Leon Fromkess, this time with Martin Mooney as associate, continues to boost PRC's stock skyhigh with 'Bluebeard.' . . . Yarn is neatly paced and builds up to climax under precise direction of Edgar Ulmer."

65. See the *Bluebeard* production budget, EGUC-AMPAS. Ulmer is listed in three separate lines on the budget, garnering a total of $3,850 in fees; Carradine is the highest paid actor with a weekly rate of $3,500; Schüfftan, not listed anywhere, can be assumed to have collected some, if not all, of credited cinematographer Jockey Feindel's $1,600 fee; finally, more than $7,000 is relegated to Erdody and to other expenses in the music department.

66. Moullet and Tavernier, "Entretien avec Edgar G. Ulmer," 6 (cited in Grissemann, *Mann im Schatten*, 210). Grissemann points out that the more plausible comparison to Hitchcock is to his psycho-thriller *Suspicion*, which appeared three years *before* Ulmer's film.

67. Despite its racy content there is no extant record of a Production Code exchange, no series of memos from the Breen Office. What does exist is a certificate from the PCA, addressed to Fromkess and dated December 26, 1944, with a typed postscript: "This certificate is issued with the understanding that the objectionable breast shot of Sally Eilers at the banquet table has been removed." What is meant by "breast shot" (a costume malfunction? an unseemly lingering focus on Eilers's low-cut dress?) remains a mystery. PCA files on *Strange Illusion*, AMPAS.

68. See Hugh S. Manon, "Fantasy and Failure in *Strange Illusion*," in Herzogenrath, *The Films of Edgar G. Ulmer*, 162.

69. Jimmy Lydon, interview by the author, Dec. 16, 2001.

70. Horwath, "Das Shining," 300.

71. "'Strange Illusion' Puts PRC in Major League Running," *Hollywood Reporter*, Feb. 12, 1945. The attention it received elsewhere was less enthusiastic. "'Strange Illusion' is okay melodrama for the PRC market," began the review in *Variety*, noting among its perceived flaws "some directorial plodding" (review of *Strange Illusion*, *Variety*, Feb. 12, 1945).

72. Eddie Muller, *Dark City: The Lost World of Film Noir* (New York: St. Martin's, 1998), 179.

73. Hoberman, "Low and Behold," *Village Voice*, 135.

74. Müller, "Zwischen Licht und Schatten," 142.

75. Everson, "Introduction," 2.

76. Grissemann suggests that this particular scene is much closer to Scorsese than to the films of Ulmer's contemporaries. See *Mann im Schatten*, 214.

77. "'Club Havana' Looks Class," *Hollywood Reporter*, Oct. 22, 1945.

78. Cited in Asper, *Nachrichten aus Hollywood*, 20. See also Hans Kafka, *Hollywood Calling: Die* Aufbau-*Kolumne zum Film-Exil*, ed. Roland Jaeger (Hamburg: ConferencePoint, 2002).

79. Shirley Ulmer, interview.

80. See Grissemann, *Mann im Schatten*, 236.

81. Lutz Koepnick, *The Dark Mirror: German Cinema between Hitler and Hollywood* (Berkeley: University of California Press, 2002), 159.

82. A. W., "Back to 1832," *New York Times*, April 8, 1946.

83. Otis L. Guernsey Jr., "On the Screen" (review of *The Wife of Monte Cristo*), April 8, 1946.

84. Review of *The Wife of Monte Cristo*, *Hollywood Reporter*, March 29, 1946.

85. Joseph I. Breen to Arnold Pressburger, Nov. 8, 1944, PCA-AMPAS. See also Joseph I. Breen to Arnold Pressburger, Nov. 16, 1944, PCA-AMPAS.

86. See Jan-Christopher Horak, "German Exile Cinema, 1933–1950," *Film History* 8 (1996): 386. The final script that was resubmitted by PRC in October 1945 ran into many of the same problems that Pressburger originally encountered; they were in the end, however, largely ignored. See Joseph I. Breen to Jack Jungmayer, Oct. 24, 1945, PCA-AMPAS.

87. Gina Kaus, *Dark Angel*, trans. Eden Paul and Cedar Paul (New York: Macmillan, 1934), 250. See also Kaus's memoirs, *Von Wien nach Hollywood* (Frankfurt: Suhrkamp, 1990).

88. Horak, "German Exile Cinema," 386.

89. Grissemann, *Mann im Schatten*, 234.

90. Review of *Her Sister's Secret*, *Hollywood Reporter*, Sept. 10, 1946; review of *Her Sister's Secret*, *Variety*, Sept. 10, 1946; review of *Her Sister's Secret*, *Film Daily*, Sept. 11, 1946.

91. "Familiar Tale Retold," *Los Angeles Times*, Sept. 12, 1946.

92. Louella Parsons, *Palm Beach Daily News*, Dec. 17, 1945.

93. John McCarten, review of *Her Sister's Secret*, *New Yorker*, Feb. 1, 1947. See also A. W., "'Her Sister's Secret' (1946) at The Gotham," *New York Times*, Jan. 23, 1947.

94. See the Loan and Security Agreements, detailing budget and costs, kept at AMPAS Core Collection. In her biography of Hedy Lamarr, Ruth Barton suggests that the film ran a million dollars over budget. See Ruth Barton, *Hedy Lamarr: The Most Beautiful Woman in Film* (Lexington: University Press of Kentucky, 2010), 159.

95. "Film Director 'Discovered' by Hedy Lamarr," *Los Angeles Times*, Jan. 4, 1947. "He wasn't an expensive talent," Lamarr later observed, "but he had a good reputation from Europe." See Hedy Lamarr, *Ecstasy and Me: My Life as a Woman* (Greenwich, CT: Fawcett, 1966), 116.

96. Halliday, *Sirk on Sirk,* 121. See also Barton, *Hedy Lamarr,* 155.

97. See Stephen Michael Shearer, *Beautiful: The Life of Hedy Lamarr* (New York: St. Martin's, 2010), 206.

98. See Barton, *Hedy Lamarr,* 155; Grissemann, *Mann im Schatten,* 238.

99. Weaver, "Shirley Ulmer," 55.

100. Lamarr, *Ecstasy and Me,* 117.

101. Hedy Lamarr and John Loder, unpublished poem, EGUC-AMPAS.

102. Weaver, "Shirley Ulmer," 56.

103. Philip K. Scheuer, "Hedy Plays Evil Woman," *Los Angeles Times,* Dec. 21, 1946. "Don't be surprised to see her win an Academy nomination for her work here," predicted Jack D. Grant in the *Hollywood Reporter* (Oct. 28, 1946).

104. Philip K. Scheuer, "Hollywood Clings to Lead as Film-Production Center," *Los Angeles Times,* Dec. 15, 1946.

105. See Barton, *Hedy Lamarr,* 159; and Shearer, *Beautiful,* 217.

CHAPTER 6. BACK IN BLACK

1. See Paul Schrader, "Notes on Film Noir," *Film Comment* 8, no. 1 (Spring 1972): 8–13.

2. James Naremore, *More Than Night: Film Noir and Its Contexts* (Berkeley: University of California Press, 1998), 9.

3. Patrick Keating, *Hollywood Lighting: From the Silent Era to Film Noir* (New York: Columbia University Press, 2010), 244. See also Edward Dimendberg, *Film Noir and the Spaces of Modernity* (Cambridge, MA: Harvard University Press, 2004).

4. See Thom Andersen, "Red Hollywood," in *Literature and the Visual Arts in Contemporary Society,* ed. Suzanne Ferguson and Barbara Groseclose (Columbus: Ohio State University Press, 1985), 141–96.

5. Sheri Chinen Biesen, *Blackout: World War II and the Origins of Film Noir* (Baltimore: Johns Hopkins University Press, 2005), 163–64.

6. Fred T. Marsh, "A Precious Pair" (review of Martin Goldsmith, *Detour*), *New York Times,* Jan. 29, 1939. For a more detailed discussion of *Detour,* Goldsmith's novel and Ulmer's film, see my monograph, *Detour* (London: British Film Institute, 2008). In the following, I draw heavily from that initial treatment and would like to thank Rebecca Barden of BFI Publishing for her input and for granting me the opportunity to write on the film in a sustained fashion.

7. See Wade Williams's account in "Edgar Ulmer's Dark Excursion into the Nightmare World of Fatal Irony . . ." *FILMFAX* 11 (July 1988): 22–25, esp. 24. A film collector and Ulmer enthusiast, Williams holds the rights to the 2000 DVD release of *Detour* by Image Entertainment. In 1992 his obsessively faithful remake of the film, including scenes from Goldsmith's script that were cut from Ulmer's production, was released. An unsigned profile of Goldsmith is also contained in the appended materials to the reprint of his complete script in *Scenario* 3, no. 2 (Summer 1997): 179.

8. Edwin Schallert, "Super Man Hunt Will Spark 'War Criminals,'" *Los Angeles Times,* Oct. 20, 1944.

9. On the extraordinary career of Ann Savage see my short tribute, "When Faces Mattered Most," *Vertigo* 4, no. 3 (Spring/Summer 2009): 64–65. See also Lisa Morton and Kent Adamson, *Savage Detours: The Life and Work of Ann Savage* (Jefferson, NC: McFarland, 2009).

10. See Eddie Muller, *Dark City Dames: The Wicked Women of Film Noir* (New York: Harper Collins, 2001), 151.

11. Williams, "Edgar Ulmer's Dark Excursion," 24. See also Stefan Grissemann's sketch of the transaction in *Mann im Schatten,* 217; and Muller, *Dark City,* 178.

12. Allegedly, Goldsmith made this (i.e., that he write his own screenplay) a condition of the sale. See the brief profile appended to his reprinted script, *Scenario* 3, no. 2 (Summer 1997): 179. This unusual move was picked up by contemporary reviewers, with Jim Henaghan of the *Hollywood Reporter* commenting, "He [Martin Mooney] is to be congratulated for breaking the rules to the extent of permitting the author to write his own screen story" (Jim Henaghan, review of *Detour*, *Hollywood Reporter,* Oct. 29, 1945).

13. Among the many choices that Ulmer and his film crew would have to make in order to mitigate any financial excesses was the decision to replace the originally selected theme song, Duke Ellington's "Sophisticated Lady," with "I Can't Believe That You're in Love with Me," a Tin Pan Alley number written by Clarence Gaskill and Jimmy McHugh. This move took the narrative in a markedly different direction and, according to the official production budget, also lopped $2,000 off the bottom line. On the choice of music see my *Detour,* 53–54. In his recent biography of Otto Preminger, Foster Hirsch notes that "Sophisticated Lady" was initially slated for use as the theme song in *Laura* (1944) until David Raksin scored his own original "Laura" theme. See Foster Hirsch, *Otto Preminger: The Man Who Would Be King* (New York: Knopf, 2007), 106–7.

14. John Belton, "Film Noir's Knights of the Road," *Bright Lights* 12 (Spring 1994): 8.

15. All citations from Goldsmith's novel, given parenthetically hereafter, are taken from the 2005 reprint of the original edition, *Detour: An Extraordinary Tale* (New York: Macaulay, 1939) by the Florida-based O'Bryan House. Citations from Goldsmith's screenplay come from the reprint in *Scenario* 3, no. 2 (Summer 1997): 133–78. All citations from Ulmer's film are from the 2000 DVD release by Image Entertainment.

16. Edgar G. Ulmer, "The Director's Responsibility," unsourced document (ca. early 1950s), EGUC-AMPAS.

17. Robert Polito, "Some Detours to *Detour*," *LIT* 13 (Fall 2007): 148.

18. Krohn, "King of the B's," 60.

19. Anthony Heilbut, *Exiled in Paradise: German Refugee Artists and Intellectuals in America from the 1930s to the Present* (Berkeley: University of California Press, 1997), 27.

20. Edward Dimendberg, "Down These Seen Streets a Man Must Go: Siegfried Kracauer, "Hollywood's Terror Films," and the Spatiality of Film Noir," *New German Critique* 89 (Spring/Summer 2003): 138.

21. Grissemann, *Mann im Schatten,* 222.

22. Edward W. Said, "Reflections on Exile," *Granta* 13 (1984): 159–72.

23. Thomas Elsaesser, *Weimar Cinema and After: Germany's Historical Imaginary* (New York: Routledge, 2000), 374.

24. Luc Moullet "Présentation Edgar G. Ulmer," *Cahiers du cinéma*, no. 58 (April 1956): 55–57. With specific regard to the music, Ivan Raykoff has argued, "*Detour* is haunted by references to frustration and failure" highlighted in particular by the inclusion of the Chopin-inspired 1940s hit "I'm Always Chasing Rainbows." See Ivan Raykoff, "Hollywood's Embattled Icon," in *Piano Roles: Three Hundred Years of Life with the Piano*, ed. James Parakilas (New Haven, CT: Yale University Press, 1999), 348–49.

25. See, e.g., Yannis Tzioumakis, "Edgar G. Ulmer: The Low-End Independent Filmmaker *Par Excellence*," in Rhodes, *Edgar G. Ulmer*, 18.

26. See Richard Schickel, *Double Indemnity* (London: British Film Institute, 1992), 63.

27. See Michael Palm's documentary *Edgar G. Ulmer: The Man Off-Screen* (Edgar G. Ulmer Preservation Corporation, 2004), released on DVD by Kino International in 2006. Earlier in the same film, B-movie specialist Gregory Mank suggests that Ulmer had "to take a rat and make Thanksgiving dinner out of it."

28. Cited in A.G., "Auteur Detour," an appendix to Goldsmith's script reprinted in *Scenario* 3, no. 2 (Summer 1997): 180. Goldsmith adds to this: "We had seven days to shoot the damn thing. This wasn't just a cheap movie, this was the cheapest movie ever made! That's what I'm most proud of" (181).

29. Ann Savage, interview by Stefan Grissemann, July 2, 2001, Sherman Oaks, CA, author's personal collection. In his interview with Bogdanovich, Ulmer explains his technique the same way: "I shot my master scene, but left for the last day the close-ups" (B 573).

30. Tim Pulleine, "16mm/*Detour* (1945)," *Films and Filming*, no. 335 (August 1982): 37.

31. Muller, *Dark City*, 178.

32. See the official PRC production budget, EGUC-AMPAS.

33. Biesen, *Blackout*, 165. Gregory Mank's comment comes from Michael Palm's 2004 documentary *Edgar G. Ulmer: The Man Off-Screen*.

34. David Kalat, "*Detour*'s Detour," in Herzogenrath, *The Films of Edgar G. Ulmer*, 148.

35. Jimmy Lydon, interview by the author, Dec. 16, 2001, Bonita, CA.

36. Ann Savage notes, in her interview with Michael Henry Wilson, "I wouldn't be a bit surprised if Edgar didn't do that on purpose. . . . Maybe his sense of humor, or something like that" (Ann Savage, interview by Michael Henry Wilson, May 6, 1996, Los Angeles, EGUC-AMPAS).

37. Andrew Britton, "*Detour*," in *The Book of Film Noir*, ed. Ian Cameron (New York: Continuum, 1993), 177.

38. Savage, Wilson interview.

39. Guy Maddin, "*Detour* (V)," *LIT* 13 (Fall 2007): 139.

40. Naremore, *More Than Night*, 149.

41. Marcus, *The Shape of Things to Come*, 135. Eddie Muller gives Savage's account of Ulmer's coaching ("Edgar snapped his fingers: *Faster! Faster! Pick up the pace!*") in *Dark City Dames*, 161.

42. Joseph I. Breen to Martin Mooney, memorandum, Nov. 1, 1944, PCA-AMPAS.

43. Savage, Wilson interview.

44. See Biesen, *Blackout,* 165–66.

45. Savage, Wilson interview.

46. Walter Salles, "Notes for a Theory of the Road Movie," *New York Times Magazine,* Nov. 11, 2008.

47. Jim Henaghan, review of *Detour, Hollywood Reporter,* Oct. 29, 1945.

48. "*Detour,*" *Daily Variety,* Oct. 29, 1945; review of *Detour, Film Daily,* March 1, 1946. A review by Mandel Herbstman, in the *Motion Picture Herald,* Nov. 10, 1945, called *Detour* an "adroit, albeit unpretentious production," while giving it a rating of "fair." In the United Kingdom, where the film's release appears to have been delayed for nearly a year, the reviewer for the *Monthly Film Bulletin* offered a blistering critique: "This very poor story has little to commend it. It tries the unusual by interspersing dialogue with commentary in the form of Al talking to himself, and fails. The direction is as poor as the story. The only bright spot is Ann Savage's performance as Vera, which she does so well that she really leaves a taste of complete revulsion in the mouth." See P.T., "*Detour,*" *Monthly Film Bulletin* 13, no. 154 (Oct. 1946): 137.

49. "*Detour* Tears Emotions," *Los Angeles Times,* Oct. 30, 1945.

50. See Meisel, "The Primacy of the Visual," 150; and J. Hoberman, "Low and Behold." See also Tony Williams, "Beyond *Citizen Kane: Ruthless* as Radical Psychobiography," in Rhodes, *Edgar G. Ulmer,* 195–209.

51. Grissemann, *Mann im Schatten,* 250.

52. Schrader, "Notes on Film Noir," 57.

53. Geoffrey O'Brien, *Hardboiled America: Lurid Paperbacks and the Masters of Noir* (1981; New York: Da Capo, 1997), 16.

54. Ibid., 8.

55. Dayton Stoddart, *Prelude to Night* (New York: Coward-McCann, 1945), 336. All subsequent citations, made parenthetically within the text, refer back to this edition.

56. Joseph I. Breen to C.W. Thornton, Oct. 23, 1947, PCA-AMPAS.

57. Grissemann, *Mann im Schatten,* 26.

58. Review of *Ruthless, Hollywood Reporter,* March 24, 1948. In the short review published in the *Los Angeles Herald-Express,* on July 10, 1948, critic W.E. Oliver hailed the film as "lush with story as black gossip."

59. Philip K. Scheuer, "'Ruthless' Powerful in Its Climaxes," *Los Angeles Times,* July 10, 1948. The unnamed critic for *Variety* was much less charitable with respect to the film's direction, calling it "clichéd and outmoded." See review of *Ruthless, Variety,* March 24, 1948.

60. T.P., "*Ruthless* at the Gotham," *New York Times,* Sept. 4, 1948.

61. See their respective accounts of the HUAC interrogation: Gordon Kahn, *Hollywood on Trial: The Story of the Ten Who Were Indicted* (New York: Boni and Gaer, 1948); and Alvah Bessie, *Inquisition in Eden* (New York: Macmillan, 1965). See also Otto Friedrich's retelling of the hearing in his *City of Nets* (303–5).

62. Reynold Humphries, "The Logic of Contradiction and the Politics of Desire in *Ruthless,*" in Herzogenrath, *Edgar G. Ulmer,* 160. See also Reynold

Humphries, *Hollywood's Blacklists: A Political and Cultural History* (Edinburgh: Edinburgh University Press, 2009).

63. Paul Buhle and Dave Wagner, *Blacklisted: The Film Lover's Guide to the Hollywood Blacklist* (New York: Palgrave Macmillan, 2003), 191.

64. Anger, *Hollywood Babylon*, 357.

65. Shirley Ulmer, interview by Michael Henry Wilson, May 6, 1996, Los Angeles, EGUC-AMPAS. In the interview that Tom Weaver conducted with Shirley Ulmer, published in *Cult Movies* in 1998, she elaborates on the same story: "I remember in particular," she tells of the G-men at her door, "they were interested at that moment in Gale Sondergaard [from *Isle of Forgotten Sins*, whose husband, Herbert Biberman, was one of the Hollywood Ten]. We didn't know anything about where she joined [the Communist Party] or what she did, so I don't think we helped them!" (Weaver, "Shirley Ulmer," 58).

66. See Grissemann, *Mann im Schatten*, 253.

67. Tag Gallagher argues that Ulmer would have been intimately familiar with the morality play tradition, given his classical education in Vienna. See Gallagher, "All Lost in Wonder."

68. See the press kit for *Ruthless*, EGUC-AMPAS.

69. See, e.g., Edgar G. Ulmer to Arianné Ulmer, Dec. 27, 1955; and the unpublished script of *Diagnostic Procedures in Tuberculosis*, both in EGUC-AMPAS.

70. Robert Warshow, "The Gangster as Tragic Hero," *Partisan Review*, Feb. 1948; repr. in Robert Warshow, *The Immediate Experience: Movies, Comics, Theatre and Other Aspects of Popular Culture* (Cambridge, MA: Harvard University Press, 2001), 101.

71. Michael Phillips, "A Minor Masterpiece Rises from the Vault," *Talking Pictures*, Sept. 25, 2009, http://featuresblogs.chicagotribune.com/talking_pictures/2009/09/a-minor-masterpiece-rises-from-the-vault.html.

72. Edgar G. Ulmer to Arianné Ulmer, Feb. 14, 1954, EGUC-AMPAS. See also Bill Krohn, "The Naked Filmmaker," in Herzogenrath, *The Films of Edgar G. Ulmer*, 175–91.

73. On Ulmer's evolving sense of home see my "Permanent Vacation: Home and Homelessness in the Life and Work of Edgar G. Ulmer," in *Caught by Politics: Hitler Exiles and American Visual Culture in the 1930s and 1940s*, ed. Sabine Eckmann and Lutz Koepnick (New York: Palgrave, 2007), 175–94.

74. In an unpublished letter Lahn asserts that she had served as secretary-treasurer of Masthead Productions and that the production of *Murder Is My Beat* lasted "something over five months" in 1954. See Lahn to "To Whom It May Concern," Oct. 27, 1969, EGUC-AMPAS. The contract for the film (working title: "The Long Chance"), filed with the Paul Kohner Agency, is dated May 17, 1954, and offers a fee of $3,150 plus 7.5 percent on net profits (PKA-DKMFF).

75. Belton, *Howard Hawks, Frank Borzage, Edgar G. Ulmer*, 167.

76. Hugh S. Manon, "See Spot: The Parametric Film Noirs of Edgar G. Ulmer," in Rhodes, *Edgar G. Ulmer*, 107.

77. Ekkehard Knörer, "The Pleasures of the 'Not-Quite Movie': *Murder Is My Beat* and *Daughter of Dr. Jekyll*," in Herzogenrath, *Edgar G. Ulmer*, 198.

78. B. P. and A. S., "*Murder Is My Beat* (1955)," in *Film Noir: An Encyclopedic Reference to the American Style,* ed. Alain Silver and Elizabeth Ward (Woodstock, NY: Overlook, 1979), 191.

79. Milton Luban, review of *Murder Is My Beat, Hollywood Reporter,* May 3, 1955; anon., review of *Murder Is My Beat, Motion Picture Daily,* April 18, 1955.

80. Joseph I. Breen to Ilse Lahn, Feb. 2, 1954, PCA file on *Murder Is My Beat,* AMPAS. All citations to the memo are taken from this document.

81. Jacques Rivette speaks of the "spirit of poverty" in "Six Characters in Search of Auteurs," cited in Naremore, *More Than Night,* 137. See also Antoine Rakovsky, "Edgar G. Ulmer ou l'esthétique du 'cheap,'" *Revue du cinéma* 467 (1991): 62.

82. Naremore, *More Than Night,* 136–37.

83. John O'Dowd, *Kiss Tomorrow Goodbye: The Barbara Payton Story* (Albany, GA: Bear Manor, 2006), 277. See also Robert Polito, "Barbara Payton: A Memoir," in *Hollywood and God* (Chicago: University of Chicago Press, 2009), 5–11.

84. Cited in O'Dowd, *Kiss Tomorrow Goodbye,* 158.

85. Barbara Payton, *I Am Not Ashamed* (Los Angeles: Holloway House, 1963), cited in Muller, *Dark City,* 179.

86. Cited in O'Dowd, *Kiss Tomorrow Goodbye,* 172.

87. Cited in ibid., 243.

88. Arthur Lyons, "Killer Career—Actor Tom Neal," *Palm Springs Life,* August 1999, www.palmspringslife.com/Palm-Springs-Life/Whispering-Palms/Killer-Career-Actor-Tom-Neal/. See also the accounts in Muller, *Dark City,* 179; and in Marcus, *The Shape of Things to Come,* 137.

89. Lyons, "Killer Career."

90. Cited in O'Dowd, *Kiss Tomorrow Goodbye,* 412. Barbara Payton had allegedly taken to writing poetry late in life; a couple of her lines could serve as a fitting epitaph to the courtroom drama and to her romance with Tom Neal— "Love is a memory / Time cannot kill." Quoted in Belton, "Edgar G. Ulmer (1900[*sic*]–1972)," 346.

CHAPTER 7. INDEPENDENCE DAYS

1. The unpublished document is kept in Berlin, PKA-DKMFF.

2. See Gallagher, "All Lost in Wonder."

3. Weaver, "Arianné Ulmer," 321.

4. See Boris Morros, *My Ten Years as a Counterspy* (New York: Viking, 1959).

5. "One-Named Baton Waiver Achieves Aim," *Los Angeles Times,* August 18, 1946.

6. Richard Brody, "The Clippings File: Edgar G. Ulmer at Carnegie Hall," *New Yorker* online, April 24, 2012, www.newyorker.com/online/blogs/movies/2012/04/edgar-g-ulmer-carnegie-hall.html.

7. Cited in Tony Tracy, "'The Gateway to America': Assimilation and Art in *Carnegie Hall,*" in Rhodes, *Edgar G. Ulmer,* 220.

8. Erik Ulman, "Edgar G. Ulmer," *Senses of Cinema* 23 (Jan.-Feb. 2003): http://sensesofcinema.com/2003/great-directors/ulmer/.

9. Virginia MacPherson, "Meet Edgar Ulmer, Expert in Handling Temperament," *Hollywood Citizen-News*, Dec. 7, 1946.

10. "Carnegie Hall Rare Tribute: Ulmer Does Parade of Musical Greats," *Hollywood Reporter*, Feb. 27, 1947.

11. Bosley Crowther, review of *Carnegie Hall*, *New York Times*, May 3, 1947.

12. James Agee, *Agee on Film*, vol. 1 (New York: Perigee, 1958), 251.

13. Olin Downes, "Musical Movies: 'Carnegie Hall' May Be Milestone Despite Story," *New York Times*, May 25, 1947.

14. Wilson, "Edgar G. Ulmer," 253.

15. Ibid.

16. Grissemann, *Mann im Schatten*, 264.

17. See Joseph I. Breen to Edgar G. Ulmer, April 28, 1950, PCA-AMPAS.

18. See Grissemann, *Mann im Schatten*, 265.

19. Review of *St. Benny the Dip*, *Variety*, June 22, 1951.

20. Viertel, *The Kindness of Strangers*, 143.

21. Franz Kafka, *Amerika: The Man Who Disappeared*, trans. Michael Hofmann (New Directions, 1996), 84.

22. Grissemann, *Mann im Schatten*, 254.

23. See Ilse Lahn to Ralph Herzog, Sept. 22, 1948, and Ilse Lahn to Edgar G. Ulmer, Oct. 15, 1948, both in PKA-DKMFF. See also Edwin Schallert, "Hayward to Follow 'Capri' with Swiss 'Blue Light,'" *Los Angeles Times*, Nov. 6, 1948.

24. Shirley Ulmer, interview by Michael Henry Wilson, May 8, 1996, Los Angeles, EGUC-AMPAS.

25. Shirley Ulmer, interview by Michael Henry Wilson, May 6, 1996, Los Angeles, EGUC-AMPAS.

26. Ibid.

27. Weaver, "Shirley Ulmer," 58.

28. Schallert, "Hayward to Follow 'Capri.'"

29. Shirley Ulmer, interview.

30. Sidney Alexander, *The Celluloid Asylum* (New York: Bobbs-Merrill, 1951), 12.

31. Shirley Ulmer to Ilse Lahn, Dec. 13, 1948, PKA-DKMFF.

32. Ibid.

33. Shirley Ulmer to Ilse Lahn, Dec. 16, 1948, PKA-DKMFF.

34. Ilse Lahn to Victor Pahlen, Jan. 31, 1949, PKA-DKMFF.

35. See Edgar G. Ulmer to Shirley Ulmer, April 22, 1949, EGUC-AMPAS.

36. Fred Hift, review of *The Pirates of Capri*, *Motion Picture Herald*, Dec. 10, 1949.

37. Review of *The Pirates of Capri*, *Variety*, Nov. 30, 1949.

38. Review of *The Pirates of Capri*, *New York Times*, Dec. 26, 1949.

39. "Films on TV," *Films in Review* 12, no. 8 (Oct. 1961): 496.

40. See Edgar G. Ulmer to Shirley Ulmer, April 22, 1949, EGUC-AMPAS.

41. Edgar G. Ulmer to Shirley Ulmer, April 25, 1949, EGUC-AMPAS.

42. Edgar G. Ulmer to Shirley Ulmer, April 13, 1949, EGUC-AMPAS.
43. See Edgar G. Ulmer to Shirley Ulmer, May 3 and May 7, 1949, EGUC-AMPAS.
44. Sidney, *The Celluloid Asylum*, 326.
45. Edgar G. Ulmer to Dario Sabatello and Anthony Havelock-Allan, Oct. 11, 1949, PKA-DKMFF. In a letter composed on New Year's Eve 1948, Kohner wrote to Lahn: "We are supposed to be Edgar's agents. We are supposed to negotiate terms for him. How can we, if Edgar goes around signing papers without either consulting us or even letting us know what he signs?"
46. Paul Kohner to Edgar G. Ulmer, June 29, 1951, PKA-DKMFF.
47. Shirley Ulmer to Ilse Lahn, June 20, 1950, PKA-DKMFF.
48. Cited in Joe Morella and Edward Z. Epstein, *Paulette: The Adventurous Life of Paulette Goddard* (New York: St. Martin's, 1985), 183.
49. See memorandum by H.H. Zehner, Jan. 29, 1952, PCA-AMPAS. The *Babes in Bagdad* pressbook is cited in Noralee Frankel, *Stripping Gypsy: The Life of Gypsy Rose Lee* (New York: Oxford University Press, 2009), 190.
50. Edgar G. Ulmer to Ilse Lahn, June 25, 1951, PKA-DKMFF.
51. Weaver, "Shirley Ulmer," 59–60.
52. Edgar G. Ulmer to Ilse Lahn, August 25, 1951, PKA-DKMFF. Two days later, Shirley reiterated the same concerns: "Ilse dear—please, please believe me when I beg you to beware of productions away from Hollywood. *Only* an Edgar could navigate *within* a budget and then he's always two days ahead of disaster. It's *hard!*" (emphasis in original).
53. Cited in Julie Gilbert, *Opposite Attraction: The Lives of Erich Maria Remarque and Paulette Goddard* (New York: Pantheon, 1995), 399.
54. Frankel, *Stripping Gypsy*, 189.
55. See reviews of *Babes in Bagdad*, *Motion Picture Herald*, Dec. 8, 1952; *Hollywood Reporter*, Dec. 8, 1952; and *Variety*, Dec. 10, 1952.
56. Herbert Schwaab, "Camp, Art Film, Classical Hollywood Cinema and *Babes in Bagdad*," in Herzogenrath, *Edgar G. Ulmer*, 194.
57. "Entrevista con Jerónimo Mehura," *Archivos de la filmoteca* 9 (1991): 45–56.
58. Tavernier, Wilson interview.
59. Dave Kehr, *When Movies Mattered: Reviews from a Transformative Decade* (Chicago: University of Chicago Press, 2011), 5.
60. Dave Kehr, "Reflections on All 200 Films," *New York Times*, March 1, 2002.
61. Edgar G. Ulmer to Ilse Lahn, March 15, 1953, PKA-DKMFF.
62. Louella O. Parsons, "Hedy Lamarr to Make TV Shorts in Mexico," *Los Angeles Examiner*, June 6, 1952.
63. John Fraser, *Close Up: An Actor Telling Tales* (London: Oberon, 2004), 104–6.
64. See Shearer, *Beautiful*, 279.
65. Edgar G. Ulmer to Ilse Lahn, Oct. 5, 1953, PKA-DKMFF.
66. Barton, *Hedy Lamarr*, 191.
67. Both pieces are cited in Shearer, *Beautiful*, 280.
68. Wilson B. Heller, "Edgar Ulmer (4/53)," EGUC-AMPAS.

69. Edgar G. Ulmer to Arianné Ulmer, Feb. 14, 1954, EGUC-AMPAS.

70. See "'Naked Dawn' New Venice Film Entry," *Valley Times,* Sept. 2, 1955.

71. Ilse Lahn to Edgar G. Ulmer, telegram, March 24, 1954, PKA-DKMFF.

72. See Bill Krohn, "*The Naked Dawn:* Production, Sources, and *Mise-en-scène*," in Herzogenrath, *Edgar G. Ulmer,* 215–24.

73. See Julian Zimet (a.k.a. Julian Halevy), in Patrick McGilligan and Paul Buhle, *Tender Comrades: A Backstory of the Hollywood Blacklist* (New York: St. Martin's, 1997), 733. See also Nina and Herman Schneider (i.e., Julian Zimet), "The Bandit," unpublished screenplay, CAL-USC. All subsequent references to the script are taken from this source.

74. Robert Warshow, "Movie Chronicle: The Westerner," *Partisan Review,* March-April 1954; repr. in Warshow, *The Immediate Experience,* 105–24.

75. See Joseph I. Breen to Josef Shaftel, Jan. 21, 1954, PCA-AMPAS.

76. Krohn, "*The Naked Dawn,*" 222.

77. Tavernier, Wilson interview.

78. Jack Moffitt, "'The Naked Dawn,' Old-Time Stuff," *Hollywood Reporter,* July 26, 1955; and review of *The Naked Dawn, Variety,* July 26, 1955.

79. Albert D. Ricketts, "Mexicans, Mandolin Dress Up Dawn," *Stars and Stripes,* Sept. 5, 1955; Marjorie Barrett, "Naked Dawn Builds Masterful Suspense," *Denver Post,* Oct. 17, 1955.

80. Truffaut, *The Films in My Life,* 155–56. All subsequent references in the text are taken from this source.

81. Edgar G. Ulmer to Ilse Lahn, Sept. 22, 1955, PKA-DKMFF.

82. Daniel Kasman, "A Rock Is a Hard Place: An Interview with Luc Moullet," July 13, 2009, www.theauteurs.com/notebook/posts/777.

83. Jean-Luc Godard, "From Critic to Film-Maker," in *Cahiers du Cinéma, 1960–1968: New Wave, New Cinema, Reevaluating Hollywood,* ed. Jim Hillier (Cambridge, MA: Harvard University Press, 1986), 67.

84. Shirley Ulmer to Ilse Lahn, June 15, 1955, PKA-DKMFF.

85. Edgar G. Ulmer to Arianné Ulmer, Oct. 26, 1955, EGUC-AMPAS; Shirley Ulmer to Ilse Lahn, July 20, 1961, PKA-DKMFF.

86. Shirley Ulmer to Ilse Lahn, Nov. 14, 1955, PKA-DKMFF.

87. Salka Viertel to Ilse Lahn, Feb. 12, 1956, PKA-DKMFF.

88. Edgar G. Ulmer to Ilse Lahn, Feb. 14, 1956, PKA-DKMFF.

89. Edgar G. Ulmer to Ilse Lahn, August 7, 1956, PKA-DKMFF.

90. Edgar G. Ulmer to Ilse Lahn, August 24, 1956, PKA-DKMFF.

91. See Philip K. Scheuer, "Cast of Three Carry Film," *Los Angeles Times,* Nov. 16, 1957.

92. Shirley Ulmer to Wilson Heller, Oct. 1, 1959, EGUC-AMPAS.

93. Shirley Ulmer, interview.

94. Cited in James McKay, *The Films of Victor Mature* (Jefferson, NC: McFarland, 2013), 162.

95. Review of *Hannibal, Variety,* June 6, 1960; and Howard Thompson, "'Hannibal' Crosses Neighborhood Screens," *New York Times,* August 4, 1960.

96. Weaver, "Arianné Ulmer," 337.

97. Edgar G. Ulmer to Ilse Lahn, Sept. 10, 1960, PKA-DKMFF.

98. Shirley Ulmer to Wilson Heller, Nov. 26, 1960, EGUC-AMPAS.

99. Bret Wood, "Edgar G. Ulmer: Visions from the Second Kingdom," *Video Watchdog* 41 (Sept./Oct. 1997): 28.

100. Edgar G. Ulmer to Ilse Lahn, August 16, 1961, PKA-DKMFF.

101. Curt Siodmak, *Wolf Man's Maker*, 91.

102. Edgar G. Ulmer to Ilse Lahn, Oct. 5, 1961, PKA-DKMFF.

103. Ulmer, "The Director's Responsibility."

104. Tom Weaver, "Jack Pollexfen," in *Interviews with B Science Fiction and Horror Movie Makers: Writers, Producers, Directors, Actors, Moguls, and Makeup* (Jefferson, NC: McFarland, 2006), 274.

105. David J. Skal, *Screams of Reason: Mad Science and Modern Culture* (New York: Norton, 1998), 177.

106. Review of *The Man from Planet X*, *Variety*, March 14, 1951.

107. Bob Skotak, "*The Man from Planet X* Files," *FILMFAX* 69–70 (Oct. 1998/Jan. 1999): 48.

108. Jay Bonansinga, "The Films of Edgar G. Ulmer," *FILMFAX* 12 (Oct. 1988): 38.

109. Weaver, "Jack Pollexfen," 274.

110. Tom Weaver, "Robert Clarke," in Weaver, *Interviews with B Science Fiction and Horror Movie Makers*, 79.

111. Review of *The Man from Planet X*, *Variety*, March 14, 1951. According to producer Pollexfen, the film went on to gross more than $1 million in rentals. See Weaver, "Jack Pollexfen," 277.

112. H.H.T., "Interplanetary Doings at the Mayfair," review of *The Man from Planet X*, *New York Times*, April 9, 1951.

113. Sarris, *The American Cinema*, 123.

114. Tom Weaver, "Gloria Talbott," in Weaver, *Interviews with B Science Fiction and Horror Movie Makers*, 337.

115. Sarris, *The American Cinema*, 143.

116. Weaver, "Gloria Talbott," 336.

117. Cited in Schaefer, "*Bold! Daring! Shocking! True!*" 301.

118. Cited in Robert Skotak, "A Grave New World: Cast and Crew on the Making of *Beyond the Time Barrier*," in Herzogenrath, *The Films of Edgar G. Ulmer*, 209.

119. Arianné Ulmer Cipes, quoted in *Edgar G. Ulmer: The Man Off-Screen*.

120. Cited in Skal, *Screams of Reason*, 180. See also J. Hoberman, *An Army of Phantoms: American Movies and the Making of the Cold War* (New York: The New Press, 2011).

121. Susan Sontag, *Against Interpretation and Other Essays* (New York: Picador, 2001), 220.

122. Edgar G. Ulmer to Ilse Lahn, July 3, 1961, PKA-DKMFF.

123. See Grissemann, *Mann im Schatten*, 334–37.

124. Tavernier, Grissemann interview. See also Bruce Cook, *Dalton Trumbo* (New York: Charles Scribner's Sons, 1977), 244.

125. "Ullmer [*sic*] as Director for Six Melcher-Day Films; Exteriors Only Overseas," *Variety*, Nov. 8, 1962.

126. See Grissemann, *Mann im Schatten*, 337. See also Bertrand Tavernier's undated and unpublished letter in which he relays to Ulmer a conversation he had with the producer of *Mata Hari:* "He confirmed everything you told us about stealing the script, of your script, by Truffaut and Jean-Louis Richard." Tavernier to Ulmer, n.d., EGUC-AMPAS.

127. Tom Weaver, "Peter Marshall on Edgar G. Ulmer," in *A Sci-Fi Swarm and Horror Horde: Interviews with 62 Filmmakers* (Jefferson, NC: McFarland, 2010), 325.

128. Brian Aherne, *A Dreadful Man* (New York: Simon and Schuster, 1979), 133–35.

129. Weaver, "Shirley Ulmer," 60.

130. Pressbook for *Neunzig Nächte und ein Tag*, PKA-DKMFF.

131. Shirley Ulmer, interview.

132. Review of *The Cavern, Variety*, Nov. 8, 1965; and Howard Thompson, "'The Cavern' Bows on Local Screens," *New York Times*, Dec. 25, 1965.

133. Arianné Ulmer Cipes, telephone interview with the author, April 22, 2013. See also Grissemann, *Mann im Schatten*, 343–45.

134. Edgar G. Ulmer to Carola (Ulmer) Kornauth, Sept. 26, 1967, EGUC-AMPAS.

135. Peter Bart, "How to Be a Loner in Hollywood," *New York Times*, March 13, 1966.

136. "M.M. Interviews Edgar Ulmer," *Modern Monsters*, August 1966, 18–19.

137. "5 Stations Sign Pact on Films," *Los Angeles Times*, March 22, 1967.

138. Shirley Ulmer to Arianné Ulmer, April 26, 1962, EGUC-AMPAS.

139. Weaver, "Shirley Ulmer," 61.

140. Shirley Ulmer, interview; Arianné Ulmer Cipes, telephone interview with the author, April 22, 2013.

141. Weaver, "Arianné Ulmer," 329.

142. Tavernier, Wilson interview.

143. Anon., unpublished eulogy for Edgar Ulmer (Mordecai ben Tzvi), EGUC-AMPAS.

144. Jimmy Lydon, interview by the author, Dec. 16, 2001, Bonita, CA.

145. Fritz Feld, "In Memoriam of Edgar Ulmer," unpublished eulogy, EGUC-AMPAS.

POSTSCRIPT

1. Belton, *Howard Hawks, Frank Borzage, Edgar G. Ulmer*, 149.

2. McCarthy and Flynn, *Kings of the Bs*, xii.

3. Meisel, "The Primacy of the Visual," 148, 152.

4. Cited in Kemp, "Ulmer, Edgar G(eorg)," 1110.

5. Kevin Thomas, "UCLA Focuses on 'The King of the B's,'" *Los Angeles Times*, Oct. 6, 1983.

6. Mike Spies, "Edgar G. Who?" *Houston Chronicle*, March 5, 1984.

7. Scott Cain, "Month of Screenings Honors Career of 'King of the B's,'" *Atlanta Constitution*, March 31, 1986.

8. Shirley Ulmer and C.R. Sevilla, *The Role of Script Supervision in Film and Television* (New York: Hastings House, 1986), 61.

9. See Aljean Harmetz, "25 Films to Become U.S. Treasures," *New York Times*, July 17, 1989.

10. There are also more explicit attempts at remakes. Rather mysteriously, a full-page advertisement in the *Hollywood Reporter* (Feb. 23, 1988) announced a planned, yet never realized, remake of *Detour*, "based on the 1946 [sic] classic film noir by Edgar G. Ulmer," by Swiss-born director Carl Schenkel. And, even more bizarre, cult film collector Wade Williams released his waxworks remake, starring Tom Neal Jr. playing his father's role, in 1992.

11. Luc Moullet, unpublished interview by Stefan Grissemann, Jan. 17, 2010, Paris.

12. Peter Bogdanovich, "Bluebeard," *Indiewire.com*, Sept. 21, 2011, http://blogs.indiewire.com/peterbogdanovich/bluebeard.

Select Bibliography

Adorno, Theodor W. *Minima Moralia: Reflections from Damaged Life*. Translated by E. F. N. Jephcott. London: Verso, 1974.

Agee, James. *Agee on Film*. New York: Perigee, 1958.

Alexander, Sidney. *The Celluloid Asylum*. New York: Bobbs-Merrill, 1951.

Alpi, Deborah Lazaroff. *Robert Siodmak*. Jefferson, NC: McFarland, 1998.

Anderson, Thom. "Red Hollywood." In *Literature and the Visual Arts in Contemporary Society*, edited by Suzanne Ferguson and Barbara Groseclose, 141–96. Columbus: Ohio State University Press, 1985.

Andrew, Geoff. *The Director's Vision: A Concise Guide to the Art of 250 Filmmakers*. Chicago: Chicago Review, 1999.

Anger, Kenneth. *Hollywood Babylon*. New York: Dell, 1975.

Asper, Helmut G. *Filmexilanten im Universal Studio*. Berlin: Bertz and Fischer, 2005.

Barton, Ruth. *Hedy Lamarr: The Most Beautiful Woman in Film*. Lexington: University Press of Kentucky, 2010.

Belton, John. "Cinema Maudit." In *Retrospective*, 149–50. Edinburgh: Edinburgh Film Festival, 1997.

———. "Edgar G. Ulmer (1900[sic]–1972)." In *American Directors*, edited by Jean-Pierre Coursodon with Pierre Sauvage, 1:339–47. New York: McGraw-Hill, 1983.

———. "Film Noir's Knights of the Road." *Bright Lights* 12 (Spring 1994): 5–15.

———. *Howard Hawks, Frank Borzage, Edgar G. Ulmer*. Vol. 3 of *The Hollywood Professionals*. New York: A. S. Barnes, 1974.

Biesen, Sheri Chinen. *Blackout: World War II and the Origins of Film Noir*. Baltimore: Johns Hopkins University Press, 2005.

Bogdanovich, Peter. "Edgar G. Ulmer: An Interview," *Film Culture* 58–60 (1974): 189–238. Repr. in *Who the Devil Made It: Conversations with Legendary Film Directors*, 558–604. New York: Ballantine, 1998.

Bonansinga, Jay. "The Films of Edgar G. Ulmer." *FILMFAX* 12 (Oct. 1988): 34–38.

Bono, Francesco, Paolo Caneppele, and Günter Krenn, eds. *Elektrische Schatten: Beiträge zur Österreichischen Stummfilmgeschichte*. Vienna: Filmarchiv Austria, 1999.

Britton, Andrew. "*Detour*." In *The Book of Film Noir*, edited by Ian Cameron, 174–83. New York: Continuum, 1993.

Brunas, Michael, John Brunas, and Tom Weaver. *Universal Horrors: The Studio's Classic Films, 1931–1946*. Jefferson, NC: McFarland, 1990.

Buhle, Paul, and Dave Wagner. *Blacklisted: The Film Lover's Guide to the Hollywood Blacklist*. New York: Palgrave Macmillan, 2003.

Cantor, Paul A. "The Fall of the House of Ulmer: Europe vs. America in the Gothic Vision of *The Black Cat*." In *The Philosophy of Horror*, edited by Thomas Fahy, 137–60. Lexington: University Press of Kentucky, 2010.

Cipes, Arianné Ulmer. "Foreword." In *When Joseph Met Molly: A Reader on Yiddish Film*, edited by Sylvia Paskin, 1–3. Nottingham, UK: Five Leaves, 1999.

Davis, Blair. *The Battle for the Bs: 1950s Hollywood and the Rebirth of Low-Budget Cinema*. New Brunswick, NJ: Rutgers University Press, 2012.

Dimendberg, Edward. *Film Noir and the Spaces of Modernity*. Cambridge, MA: Harvard University Press, 2004.

Dixon, Wheeler W., ed. *Producers Releasing Corporation: A Comprehensive Filmography and History*. Jefferson, NC: McFarland, 1986.

Eisenschitz, Bernard, and Jean-Claude Rohmer. "Entretien avec Edgar G. Ulmer." *Midi-Minuit fantastique* 13 (Nov. 1965): 1–14.

Eisner, Lotte. *The Haunted Screen: Expressionism in the German Cinema and the Influence of Max Reinhardt*. Translated by Roger Greaves. Berkeley: University of California Press, 1969.

———. *Murnau*. Berkeley: University of California Press, 1973.

Elbin, Günther. *Am Sonntag in die Matinee: Moriz Seeler und die Junge Bühne*. Mannheim: Persona, 1998.

Elsaesser, Thomas. "Ethnicity, Authenticity, and Exile: A Counterfeit Trade? German Filmmakers in Hollywood." In *Home, Exile, Homeland: Film, Media, and the Politics of Place*, edited by Hamid Naficy, 97–123. New York: Routledge, 1999.

———. *Weimar Cinema and After: Germany's Historical Imaginary*. New York: Routledge, 2000.

Everson, William K. *Classics of the Horror Film*. Secaucus, NJ: Citadel, 1974.

———. "Horror Films." *Films in Review* 5, no. 1 (Jan. 1954): 12–23.

———. "Introduction: Remembering PRC." In Dixon, *Producers Releasing Corporation*, 1–7.

Farber, Manny. *Farber on Film: The Complete Writings of Manny Farber*, edited by Robert Polito. New York: Library of America, 2009.

Francke, Lizzie. "Edgar G. Ulmer." In *Retrospective*, 148. Edinburgh: Edinburgh Film Festival, 1997.

Frankel, Noralee. *Stripping Gypsy: The Life of Gypsy Rose Lee.* New York: Oxford University Press, 2009.

Fraser, John. *Close Up: An Actor Telling Tales.* London: Oberon, 2004.

Friedrich, Otto. *City of Nets: A Portrait of Hollywood in the 1940's.* Berkeley: University of California Press, 1997.

Gabler, Neal. *An Empire of Their Own: How the Jews Invented Hollywood.* New York: Crown, 1988.

Gallagher, Tag. "All Lost in Wonder: Edgar G. Ulmer." *Screening the Past* 12 (March 2001): http://tlweb.latrobe.edu.au/humanities/screeningthepast /firstrelease/fro301/tgafr12a.htm.

Gemünden, Gerd. *A Foreign Affair: Billy Wilder's American Films.* New York: Berghahn, 2008.

———. *Continental Strangers: German Exile Cinema, 1933–1951.* New York: Columbia University Press, 2014.

Gevinson, Alan. *Within Our Gates: Ethnicity in American Feature Films, 1911–1960.* Berkeley: University of California Press, 1997.

Gilbert, Julie. *Opposite Attraction: The Lives of Erich Maria Remarque and Paulette Goddard.* New York: Pantheon, 1995.

Giovacchini, Saverio. *Hollywood Modernism: Film and Politics in the Age of the New Deal.* Philadelphia: Temple University Press, 2001.

Goldsmith, Martin M. *Detour: An Extraordinary Tale.* New York: Macaulay, 1939. Reprint, Oakland Park, FL: O'Bryan House, 2005.

Grafe, Frieda. "Wiener Beiträge zu einer wahren Geschichte des Kinos." In *Aufbruch ins Ungewisse: Österreichische Filmschaffende in der Emigration vor 1945,* edited by Christian Cargnelli and Michael Omasta, 227–43. Vienna: Wespennest, 1993.

Grissemann, Stefan. *Mann im Schatten: Der Filmemacher Edgar G. Ulmer.* Vienna: Zsolnay, 2003.

Halliday, Jon, ed. *Sirk on Sirk.* London: Faber and Faber, 1997.

Heilbut, Anthony. *Exiled in Paradise: German Refugee Artists and Intellectuals in America from the 1930s to the Present.* Berkeley: University of California Press, 1997.

Herzogenrath, Bernd, ed. *Edgar G. Ulmer: Essays on the King of the B's.* Jefferson, NC: McFarland, 2009.

———, ed. *The Films of Edgar G. Ulmer.* Lanham, MD: Scarecrow, 2009.

———. "Introduction: The Return of Edgar G. Ulmer." In Herzogenrath, *Edgar G. Ulmer,* 3–21.

Hillier, Jim, ed. *Cahiers du Cinéma, 1960–1968: New Wave, New Cinema, Reevaluating Hollywood.* Cambridge, MA: Harvard University Press, 1986.

Hirsch, Foster. *Otto Preminger: The Man Who Would Be King.* New York: Knopf, 2007.

Hoberman, J. "Bad Movies." *Film Comment* 16, no. 4 (July/August 1980): 7–12.

———. *Bridge of Light: Yiddish Film between Two Worlds.* New York: Museum of Modern Art/Schocken, 1991.

———. "Low and Behold." *Village Voice,* Nov. 17, 1998.

Hoberman, J., and Jeffrey Shandler. *Entertaining America: Jews, Movies, and Broadcasting*. Princeton, NJ: Princeton University Press, 2003.

Horton, Robert. *Billy Wilder: Interviews*. Jackson: University Press of Mississippi, 2002.

Horwath, Alexander. "Das Shining: *Strange Illusion* von Edgar G. Ulmer (1945)." In *Schatten. Exil: Europäische Emigranten im Film Noir*, edited by Christian Cargnelli and Michael Omasta, 296–309. Vienna: PVS, 1997.

———. "Working with Spirits—Traces of Sternberg: A Lost Film about the 'City of My Dreams.'" Translated by Peter Waugh. In *Josef von Sternberg: The Case of Lena Smith*, edited by Alexander Horwath and Michael Omasta, 9–42. Vienna: Synema, 2007.

Huesmann, Heinrich. *Welttheater Reinhardt*. Munich: Prestel, 1983.

Humphries, Reynold. *Hollywood's Blacklists: A Political and Cultural History*. Edinburgh: Edinburgh University Press, 2009.

Isenberg, Noah. *Detour*. London: British Film Institute, 2008.

———. "Perennial Detour: The Cinema of Edgar G. Ulmer and the Experience of Exile." *Cinema Journal* 43, no. 2 (Winter 2004): 3–25.

———. "Permanent Vacation: Home and Homelessness in the Life and Work of Edgar G. Ulmer." In *Caught by Politics: Hitler Exiles and American Visual Culture in the 1930s and 1940s*, edited by Sabine Eckmann and Lutz Koepnick, 175–94. New York: Palgrave, 2007.

———, ed. *Weimar Cinema: An Essential Guide to Classic Films of the Era*. New York: Columbia University Press, 2009.

———. "When Faces Mattered Most." *Vertigo* 4, no. 3 (Spring/Summer 2009): 64–65.

Israel, Nico. *Outlandish: Writing between Exile and Diaspora*. Stanford, CA: Stanford University Press, 2000.

Kanfer, Stefan. *Stardust Lost: The Triumph, Tragedy, and Mishugas of the Yiddish Theater in America*. New York: Knopf, 2006.

Keating, Patrick. *Hollywood Lighting: From the Silent Era to Film Noir*. New York: Columbia University Press, 2010.

Kehr, Dave. *When Movies Mattered: Reviews from a Transformative Decade*. Chicago: University of Chicago Press, 2011.

Kemp, Philip. "Ulmer, Edgar G(eorg)." In *World Film Directors*. Vol. 1, *1890–1945*, edited by John Wakeman, 1107–12. New York: H.W. Wilson, 1987.

Klawans, Stuart. *Film Follies: The Cinema Out of Order*. New York: Cassell, 1999.

Koepnick, Lutz. "The Bearable Lightness of Being: *People on Sunday* (1930)." In Isenberg, *Weimar Cinema*, 237–53.

———. *The Dark Mirror: German Cinema between Hitler and Hollywood*. Berkeley: University of California Press, 2002.

Kohner, Frederick. *The Magician of Sunset Boulevard: The Improbable Life of Paul Kohner, Hollywood Agent*. Palos Verdes, CA: Morgan Press, 1977.

Koszarski, Richard. *Hollywood on the Hudson: Film and Television in New York from Griffith to Sarnoff*. New Brunswick, NJ: Rutgers University Press, 2008.

Krohn, Bill. "King of the B's." *Film Comment* 19, no. 4 (July-August 1983): 60–64.

Kuropas, Myron B. *The Ukrainian Americans: Roots and Aspirations, 1884–1954*. Toronto: University of Toronto Press, 1991.

Lipsitz, George. "The New York Intellectuals: Samuel Fuller and Edgar Ulmer." In *Time Passages: Collective Memory and American Popular Culture*. Minneapolis: University of Minnesota Press, 1990.

Lyons, Arthur. *Death on the Cheap: The Lost B Movies of Film Noir*. New York: Da Capo, 2000.

Madsen, Axel. *William Wyler*. New York: Crowell, 1973.

Mandell, Paul. "Edgar Ulmer and *The Black Cat*." *American Cinematographer*, Oct. 1984, 34–47.

Mank, Gregory William. *Bela Lugosi and Boris Karloff: The Expanded Story of a Haunting Collaboration*. Jefferson, NC: McFarland, 2009.

Marcus, Greil. *The Shape of Things to Come: Prophecy and the American Voice*. New York: Farrar, Straus and Giroux, 2006.

McCarthy, Todd, and Charles Flynn, eds. *Kings of the Bs: Working within the Hollywood System*. New York: E. P. Dutton, 1975.

McGuire, James. *Impresario: The Life and Times of Ed Sullivan*. New York: Random House, 2006.

Meisel, Myron. "The Primacy of the Visual." In McCarthy and Flynn, *Kings of the Bs*, 147–52.

Morella, Joe, and Edward Z. Epstein. *Paulette: The Adventurous Life of Paulette Goddard*. New York: St. Martin's, 1985.

Morton, Frederic. *Thunder at Twilight: Vienna, 1913/1914*. New York: Da Capo, 2001.

Morton, Lisa, and Kent Adamson. *Savage Detours: The Life and Work of Ann Savage*. Jefferson, NC: McFarland, 2009.

Moullet, Luc. "Présentation Edgar G. Ulmer." *Cahiers du cinéma*, no. 58 (April 1956): 55–57.

Moullet, Luc, and Bertrand Tavernier. "Entretien avec Edgar G. Ulmer." *Cahiers du cinéma*, no. 122 (August 1961): 1–16.

Muller, Eddie. *Dark City: The Lost World of Film Noir*. New York: St. Martin's, 1998.

———. *Dark City Dames: The Wicked Women of Film Noir*. New York: Harper Collins, 2001.

Naremore, James. *More Than Night: Film Noir and Its Contexts*. Berkeley: University of California Press, 1998.

Nau, Peter. "Das Geheimnis der Form in den Filmen Edgar G. Ulmers." In *Aufbruch ins Ungewisse: Österreichische Filmschaffende in der Emigration vor 1945*, edited by Christian Cargnelli and Michael Omasta, 117–31. Vienna: Wespennest, 1993.

Nebesio, Bohdan Y. "*Zaporozhets za Dunaiem* (1938): The Production of the First Ukrainian-Language Feature Film in Canada." *Journal of Ukrainian Studies* 16, no. 1–2 (Summer-Winter 1991): 115–29.

O'Brien, Geoffrey. *Hardboiled America: Lurid Paperbacks and the Masters of Noir*. 1981. New York: Da Capo, 1997.

O'Dowd, John. *Kiss Tomorrow Goodbye: The Barbara Payton Story*. Albany, GA: Bear Manor, 2006.

Polito, Robert. "Some Detours to *Detour.*" *LIT* 13 (Fall 2007): 144–61.

Reinhardt, Gottfried. *The Genius: A Memoir of Max Reinhardt.* New York: Knopf, 1979.

Rhodes, Gary D., ed. *Edgar G. Ulmer: Detour on Poverty Row.* Lanham, MD: Lexington Books, 2008.

Rosar, William H. "Music for the Monsters: Universal Pictures' Horror Film Scores of the Thirties," *Quarterly Journal of the Library of Congress* 40, no. 4 (1983): 391–421.

Said, Edward W. "Reflections on Exile." *Granta* 13 (1984): 159–72.

Sannwald, Daniela. "Metropolis: Die Wien-Berlin-Achse im deutschen Film der 1oer und 2oer Jahre." In Bono, Caneppele, and Krenn, *Elektrische Schatten,* 139–48.

Sarris, Andrew. *The American Cinema.* New York: Dutton, 1968.

Schaefer, Eric. *"Bold! Daring! Shocking! True!" A History of Exploitation Films, 1919–1959.* Durham, NC: Duke University Press, 1999.

Schatz, Thomas. *Boom and Bust: American Cinema in the 1940s.* Berkeley: University of California Press, 1997.

Schildkraut, Joseph. *My Father and I.* New York: Viking, 1959.

Schorske, Carl. *Fin-de-siècle Vienna: Politics and Culture.* New York: Pantheon, 1980.

Schrader, Paul. "Notes on Film Noir." *Film Comment* 8, no. 1 (Spring 1972): 8–13.

Shearer, Stephen Michael. *Beautiful: The Life of Hedy Lamarr.* New York: St. Martin's, 2010.

Sikov, Ed. *On Sunset Boulevard: The Life and Times of Billy Wilder.* New York: Hyperion, 1998.

Sinyard, Neil. *Fred Zinnemann: Films of Character and Conscience.* Jefferson, NC: McFarland, 2003.

Siodmak, Curt. *Wolf Man's Maker: Memoir of a Hollywood Writer.* Rev. ed. Lanham, MD: Scarecrow, 2001.

Siodmak, Robert. *Zwischen Berlin und Hollywood: Erinnerungen eines großen Filmregisseurs.* Edited by Hans C. Blumenberg. Munich: Herbig, 1980.

Skal, David J. *The Monster Show: A Cultural History of Horror.* Rev. ed. New York: Faber and Faber, 2001.

———. *Screams of Reason: Mad Science and Modern Culture.* New York: Norton, 1998.

Skotak, Bob. "The Man from Planet X Files." *FILMFAX* 69–70 (Oct. 1998/Jan.1999): 44–49.

Sontag, Susan. *Against Interpretation and Other Essays.* New York: Picador, 2001.

Stoddart, Dayton. *Prelude to Night.* New York: Coward-McCann, 1945.

Thomajan, Dale. "Ready When You Are, Mr. Ulmer," *Film Comment* 26, no. 3 (March-April 1990): 67–68.

Thomson, David. *The New Biographical Dictionary of Film.* New York: Knopf, 2002.

Truffaut, François. *The Films in My Life.* Translated by Leonard Mayhew. 1975. New York: Da Capo, 1994.

Ulman, Erik. "Edgar G. Ulmer." *Senses of Cinema* 23 (Jan.-Feb. 2003): http://sensesofcinema.com/2003/great-directors/ulmer/.

Ulrich, Rudolf. *Österreicher in Hollywood*. Vienna: Edition S, 1993.

Vangelisti, Paul, ed. *L.A. Exile: A Guide to Los Angeles Writing, 1932–1998*. New York: Marsilio, 1999.

Vieira, Mark. *Irving Thalberg: Boy Wonder to Producer Prince*. Berkeley: University of California Press, 2009.

Viertel, Salka. *The Kindness of Strangers: A Theatrical Life. Vienna, Berlin, Hollywood*. New York: Holt, Rinehart and Winston, 1969.

Warshow, Robert. *The Immediate Experience: Movies, Comics, Theatre and Other Aspects of Popular Culture*. Cambridge, MA: Harvard University Press, 2001.

Weaver, Tom. "Arianné Ulmer." In *Science Fiction and Fantasy Film Flashbacks: Conversations with 24 Actors, Writers, Producers and Directors from the Golden Age*. Jefferson, NC: McFarland, 1998.

———. "Her Father's Keeper: Arianné Ulmer Cipes." *Video Watchdog* 41 (Sept./Oct. 1997): 32–49.

———. *Interviews with B Science Fiction and Horror Movie Makers: Writers, Producers, Directors, Actors, Moguls, and Makeup*. Jefferson, NC: McFarland, 2006.

———. "Shirley Ulmer." *Cult Movies* 25 (1998): 52–61.

Williams, Wade. "Edgar Ulmer's Dark Excursion into the Nightmare World of Fatal Irony . . ." *FILMFAX* 11 (July 1988): 22–25.

Wilson, Michael Henry. "Edgar G. Ulmer: 'Let There Be Light!'" In *Divini Apparizioni: Edgar G. Ulmer, Joseph Losey, Leonid Trauberg*, 249–55. Milan: Transeuropa, 1999.

Wood, Bret. "Edgar G. Ulmer: Visions from the Second Kingdom." *Video Watchdog* 41 (Sept./Oct. 1997): 22–31.

Wood, Ed, Jr. *Hollywood Rat Race*. New York: Four Walls Eight Windows, 1998.

Zweig, Stefan. *The World of Yesterday*. Lincoln: University of Nebraska Press, 1964.

ARCHIVES

CAL-USC. Universal Archives, Cinematic Arts Library, University of Southern California.

EGUC-AMPAS. Edgar G. Ulmer Collection, Margaret Herrick Library, Academy of Motion Picture Arts and Sciences, Los Angeles.

PCA-AMPAS. Production Code Administration Files, Margaret Herrick Library, Academy of Motion Picture Arts and Sciences, Los Angeles.

PKA-DKMFF. Paul Kohner Archive, Deutsche Kinemathek Museum für Film und Fernsehen, Berlin.

UNPUBLISHED SOURCES

Alexander, Arthur. Personal correspondence, 1969. EGUC-AMPAS.

Beverley, Helen. Interview by Michael Henry Wilson. May 8, 1996, Los Angeles. EGUC-AMPAS.

Breen, Joseph I. Personal correspondence, 1934–1963, PCA-AMPAS.

Cipes, Arianné Ulmer. Email correspondence with the author.

———. Interview by Bob Baker. June 15, 1998, Los Angeles. EGUC-AMPAS.

Feld, Fritz. "In Memoriam of Edgar Ulmer." Oct. 3, 1972. EGUC-AMPAS.

———. Personal correspondence, 1969. EGUC-AMPAS.

Fromkess, Leon. Personal correspondence, 1969. EGUC-AMPAS.

Heller, Wilson. Personal correspondence, 1954–1961. EGUC-AMPAS.

Kohner, Paul. Personal correspondence, 1945–1967. PKA-DKMFF.

Laemmle, Carl, Jr. Personal correspondence, 1969. EGUC-AMPAS.

Lahn, Ilse. Personal correspondence, 1948–1961. PKA-DKMFF.

Lydon, Jimmy. Interview by Noah Isenberg. Dec. 16, 2001, Bonita, CA.

Mitchell, Joen. Interview by Noah Isenberg. August 4, 2009, Los Angeles.

Moore, Dick. Interview by Noah Isenberg. June 12, 2012, New York.

Moullet, Luc. Interview by Stefan Grissemann. Jan. 17, 2010, Paris.

Savage, Ann. Interview by Stefan Grissemann. July 2, 2001, Sherman Oaks, CA. Author's personal collection.

———. Interview by Michael Henry Wilson. May 6, 1996, Los Angeles. EGUC-AMPAS.

Steiner, Joseph. Personal correspondence, 1969. EGUC-AMPAS.

Tavernier, Bertrand. Interview by Stefan Grissemann. Feb. 9, 2009, Berlin. Author's personal collection.

———. Interview by Michael Henry Wilson. Nov. 7, 1997, Paris. EGUC-AMPAS.

Turner, D.J. Email correspondence with the author.

Ulmer, Edgar G. "Beyond the Boundary." Unfinished novel, 1935. EGUC-AMPAS.

———. "The Director's Responsibility." Unsourced document, early 1950s. EGUC-AMPAS.

———. "The Loser." Screenplay, 1969. EGUC-AMPAS.

———. Personal correspondence, 1927–1968. EGUC-AMPAS.

Ulmer, Shirley. Interview by Michael Henry Wilson. May 6–8, 1996, Los Angeles. EGUC-AMPAS.

———. Personal correspondence, 1939–1973. EGUC-AMPAS.

Zimet, Julian. "The Bandit" (i.e., *The Naked Dawn*). Screenplay, CAL-USC.

Zinnemann, Fred. Personal correspondence, 1929. PKA-DKMFF.

Acknowledgments

When I began work on this project, more than a decade ago, I could not possibly have foreseen how many people would help guide me toward its completion. In addition to the various funding agencies that provided generous grants, fellowships, and residencies, countless individuals—some of whom will necessarily, if unwittingly, go unmentioned here—have supported the project and offered invaluable input.

Beginning with the foundations, funding sources, and institutions, I would like to express a deep gratitude to the National Endowment for the Humanities for a collaborative grant (enabling my colleague Robert Polito and me to organize a three-day Ulmer symposium at the New School in 2002) and for an individual research fellowship in 2002–3. Thanks to a short-term grant in Exile Studies from the Feuchtwanger Memorial Library at USC, I was able to spend a critical week in Los Angeles in early 2002, gathering preliminary materials. At USC's Cinematic Arts Library, Ned Comstock provided expert advice and invaluable material for the project, and I owe him my sincere gratitude. Also in Los Angeles, Howard Prouty, Barbara Hall, Michael Pogorzelski, and Kristine Krueger of the Academy of Motion Picture Arts and Sciences and the Margaret Herrick Library have been remarkably generous and supportive throughout—a big, hearty thanks to them. The Austrian Fulbright-Kommission and the International Research Center for Cultural Studies (IFK) made it possible for me to spend a semester in residence in Vienna in spring 2003, where

I undertook initial archival research. At the Austrian Film Museum, I'd like to thank Alexander Horwath, Regina Schlagnitweit, and Elisabeth Streit. In 2008–9 the Alexander von Humboldt Foundation provided me with a full year of support in Berlin to work with the papers of the Paul Kohner Archive at the Deutsche Kinemathek—Museum für Film und Fernsehen. There I wish to thank the executor of the Kohner papers, Gerrit Thies, for his kind help. In a similar vein I wish to thank my academic host, the eminent film scholar Gertrud Koch, who offered terrific encouragement—both intellectual and culinary nourishment—during my year in Berlin. The Dietrich W. Botstiber Foundation, together with the Austrian Cultural Forum and Deutsches Haus at NYU, helped underwrite a small tribute to Ulmer on the fortieth anniversary of his death, in October 2012.

Along the extended path of writing, I incurred many more debts of gratitude. The first published piece, "Perennial Detour: The Cinema of Edgar G. Ulmer and the Experience of Exile," appeared in the winter 2004 issue of Cinema Journal (my thanks go to Jon Lewis, then editor of the journal, and to anonymous readers who offered valuable feedback), parts of which I have drawn on in highly revised and expanded form. I wish to thank Lutz Koepnick and Sabine Eckmann for including another early extract from this project, "Permanent Vacation: Home and Homelessness in the Life and Work of Edgar G. Ulmer," in their 2007 volume Caught by Politics: Hitler Exiles and American Visual Culture in the 1930s and 1940s, which, in the meantime, has been reprinted in Bernd Herzogenrath's 2009 anthology The Films of Edgar G. Ulmer. In 2008, as part of the BFI Film Classics series, I published my monograph on Detour, which benefited from the astute editorial guidance of Rebecca Barden and from critical input of members of the BFI's editorial board. At the Criterion Collection, Liz Helfgott offered exceptional insight and precision to the liner notes I wrote for the 2011 release of People on Sunday, sections of which are included here. Thanks, too, to Kim Hendrickson and Issa Clubb, at Criterion, for their keen interest and support. Finally, in April 2013, Dennis Lim posted an advance extract from the book at Moving Image Source, and I'd like to offer my thanks to him and to the website.

Over the years, I have benefited from presenting portions of the book, in its various incarnations, in public lectures. In this vein I wish to thank Henry Abelove, then Director of Wesleyan University's Center for the Humanities; Marje Schuetze-Coburn at the Feuchtwanger Memorial Library; Lutz Musner at the IFK in Vienna; Jack Kugelmass at the Center for Jewish Studies of the University of Florida; Alexander Horwath of the Austrian Film Museum; Paul Reitter and Dave Filipi at the Wexner Center for the Arts in Columbus, Ohio; Florence Almozini at BAMcinématek; Jed Rapfogel at Anthology Film Archives; Hannah Liko of the Austrian Cultural Forum; Martin Rauchbauer of Deutsches Haus at NYU; Fatima Naqvi in German and Cinema Studies at Rutgers University; Steve Taubeneck and the Ziegler Lecture series at the University of British Columbia in Vancouver, Canada; Eric Ames and the Department of Germanics, together with the Stroum Program in Jewish Studies and the Moving Images Research Group, at the University of Washington; and Sunka Simon and Patricia White of the Department of Film and Media Studies at Swarthmore College.

The intense dialogues that I have enjoyed with students, at the undergraduate and graduate level, have had a major impact on this project and on my intellectual development more generally. From my years at Wesleyan I wish to thank, among others, Paul Brunick, Max Goldberg, Max Goldblatt, Caddie Hastings, Oliver Henzler, Alex Horwitz, Keefe Murren, Mary Robertson, Jason Schwartz, Dahlia Schweitzer, Ben Simington, Kerry Wallach, and Sam Wasson. At the New School I owe thanks to Kaylynn Arnett, Zeba Blay, Suzanne Coote, Cullen Gallagher, Morten Høi Jensen, Liz Hynes, Aaron Light, Rachelle Rahme, Hannah Read, Meghan Roe, Max Schneider-Schumacher, Michael Stewart, and others. My students and colleagues in the Department of Culture and Media, and in the program in Screen Studies, at Eugene Lang College—The New School for Liberal Arts, deserve special gratitude, as do my students and colleagues in the interdisciplinary M.A. program in Liberal Studies at the New School for Social Research.

At the University of California Press, former commissioning film editor Eric Smoodin contracted the book more than a decade ago. In the meantime Mary Francis has helped, in more ways than I can enumerate, to oversee the project's development from a more traditional work of film scholarship to a critical biography aimed at a wider audience. She has read and critiqued drafts of each chapter, has shown boundless patience and encouragement, especially when the project's fruition seemed, if not in complete jeopardy, like a distant prospect, and has been a superb editor and a great friend throughout. Also at UC Press, Kim Hogeland, Suzanne Knott, and Jessica Moll have helped guide the project through the thickets of editorial production, and I offer them my deepest gratitude. For his expert skills as copyeditor, Joe Abbott has earned my indebtedness again and again. I also owe many thanks to

James Naremore and an anonymous reader for the press for their critical evaluations of the manuscript.

For the use of photos—productions stills as well as snapshots—I express my sincere gratitude to Robert Ulmer, John Belton, D. J. Turner, and Arianné Ulmer Cipes. Ms. Cipes's magnanimous support of the project from start to finish included everything from family photos, unpublished documents, private correspondence, rare prints, audiocassettes, DVDs, and much more. Others who helped provide photos include Ron and Howard Mandelbaum at Photofest in New York; Wolfgang Theis and Julia Riedel in the stills archive of the Deutsche Kinemathek in Berlin; Sharon Rivo and Dave Ortega at the National Center for Jewish Film in Waltham, Massachusetts; and Dave McCall at the BFI Film Stills Collection in London. Finally, I wish to express genuine gratitude to the talented staff of Print Space Lab in New York City, who helped with the retouching of old, otherwise unusable, photos.

Several individuals supported the project in profound and lasting ways, offering extensive input on the manuscript, sharing research materials, and serving as interlocutors in countless animated conversations over the years. The Vienna-based film critic and scholar Stefan Grissemann, whose 2003 German-language biography *Mann im Schatten: Der Filmemacher Edgar G. Ulmer* stands as a landmark achievement in the critical reception of Ulmer, contributed immeasurably to my understanding of the director and his life. Stefan has been a wonderful colleague and true friend throughout the entire process. Similarly, Gerd Gemünden and Dana Polan have exceeded the call of duty, inspecting each and every chapter of the book, offering sage advice and important feedback. D. J. Turner has also cast his discerning eye on the manuscript in its entirety, catching numerous slips of the pen and sharing his own vast research on Ulmer. Other scholars, critics, mentors, and friends have offered material and input at various junctures: Ruth Barton, Jeanine Basinger, John Belton, Peter Bogdanovich, Lisa Dombrowski, Sonia Beth Gollance, Molly Haskell, Bernd Herzogenrath, J. Hoberman, Anton Kaes, David Kalat, Dave Kehr, Stuart Klawans, Richard Koszarski, Carola Krempler, Bill Krohn, Phillip Lopate, Jimmy Lydon, Guy Maddin, Greg Mank, Joen Mitchell, Dick Moore, Michael Omasta, Zoë Pagnamenta, Michael Palm, Claudia Pummer, David J. Skal, Johannes von Moltke, Tom Weaver, and others. And finally, without the exceptional support of Arianné Ulmer Cipes, who repeatedly read draft after draft and helped me to fill in vital gaps, the book could not have been written. Needless to say, any remaining errors and infelicities are mine alone.

The book is dedicated to three people who have lived through much if not all of the process, two of them, Jules and Bruno, born in the midst of it. As always, Melanie Rehak has revved up the editorial engines whenever called upon and has helped steer things along both by the sterling example she herself sets, as an accomplished critic and author, and by encouraging me to keep inching my way toward that ever-elusive finish line. Before I hit that line, we lost two beloved parents, both of whom would have taken considerable joy in seeing the final publication. The book is also dedicated to their memory.

Index

S

WEIMAR AND NOW: GERMAN CULTURAL CRITICISM

Edward Dimendberg, Martin Jay, and Anton Kaes, General Editors